America's Forgotten
Middle East Initiative

'The King–Crane Commission Report may be the most detailed account extant of the Wilsonian imaginary applied to a particular region. Patrick's lucid and beautifully written study brings to life all manner of paths not taken in the post-Ottoman Middle East. Historians, regional specialists across disciplines and international relations scholars will all find this book essential reading.'

Leonard V. Smith, Frederick B. Artz Professor of History, Oberlin College

'This admirably fair-minded book provides a reliable and deeply engaging account of one of the least-understood episodes in the history of America's relationship with the Middle East. Anyone interested in how the United States has sought to engage a post-colonial world can profit from Andrew Patrick's splendid research and judicious analysis.'

David A. Hollinger, Preston Hotchkis Professor of History Emeritus, University of California, Berkeley

'Andrew Patrick's meticulously researched study presents a shrewd assessment of the King–Crane Commission of 1919, an episode in the history of the Middle East that has been long overdue for an in-depth historical investigation. Writing with admirable clarity, Patrick offers an absorbing analysis that is even-handed and firmly rooted in the sources, salvaging the King–Crane Commission from ahistorical and sometimes ill-informed appropriation by present-day controversies. While this book will be read profitably by those interested in the history of American foreign relations, Patrick's book is also a significant and timely contribution to modern Middle Eastern history.'

Oliver Bast, Senior Lecturer in Middle Eastern History, the University of Manchester

AMERICA'S FORGOTTEN MIDDLE EAST INITIATIVE

The King–Crane Commission of 1919

ANDREW PATRICK

I.B.TAURIS
LONDON • NEW YORK • OXFORD • NEW DELHI • SYDNEY

I.B. TAURIS
Bloomsbury Publishing Plc
50 Bedford Square, London, WC1B 3DP, UK
1385 Broadway, New York, NY 10018, USA

BLOOMSBURY, I.B. TAURIS and the I.B. Tauris logo are trademarks of Bloomsbury Publishing Plc

First published in Great Britain 2015
This edition published in 2020

Copyright © Andrew Patrick 2015

Andrew Patrick has asserted his right under the Copyright, Designs and Patents Act, 1988, to be identified as Author of this work.

Cover design: Mark Cavanagh
Cover image: The King–Crane Commission at the Paris Peace Conference, 1919 (© Oberlin College Archives)

All rights reserved. No part of this publication may be reproduced or transmitted in any form or by any means, electronic or mechanical, including photocopying, recording, or any information storage or retrieval system, without prior permission in writing from the publishers.

Bloomsbury Publishing Plc does not have any control over, or responsibility for, any third-party websites referred to or in this book. All internet addresses given in this book were correct at the time of going to press. The author and publisher regret any inconvenience caused if addresses have changed or sites have ceased to exist, but can accept no responsibility for any such changes.

A catalogue record for this book is available from the British Library.

A catalog record for this book is available from the Library of Congress

ISBN: PB: 9781788314558
HB: 9781784532741
ePDF: 9780857727008
eBook: 9780857737588

To find out more about our authors and books visit www.bloomsbury.com and sign up for our newsletters.

For Jami

CONTENTS

List of Illustrations   viii
Acknowledgements   xi

1. Introduction   1
2. Backdrop of the King–Crane Commission   9
3. Paris Peace Conference 1: The Idea of a Commission   28
4. Paris Peace Conference 2: Topsy-Turvydom   51
5. Pre-Journey Opinions   78
6. Istanbul and Palestine   98
7. Syria and Lebanon   130
8. Istanbul, Paris and the Recommendations   165
9. Accounting for the Differences 1: The Ability to Become Modern   182
10. Accounting for the Differences 2: The King–Crane Commission and Wilsonian Ideals   222
11. Conclusion   256

Notes   264
Selected Bibliography   300
Index   309

LIST OF ILLUSTRATIONS

Map

Map 1. The main locations visited by the King–Crane Commission. The places where they spent several nights are numbered and in bold. (Adapted from a map on the website of the King–Crane Commission Digital Collection: http://www.oberlin.edu/library/digital/king-crane/map.html). xii

Figures

Figure 2.1. Amir Faysal leaving the Hotel Victoria after a conference with General Allenby on 3 October 1918. (Source: World War I Photograph Album, 1918–19, American University of Beirut/Library Archives). 20

Figure 4.1. The five main members of the King–Crane Commission at the Paris Peace Conference. They are, from left to right, George Montgomery, Charles R. Crane, Henry Churchill King, Albert Lybyer and William Yale. (Source: Oberlin College Archives, Oberlin, Ohio). 57

Figure 6.1. Members of the King–Crane Commission (in their car) and delegations in front of the Church of the Nativity in Bethlehem on 17 June 1919. (Source: Oberlin College Archives, Oberlin, Ohio). 122

List of Illustrations

Figure 7.1. Charles Crane with the 'Daughters of the Arab Martyrs'. (Source: World War I Photograph Album, 1918–19, American University of Beirut/Library Archives). 138

Figure 7.2. Delegations awaiting their audience with the commission in Amman. (Source: Oberlin College Archives, Oberlin, Ohio). 140

Figure 7.3. The King–Crane Commission at the Hotel Royal in Beirut. In the back row (left to right) are Dr. Sami Haddad, Yale, Lybyer, Montgomery, Captain Donald Brodie and Laurence Moore. In the front are King (left) and Crane (right). (Source: Oberlin College Archives, Oberlin, Ohio). 146

Figure 7.4. The reception of the commission at Tripoli, 12 July, 1919. (Source: Oberlin College Archives, Oberlin, Ohio). 152

Figure 7.5. The reception of the commission at Latakia, 14 July 1919. (Source: World War I Photograph Album, 1918–19, American University of Beirut/Library Archives). 155

Figure 7.6. The commission stopping at a village north of Homs. (Source: World War I Photograph Album, 1918–19, American University of Beirut/Library Archives). 156

Figure 7.7. Representatives of the 'wards of the city of Aleppo'. (Source: Oberlin College Archives, Oberlin, Ohio). 158

Figure 7.8. The commission's 'special train' to Adana. (Source: World War I Photograph Album, 1918–19, American University of Beirut/Library Archives). 160

Figure 9.1. Delegates at Quneitra led by the mayor (centre) with commission members Laurence Moore (fifth from the left) and Montgomery (centre), 25 June, 1919. The varied styles of clothing were indicative of what the commission saw in the region. (Source: World War I Photograph Album, 1918–19, American University of Beirut/Library Archives). 188

Figure 9.2. The 'ultra modern' Boy Scouts in Damascus. (Source: World War I Photograph Album, 1918–19, American University of Beirut/Library Archives). 191

ACKNOWLEDGEMENTS

Before I begin, I must briefly thank the people who made this book possible. Quite a few generous academics have helped me during the writing process, the foremost of whom is Oliver Bast. Oliver served as a fine mentor and editor during the production of this book's previous incarnation as a PhD thesis at the University of Manchester. Moshe Behar also provided valuable feedback for which I am immensely grateful, and Feroze Yasamee gave me much beneficial criticism along the way as well. I must also thank Eugene Rogan, who contributed excellent comments as my external examiner, and John Milton Cooper, who volunteered to read my PhD thesis and offered many helpful suggestions. Further thanks goes to Roberto Mazza who read this manuscript in its final stages and helped to improve it immensely. Others have given helpful critiques at various points in the writing process, including Erik Goldstein, Mustafa Aksakal, Graham Ward and Michael Harvey. Archivists have been helpful in all of my stops (though I lack the space to thank them all) and I have received funding help from various organisations to visit these archives. Special thanks goes to the British Society for Middle Eastern Studies, the Council for British Research in the Levant, New York University-Abu Dhabi, Zayed University and the National Endowment for the Humanities. The fine people at I.B.Tauris have guided me through the editorial process, with Tomasz Hoskins and Iradj Bagherzade being especially deserving of my gratitude. Most importantly, I thank my wife for supporting me in my studies. This book is for you Jami.

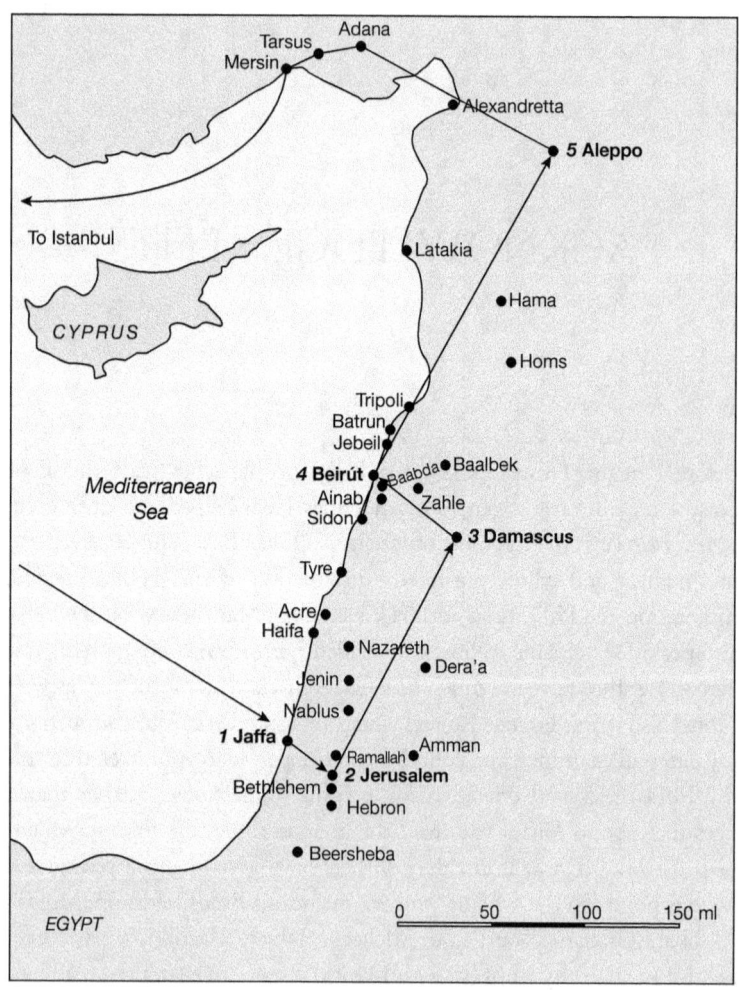

Map 1 The main locations visited by the King–Crane Commission. The places where they spent several nights are numbered and in bold. (Adapted from a map on the website of the King–Crane Commission Digital Collection: http://www.oberlin.edu/library/digital/king-crane/map.html).

CHAPTER 1

INTRODUCTION

The King–Crane Commission of 1919 was controversial from its inception. At the end of World War I, the leaders of the victorious powers gathered in Paris in order to decide the fate of their wartime enemies, with Britain, France, Italy and the United States playing the most prominent roles in the negotiations. In some of the early discussions regarding the defeated Ottoman Empire, US President Woodrow Wilson advocated the sending of an 'Inter-Allied' fact-finding commission to the Ottoman lands and this proposal triggered unease among his fellow leaders at the peace conference. This unease stemmed from the commission's proposed objective, which was to ascertain the political attitudes of the Ottoman Empire's inhabitants so that these attitudes could be taken into consideration when framing the region's peace settlement. Britain, France and Italy, afraid that such a commission might infringe upon their claims to the Ottoman lands, were reticent about it at first, then agreed to participate, then delayed and finally backed out. The Americans completed the work of the commission on their own and the final recommendations of what is now commonly referred to as the King–Crane Commission have been the subject of a simmering debate ever since.

The controversy surrounding the King–Crane Commission comes primarily from its recommendations pertaining both to Zionism and to the future control of the Ottoman lands. The commission's final report stated that the opposition to Zionism in the region was so intense that any future Jewish immigration to Palestine would cause great conflict. In line with this, the commission argued that a French presence in the region would be resisted and, hence, they could not recommend such a policy. Furthermore, the commission's report stated that the people of the Ottoman lands (with the exception of Iraq) would greatly benefit from US tutelage and hence the United States should take 'mandates' for Anatolia, Greater Syria (including what is now Syria, Lebanon, Palestine/Israel and Jordan), Armenia and a newly formed 'Constantinopolan State' around Istanbul. In light of the current realities in the region, one could be forgiven for seeing both prescience and irony in these recommendations. The King–Crane Commission's findings were, however, largely ignored by policy makers of the era and have gone down as a great 'what if' in the history of the modern Middle East, providing the basis for some rather stunning, if improbable, counterfactuals.

The controversial nature of these recommendations alone make the King–Crane Commission a fascinating object of study, and the general lack of scholarship specifically on the commission is one of the primary justifications for this book. The only other major study dealing with the King–Crane Commission is Harry N. Howard's rather dry but meticulous account published in 1963. Interestingly, this book was written between 1939 and 1941 but publication was delayed because Howard took a job in the US Department of State during World War II and was not allowed to publish anything that 'dealt too much with current political topics'.[1] Howard remained with the State Department until 1956 and later published the manuscript without doing any substantial new research. As could be expected, there are many more primary and secondary materials available now than there were during Howard's time, many of which have been drawn on for this study.

Although the need for a new analysis of the King–Crane Commission provides part of the impetus for this book, the subsequent disparate and often cursory assessments of the commission offer further justification. The commission has been given substantive mention in at least 300 academic works and has appeared in the public realm through occasional newspaper references and, more recently, dozens of web pages.[2] As frequently happens with events that are ensconced in the highly politicised history of the Israeli–Palestinian conflict, scholars have often interpreted aspects of the commission to suit their particular political leanings. Most scholars who have assessed this event have concluded that the commission accurately reflected the will of the region's people and was prophetic on the issues of both Zionism and the French occupation.

The most prominent initial proponent of this view was George Antonius who, in his famed 1937 volume *The Arab Awakening*, described the report as 'disinterested', 'wholly objective' and 'penetrating', further noting that the conclusions drawn by the report's authors accurately displayed 'the wishes of the people' with 'shrewdness' and 'unmistakable honesty'.[3] More recently, historian Ussama Makdisi has argued in a similar manner that the commission's report 'laid out in extraordinary detail precisely what the people of Syria, including Lebanon and Palestine, desired in their overwhelming majority'.[4] These discussions of the King–Crane Commission are representative of many others like them and their general line of argument is fairly uniform: the commission was largely impartial, its report reflected the fears and aspirations of the region's people and its recommendations were unjustly ignored.[5]

In contrast to these assessments, other scholars have argued that the commission, having been unduly influenced by both the region's Arabs and its American missionaries, were prejudiced against the interests of the Zionists and the other imperial powers. Perhaps the most significant early appearance of this assertion came in Frank Manuel's 1949 book entitled *The Realities of American–Palestine Relations*. In his book, Manuel contends that the commission was the product of missionary pressure on Wilson and, hence, a 'triumph' for the missionaries. Once it got to the region, the commission was fooled by 'Arab propaganda' that 'fomented' anti-Jewish feeling 'in a synthetic manner'.[6] Building on this line of criticism in his recent book about United States–Middle East relations, historian Michael Oren has also argued that American missionaries were behind the commission and that the chosen commissioners were 'obviously predisposed against European and Zionist objectives in the Middle East', with Commissioner Charles Crane being a particularly proud 'anti-Semite'.[7] While there are numerous other assessments of this type, these two are representative of the general trend.[8]

In general, these viewpoints exemplify the wide interpretive gulf in the existing scholarship about the King–Crane Commission. Although such incongruity is not unusual in academic works on the history of the modern Middle East, this disparity must appear questionable to historians who strive to keep present-day politics out of their work (as much as is possible). One of the primary purposes of this study, then, is to provide a new analysis of the King–Crane Commission that moves away from the partisan rancour often present in these past assessments.

In addition to this, most scholars have ignored the fact that the commission's final report represented the opinions of only three of its five main members. The disagreement within the commission provides one of this book's analytical points of departure. As drawn from these two issues, the question that this study attempts to answer is, on the surface, rather simple: Why did the King–Crane Commission members arrive at their respective conclusions? Yet the question of 'why' is a deceptively difficult one to answer because it is impossible to determine precisely what a person was thinking at a given moment in history. It is possible, however, to come close to such a determination if there are enough primary sources regarding a specific decision that a person has made.

The answer to this study's research question comes from an intermingling of three elements that will be apparent throughout the book. The first, and most straightforward, element consists of the diplomatic constraints placed on the commission. Woodrow Wilson instructed the commission that numerous requests, such as giving immediate independence to any new regional state, would not be granted. The commission's possible conclusions, then, were delimited by their instructions, which they followed to the letter.

The second element that influenced the commission's recommendations was the testimony of the region's people. The veracity of this testimony was the source of much controversy within the commission but the recommendations in the commission's report do reflect much of what its members were told during their time in the region. Although much energy has been spent trying to portray statements made before the commission as being the fruit of well-organised propaganda campaigns, this book treats these various statements as legitimate political choices (with a few exceptions in cases of bribery or physical coercion). The encouraging trend of recent scholarship on the Middle East has been to stop treating the people of the region as bystanders in their own history. In this case, delegations from the region made informed political decisions about what they would say to the King–Crane Commission. Although it is difficult to know how representative of the Ottoman population these delegations were, it is important to note that people from the region made a concerted effort to play a prominent role in their own destiny in 1919 and their pleas were largely ignored by the world leaders they were attempting to influence.

The final, and perhaps most important, element shaping the commission's recommendations was its members' preconceptions about the Middle East, which would have been partly ingrained in their world view or 'social imaginary', to borrow Charles Taylor's term.[9] More specifically, the commission members would have been inculcated with a shared 'Western' social imaginary and the discourses embodied within it. An element rooted in the social imaginary of Western elites at this point was the tendency to essentialise groups, be they racial, religious or other, and this played a major role in their thinking about the people of the Ottoman Empire.[10] As Timothy Mitchell has argued, nineteenth century colonialism played a large role in Western thinking, with 'the Orient' and its inhabitants representing the negation of the West in the minds of most Western elites, meaning that it was 'backward, irrational, and disordered, and therefore in need of European order and authority'.[11] Although this generally held true, there were distinct differences of opinion within the commission about their final recommendations, which indicates the existence of discord in American conceptions of the Middle East. Any historical period, as Michael Shapiro has argued, 'has forces at work producing interpretations and overcoming rival ones' and this was certainly the case in this instance.[12] Along these lines, this book examines the commission members' disagreements in terms of discourses that would have been far less ingrained in their social imaginary and hence would have been more contentious in the era. These 'rival' discourses pertained to topics such as the basis for the international system of states and America's place in that system, as well as the ability of the 'non-Western' people of the world to become modern. The broad contention of this study, then, is that discourses pertaining to race, religion, modernity and self-determination most heavily influenced the King–Crane Commission members' conflicting recommendations. With this in mind, the manifestation of the King–Crane Commission provides a valuable episode from which to gauge American discourses about the Middle East in the early days of American ascendancy in the region.[13]

This study sheds light on the history of the region in one further way. Just as many of Greater Syria's Arabs sought to ensure that the King–Crane Commission was exposed to their preferred political programme, so too did the Zionists. As will be seen, the Zionists knew that most people in the region did not favour their cause and that Zionism was not even universally supported by all of Greater Syria's

Jews. With this in mind, the Zionists sent representatives to try to rally support for the Zionist cause among the Jewish communities of the region and, to a far lesser extent, among some possibly sympathetic non-Jewish groups. By the time the commission left Greater Syria, the Zionists had been successful in obtaining varying degrees of support from the region's major urban Jewish leaders but had failed almost entirely in getting support from the non-Jewish groups. This, paired with the anti-Zionist rhetoric of the vast majority of the petitioners, indicates that 1919 was one of the key moments of cleavage between the region's Jewish and non-Jewish populations.

In the end, the story of the King–Crane Commission is one of elevated expectations and dashed hopes in the minds of the Americans involved in the commission and, more importantly, many people in the Ottoman lands. On the US side, it is a story of a well-intentioned foray into the Middle East that was met with enthusiasm by the people who believed they would have a say in their own future and silence by the people it was meant to influence. It was also one of the first attempts to apply the vision of Woodrow Wilson to the postwar world and, as elsewhere, this turned out to be controversial and confusing. The commission's final report is, however, an early and bold statement of what was to become a dissenting discourse in US policy discussions about the Middle East, a discourse in which the rights of all of the region's people were placed on equal footing and grander geopolitical ambitions played little role. It is the story of a commission that had little discernible impact on US (or European) policy towards the region but had concrete implications for the region in general. The failure of the Western powers to take the people of the Ottoman lands seriously in 1919 helped to initiate the cycle of violence that still engulfs much of the region. While the recent Arab uprisings offer at least some hope that this cycle may yet be broken, the residues of the World War I era remain as impediments to the realisation of such hope. The King–Crane Commission, then, endures as a forlorn reminder that it did not have to be this way, and this is its history.

***

The primary goals of this book are rather simple: the first is to provide a detailed yet readable narrative of the commission's journey, and the second is to answer the research question through a close reading of the commission members' writings. The book is arranged in a fairly chronological fashion, with certain chapters (2–4, 6–8) laying out the narrative of the commission and the others (5, 9–11) being much more analytical. The next chapter (2) gives the backdrop of the commission, with a brief recounting of the Ottoman Empire during World War I and US attitudes about the people of the world in this era. It concludes with a discussion about the interactions between the United States and the Ottoman Empire during the war. The book continues with two chapters (3 and 4) about the formation of the commission at the Paris Peace Conference, and a chapter (5) about the commission members' views on the questions with which they were faced before they arrived in the Ottoman lands. Chapters 6, 7 and 8 recount the commission members' time in and return from the region. The next two chapters (9 and 10) are the analytical heart of the book, examining the commission members' contrasting recommendations in depth. The concluding chapter (11) brings the various analytical threads of the book together.

This is a focused monograph and the sources employed in this study are many but are also limited. All available papers of the commission members have been scoured, as have the State Department records in the National Archives of the United States. These have yielded both a solid overview of the US side of the story and many sources written by the people of the region. Because this study is essentially an examination of US discourses about the Middle East at the time of the King–Crane Commission, it depends almost entirely on contemporary sources. Commission members Charles Crane and William Yale both wrote unpublished memoirs later in their lives but these have been employed only when their recollections were consistent with what they were writing in 1919. Beyond this, a visit to the Central Zionist Archives in Jerusalem proved fruitful and has yielded new information about Greater Syria. Primarily, though, this study focuses on US perceptions of the Ottoman people in 1919.

The source material is largely in English, Arabic, French and Ottoman. Little Arabic translation has been required because the commission's translator, Dr Sami Haddad, did an admirable job in translating or summarising many of the petitions given to the commission. The author is responsible for the little Arabic and French translation that has been required. For the purposes of this study, the sources written by people from the region yielded little new information, which is why the study has analysed the US perspective in the most depth. This is not to say that another researcher might not find fascinating material for other projects in these sources. Furthermore, the author has employed commission member George Montgomery's Ottoman-to-English translations and summaries. Limitations of time, finance, linguistic ability, deadlines and family, along with the political upheavals in the Middle East, have curtailed further research. With this in mind, the study's research question and conclusions have not gone beyond the sources it employs.

CHAPTER 2

BACKDROP OF THE KING-CRANE COMMISSION

In the early twentieth century, the United States was establishing itself as a major world empire to rival its European counterparts. The Ottoman Empire, on the other hand, was struggling to modernise and strengthen itself in order to stave off the constant encroachment of its imperial adversaries. World War I (1914–18) showed this contrast more than any other event: it was an important moment of global engagement for the Americans and brought the downfall of the Ottoman Empire, an event that the European powers had been expecting (with some trepidation) for centuries. As was true of the Austrian and German imperial demise at the war's conclusion, the end of the Ottoman Empire was a contentious world event in which a huge number of powers and regional groups had a stake. The political moment, which represented the denouement of the 'Eastern Question', could hardly have been more charged and important for the parties involved. The United States was also debating the future of its role in the world, though few Americans cast covetous glances in the direction of the Ottoman lands.

This chapter lays out the context from which the King–Crane Commission members came and into which they proceeded. The sections of this chapter are disparate but necessary. The first section discusses the US conception of the world in this era and hence frames the social imaginary of the commission members as it pertained to the people of the Middle East. The next section briefly recounts the context of the Ottoman Empire in the summer of 1919. Finally, the last section concisely summarises the interaction between Ottomans and Americans both before and during the war.

Americans and the World

In the nineteenth and early twentieth centuries, American elites (which included the King–Crane Commission members) increasingly viewed their society as the pinnacle of civilisation, asserting the supremacy of, among other things, the American style of governing, societal organisation, economic production and general way of life. The vast majority of these elites believed that the historical trajectory of the United States was the path that the rest of the world should follow into the future; the United States was both the best model for less-developed nations to emulate and the most able purveyor of this model to these nations.[1] This belief had concrete ramifications for US interactions with the world. As historian Frank Ninkovich has argued, 'this argument from civilization [...] was the central ideological theme behind *all* of American foreign policy in the twentieth century'. This foreign policy, according to Ninkovich, 'featured a strong emphasis on creating stable, prosperous societies in nations that seemed incapable of self-modernization'.[2] The United States, it was believed by a large portion of these elites, could and should bring civilisation to the world.

This conception of history in its more general form, meaning the belief that societies inexorably moved from 'traditional' (agrarian, rural) to 'modern' (industrial, urban) ways of life in a manner similar to that of Western Europe and the United States, had been formalised into theory by numerous academics of the era and had become an accepted part of the Western elite social imaginary by the early twentieth century. The shifting meaning of the term 'modern', which by the late nineteenth century was being used to describe American (and Western European) society, reflected this belief: earlier in the nineteenth century modern had simply meant recent or current, but by the twentieth century modern had morphed into a more qualitative term, meaning 'improved or satisfactory or efficient'. It also began to be 'used to indicate something unquestionably favourable or desirable', thereby adding to the temporal character of its meaning.[3]

In the early twentieth century, many Americans believed that they were uniquely well positioned to spread their 'modern' way of life to the less-developed parts of the world. American elites were convinced that the United States had become, in the words of historian Emily Rosenberg, the 'vanguard of world progress', which meant that Americans alone had the ability to 'perfect and apply laws of progressive betterment' and 'uplift those lower on the evolutionary scale'. The development of the discourse encompassing these ideas, which Rosenberg has aptly labelled 'liberal-developmentalism', matured in the later nineteenth century, and the basic elements of it were more or less fully formed in the minds of most American elites by the century's end. The tenets of this discourse were rather simple: all nations should accept the capitalist and liberal ideals of the United States, with the central core of these ideals being free private enterprise, free international trade and free speech, all protected by a liberal, representative government. Liberal-developmentalism acted as both a framework for the modernisation of the world and a justification for the growing American role in this process. This discourse was internalised and reproduced by Americans who dealt with the world in a diverse set of ways. American businessmen hawking their wares and investors seeking new opportunities saw the modernisation of the rest of the world as a path to increased profits. Government officials, noting the success of and being increasingly pressured by these businessmen and investors, believed that the opening of the rest of the world to American private enterprise was an integral part of future American prosperity. American missionaries, faced with limited success in their nineteenth century evangelism, shifted the primary focus of their endeavours to modernisation, which, in their minds, was also the work of God and would likely lead to mass conversion in the future. For all of these Americans, the advocacy of global modernisation would greatly benefit the United States, and, because the path of the United States was without doubt the best way forward for the world, there was 'no fundamental conflict between national advancement and global progress'.[4]

In this era, the discourse of liberal-developmentalism had manifested itself in US policies and was increasingly being practised in a variety of laboratories ranging from the American West to the Philippines. However, American elites were not always in agreement on the ability of the world's non-Western people to move towards modernity or about the method through which modernity should be spread. Elites trying to explain or justify the civilisational superiority of the West often did so by employing essentialising discourses usually tied to the concept of race. These discourses generally linked disparate biological or cultural characteristics of a group (such as average skull size, perceived diligence, excessive consumption of alcohol, or chosen religion) with their inherent abilities. In line with this, it became widely accepted both academically and in the broader public sphere that the 'differences in levels of culture or civilisation which occurred among the diverse peoples of the world derived from differences in their biological capacities'.[5] Scholars studying the concept of race have variously referred to it as a 'scavenger ideology' and 'rubbery', meaning that people could (and did) alter their conception of race in order to satisfy the needs of a particular political project, even jettisoning biology altogether if it no longer suited the project.[6] Hence, the conception of race produced by people trying to prove Western civilisational superiority did not reveal truths about various existing groups as they purported to. Instead, people continually constructed new and different conceptions of race in order to further their particular political objectives.[7] Whether or not the basis for the conception of a race was grounded in biology or culture mattered little; what mattered was that groups of people were assigned characteristics and potentials, hence being constructed as inferior to Europeans and Americans in the mind of the Western elites.

That this essentialising discourse gained strength in the era of imperialism was not a coincidence. The development of race as a concept helped to justify a world order in which Western Europeans and certain Americans were unquestionably superior to other peoples of the world because of the 'advanced' civilisation they had been able to create, thus legitimising various forms of domination.[8] Yet in the case of the United States, a country with an arguably less grand imperial history than its Western European counterparts, the domestic situation of the country played a greater role in the formation of this racist discourse. To be more specific, the construct of race in the early twentieth century United States was conditioned by the legacy of slavery and the marginalisation of Native Americans, and characterised by the employment of nineteenth century intellectual discourses that tended to reify race in scientific fact.[9] In the immediate context of this era, factors such as encounters with new waves of immigrants, increased exposure to world populations and the emergence of discourses surrounding Darwinian evolution served to sculpt American constructs of race. In a sometimes overt, sometimes unconscious endeavour to maintain their political and economic primacy at home and expand their economic dominance abroad, the self-styled 'Anglo-Saxons' of the United States did not consider all people of European heritage 'white'; this would have been tantamount to accepting all people of European origins as racial equals. Instead, they variously split the inhabitants of Europe (and increasingly the United States) into races such as Anglo-Saxons, Celts, Slavs, Iberians and Teutonic peoples. Each 'race' was assigned qualities that assessed their general worth to society and that suited the particular political project of the person assigning these qualities.[10] The people of non-Anglo-Saxon groups were often described as existing in less advanced stages of both human evolution and historic time. In dealing with foreigners, many Americans argued that the United States, being the most advanced country in the world, was the appropriate tutor to whom these people should turn in order to move from primal chaos into modernity. Christianity (preferably of a Protestant variety) was frequently seen as a sign of relative advancement, or at least advancement potential, among non-Anglo-Saxons because it was accepted by the most 'advanced' civilisations.[11]

It is interesting to note, however, that race played a somewhat indeterminate role in the formation of US foreign policy and especially in the debate about overseas expansion during the late nineteenth and early twentieth centuries. Each side in this fairly bitter debate employed the concept of race as primary evidence in the exposition of their views. American advocates of overseas expansion argued that it was the destiny and/or duty of Anglo-Saxons to guide the inferior races of the globe towards modernity, while anti-imperialists often argued that contact with and, worse still, the assimilation of these other races would be detrimental to American society. There were others, like Mark Twain, who bemoaned American mistreatment of the 'savages' in the Philippines and questioned the sagacity of forcing American-style modernity upon these people. Race, then, played a major role in the debates over American imperialism because it was such an influential concept in the era, but the malleability of the concept made it useful for many opposing positions within a single debate.[12]

Conceptions of religion in the United States were often intertwined with race during this era, in that a chosen religion somehow showed a group's relative potential for advancement. As previously noted,

American elites saw Protestant Christianity, the dominant faith in their country, as the most modern of religions and as a worldwide 'vehicle for both spiritual and material development'. According to these elites, Protestant Christianity held within it the seeds of prosperity whereas the other religions of the world generally did not.[13] Islam, to use an example pertinent to this study, was seen as greatly flawed. As historian Ussama Makdisi has observed, most Americans saw Islam as 'wrong and hateful', 'backward' and 'uniquely unsuited to modern civilization'.[14] Judaism (generally referred to as both a religion and a race), like Christianity, held within it seeds of prosperity but also held some less desirable traits like 'a vicious, race-specific brand of individualism and materialism'.[15] In general, American elites discussed religious groups in a similar manner to the way in which they discussed races and ethnicities, that is by assigning these religions enduring traits and potentials.

While the above-described conceptions of race and religion were the dominant beliefs in this era, not everyone accepted these views. Among the underlying strands of dissenting discourse, two appear to have been especially significant to the members of the King–Crane Commission. In one such strand, contemporary anthropologist Franz Boas and his followers maintained that although certain divisions between races may exist, there was no proof that one race was inherently superior to the others. While Boas did not question that there were different levels of development among world races, he contended that this was due to cultural, not biological, differences.[16] Others argued that the West did not have the monopoly on the proper way to live and may have even got a few things wrong. Historian Matthew Frye Jacobson has offered an apt summary of this view: 'Shadowing the aggressive literature of social evolution and world supremacy was a quiet antimodern envy, a muted suspicion that the benighted regions of the globe might actually embody a few lessons worth learning.'[17]

Beyond these more essentialising discourses, there was another, perhaps even more immediately influential idea that shaped the minds of the era's American elites. In the post-World War I diplomatic environment, the quandary of how to reshape the world in such a way as to avoid future conflagration took precedence in many people's thinking, and the implementation of the concept of self-determination was part of Woodrow Wilson's solution to this problem. Having only been deployed by Wilson in 1918, the concept remained a contested signifier within

American policy circles: although self-determination had strong affiliations to other concepts previously existing in American minds, it came across to many people as being the basis for a complete reshuffling of world politics. Discussion of its application, however, seemed to raise as many questions as it answered. The opacity of self-determination as a concept and the role that it should play in state creation were the sources of major disagreement among American policy elites.

Although the term 'self-determination' had previously existed in various contexts, it was first prominently deployed in this era by the Bolsheviks, with Lenin and Trotsky both using it in 1917 to specifically call for the dismembering of the world's colonial empires along 'national' lines. In early 1918, British Prime Minister David Lloyd George co-opted the term in a speech to a group of union leaders, stating that Britain would respect 'the right of self-determination or the consent of the governed' in the postwar division of lands. Wilson, who, like Lenin, sought a changed postwar order but, like Lloyd George, wanted no revolutions, first used the term in February 1918. In line with Lloyd George, Wilson employed self-determination as synonymous with 'the consent of the governed', which was a term he had been using for a number of years. By this, he did not mean that the people of the now defunct German, Austrian, and Ottoman Empires would be able to choose their future government, but that the powers should 'respect' any 'national aspirations' of these people, and that only the most 'well-defined' versions of these aspirations 'shall be accorded the utmost satisfaction that can be accorded them'.[18] These national aspirations, in Wilson's mind, had less to do with ethnic nations and more to do with popular sovereignty of people (regardless of race or religion) within a given territory. Wilson's formulation boded well for European regions that sought independence and were likely to have (in Wilson's mind) the most 'well-defined' national aspirations; it was less auspicious for the non-European peoples of the world, who were more likely to harbour, according to Wilson, poorly defined national aspirations. Such people were not yet ready to govern themselves but could, perhaps, be led in this direction. According to Wilson, then, it was not that most people in the world would have the right to determine their political future, but that they at least had the right to be consulted about their preferences.[19] The people of the Ottoman lands, in Wilson's mind, fell into the group who had less well-defined national aspirations and required extensive tutelage before they would be ready for independence.

The commission members, then, were not simply blank slates (which is something that both they and Wilson sometimes implied). They harboured a social imaginary that proclaimed the superiority of certain American and Western European Christians as the creators and bearers of the highest form of civilisation the world had yet seen. Discourses of modernity, race and religion, along with the more contemporary and controversial concept of self-determination, governed the minds of the commission members. Yet the differing strands of discourse not yet incorporated into their social imaginary, along with discourses that challenged the framework of this imaginary, allowed for the possibility of differences in their opinions.

The Ottoman Empire in the Early Twentieth Century[20]

The Ottoman Empire entered the twentieth century with a proud history and an uncertain future. Although the Ottoman realm was significantly smaller than it had been at the start of the nineteenth century, its territory still included large portions of what is today Turkey, the Balkans, Thrace, Iraq, Syria, Lebanon, Jordan, Israel/Palestine, Saudi Arabia, Yemen and Libya. In an effort to remain viable, the empire was in the midst of a long modernising scheme initiated in the nineteenth century during which the government had extended things like schooling, railroads and medical care to many parts of the empire. The Ottoman military had also been improved through modernisation and training, though it still relied largely on European countries for the technology of warfare. The government was, however, saddled with debt and at the financial mercy of Europe's most powerful empires (Britain, France and Germany). Furthermore, the Russian and Austro-Hungarian Empires, along with smaller countries like Greece, coveted Ottoman lands. In sum, the Ottoman Empire was a modernising but internally flawed polity under great external pressure in the years before World War I.

In hopes of remedying the empire's problems, a group of army officers, calling themselves the Committee of Union and Progress (CUP), overthrew the government of Sultan Abdulhamid II in 1908 (often referred to as the Young Turk Revolution). This group reinstated the Constitution of 1876, which checked the Sultan's power and established an elected legislature. They also sought to reinvigorate the empire through the continuation and acceleration of the modernising projects of the nineteenth century. The CUP reforms brought in many changes, including an era of elections and the renewed appeal of imperial citizenship (Ottomanism), both of which fostered goodwill among the varied populations of the empire. Problems began to cloud these seemingly positive changes: an attempted counterrevolution in 1909 made it clear to the CUP that their new government was fragile and they began to centralise power in their own hands. Revolts in Albania and Yemen, along with the Italian seizure of the Ottoman provinces in what is now Libya, made the empire's situation more precarious, and problems in the Balkan provinces compounded this. In 1912, several Balkan states (Serbia, Montenegro, Bulgaria and Greece), having observed the Ottoman military's weakness against Italy, sought to remove more land from Ottoman control. The subsequent Balkan Wars of 1912–13 were a disastrous episode for the Ottomans, partly because they lost their relatively prosperous Balkan provinces that had been part of the empire for hundreds of years. There was also a massive influx of Muslim refugees from the Balkans and their resettlement in the empire caused major problems. Finally, the loss of the Balkan populations marked a major demographic shift in the empire, making it more ethnically Turkish and religiously Muslim than it had been previously. By this time, the moment of good will towards the CUP and Ottomanism in general was waning. The wars had hindered the ability of the central government to carry out effective reforms and the competing aims of the empire's various internal communities often clashed with the realities of a centralised and increasingly authoritarian Ottoman state.

In terms of the Ottoman Empire's future, it had long been accepted by the European powers that it would some day be dismantled, though many of these powers had sought to keep the empire intact on numerous occasions in order to maintain the tenuous European balance of power. For years, the Ottoman's rivals had been trying to position themselves advantageously in anticipation of the empire's eventual dismantling. Britain was interested in Mesopotamia and Palestine, and had already occupied Egypt with an eye to keeping their lifeline to India, the Suez Canal, firmly in their hands. They also had been moving to control Iran, adjacent to both the Ottoman Empire and British India. France, having occupied the former Ottoman provinces of Algeria and Tunisia by this time, was also trying to spread its influence in Greater Syria. Russia, seen by many Ottomans as their empire's greatest threat, had expanded its holdings in eastern Anatolia during the 1878 War and had coveted the Bosphorus and Dardanelles – the Straits – for years. The Germans also had expanded their economic influence in the region, having been behind the building of a railroad that extended from Istanbul to Basra (unfinished at the beginning of the war) and having also funded public works in Jerusalem. Lastly, Austria had been competing with the Ottomans for influence and territory in the Balkans for centuries and continued to do so.

The events of 1914 in Europe were foreboding for the embattled Ottoman Empire. The CUP, believing that their empire's very existence was at stake should some sort of major war break out, sought an alliance that would give them the best chance of survival. By the spring of 1914, the only real option for the Ottomans appeared to be an alliance with Germany, partly because France and Britain had already concluded an alliance with Russia, which was arguably the empire with the longest standing designs on Ottoman territory. As war broke out in Europe in the summer of 1914, the Ottomans delayed their entry into the war as long as possible, knowing that they were ill-prepared for such a conflict. Finally, in late October (after having convinced the Germans to give them a major loan and to send them a large amount of materiel), two new Ottoman/German warships sailed into the Black Sea and attacked Russian maritime interests. The formal Ottoman role in the conflict had begun. They joined the war on the side of the Central Powers (Germany, Austria–Hungary and eventually Bulgaria) against the Triple Entente (Britain, France, Russia and a number of smaller countries – often referred to as 'the Allies'). Italy became a member of the Entente in 1915, and the United States joined as an 'associated power' in 1917.

Militarily, the war was interspersed with disasters and successes for the Ottomans. The initial two campaigns, attacks on the Russians in eastern Anatolia and the British at the Suez Canal, were disasters. In the winter of 1914–15, CUP Minister of War Enver Pasha personally led 100,000 troops through eastern Anatolia (where modern transport was virtually non-existent) in order to attack Russian positions in the Caucasus. The Russians, assisted by disease and freezing temperatures, wiped out most of this Ottoman army, leaving the front vulnerable to Russian advances. Jamal Pasha, also a major leader of the CUP, led his troops to the edge of the Suez Canal but the well-entrenched British easily defeated his army. Conversely, 1915 and 1916 saw two major Ottoman successes. In the spring of 1915, the British and French tried to take control of the Dardanelles but the Ottomans were able to repulse them after intense and lengthy fighting at Gallipoli. In the spring of 1916, the Ottomans also captured British forces at Kut in Mesopotamia after a long siege. Despite these successes, the Ottoman army was nearly a spent force by the end of 1916, with disease ravaging the troops and overall poor conditions causing mass desertions. By the time General Edmund Allenby and the British forces began their march north from Egypt, the Ottomans, though often still fighting valiantly, had little chance of successfully resisting. The so-called 'Arab Revolt' also abetted Allenby's campaign, with Bedouins and Ottoman prisoners of war (under the command of Amir Faysal of the Hejaz and British Captain T.E. Lawrence) harassing Ottoman supply roots and capturing key outposts. The British had taken all of Greater Syria and Mesopotamia by the time the war ended in 1918.

During the war, conditions in the Ottoman Empire for its civilians were terrible. Famine gripped large parts of the empire, having been caused by the combination of a lack of workers in the fields, a major locust plague in 1915, various types of harsh weather, Ottoman bureaucratic moves that kept grain away from the coast and a blockade by the British and French. In Greater Syria, Jamal Pasha tried to root out all subversion (real or imagined) and executed many accused traitors. In eastern Anatolia, the Armenian populations, because of their alleged disloyalty to the empire, were forcibly removed from their villages and were mostly sent south towards Greater Syria, with hundreds of thousands dying or being killed along the way. These events captured the attention of the United States, and in 1915 the American Committee for Armenian and Syrian Relief (ACASR, later referred to as Near East Relief) began providing humanitarian aid to the region. The horrific deprivations of the war served to undermine the allegiance of non-Turkish subjects to the Ottoman Empire and helped lead to a postwar situation in which many members of these groups called for independence from the Turks.

On 30 October 1918, Ottoman and British officials signed the Armistice ending Ottoman involvement in World War I. The events of September (with neighbouring ally Bulgaria leaving the war and the

Figure 2.1 Amir Faysal leaving the Hotel Victoria after a conference with General Allenby on 3 October 1918. (Source: World War I Photograph Album, 1918–19, American University of Beirut/Library Archives).

British making a major push on the Syrian front), paired with the empire's diminishing material ability to wage war, led the majority of the Ottoman leadership to agree that defeat had become inevitable. Following the cessation of hostilities, the British and French occupied Istanbul and divided Greater Syria into 'Occupied Enemy Territory Administrations' (OETA) with France controlling the 'West' and the 'North' (encompassing the coast from Lebanon to Cilicia), and Britain overseeing a government led by Amir Faysal in the 'East' (largely what now constitutes Syria and Jordan, minus the coast). Britain also controlled the 'South' (Palestine) and Mesopotamia. The Ottoman Empire, the borders of which had been receding for years, placed itself at the mercy of the Allies, though elements of the Ottoman army regrouped in central Anatolia and prepared to resist occupation by foreign powers.

Unbeknown to the countries not involved (though not unsuspected by them), Britain, France, Italy and Russia had been secretly divvying up the lands of the Ottoman Empire during the war. In the most notable of these understandings, the Sykes–Picot Agreement of 1916, the British and French divided Greater Syria and Mesopotamia between them, with France slated to receive what is now Lebanon, Syria and northern Iraq, and the British to receive what is now Palestine, Jordan and southern Iraq. The Russians were also promised the Straits and portions of eastern Anatolia, while the Italians were promised islands and land in Anatolia around Antalya. The Greek government had also aided the British in their campaign against the Ottomans and were hoping to gain territory around Smyrna after the war. Though this could have set the stage for a rather simple postwar distribution of the Ottoman spoils, numerous disagreements and changes in circumstances created an uncertain postwar situation regarding this matter.

The factors that complicated this potentially simple settlement were numerous. The Bolsheviks had taken control of the Russian government in 1917 and pulled out of treaty obligations made by the previous regime, hence technically undermining the basis of any treaties to which Russia had been a party. The Arab contribution to the war effort, which the British had coaxed with a vague commitment to 'support Arab independence' given to Sherif Hussein of Mecca, had led to heightened expectations for autonomy among many people in the region, as did the so-called 'Anglo-French Declaration' of November 1918, in which the British and French pledged to 'encourage and assist in the establishment of indigenous governments' in the region. The British had also promised European Zionists in the 'Balfour Declaration' that they would 'facilitate' the establishment of a 'Jewish national home' in Palestine. The contrasting nature of these equivocally worded documents and the expectations they had sown among the people involved made it extremely difficult to create a postwar Middle East that would satisfy all inhabitants of the region.

Postwar wrangling between the victorious powers was also causing tension. British forces, having spearheaded the war effort in the Middle East, occupied most of Greater Syria and Mesopotamia, leading Lloyd George and many other British officials to wonder if Britain should honour the wartime agreements with the French because they had contributed little to the Middle East war effort. Georges Clemenceau, angry at the British for not allowing the French to be involved in the signing of the Armistice with the Ottomans and fearful that the British would renege on their previous agreements pertaining to the region, was determined to ensure that France got a substantial share of the Middle East. In an attempt to finalise the division of the ex-Ottoman provinces outside of the peace conference (one of many such attempts in the year or so that followed), Clemenceau and Lloyd George informally modified the Sykes–Picot Agreement, with Clemenceau ceding Mosul and Palestine to Britain in exchange for guarantees that France would have Syria. The French had also landed troops on the coast around Beirut in October 1918, much to the chagrin of Amir Faysal and his backers. In addition, Italy and Greece were both determined to control the parts of Anatolia that they deemed rightfully theirs, either through wartime promises (Italy) or by heritage (Greece). All of these agreements made it nearly impossible to reapportion the Ottoman lands to the satisfaction of every interested party.

The United States and the Ottoman Empire during World War I

On the eve of World War I, the United States was less involved with the Ottoman Empire than the other major powers but Americans did have a number of interests in the region. The group of Americans with arguably the most at stake in the empire were missionaries and their benefactors in the United States. The presence of American missionaries had been increasing over the previous century and this had culminated in, among other things, the building and maintenance of numerous schools and hospitals. Additionally, missionaries had helped to spur a huge relief effort (ACASR) to alleviate the suffering of the Ottoman subjects during the war and this brought many more Americans to the region. While the missionary footprint in the empire was significant, American business interests were relatively minor, with the largest imports from the region being tobacco, liquorice root and dates. The presence of American oil companies in the Ottoman lands was negligible at this point: it was only just before the war that the Standard Oil Company of New York had entered the early stages of exploration work in the region. Exports from the United States were also not sizeable, though the Middle East had proven to be a valuable market for American petroleum products and sewing machines.[21] In sum, the United States did have interests in the region before and during World War I, but these interests were minor in comparison to the other major powers.

Partly because the United States had relatively few connections to the Ottoman Empire, it figured little in Woodrow Wilson's presidency and foreign policy. The empire, however, had been part of his general thinking on American involvement in both the war and in the remaking of the postwar world. Wilson believed, at least from January 1917, that 'Turkey should cease to exist' in a postwar world but ultimately, after great consideration, he decided not to declare war on the Ottoman Empire.[22] In public, Wilson argued that he would not rule out going to war with Turkey, mainly because the inhabitants of the empire had to be liberated from the 'misrule'[23] of its government which was in turn under 'the impudent and alien dominion of the Prussian military and commercial autocracy'.[24] In private, he usually stated that his reasons for not going to war with Turkey were the lack of available American military resources and his concern for both the American missionaries and the Christian 'natives' in the region.[25] Wilson was influenced on this issue by his friend and wealthy political patron Cleveland Dodge, who informed him that an American declaration of war on Turkey would be a 'serious blow' to American missionary and relief efforts. Furthermore, Dodge argued that intervention would 'jeopardize many American lives besides stopping the work we are doing in saving the lives of hundreds of thousands of natives'. Among these missionaries were two of Dodge's children.[26] Wilson often voiced these concerns in more drastic terms, telling his close adviser 'Colonel' Edward House that he did not want to go to war with Turkey because 'the Turks would massacre the entire Christian population' of the territory under their control.[27] He repeated this rationale for not going to war with Turkey to the British, stating that he was convinced 'a terrible outburst of savagery would follow on a declaration of war'.[28] In an attempt to get the Ottomans to leave the war in 1917, Wilson had even secretly sent Henry Morgenthau, the American Ambassador to the Ottoman Empire during much of the war (1913–16), to try to negotiate with the Turkish leadership. Morgenthau abandoned his mission on the way to Istanbul after being convinced by British and Zionist envoys that his trip had little chance of success.[29]

In his public speeches, Wilson's most prominent mention of the Ottoman Empire came in his Fourteen Points speech of 8 January 1918. Wilson, as the 'most punctilious of stylists to sit in the White House' according to historian John Milton Cooper, generally selected the phrasing of his speeches carefully, and his comments on colonialism and the Ottoman

Empire in this speech were no exception.[30] Point Five, the general point about postwar colonial 'adjustments', called for the following:

> A free, open-minded, and absolutely impartial adjustment of all colonial claims, based upon a strict observance of the principle that in determining all such questions of sovereignty the interests of the populations concerned must have equal weight with the equitable claims of governments whose title is to be determined.

Though this was hardly an unequivocal condemnation of the world imperial system, it did highlight Wilson's belief that the rather ambiguous 'interests' of colonised peoples needed to be considered when the Allies reapportioned the lands of the defeated empires. Importantly, though, he made no mention of how the 'interests of the populations' would be determined and explicitly did not state that these populations would be responsible for determining their own interests.

The point specifically about the Ottoman Empire (Point Twelve) also displayed similarly particular wording:

> The Turkish Portions of the Ottoman Empire should be assured a secure sovereignty, but the other nationalities which are now under Turkish rule should be assured an undoubted security of life and an absolutely unmolested opportunity of autonomous development, and the Dardanelles should be permanently opened as a free passage to the ships and commerce of all nations under international guarantees.

In employing the term 'a secure sovereignty', Wilson was likely making the point that the 'Turkish Portions' of the empire should not be divided up between the Allies and instead should remain 'sovereign' but not necessarily independent. His choice of the phrases 'unmolested opportunity of autonomous development' and 'undoubted security of life' for these 'other nationalities' certainly represented a rhetorical step up from 'secure sovereignty' but also fell decidedly short of independence. Wilson did believe that all people deserved to have some say in their own governance, which is what he meant by 'self-determination', a term he began using shortly after this speech. Yet he also believed that much of the world's population (including the entire population of the Ottoman Empire) required tutoring in the best methods of self-governance in order to become successful members of the international community. Therefore, these nascent countries needed an 'advanced' nation to tutor them in the ways of modern governance until they were ready for independence. Wilson further believed that these countries should be consulted about the 'advanced' nation from which they wanted to receive their political education.[31] The difference between the Turks and these 'other nationalities' was important here: the Turks, though they did not deserve to become a colonised people, had proven themselves so inept at governing that Wilson was unsure when they would be ready for, or could be trusted with, independence. The 'other nationalities', having been under Turkish rule for so long, would require help governing themselves for the foreseeable future. Wilson likely believed that some of these nationalities might advance quickly (the Armenians) while others might simply not have the capacity for self-governance (the Arabs). Generally speaking, though, the inclusion of Point Twelve confirmed that Wilson believed that his principles should be a significant factor in the reconfiguration of the Ottoman lands. As will be seen in subsequent chapters, Point Twelve was noted by nationalists in the region, many of whom thought that it represented a commitment to help them attain a just political solution for their future.

Zionism also played a role in Wilson's thinking about the Ottoman lands. Wilson appears to have supported Zionism by the war's end yet this support remained somewhat equivocal. Zionism was a relatively minor movement in the early twentieth century United States and it divided American Jews. This was partly because Jews had faced staunch suspicion of their ability to be 'American first and Jewish second'. Many Jews had fought hard to establish themselves as assimilated Americans and believed that they could be accused of divided loyalties if they supported the establishment of a new Jewish state, thus leading to the lacklustre American Jewish support for Zionism.[32] Wilson, therefore, had little electoral impetus to wholeheartedly endorse the Zionist project.

During the war, however, American Zionists lobbied Wilson extensively and were successful in getting him to express sympathy for their cause. In a private 1917 meeting with leading Zionist (and Wilson Supreme Court appointee) Louis Brandeis, for example, Wilson stated that he was 'sympathetic' to the goal of the Zionist movement that, in his understanding, was 'to establish a publicly assured, legally secured homeland for the Jewish people in Palestine'.[33] The British also sought his backing for their government policy towards Zionism as stated in the Balfour Declaration, but Wilson believed that it was best only to express 'sympathy' for the movement rather than make 'any real commitment'.[34] In 1918, Wilson wrote a letter to another prominent American Zionist (Rabbi Stephen Wise) stating that he welcomed the opportunity to express 'satisfaction' with the progress of the Zionist movement, but he felt compelled to state that he was backing Zionism 'with the understanding that nothing would be done to prejudice the civil and religious rights of non-Jewish people in Palestine'.[35] Wilson also acknowledged other problems with his quiet policy of favouring Zionism (as pointed out to him by Secretary of State Robert Lansing): the United States was not at war with the Ottomans and hence had no right to discuss matters that concerned Ottoman lands; American Jews were not all supportive of Zionism, hence backing Zionism could be politically 'unwise'; and many Christians might 'resent' turning over their 'Holy Land' to the Jews. Wilson told Lansing that 'very unwillingly he was forced to agree' with him on these points but stated in an oddly passive fashion that 'he had an impression that we had assented to the British declaration regarding returning Palestine to the Jews'.[36]

***

Shortly after the Ottomans left the war, the conflict as a whole ended, with Austria-Hungary and Germany conceding defeat in November 1918. The Paris Peace Conference, where the wartime victors were to decide the fate of the vanquished, convened the following January. Wilson, having for years been making lofty, well-publicised pronouncements of his ideas for the postwar world, decided that he must attend the conference and play a key role in its settlements. In December 1918, Wilson arrived in Europe to great fanfare. Crowds lined the streets to cheer his arrival throughout his short pre-conference European tour. Wilson's idealism, paired with the jubilation that accompanied the end of such a devastating conflict, had planted optimism that ranged from guarded to unreserved among both the victors and the vanquished; the public expectation that came with American involvement in the peace conference could hardly have been higher. Wilson's words also greatly excited colonial subjects throughout the world; in their minds, Wilson was advocating their anti-colonial causes.[37] However, his Allied counterparts generally did not see his popularity as helpful to their respective postwar plans. France, Great Britain and Italy had taken far more losses than the United States during the war and were hoping to have something to show for these losses at the end of their negotiations. These goals often conflicted with Wilson's rhetoric.[38] The stage was thus set for acrimony among the victorious powers.

CHAPTER 3

PARIS PEACE CONFERENCE 1: THE IDEA OF A COMMISSION

The Paris Peace Conference of 1919 was one of the most momentous events in modern history. At the end of an obscenely destructive war, the leaders of the victorious powers gathered in Paris to decide the terms of the postwar peace. The complexity and diversity of the tasks in front of these leaders (nothing less than reapportioning major chunks of the globe) were daunting to say the least. The fate of the Ottoman lands, though not the top priority for this select group of world leaders, was a particularly prominent item on the agenda. The powers had decided that a settlement was going to be imposed upon the Ottoman Empire and that the empire was going to be dismantled. These powers did, however, hear testimony from various groups representing populations in the Ottoman lands. The list of those allowed to give testimony included Amir Faysal (who, while officially representing the Hejaz, claimed to speak for the people of Greater Syria) as well as delegations of Armenians, Kurds, Zionists, Syrian expatriates and, eventually, the Ottoman government. This testimony played little role in the decisions made about the future disposition of Ottoman territories, with Britain and France both showing a strong determination to craft a settlement in line with their own interests.

So in this unfavourable context, how did the King–Crane Commission come to be? As will be shown in the next two chapters, Woodrow Wilson sent the commission for two main reasons. First, figures like Amir Faysal, Syrian Protestant College President Howard

PARIS PEACE CONFERENCE 1: THE IDEA OF A COMMISSION 29

Bliss and British General Edmund Allenby convinced Wilson that the sending of a fact-finding commission to the Ottoman lands would be beneficial and informative. Second, Wilson deemed such a commission to be in line with his ideals and contrary to the 'old diplomacy' that he believed was still being practised by the British and French in the division of the Ottoman lands. After the commission was proposed, many people attempted to ensure that it would not go, including French and British officials, Zionists and even a number Americans. The commission, then, emerged from the fractious atmosphere caused by wrangling about the disposition of the Ottoman lands and began under a cloud of controversy from which it has never entirely escaped.

The Initial Idea

Woodrow Wilson arrived in Paris with a set of ideals that challenged the international status quo. He argued that any agreement reached in Paris should be far less punitive than past peace settlements so that resentment would not cause future wars. In line with this, he championed a new 'League of Nations' which would, among other things, seek to shift the dominant mode of inter-state dispute resolution from war to arbitration.[1] Wilson also arrived in Paris with little personal knowledge of the Ottoman lands and few advisers who knew the region well. The fact that the group of American commissioners he selected for the peace conference (consisting of Colonel House, Secretary of State Lansing, career diplomat Henry White and General Tasker H. Bliss) had little experience with, or knowledge of, the Middle East was a telling example of this.

Somewhat surprisingly, the same was largely true of Wilson's 'expert' advisers on the region. Wilson did have access to numerous reports about the Ottoman lands prepared by the Inquiry (the American group of academics commissioned to advise the president on peace settlements), though the quality of these reports was low and the credentials of their authors were questionable. An internal (and forthright) 1918 meta-analysis of the Inquiry's reports on the Ottoman Empire noted, for example, that 'the study of Turkey is of course enormously difficult owing to the extreme complexity of the problem, the unreliability of official statistics, and the great changes caused by the war'. The report further noted that 'the Inquiry is not prepared to speak with any authority on Turkish questions' and that more time would be required to 'develop a group of men who can speak with expertness', insinuating that little such expertise existed among this elite group of scholars.[2]

At the peace conference, the main report on the Middle East that Wilson would have had at his disposal was primarily written by William Westermann, the head of the 'Western Asia' section of the Inquiry in Paris. Westermann was chiefly an historian of ancient Egyptian, Greek and Roman societies and had what seems to have been only a passing knowledge of the Middle East. He was aided by Leon Dominian, who had been born in the Ottoman Empire but was primarily an expert on European languages. Others were brought in because of their supposed expertise such as David Magie (a professor of classics at Princeton) and Isaiah Bowman (a geographer who was known for books like *Well-Drilling Methods* and *The Andes of Southern Peru*). While these people sought advice from American diplomats and missionaries who had spent time in the region, Wilson's main counsellors on the division of the Ottoman Empire could hardly be considered experts on the subject. Despite this, the 'Western Asia' section delivered their recommendations to the president in January of 1919, proposing that the Ottoman Empire should be divided into six sections (Armenia, Anatolia, Mesopotamia, Syria, Palestine and Arabia) and that all of the Ottoman lands should be supervised by Western powers for the foreseeable future. In addition, the report recommended that a Jewish 'national home' (which they used synonymously with 'Jewish State' in the report) should be established in Palestine.[3] These recommendations were not far from the basic framework for the reapportioning of the Ottoman lands brewing in the minds of their European colleagues.

When negotiations began at the peace conference on 18 January 1919, the main concern of the victorious powers was the final treaty with Germany. The Ottoman Empire, being a somewhat secondary concern, was mentioned only in passing in the Supreme Council[4] until 30 January, when the council was debating the details of the League of Nations. The specific document they discussed on this day was entitled the 'Draft Resolutions in Reference to Mandatories', which Wilson saw as the partial fulfilment of his ideals. 'Mandatories' were a seemingly novel geopolitical category. The idea was that the colonial holdings of the defeated empires, including those of the Ottoman Empire, should not be simply annexed by the Allies but should instead be presided over as 'mandatories' by the League of Nations, though the League would assign a specific power to each mandatory. These mandatories would be tutorial (not colonial) polities in which an 'advanced' power would lead the less advanced people of a given region towards self-government.[5] In this sense, the 'theory of mandates', as Wilson later argued, was not 'a theory of permanent subordination' but was instead a 'theory of development'.[6]

In its discussion of the Ottoman lands, the 'Mandatories' document argued for the complete dismantling of the Ottoman Empire. This needed to be done 'because of the historical mis-government by the Turks of the subject peoples and the terrible massacres of Armenians and others in recent years'. 'Armenia, Syria, Mesopotamia, Palestine and Arabia,' it continued, 'must be completely severed from the Turkish Empire'. While most European territories being formed in the wake of the war were advanced enough for self-government, these new post-Ottoman territories were 'inhabited by peoples not yet able to stand by themselves' and would require 'the rendering of administrative advice and assistance by a mandatory power until such time as they are able to stand alone'. 'The wishes of these communities', the document continued, 'must be a principal consideration in the selection of the mandatory power'.[7] Hence, mandatory overseers were to be obligatory for territories taken from the Ottomans and, in an apparent victory for Wilson, the wishes of these territories' inhabitants were to be considered in the selection of the mandatory power. While seeing something resembling his rhetoric officially placed on paper may have pleased Wilson, the deliberate ambiguity of the language made it possible for his principles to be circumvented.

Although this 'wishes of the people' rhetoric may have looked good on paper, it raised the question of how these wishes could best be ascertained in the Ottoman Empire. When the Paris Peace Conference attempted to learn such 'wishes', they employed two main methods. The first and most convenient (because it could usually be done in Paris) was to learn the desires of a particular region's people by consulting with both selected representatives from the region in question and with experts who had knowledge of the region. The second, which (if it happened) usually occurred after the first had been utilised, was to consult the people of a region directly via some form of plebiscite or fact-finding commission. There were several plebiscites held as a result of the postwar reapportioning of the globe but, predictably, these generally occurred in Europe where nationalism and democracy would have been considered 'more developed'.[8] In view of the dismissive attitude of the diplomats at the Paris Peace Conference towards the people of the Ottoman lands and the covetous tendencies of France, Britain, Italy and Greece towards the region, it is not surprising that undertaking some sort of formal Ottoman plebiscite was never seriously contemplated.[9] Although specific reasons were never given for this, it is easy to surmise the primary objection: the region had a poorly educated populace that was not yet prepared for democracy (wilfully ignoring the fact that there had been a number of elections held in the Ottoman Empire's recent past).

A fact-finding commission to the Ottoman lands seemed to make more sense to Wilson, although it was not his idea. The US government had recently been appointing many such commissions to investigate a wide variety of issues, including the situation in the Philippines (the Philippines Commission of 1899), industrial working conditions (the Factory Commission of 1911) and the situation in postwar Russia (the Bullitt Mission of 1919). These panels were often filled with influential Americans, including wealthy businessmen, political figures, university presidents, military generals and prominent journalists. Such commissions were commonplace in the United States and would become commonplace at the peace conference as well. In January, members of the Inquiry started planning a fact-finding commission to the Ottoman Empire, which was to be similar to others that had already gone to Germany, Austria-Hungary and Russia. Although it is possible that such a commission was being discussed before this, it appears that Gabriel Bie Ravndal (an American diplomat with extensive experience in the region) first suggested the 'sending of a special mission into Turkey' to the American Commission to Negotiate Peace in December of 1918. In its initial incarnation, it was to be led by Leon Dominian and its task was to travel through the Ottoman lands and report on the 'conditions' therein.[10]

Despite preparations for this commission occurring among the Americans, Amir Faysal was in fact the first to openly suggest to the Supreme Council that a commission should survey the Ottoman lands.[11] Faysal was one of the more storied figures of the Paris Peace Conference. As a Hashemite (hence purportedly the direct descendant of the Prophet Mohammad) with a regal Bedouin appearance, Faysal looked to many people at the Conference like someone directly from a storybook. 'His voice', stated Robert Lansing, 'seemed to breathe the perfume of frankincense.'[12] Though he did not speak English, Faysal was well-educated and was a past member of the Ottoman Parliament. He was also the son of Sharif Hussein of Mecca and had learned to articulate his position in Wilsonian terms (usually through the translation of T.E. Lawrence).[13] The American Middle East 'expert' William Westermann, for his part, was initially dismissive of Faysal when they met on 12 January, claiming that Lawrence was 'Faisal's brain as well as his mouthpiece'. In support of this opinion, Westermann cited the rumour that Faysal had 'recited a certain portion of the 4th book of the Koran' at a speech in Edinburgh before the peace conference and Lawrence had 'said what he wanted to in translating' the speech.[14] Westermann changed his opinion after having dinner with Faysal on 20 January. At this dinner, attended by many of the American Middle East experts, Faysal jokingly recounted a story about recently being handed 'a card asking him to vote' on whether or not Emperor Wilhelm II of Germany should be tried. Instead of voting on this matter, Faysal noted that he scratched out Wilhelm's name and 'wrote four names in its place': Jamal Pasha, Mark Sykes, François Georges-Picot (both of the Sykes–Picot Agreement) and Jean Goût, an influential proponent of French colonial incursions into the Middle East. Furthermore, when his dinner companions asked Faysal about his official position on the reapportioning of the Ottoman lands, he began by writing a word in Arabic on a sheet of paper and stated he hoped that it was a word on which they all would agree after they had heard his position. These 'experts' on the Middle East, none of whom knew Arabic, went along with Faysal's ruse and listened to him tell a 'dramatic' and 'wonderfully told' story about the Arab Revolt and the intransigence of the French. At the end, the meaning of the word was revealed; it was *istiklal* (independence). Faysal concluded by asking whether the people at the dinner agreed with him that such a thing was appropriate for Greater Syria. Westermann, being duly impressed by this showing, declared that: 'This is a remarkable man really. Lawrence is not his brains as I thought. Lawrence says that he can help him on details, but when he starts on principles Faisal goes off like a 60 [horse] power car.' He concluded, 'Great is Faisal. I am a convert.'[15]

Faysal's first mention of a commission in a semi-official setting also appears to have come on 20 January. Although in late 1918 he had mentioned the possibility of a 'mixed' or American commission to judge public opinion on matters concerning the future of the region, he does not appear to have come to the Conference set on such a commission.[16] In a 1 January 1919 memorandum, for example, Faysal noted his basic aims for the conference but did not mention a commission of any sort.[17] On 20 January, however, Faysal listed such a commission as one of the central parts of his platform in a conversation with William Westermann, stating that he now planned 'to ask the Conference, and he wants American help, to send a Mixed commission out to Syria and find out what the people want and let that finding be adopted'. Faysal claimed he was making this request because the French had attempted to tell him that he could not have a voice at the peace conference unless he agreed to French control in Syria.[18] T.E. Lawrence later backed this version of this story, claiming Faysal's call for a commission was 'prompted by the failure of the French authorities to approach the Amir Faysal in a conciliatory way'.[19] Also on 20 January, Faysal requested a 'plebiscite to ascertain opinion in [the] Arab lands' in a meeting with Colonel House and, on 23 January, made a similar appeal in a brief audience with Woodrow Wilson. Wilson would not commit to supporting such an endeavour at this point, according to Rustum Haydar (Faysal's secretary).[20] At a time when commissions of various sorts were active in Paris and throughout Europe, Faysal understood that such a commission might help to advance his goals. Westermann supported Faysal on this and decreed that he was 'trying to get one of the American commissioners to introduce a resolution that a committee should be sent to Syria to find out what the natives really want in the way of a government'.[21]

On 29 January, Amir Faysal submitted a short written statement of his position to the Americans. Speaking in his official capacity as a representative of his father, Sharif Hussein of Mecca, Faysal made the rather bold request that 'the Arabic-speaking people of Asia [...] be recognized as independent sovereign peoples'. The boundaries of the newly formed states would be decided 'between us [the Arabs], after the wishes of their respective inhabitants have been ascertained'. The last paragraph and the appendix of this concise document were devoted to Wilson's rhetoric, in which he paraphrased from the Second Point of Wilson's Four Points speech of 11 February 1918, stating:

I base my request on the principles enunciated by President Wilson (attached [in the appendix]), and am confident that the Powers will attach more importance to the bodies and souls of the Arabic-speaking peoples than to their own material interests.

Faysal, having devoted approximately one-third of this concise request for independence to either quoting or summarising Wilsonian principles, was pinning his hopes on both the influence of Wilson's vision in the drafting of the peace settlement and, implicitly, on the United States to ensure that the wishes of the people were considered in this drafting.[22]

Meanwhile, the American diplomats appeared to have reacted quickly to Faysal's request for a commission. In a 1 February meeting of the 'plenipotentiary' of the American commissioners to the peace conference (Lansing, House, White and Bliss), Lansing noted that he believed that there should be a commission to Turkey, apparently unaware that another such commission was already in the works. This plan, which Lansing claimed had been approved by Wilson, was to send two Americans – noted progressive Frederic C. Howe (who was in Paris) and experienced Middle Eastern missionary James L. Barton – on a mission to Ottoman lands in order to gain insight into the political desires of the region's population. Barton was in Rome at this point (or so they thought) and, after receiving instructions on his mission, Howe was sent to meet him there. From Rome, they were supposed to travel to the Ottoman lands together. Howe left for Italy shortly after this meeting and the previously planned commission led by Leon Dominian was put on hold.[23]

On 3 and 4 of February, another figure was laying out the claims of his country to Ottoman lands before the peace conference. The charismatic Greek Prime Minister Eleutherios Venizelos, who charmed the leaders of the Great Powers at least as much as Faysal, saw the end of the war as a way to expand the borders of his country. Using Wilson's aforementioned Point Twelve, Venizelos argued that the best way to give the Greeks in Anatolia (one of the 'other nationalities' living under Turkish rule) a chance for 'development' was to place them under the rule of Athens. More specifically, Venizelos was requesting that Greece be given control of the Anatolian shores stretching from Smyrna to the Dardanelles and even further along the Sea of Marmara. These were, in his reckoning, the places where the most substantial populations of Greeks lived, though some of the American experts on Greece thought that the statistics he used were inflated. Venizelos used terms to denigrate the Turks that would have been acceptable and familiar to his audience, stating that 'Asia Minor':

> was inhabited by two races differing so greatly; the one representing an old and advanced civilisation, the other unable to establish a Government acceptable to foreign races. The Turks were good workers, honest in their relations, and a good people as subjects. But as rulers they were insupportable and a disgrace to civilisation.[24]

The requests of Venizelos were extremely ambitious, though he was ably couching them in modest and modern rhetoric that dazzled the leaders of the Great Powers. William Westermann, for his part, recognised the ambition behind this agreeable façade, stating that 'M. Venizelos' appetite grows with feeding.'[25] A commission with representatives from each of the Great Powers was set up to weigh these claims and to recommend a final decision on these and other Greek requests. Like much else at the peace conference, the Greek commission's work was quickly caught up in squabbling among the Allies, with the British and French largely supporting Venizelos's requests, the Americans taking a moderate stance and Italians attempting to deny any Greek expansion.[26]

In continuing their focus on the Ottoman Empire, the Supreme Council received Amir Faysal on 6 February. In his speech, Faysal requested independence for 'all of the Arabic speaking peoples in Asia'. Faysal framed his plea for independence in modern terms, claiming that the region was socially and economically coherent, as well as linguistically and racially pure (Arabic and Semitic). The region's inhabitants, as a race, were the descendants of a people who had created one of history's great civilisations (meaning medieval Arab society) and hence had an inherent 'capacity to play their part in the world'. Furthermore, the region's people realised that their 'country lacked development' and consequently had a 'zeal for betterment'. The Arabs would, according to Faysal, 'seek help from everyone who wished them well'. In addition, Faysal buffered his argument by noting that the Arabs had been loyal to the Allies, had suffered great losses, and had been promised much during the war. In terms of territory, Faysal spoke of a rather vague 'confederation' of countries in the 'liberated Arabic speaking' lands of Asia, with Greater Syria (perhaps including 'the present province of Lebanon') and the Hejaz accounting for at least two of these countries. Palestine, he stated, could be 'left on one side for the mutual consideration of all parties interested' because of its 'universal character'.[27]

At the end of his plea for the independence of the Arab people, Faysal asked for a commission to the region, stating that:

> The various Provinces, on the principle of self-determination, should be allowed to indicate to the League of Nations the nature of the assistance they required. If the indications before the Conference in any one case were not conclusive as to their wishes for their complete independence or for their mandatory power [...] [then] an international inquiry, made in the area concerned, might be a quick, easy, sure and just way of determining their wishes.[28]

After his speech, he entertained numerous questions from those present, including some loaded ones from Lloyd George about how much the Arabs had helped in the conquest of Mesopotamia, to which Faysal answered that, though they had not fought in this region, many people from Mesopotamia had served in his army in order to 'vindicate their rights to self-government'. Wilson stepped in and asked Faysal which countries he would want as mandatory powers to oversee the region, with this having already been written into the League of Nations Covenant. Faysal replied that 'it must be for the Arab people to declare their wishes' on this matter and that he was in Paris only to 'ask for the independence of his people and for their right to choose their own mandatory'. He ended his response to Wilson with what surely would have been seen by the Americans present as an eloquent plea:

> The Arabs were an ancient people, civilized and organized at a time when the nations represented in this room were unformed... The Arabs had tasted slavery: none of the nations gathered in the room knew what that meant. For 400 years [Ottoman rule] the Arabs had suffered under a violent military oppression, and as long as life remained in them, they meant never to return to it.

After further questioning mainly by the British and French, Faysal concluded his appearance before the council.[29] His oratorical skills were praised by the Americans, with Robert Lansing stating that it was 'a very dignified and interesting presentation'.[30] The influence of Faysal's testimony among the Americans was almost immediate, with General Tasker Bliss suggesting to Wilson on 8 February that 'the Conference should adopt the proposal made by Amir Faysal' for an inter-Allied commission to the Ottoman lands in hopes of, among other things, lessening the tension that existed between the Arabs and the French.[31]

The French still believed, with increasing reason, that Faysal posed a serious threat to their Syrian claims and this prompted them to renew their previous efforts to settle the matter bilaterally with the British. On the day of Faysal's presentation (6 February), French diplomats proposed a settlement to the British based on the boundaries that Clemenceau and Lloyd George had agreed upon in December 1918. Importantly, the French agreed to install Faysal as ruler in Damascus as part of the agreement. The British, perhaps sensing the weakness of France's position, delivered a counter-proposal on 8 February in which the size of French Syria was significantly smaller. Unsurprisingly, this infuriated the French. Clemenceau, for whom Syria had previously only registered as a minor concern, had now been transformed into a 'passionate defender of French rights in Syria'. The tension created by this issue was only just beginning.[32]

Support for Faysal's general point of view arrived in Paris in the form of Howard Bliss, the President of the Syrian Protestant College in Beirut (later the American University of Beirut), and this support accelerated among the Americans thereafter. Having been born and raised in Lebanon (the son of Daniel Bliss, founder of the Syrian Protestant College), Bliss was one of the most respected expatriates in the Ottoman Empire. His reputation was stellar among most Americans and Europeans with knowledge of the region, with, for example, T.E. Lawrence praising him as 'the route of all good in the Near East'.[33] Bliss's official attempts to sway Wilson in support of a commission to the Ottoman lands began on 7 February, when he wrote a letter to the president stating that the people of Syria, having knowledge of Wilson's 'twelfth point and the Anglo-French Declaration', desired 'a fair opportunity to express their political aspirations'.[34] A few days later, Bliss wrote to Wilson again, stating that 'if an Inter-Allied commission of Inquiry is to be sent to Syria – a most desirable arrangement – no time should be lost in sending it'.[35]

At Wilson's behest, Howard Bliss received a hearing before the Supreme Council on 13 February in which his primary aim was to argue in favour of a commission. At the opening of his speech, he stated the following:

> My plea before this body on behalf of the people of Syria is this: that an Inter-Allied or a Neutral commission, or a Mixed commission, be sent at once to Syria in order to give an opportunity to the people of Syria – including Lebanon – to express in a perfectly untrammelled way their political wishes and aspirations, viz: as to what form of Government they desire and as to what power, if any, should be their Mandatory Protecting Power.

Furthermore, he argued that the people of the region would 'honestly work with' a mandatory power if they felt 'confidence in the fact that the promise held out to the people to express themselves had been fulfilled'. Sending such an 'Inter-Allied commission', Bliss contended, would be part of a delicate but necessary political trust-building exercise between the Allies and the people of the region.[36]

The French were particularly unhappy with this testimony. William Westermann, who was at the meeting, observed that the French showed great 'sensitiveness' about the proposed commission because they assumed 'with some justice' that this proposal was 'directed against their future hold on' Syria. In the time allotted for questions after Bliss's statement, French Foreign Minister Stephen Pichon asked Bliss whether or not his comments applied to 'all the populations who had been living under Ottoman rule in the Ottoman Empire – in Syria, Palestine, Mesopotamia and Armenia, or did these proposals apply only to Syria?', implicitly suggesting that if French claims to Syria could be jeopardised by this commission, then the British claims to Mesopotamia and Palestine should be jeopardised as well. Bliss replied that he 'spoke only for Syria' because 'he knew the conditions existing in that territory', though he did note 'his remarks should apply also to other religions and to other populations'.[37] Following Bliss's appearance, a Parisian–Syrian delegation gave over two hours of 'deadly dull' and transparently manufactured pro-French testimony. According to Westermann, 'President Wilson got up and moved about the room. Lansing did also. The British talked aloud. Clemenceau was bored.' Another pro-French Lebanese delegation, handpicked by the French military administration in Lebanon, gave an effusive pro-French statement to the Supreme Council on 15 February. This turned out to be another deception: William Westermann met with this group and discovered that only two out of its five members were actually in favour of a French protectorate, with one of them having agreed to give such testimony in order to get a free trip to Paris. Wilson did not hear this testimony because he had departed for a short visit to the United States on 14 February. Much to the ire of the rest of the American delegation, he left no further instructions on how to negotiate about the disposition of the Ottoman lands.[38]

In the meantime, the confusion over the solely American commissions to the region continued. The proposed Howe–Barton commission to the Ottoman Empire had stalled. In early February, Frederick Howe had gone to Rome in search of James Barton. In Rome, Howe was told that Barton had gone to the port town of Brindisi. Howe then continued on and attempted to find Barton there, with no better luck. After becoming ill and growing disgusted with Brindisi, a port town full of 'drunken sailors' and 'dark-skinned murderers', Howe decided to return to Paris. Back in Paris on 20 February, he reported to Henry White that he had chosen to abandon the commission because he believed he could not have undertaken the task alone and 'that under the present conditions of British and French occupation he would be unable to do any useful work'. He did, nonetheless, insist on being reimbursed for his aborted journey, which irritated some members of the American delegation. He later wrote that he had become disillusioned with the whole enterprise of the commission because he believed that the British and French were destined to quarrel over the region with little regard for its inhabitants and, furthermore, that becoming involved in the Middle East at this point would have been a mistake for the United States because it would 'embroil us forever in European affairs'.[39] Barton, having been in Istanbul (not Rome or Brindisi), heard that Howe was returning to Paris and requested on 18 February that he be released from the commission in order to continue his work for Near East Relief.[40] On 22 February, the plenipotentiary debated whether or not to send another commission of this sort. Secretary of State Lansing was especially dubious of the merits of such a commission and he suggested that they could simply call upon the expertise of Americans already in Paris, with Westermann and Howard Bliss being mentioned in particular. In the end, the members of the meeting agreed that a recommendation about the partition of the Ottoman Empire should be made to President Wilson 'on the basis of reports from these two men'.[41] At the same time, Joseph Grew (Secretary General of the American Commission to Negotiate Peace) and members of the Inquiry resurrected the previously shelved Dominian Commission and planning for this continued into March.[42]

Discussions about the Ottoman Empire carried on while Wilson was away. The issue of Armenia was addressed by the Supreme Council on 26 February. After being coached by a highly sympathetic William Westermann, Armenian representatives orally presented the Council with a request for a large Armenia with ports on both the Black Sea and the Mediterranean (in Cilicia). Interestingly, the Armenian delegation chose not to dwell on the massacres that had occurred during the war as support for this request. Instead, justifications for their appeal included the following:

- Armenians had been belligerents on the side of the Entente during the war and thus deserved preferential treatment;
- before the war, Armenians had constituted a majority of the population in the area they were requesting for their state;
- the region's Armenians were more modern than the other groups in eastern Anatolia;
- Armenians needed a large country in order to maintain racial cohesion: 'Bonds of race, blood, religion and language', they argued, existed between the 'Turkish' and the 'Caucasian' Armenians that could not be broken.

They ended by asking to be protected by a power during their formative years as a new nation.[43] The written Armenian statement of these demands raised these same points but focused more on the wartime massacres. Pre-war population figures, they argued, had to be utilised when determining who should control the lands of eastern Anatolia because doing otherwise would reward the propagators of these massacres. 'The voice of the dead', they stated, 'must be heard as much as that of the living.' The Armenians summarised their justifications at the end of this document with a telling emphasis on modernisation, contending that 'the peace conference may rest assured that under a regime of Peace and Liberty the Armenian State will be one of the strongest agents of Civilisation in the East'.[44] The Armenians knew that sympathy for the Armenian plight alone, while certainly important to the members of the peace conference, could not justify the establishment of a new Armenian state. They realised (or had been told) that testimony emphasising the 'spreading of civilisation' would resonate with the members of the peace conference. Without convincing the Supreme Council of their potential to do this, they had little chance of gaining independence.

Also on 26 February, Howard Bliss appeared before the American plenipotentiary of Wilson's main advisors to again argue for a commission to Syria. He repeated many of the same points he had made in front of the Supreme Council and candidly stated that such a commission, 'whatever might be its findings', would 'satisfy the demands of honor'. Lansing informed him that he had proposed such a commission to Stéphen Pichon but the idea was turned down 'under orders from Clemenceau'. Lansing argued that if a commission were to go, it would require much delicate diplomacy with the British and the French. Henry White voiced scepticism about the ability of a commission to get accurate information in the region 'because of the propaganda of both the British and the French', with Bliss replying that such a task was 'difficult, but not impossible'. The meeting ended with Lansing stating that 'no decision was imminent' on the matter.[45] Before leaving Paris, Bliss wrote one final appeal to President Wilson on 10 March, lamenting that 'the old order of the world is reasserting itself' and he finished the letter with a plea for Syria:

> No self respecting man could face the people of Syria without shame, if a Government is imposed upon them before they have been consulted. Syria is a little country but a big principle is involved in the settlement of its political future.[46]

If Wilson read this, Bliss's pessimism and moralistic tone may well have resonated with him.

The Zionist Organisation presented their request for a 'Jewish national home' in Palestine to the Supreme Council on 27 February, receiving a cordial reception. The Zionists stated that their goal was to 'settle Jews in the empty spaces of Palestine' and that they could do so 'by the expenditure of their own money and the exercise of their brains'. There was 'room for an increase of at least four to five million people' in Palestine, they contended, and this sort of increase could occur 'without encroaching on the legitimate interests of the people already there'. Lansing posed the only question at the session, asking the Zionists to 'clear up some confusion in his mind as to the correct meaning of the words "Jewish National Home"'. The Zionists carefully replied that they 'did not want an autonomous Jewish Government' until they 'formed a large majority' of the population and had time to 'build up gradually a [Jewish] nationality'.[47] Lansing's question exemplified the quiet scepticism about Zionism among many of the Americans at the conference. Some believed that the Zionists were actually seeking a 'state' rather than a 'home' and that they could not do what they proposed without 'encroaching' on the rights of Palestine's current inhabitants. Despite these misgivings, the Americans at the Conference remained generally supportive of Zionism.[48]

Wilson's Return

After Wilson returned from the United States (14 March), the Ottoman Empire continued to be a prominent item on the peace conference agenda. Colonel House had continued negotiating a settlement for the region in Wilson's absence and, on 7 March, he indicated to Clemenceau and Lloyd George (probably in a more assured fashion than Wilson would have liked) that the United States 'would be willing' to take mandates for Istanbul and Armenia.[49] On 20 March, the Ottoman Empire was the main item for discussion in a meeting of the Supreme Council.[50] The meeting began with Stéphen Pichon reviewing the agreements made about the Middle East during and shortly after the war. Pichon recounted the Sykes–Picot agreement of May 1916 and its subsequent modifications, providing maps of the agreement and a narrative of the later meetings in which it was modified. He also discussed Lloyd George's wish to lessen Britain's burden of occupation and France's desire to station troops in the areas it had been granted by these wartime agreements. Pichon noted that there were seeds of ill will between France and Britain on numerous issues in the region and that France hoped to resolve all of these matters at the Paris Peace Conference. Lloyd George then discussed the possible issues arising from a French occupation of Syria, the most serious of which being the breach of the British commitments to King Hussein pledging support for Arab independence in some of the lands desired by France. Pichon countered this point by stating that France had not been signatories on these commitments and was not bound by them, which was a comment that surely irritated the British.[51]

At this rather contentious moment, Wilson interjected himself into the debate. He began his argument using traditional diplomatic terms, stating that because one of the parties to the '1916 [Sykes–Picot] agreement' had 'disappeared' (by which he meant Russia), then the 'partnership of interest was dissolved' and the basis of the whole agreement had been altered. Hence, according to Wilson, the Council had to move beyond the wartime agreements of partition. With these agreements cast aside, Wilson then introduced his professed ideals as the grounds for his argument, contending that 'one of the fundamental principles to which the United States adhered was the consent of the governed'. Because of this, the United States was 'indifferent to the claims both of Great Britain and France over peoples unless those peoples wanted them' and was therefore more worried about whether 'France would be agreeable to the Syrians' and 'Great Britain would be agreeable to the inhabitants of Mesopotamia'. Wilson reminded the members of the Council that according to the document they had agreed upon earlier in the conference, the choice of a mandatory power had to take the 'desires of the people over whom the mandate was to be exercised' into consideration.[52]

General Edmund Allenby, the head of the region's occupying forces (recently arrived in Paris), then gave testimony about the probability of trouble in the region, especially if the French were to be given a mandate. This was followed by a short adjournment, after which Wilson launched his appeal for an inter-Allied commission to the region. He suggested the following:

> The fittest men that could be obtained should be selected to form an Inter-Allied commission to go to Syria, extending their

inquiries, if they led them, beyond the confines of Syria. Their object should be to elucidate the state of opinion and the soil to be worked on by any mandatory. [...] The commission should be composed of an equal number of French, British, Italian and American representatives [...] [and they would have] carte blanche to tell the facts as they found them.

While he acknowledged that there was plenty of expertise on the region in Paris, as exemplified by the testimonies of Bliss and Allenby, he believed that the commission would also 'convince the world that the Conference had tried to do all it could to find the most scientific basis possible for a settlement'.[53]

Clemenceau and Lloyd George each gave measured responses to this proposal. Clemenceau immediately agreed 'in principle to an inquiry' (which 'alarmed' those in the French foreign policy establishment advocating a mandate over Syria)[54] but noted that he had certain reservations. First, he stated that Syria must not be the only destination for the commission, insisting that 'Palestine, Mesopotamia and Armenia, and other parts of the Turkish Empire' be investigated as well. Second, he argued that 'many Syrians were not Arab' and there had to be assurances that all people could speak without intimidation from Faysal who was 'practically a soldier of England'. Third, Clemenceau stated that Orientals were 'very timid and afraid to say what was at the back of their mind' making it 'very difficult to get the real feelings of the people' (rehashing a common refrain about the region's people at the time). Finally, Clemenceau noted that although he agreed with 'the principles propounded by President Wilson', he countered that 'something must be said for historical claims', referring primarily to the institutions established by the French in Greater Syria.[55]

Lloyd George then stated that he had 'no objection' to the proposed commission but that he was concerned about the amount of time the commission might take to complete its work. The reasons behind his worry were twofold: first, the British were bearing the financial and martial burden of the region's occupation; and, second, Turkey was uneasily awaiting its fate and he thought it was 'entitled to know who would be the mandatory for Turkish territory'. Wilson, ignoring Lloyd George's first concern, replied that he failed to see this second reason as a problem because

Turkey, not being entitled to anything, only needed to be told how much land would remain Turkish with the question of the mandatory power being of secondary concern. 'For the purposes of peace', Wilson stated, 'all that was necessary to tell Turkey was that she would have nothing.' Lloyd George then raised another objection: fearing that the people of Mesopotamia (or elsewhere) did not want Britain as a mandatory power, Lloyd George noted that the British could conceivably not receive a mandate anywhere in the Ottoman lands, which he (implicitly) believed they deserved. Despite his reservations, Lloyd George requested that Wilson draft 'terms of reference' for the commission, a task that Wilson accepted, and this portion of the meeting was ended.[56]

President Wilson immediately wrote the secret 'terms of reference' for the commission, a draft of which was ready by 22 March. In this document, the commissioners (not yet chosen) were instructed as follows:

> It is the purpose of the Conference to separate from the Turkish Empire certain areas comprising, for example, Palestine, Syria, the Arab Countries to the east of Palestine and Syria, Mesopotamia, Armenia, Cilicia, and perhaps additional areas in Asia Minor, and to put the development of their people under the guidance of Governments which are to act as Mandatories of the League of Nations.

After stating that the above task would have to be 'done in accordance' with the Resolution on Mandates of 30 January and 'in the spirit of' the Anglo-French Declaration of 9 November 1918 (quoting extensively from them both), the document gave the commission two assignments. First, it stated that the conference felt 'obliged to acquaint itself as intimately as possible with the sentiments of the people of these regions with regard to the future administration of their affairs'. Following from this, the commission was instructed to 'visit these regions to acquaint yourselves as fully as possible with the state of opinion there with regard to these matters, with the social, racial and economic conditions, a knowledge of which might serve to guide the judgement of the Conference'. Second, the document asked the commission to

> form as definite opinion as the circumstances and the time at your disposal will permit, of the divisions of territory and assignment of

mandates which will be most likely to promote the order, peace and development of those peoples and countries.

Wilson further ordained that mandatory powers were compulsory and independence, even if it was overwhelmingly requested, was not an option. Put more simply, the commission's task was to learn the political desires of the Ottoman Empire's inhabitants and then to craft recommendations for the future configuration of the Ottoman lands. Importantly, these instructions did not indicate that there needed to be any correlation between these two things. The wording of Point Five of the Fourteen Points was being put into practice: the people of the Ottomans lands would be consulted about their political desires but the commission members were not bound to craft recommendations in line with these desires. What was in the best interest of the people could easily be different from what these people requested. The Supreme Council 'agreed to' this document on 25 March, and thus despite the initial reservations of Lloyd George and Clemenceau, a full inter-Allied commission looked likely to move forward at this point.[57]

The proposed commission immediately received both praise and criticism. Faysal wrote a letter to President Wilson on 24 March that thanked him profusely for giving the 'Arab peoples', who had been 'so long under the yoke of a barbarous militarism', the chance to express 'their own purposes and ideals for their national future'. This foreshadowed the elevated expectations he would bring back to Syria.[58] On 29 March, Faysal also told Colonel House that the proposal for the commission was 'the best thing he had ever heard in his life'.[59] Lawrence told Westermann that when Faysal heard about the decision, he 'drank champagne for the first time'. After this he 'rode out and threw cushions at the Hotel Crillon, the Majestic and the Quai d'Orsay [all inhabited by French diplomats], saying that he had no bombs, but could express his feelings this way'.[60] British Foreign Minister (and advocate of Zionism) Arthur Balfour raised objections to the commission shortly after Lloyd George tentatively agreed to it. On 22 March, he told Lloyd George and Wilson that a commission to the region would discover that 'the present inhabitants of Palestine, who in large majority are Arab, do not desire to see the administration of the country so conducted as to encourage the relative increase of the Jewish population and influence'. If this was the case, then Balfour believed countries that were 'anxious to promote Zionism' like 'England and America' would 'find that the difficulties of carrying out a Zionist policy have been much increased'.[61] The French imperial establishment was greatly angered by Clemenceau's acceptance of the commission, believing that there would be little support for a French mandate in Syria. Clemenceau (who knew next to nothing about the region) could not imagine that this was true and thus did not see the danger posed by the commission. A number of Clemenceau's advisers, in hopes of changing his mind, planted articles opposing the commission in some of France's most prominent newspapers.[62] Despite having supported the formation of a commission in January, William Westermann believed that holding all major decisions about the Ottoman lands until such a commission had finished its work was 'foolish' and could greatly harm the situation in the region. He argued that 'a wrong decision now will do less harm than a correct decision in two months or five months'. Westermann also spoke with Gertrude Bell, the British specialist on Mesopotamia, who was against the commission for the same reason he had noted (i.e. a decision needed to be made quickly). She further stated that such a commission could not get accurate information because 'no Oriental ever told what he actually thought about matters openly and in a public way'.[63]

Further opposition came from American Zionist Felix Frankfurter, who was angered by the decision to send a commission, contending that it was inconsistent with Wilson's professed support for Zionism. Frankfurter had believed that all was going well for the Zionist cause at the peace conference, especially because of his encouraging correspondence with Amir Faysal in early March. Faysal initiated the exchange of notes, writing a letter to Frankfurter on 1 March (likely crafted by Lawrence[64]) that stated in a very general manner that he was sympathetic to the Zionist movement and that 'there was room in Syria for both of us'. The rest was simply a matter of 'details' that could be 'easily adjusted'. Frankfurter replied in an equally cordial manner, stating that he believed Arabs and Jews could easily 'live side by side as friends' while they 're-build two great civilizations that have been suffering oppression and misrule for centuries'.[65] The correspondence was so satisfying to Frankfurter that he alerted Brandeis in a 3 March letter that 'the Arab question has ceased to exist as a difficulty to the realization of our programme before the peace conference' mainly because it seemed that Faysal was 'a genuine friend' to the Zionists. In general, he appraised

Faysal as 'a very superior person, shrewd as every Easterner is supposed to be shrewd but I am sure a man of spiritual depth'.[66] Just as the Zionists had seemingly removed one impediment to their plan, however, another appeared in the form of the commission. On 26 March, Frankfurter went to see House in an 'excited' state and told him he believed that the commission was going to 'cheat the Jewry of Palestine'. House was able to momentarily calm his fears, though Frankfurter would later seek assurances on this matter from Wilson himself.[67]

Perhaps the most prominent meeting to take place outside of the Supreme Council concerning the commission was the 25 March 'informal meeting of British and French experts on the Syrian question'. The meeting was arranged by *The Times* editor Henry Wickham Steed because he feared that the 'Syrian problem' might 'poison the whole conference'.[68] At the meeting, the British representatives (T.E. Lawrence, Gertrude Bell and the journalist/diplomat Sir Valentine Chirol) discussed the Syria question and the idea of a commission with a number of important French figures, who included a mix of influential colonial lobbyists (Robert de Caix and Henri Brenier), journalists (Phillippe Millet and Auguste Gauvain) and a government official (Sabatier d'Espeyran). The main objective of this nearly six-hour discussion was to negotiate the parameters of the approved inter-Allied commission to the Ottoman lands in hopes of soothing British–French relations on the matter. The members of the meeting agreed that the sending of such a commission was not a good idea because it would 'unsettle the country' and 'make it appear that the conference had been unable to reach any decision' which would then 'open the door to intrigues and manifestations of all kinds'. They went on to agree that, should a commission be sent, it would be preferable for France to reach a basic 'settlement' with Faysal in which France's relationship as the mandatory power would be similar to that which Britain had with Egypt and India. By assuaging France's fear of being excluded from the Middle East through a pre-agreement that would assure them Syria would be theirs in some manner, the French would then likely be amenable to this international commission because it posed no real threat to their claims.[69]

The matter came up again in the Supreme Council meeting on 27 March. This time, Lloyd George expressed further misgivings about the commission, stating that he had been told that such a commission 'might stir up trouble in this region' and that 'it could only gather inadequate information, since Oriental peoples are suspicious and do not easily open up to newcomers'. He also stated that he had received a petition stating that the people of Mesopotamia preferred the 'direct administration of Europeans' to that of an 'Arab Emir'. Wilson steadfastly replied that the 'decision to hold an inquiry be maintained' and that the benefits of the 'impression' such a commission would make outweighed any deleterious effect it might have. Clemenceau, wanting to move on to other matters, agreed with Wilson, stating that he hoped (perhaps disingenuously) that the 'inquiry will proceed without loss of time'.[70]

***

By the end of March, the commission appeared destined to go, with the Supreme Council having given it their tentative approval. Many of the policy elites of these countries, however, paid little attention to the commission because they did not believe it would ever come to fruition and that it was just part of the diplomatic game being played by Lloyd George and Clemenceau over the division of the Ottoman lands. Arthur Balfour harboured such doubts about the commission, stating 'a great deal of time must elapse before the commission can set to work in Palestine and Armenia – and much may happen in the interval'.[71] Similarly, William Westermann told Gertrude Bell that he thought 'the chances' seemed to be 'about even that this commission would not go out'.[72] Wilson, for his part, dared to enter this game with his only real leverage being the moral heft of his 'wishes of the people' rhetoric. The commission then took on significance to Wilson as a symbol of the 'new diplomacy' he espoused in opposition to the 'old diplomacy' he despised. Although it may have seemed like a victory for his vision at the time, the commission was not nearly as close to fruition as he believed.

CHAPTER 4

PARIS PEACE CONFERENCE 2: TOPSY-TURVYDOM

As the peace conference wore on, many Americans in Paris began to believe that the victorious powers were making grave mistakes, and that these were the very same mistakes that Wilson had been pointing out during the war. In the words of Charles R. Crane, who was a keen observer of the peace conference before he was asked to join the King–Crane Commission:

> This is the biggest kind of a man's job, for which the biggest, and best, and most experienced, are hopelessly unequal [. . .] Of course the central difficulty is that all of the men with whom and through whom the President has to work are not only inadequate from every point of view but they are all the authors of the secret treaties, are trying in every way to keep them secret and still make them work, and they have no understanding of the Fourteen Points or real sympathy for them. I fear that a more or less naïve world which imagines that the Council is sitting around a table trying to apply these principles in a conscientious way to its great problems, is due for a great awakening.[1]

The proposed inter-Allied commission to the Ottoman lands, in many American minds, was one way to honestly apply Wilson's principles, thus creating a platform for continued peace in what many saw as an important and volatile part of the world. Despite the fact that

Lloyd George, Clemenceau and Italian Prime Minister Vittorio Orlando had agreed to send a commission to the Ottoman lands, President Wilson was the only member of the Supreme Council with any enthusiasm for the project. Having already drafted the 'terms of reference' for the commission, he went about choosing his commissioners immediately and expected the others to do the same. His colleagues on the Supreme Council chose instead to delay, likely figuring postponement might sink the commission altogether. The story of the commission in Paris, then, was one of undulating fortunes, with many forces fighting against its formation.

Choosing the American Commission Members

The American section of the commission materialised in a somewhat haphazard fashion. President Wilson seemed to know little about the proposed Dominian Commission to Turkey, which had both personnel and a budget by late March. Once the leading American diplomats in Paris were informed that Wilson now wanted an inter-Allied commission to travel to the region, the Dominian Commission was called off.[2] Wilson commenced the task of choosing commissioners on 20 March, the same day that the Supreme Council tentatively accepted the idea of a commission. Funding was immediately allocated for 'five officials and four Field Clerks' to make the journey, and Wilson asked his press secretary, the noted journalist Ray Stannard Baker, for suggestions, stating 'I want the ablest American now in France'.[3] Baker responded on the following day, proposing a short list of candidates, which included Henry Churchill King, who Baker believed commanded 'very high respect and esteem in America' and was 'a man liberal in spirit'. Baker also recommended that William Westermann accompany the commission in order to give technical advice.[4] King, who was in Koblenz, Germany doing work for the Young Men's Christian Association (YMCA) at the time, received a message from Baker on the evening of 23 March stating that Colonel House wanted to see him. King subsequently hurried back to Paris.[5] House, wanting to learn whether or not King was made of 'suitable timber for the Syrian mission', met with King and Baker on 26 March. House approved of King, stating that he was 'an intelligent vigorous fellow', and King immediately accepted a place on the commission.[6]

Henry Churchill King (1858–1934) was the President of Oberlin College, a small Protestant university in Ohio. King was born in Michigan to devout Christian parents and was educated at Oberlin, Harvard and the University of Berlin, becoming an ordained Congregationalist minister along the way. He had gained academic distinction by this point in his career, with numerous publications in theology and philosophy. As a progressive Christian, King saw Wilson's idealistic pronouncements as being rooted in activist Christian values akin to his own and agreed with Wilson that the United States had a moral obligation to help craft a peaceful international order.[7] He had been a proponent of American involvement in the war as a way for the United States to engage in 'a true social program, by and through the war, as well as after it, to make certain that this world cataclysm shall bear its full fruit in a better civilization than the world has yet seen'.[8] King further believed that this was a 'war *for* the preservation of ideal views [...] that is, for the great values of what we call a Christian civilization, as President Wilson has interpreted it in his attempt to apply Christian principles to international relations'.[9] The commission, for King, became a way to play his role in improving the world.

Before his time on the commission, King had already decided to do his part for the war effort. In August 1918, King took a leave of absence from Oberlin in order to volunteer for the YMCA in Europe. In Paris, he was the Director of the YMCA's 'Religious Works Division for France', which meant he helped to organise services to provide for the 'moral, spiritual, and intellectual needs' of American soldiers. King had gone to the frontlines in France and Italy (having met Ray Stannard Baker in the latter), and made stops in various YMCA facilities around Western Europe. Once King accepted a position on the commission, he immediately sought to educate himself about a region that he knew primarily through missionary accounts, newspapers and the Bible. Despite being fairly well travelled for an American of the era, the Middle East had merely been an accidental destination for King: the only time he spent in the region was an impromptu six-day visit to Egypt as part of an 'Oriental Tour' of missionary stations in 1909 after he missed his scheduled ship to India.[10] Although King was reluctant to prolong his absence from his family and job, he was excited to have the opportunity to serve his country and to see the region, telling his wife that 'I should be visiting the lands I've always wanted to visit, and that I first planned to visit on my world trip, but missed.'[11]

Also on 26 March, House told King that Wilson named his informal adviser Charles R. Crane as the other commissioner. Crane (1858–1939) was a prominent figure in the American political landscape largely because of his ability to donate substantial sums of money to causes he deemed worthy of support. He was heir to his father's hugely successful plumbing fixture company in Chicago, though the business was never his passion. He instead spent his life as a world traveller, generous philanthropist and political dabbler. Crane never finished a university degree, ostensibly having dropped out because of health problems though it is more likely that he simply disliked formal education. Instead of university, Crane travelled the globe and eventually sold his share of the family business to his brother, subsisting lavishly on these funds and various other investments for the rest of his life. Crane was by no means a common traveller: because of his wealth and connections, he was usually able to arrange meetings with some of the world's leading figures. For example, Crane met with Tsar Nicholas II and Leo Tolstoy on numerous occasions during his visits to Russia. Russia was Crane's primary fascination and was the place where he spent most of his time abroad. During World War I, he advised Wilson extensively on policy matters having to do with Russia and travelled there in 1917 in order to give the president a firsthand account of the revolution. China was Crane's second major interest, and his first near-foray into diplomacy came in 1909 when President William Howard Taft nominated him as Ambassador to China. The nomination was withdrawn after Crane made some off-hand remarks about American policy in the region, though he later did serve as Wilson's Ambassador to China in 1920–1. Crane had travelled in the Middle East, most recently in 1911, but it was a region that had not piqued his interest to the same degree that Russia, China and Eastern Europe had at this point in this life.[12] He was also a major benefactor of Robert College and Constantinople College (both in Istanbul). Initially, Crane was not enthusiastic about being named as a commissioner because he did not have in-depth knowledge about the region (claiming he knew 'most about the Balkans') but he stated that 'if Pres. [President Wilson] wishes, [he] would go'.[13] In early April, it even appeared that Crane might back out, with another commission member marking in a notebook that there could be a 'possible change of Crane to another'.[14]

After being officially appointed to the commission, Crane continued his normal routine at the peace conference, which meant dining with elites and counselling Wilson when asked, while King began looking for someone who could advise him on the Ottoman lands. On 31 March, King met with Albert Lybyer (an old acquaintance who had taught at Oberlin) in order to discuss the commission and ask questions about the region. Lybyer was a professor of history at the University of Illinois and was an ordained minister, having been educated at Princeton Theological Seminary. He had also spent substantial time in Istanbul, teaching at Robert College from 1900 to 1907, after which he returned to the United States in order to study for his PhD, which he received from Harvard in 1909. Lybyer's PhD thesis was published in 1913, entitled *The Government of the Ottoman Empire in the Time of Suleiman the Magnificent*. Lybyer's book became a widely used text on this era of Ottoman history, even though he wrote it without knowing how to read Ottoman Turkish. During the war, Lybyer was a member of the Inquiry and was in Paris as an 'Assistant to the Balkan Division' of the American Commission to Negotiate Peace.[15] His time in Paris was about to end when King contacted him. While King did not initially ask Lybyer to become a member of the commission, a friend convinced Lybyer to seek appointment because serving on a commission with King and especially Crane would be 'a great opportunity' and could immediately make him 'famous'. Lybyer was convinced and went on a small lobbying campaign for himself, visiting people like Joseph Grew in order to get himself 'on the map'.[16] On 3 April, King appointed Lybyer as an adviser, stating that he would be 'glad to have' him on the commission, and together they started to fill out the commission's ranks. Crane took little interest in these preparations.[17]

Also on 3 April, Lybyer went to see William Westermann for advice on personnel. The conversation, according to Lybyer, was 'intense' because Westermann, who had turned down the opportunity to be part of this commission, believed that the project threatened to overshadow the work that he and his staff had undertaken for the Inquiry. In a conversation two days prior, Westermann told Lybyer that he had recommended this commission in January but he was 'now against [the] project'.[18] A colleague would later state that Westermann opposed the commission because he felt that 'the destinies of the region were in the main determined' by the agreements made during the war, and that any 'contradiction could be best ironed out in Paris'.[19] In a compromise, Lybyer promised Westermann that he would place 'one or two men from his office on the staff' and Westermann stated that 'he would put nothing in my [Lybyer's] way'.[20] The two people that Westermann recommended were George Montgomery and William Yale, and by 6 April these two had been added to the commission's staff list.

George Montgomery, appointed the 'Technical Adviser for the Northern Regions of Turkey', was an itinerant academic and church pastor who had spent much time in the Ottoman lands. Born in 1870 to missionary parents in Maraş (now Kahramanmaraş), Montgomery was raised in the Ottoman Empire and was fluent in Turkish, German and French. He was educated at Yale and the University of Berlin, and had published books on language and philosophy. Montgomery maintained an interest in Turkey throughout his life, returning there on numerous occasions as an adult. He was employed as the Turkey correspondent for the *London Standard* during the Greco-Turkish War in 1896–7, for example, and served as a special assistant to the American Ambassador in Istanbul in 1916. By 1919, he had taught at three different universities and was an ordained Congregationalist minister who had served as the pastor of two churches.[21]

The 'Technical Adviser for the Southern Regions of Turkey' was William Yale, the youngest of the five main members of the commission (turning 32 during the commission's time in the Ottoman lands). Yale had a degree in engineering from Yale University and was a descendant of the university's founder. His first visit to the Ottoman lands came in 1913 via employment with the Standard Oil Company of New York (SOCONY), which sent him to Palestine to search for oil. He became SOCONY's representative in Jerusalem where he helped to orchestrate the purchase of several plots of land for drilling. In 1917, he was recruited as the US government's 'Chief of Intelligence' in the region, sending back numerous reports throughout 1917 and 1918. He was also attached to the British Expeditionary Force during the latter part of its campaign in Greater Syria. According to Yale, he knew 'all of the leading Arabs in Palestine' and spoke some Arabic. He also had a reputation as a philanderer and seemed quite proud of this.[22] T.E. Lawrence, who met Yale during the war, did not like him for this reason, stating to Westermann that 'Yale spent his time in Jerusalem visiting brothels' and further remarking that 'men of our set don't do that sort of thing. It would be all in order for Italians, but Anglo-Saxons don't do it.'[23] With many of the commission members being ordained ministers, Yale considered himself the most 'ungodly' participant in the commission.[24]

Paris Peace Conference 2: Topsy-Turvydom

Figure 4.1 The five main members of the King–Crane Commission at the Paris Peace Conference. They are, from left to right, George Montgomery, Charles R. Crane, Henry Churchill King, Albert Lybyer and William Yale. (Source: Oberlin College Archives, Oberlin, Ohio).

King and Lybyer also promptly assembled the rest of the commission's American contingent, eventually bringing the total number to 11. Lybyer lined up two of his acquaintances to be involved. Laurence Moore, who joined the commission as business manager, had been a colleague of Lybyer's at Robert College and was in Paris after having volunteered to drive ambulances during the war. Michael Dorizas, who was chosen to serve as an interpreter of Turkish and Greek, had been born and raised in Istanbul's Greek community and was one of Lybyer's former students at Robert College. Dorizas received his undergraduate degree from the University of Pennsylvania in 1914 and continued his graduate studies at this same institution. Despite being close to the completion of his PhD when the United States entered the war, he chose to become a naturalised US citizen and join the army. Interestingly, he was also a champion heavyweight Greco-Roman wrestler and, at the 1908 London Olympics, had won the silver medal in the 'freestyle javelin throw' as a representative of Greece.

Henry Churchill King gave the job of secretary to US Army Captain and Chaplain Donald Brodie, a young graduate of Oberlin College who was stationed in Paris. Brodie would later become Charles Crane's longtime personal secretary. The commission also gleaned two stenographers (Ross Lambing and Paul Toren) from the ranks of the American Commission to Negotiate Peace, with Toren having worked for Westermann in Paris. Finally, with the help of Edward Nickoley (acting President of the Syrian Protestant College in Bliss's absence), the commission was also able to secure the services of Dr Sami Haddad as interpreter and physician, though Haddad would not join the commission until it arrived in Greater Syria. Haddad, a Lebanese Protestant, was a graduate of the Syrian Protestant College and was fluent in English, Arabic, Turkish and French. The American participants in the commission, then, were mostly appointed by mid-April 1919.[25] The final roster went as follows:

- Henry C. King, Commissioner
- Charles R. Crane, Commissioner
- Albert H. Lybyer, 'General Technical Adviser'
- George R. Montgomery, 'Technical Adviser for the Northern Regions of Turkey'
- William Yale, 'Technical Adviser for the Southern Regions of Turkey'
- Donald Brodie, 'Secretary and Treasurer'
- Laurence S. Moore, 'Business Manager'
- Michael Dorizas, medic and interpreter of Turkish and Greek
- Sami Haddad, 'Physician and Interpreter'
- Paul O. Toren, stenographer
- Ross Lambing, stenographer[26]

It is important to note that although the commission had 11 members, only the two commissioners and three technical advisers were in a position to influence its outcome. These five main members of the commission were American elites. They were educated, connected and Protestant (with King, Lybyer and Montgomery being ordained ministers). Neither of the two commissioners claimed to have any specialist knowledge about the Middle East, though Crane had visited the region on at least two occasions. This fit into a general pattern for Wilson, at least according to Robert Lansing: Wilson was 'against appointing on Inter-Allied commissions for the investigation of political and territorial questions persons who are familiar with the subject'. Wilson believed (again, according to Lansing) that 'an empty mind is more receptive of the truth than one affected by experience and study'. 'Ignorance', Lansing noted derisively, was an 'essential qualification for an investigator'.[27] The three technical advisers, however, were far more 'familiar with the subject', having all lived in and studied the region for significant amounts of time.

These commission members cited a mixed set of rationales for accepting their places on the commission. All five of them would have professed to support Wilson's liberal ideals to a large extent and all, except perhaps Crane, would have considered serving on the commission a great honour. Henry Churchill King framed his rationale mainly in humanitarian and personal terms: 'the problem that I'm asked to face [...] involves such possibilities of service to some millions of human beings and it holds such opportunities of growth for myself and for my future work for the College'. King also decreed his own impartiality on the issues facing them, stating 'I can hope to bring an honest, open mind to the task, I think, with no selfish reasons of my own to block conclusions'.[28] Charles Crane was rather ambivalent about the project at first and, as the commission's secretary would later write, Crane 'did not participate to any great extent in the preliminary conferences or studies of the commission'.[29] As previously stated, however, Crane accepted his role out of loyalty to the president. Albert Lybyer saw the commission both as an opportunity to help the region's populace, claiming it was 'Syrian and Armenian relief of the highest sort', and as an important career-enhancing chance for himself, or in his words, 'it is beyond all question the greatest opportunity of my life so far'. He hoped to gain prestige that would remove him from the 'relative obscurity of Urbana [the location of the University of Illinois]', perhaps leading to a better teaching position or 'some influential post in the Near East'.[30] Similarly, Montgomery hoped the commission would, in some way, help him find a new job, specifically mentioning his desire to obtain a teaching position at Oberlin.[31] The only motive William Yale recorded for accepting a position on the commission was that he wanted to make sure that William Westermann's viewpoint (with which he largely agreed) was represented.[32] In general, the motives of these people for joining the commission stemmed in part from a belief in the principles espoused by the president, in part from loyalty to the president, and in part from personal ambition.

The Early Days of the Commission

The commission got off to a slow start, with King and Lybyer being the only two people who were readying themselves for the project. King wrote to his wife that the whole enterprise seemed to have an 'up-in-the-airness' about it, with no concrete plans in place and no other countries naming their commissioners. Despite this, King began preparing in earnest for the commission, reading 'the main documents and information so far as Syria is concerned [...] and taking notes along various lines – physical, economic, social, racial, religious, political, etc.' He only learned on 3 April that the commission was 'not confined to Syria' despite the fact that all of the people he had spoken with 'talked as if Syria were all I had to deal with'.[33] Westermann noted King's assiduousness, stating that 'King is working hard and comes in daily for material from us'. Westermann also noted that Charles Crane was ambivalent about the project, stating that he 'does not seem interested and is said to be loath to go'.[34] Once King and Lybyer had invested themselves in the project, they became the commission's strongest advocates and began urging their most influential acquaintances to push for its departure.[35]

Reactions to the commission continued to be mixed among other people with an interest in the region, with the French being especially opposed. The French colonial establishment was not pleased that Clemenceau had agreed to the commission. Westermann received a rather frank assessment of Robert de Caix's interpretation of French intentions over tea on 4 April. The French, de Caix argued, would accept nothing less than what they were promised in the Sykes–Picot agreement because of 'political, sentimental and traditional reasons'. He also claimed that they had been the ones to offer 'traditional protection' for the region's Christians (a belief that, according to Westermann, was 'only in their mind's eye. It has really never meant anything'). De Caix further stated that France was interested in 'intellectual penetration and leadership in the Near East'. This 'moral and intellectual leadership' was 'bound up with political leadership' and hence France needed to control Syria at the very least. De Caix's attitude was geopolitical and historical as well. 'The loss of Egypt', he stated, 'had been a terrible blow to their [France's] moral prestige.' Because Britain 'had Egypt', 'would keep Mesopotamia' and 'would work its will in Persia', France 'would be lost if she could not keep Syria'. Westermann also dined with François Georges-Picot (negotiator of the Sykes–Picot Agreement) on 7 April, who he noted was 'dead against the going of the Interallied commission to Syria' because 'the impression in Syria will be against the French, except in Maronite Lebanon'.[36] Albert Lybyer heard similar views in a meeting with de Caix and French colonial administrator Jean Goût (the two probable French commissioners) on 10 and 11 April. Both were emphatically against the commission, though they noted that Clemenceau had written up instructions for his commissioners, stating, tellingly, that they should consult the people 'regarding local government', as opposed to national government.[37]

American discussions with the French about the commission were never without tension. Westermann had a further conversation with de Caix and Henri Brenier on 12 April. In this conversation, de Caix reiterated French opposition to the commission and stated that, if it did go, the commission should go to all areas of the Ottoman Empire including Mesopotamia and not to 'Syria alone'. The French, he threatened, would then 'buy up some people in Mesopotamia at a franc a head to make an outcry against British control there, which, he said, could be easily done'. De Caix and Brenier argued that Faysal needed French 'support' in the towns that were favourable to France, and that France wanted to be in a position of power to stop Faysal when 'he started to hang people' who opposed him.[38] After this meeting, de Caix suspiciously forgot a document outlining French thoughts about the Ottoman lands in Westermann's office. The document merely reiterated French opposition to the proposed commission and also contended that such a commission would only get information that the French, British, Faysal and the Zionists wanted them to get, meaning that it could not learn the 'desires of the people' in any true sense. Although the document may have been crafted for the Americans, it did illuminate many of the political complications motivating French behaviour. It also appeared to cement Westermann's fickle attitude towards the commission, as he stated that he was now 'absolutely opposed' to the sending of it in any form.[39] On 14 April, Albert Lybyer had a similar discussion with Jean Goût, who noted that he still thought that their plan was 'a blunder' but that the French were 'about reconciled to its going because the Americans wish it'.[40]

Partly because of the French opposition, the commission was far from a sure thing at this moment and the events of 15–22 April exemplify the uncertainty that the American commission members faced while in Paris. Wilson realised that the other powers were not keen on the idea of a commission, acknowledging to Joseph Grew on 15 April that these powers had 'virtually withdrawn from their agreement to send commissioners'. In this same correspondence, Wilson was already making reference to a solely American commission, telling Grew that he should still officially authorise the appointment of King and Crane as commissioners 'in case we send them alone'.[41] On the morning of 16 April, however, it seemed likely that the commission would go as an inter-Allied undertaking. King and Lybyer learned that the British had finally appointed their commissioners: Sir Henry McMahon (former British High Commissioner in Egypt) and David Hogarth (renowned Middle Eastern archaeologist and head of the British 'Arab Bureau' in Cairo for part of the war). Arnold Toynbee (later an eminent historian) was to be their secretary. By mid-afternoon, however, King and Lybyer were told that the commission was abandoned: Crane stormed into their office after having lunch with President Wilson and stated that the project 'was all off' because Wilson had received information that 'the Europeans were double-crossing him behind his back'.[42] Lybyer was disappointed ('Consternation!') but the fact that he and King were both homesick and had commitments elsewhere softened the blow. They contentedly, if lamentably, made plans to return to the United States.[43] In order to finalise the disbanding of the American portion of the commission, Lybyer went to see Joseph Grew late in the afternoon of 16 April. To his surprise, Grew told him that the commission could still go as a wholly American endeavour and that he should draft a 'memo authorizing' this limited version of the commission.[44] Lybyer wrote this memo on 17 April, but on the following day King spoke with Colonel House, who told him that 'the President felt the circumstances were such that it was hardly wise [or] possible to send the commission and that the Com. was abandoned'.[45] Lybyer declared this development to be 'more topsy-turvydom' and it caused him to make some fairly bitter remarks in a letter to his wife: 'You can have no idea of the amount of jealousy, self-seeking, and undermining that goes on around here. It is a revelation. [...] Personalities amount to a great deal in the [sic] high politics. They are all very human, and mix the great ideas with small traits and curious weaknesses.' He went to see a Charlie Chaplin movie that evening to lift his spirits.[46]

Charles Crane, annoyed by the political wrangling surrounding the commission (and with his penchant for impetuosity), decided to go to the region on his own in order to attend the commencements of Robert College and Constantinople College. He asked Lybyer (being an ex-Robert College professor) to accompany him, and Lybyer accepted the offer. The journey, however, was to have a secondary purpose, which Lybyer described to his wife as follows: 'At the same time you may make guesses that we will try to learn what the people whom we may meet think.' This surreptitious commission of two was to last for about two months and return with an unofficial report about the desires of the region's people, which Crane would certainly have passed to Wilson. They booked tickets on the Orient Express for departure on 22 April.[47]

To further the confusion, Lybyer called on Toynbee on 19 April to tell him the American portion of the commission was disbanding because they had been told that the undertaking was finished. Toynbee 'had not heard' this and told Lybyer that the British commissioners were arriving in Paris that evening. Toynbee informed Lybyer that the British had received a telegram from General Allenby stating that the commission was needed in order to 'quiet the country'.[48] T.E. Lawrence entered Toynbee's office during this conversation and told them that Lloyd George, with whom he had just been speaking, 'expected the Com[mission] to go'.[49] Finally, on 22 April, Ray Stannard Baker informed King, who had already booked passage home, that President Wilson 'was now very anxious to have the commission go and felt it more important than ever'. An office was arranged for the commission in the Hôtel de Crillon (where the more important members of the American delegation were headquartered) and the commission members accelerated preparations for their departure.[50] With the apparent reinstatement of the commission, Lybyer and Crane cancelled their trip to Istanbul.[51] Lybyer reported that even the sceptical William Westermann was now 'warmly in favour' of the commission, largely because of Allenby's telegram.[52]

Meanwhile, the British and French continued to quietly manoeuvre for position in the region. Clemenceau met Faysal directly in hopes of coming to an agreement and avoiding the commission altogether, though no agreement was forthcoming. Lloyd George, whose officials had not been able to come to an understanding with the French behind the scenes, now saw the commission as further diplomatic leverage and as a way of 'softening up the French'. Most British sources in Greater Syria believed that the people of the region were largely against French occupation and so a fact-finding commission would only serve to weaken the French position. The French recognised this and quietly laid the foundation to undermine the endeavour, stating that they would not send their commissioners unless the British allowed the French to occupy Syria, which was a request they knew the British would be loath to grant. Furthermore, Georges-Picot had already been sent to Greater Syria with two million francs to spend 'stimulating the zeal' of French allies.[53] The British were in a far better position in the region, having control over most of the areas in question and also being the country that provided Amir Faysal with his governmental budget. While the British certainly had something to lose if the commission reported anti-British sentiment, the French feared that the commission would further loosen their already weak grip on their coveted territories.

For the rest of April and into May, the departure of the commission seemed imminent but a number of things still stood in its way. Although the British were readying to take part in the commission, with their participants (Hogarth and McMahon) returning to England to prepare for the journey, the French still had not officially named their commissioners.[54] Amir Faysal, confident that the commission would soon travel to the Ottoman lands, left for Syria on the night of 21 April but some of his entourage remained in Paris to watch over the proceedings. King and Lybyer were still the most active members of the commission, filling their days compiling information and meeting with (mainly) American regional experts.[55] Lybyer built a substantial collection of books pertaining to the region both for King's voracious literary appetite and for reference during their journey. Bureaucracy stood in the way of them moving quickly on many matters. Not having yet received official 'letters of appointment', for example, made it impossible for them to purchase their supplies for the journey.[56]

The other main members of the commission still seemed leery of spending much effort on the endeavour until they knew that it was definitely going, though they did attend a number of meetings organised by King and Lybyer. George Montgomery, who was never quite convinced the commission would go (stating on 30 April that he would 'believe that it was going when we start'), remained unenthusiastic about the trip partly because he felt the pay was too low.[57] Charles Crane remained rather indifferent to the commission. According to commission secretary Donald Brodie, Crane did not bother to read 'any of the documents and reports relating to the problems that the commission was to consider' and, in late April, Crane wrote a letter to his wife not even mentioning the commission.[58] In Lybyer's estimation, however, Crane was 'well-disposed to the plan' by this time.[59] Crane did solicit the opinion of his friend C. Snouck Hurgronje, a prominent Dutch Orientalist scholar, and he advised Crane to seek both the abolition of the Caliphate and limited Western mandates over the whole of the Middle East.[60] Crane relayed Hurgonje's thoughts to Wilson who replied (rather tellingly) 'I get so many opposite views in these matters that I must admit that I am very much at a loss what judgment to follow.'[61]

Wrangling over the commission continued into May. The consensus among the American contingent at the peace conference was that France, with its persistent refusal to name its commissioners, was the main cause of the delay.[62] King went so far as to write a letter to Wilson branding the French as the main impediment to the commission. He further requested that the French be warned that the delay 'inevitably prejudices their case, and tends to drive the Americans into the arms of the British'.[63] The French continued to seek a 'definite and written agreement' for the splitting of the region that established their control over the northern portions of Greater Syria before any commission was sent. At various times in May, new proposals for the partition of the Ottoman Empire were put forward (usually by Lloyd George), with many of these including American mandates or at least temporary American troop deployment. For example, Lloyd George proposed to the Supreme Council on 5 May that, in anticipation of a settlement, American troops should be sent to Armenia, and that French and Italian troops should relieve the British forces in Greater Syria and the Caucasus respectively.[64]

Wilson continued to receive pressure from influential Americans on the matter of the commission throughout May as well. Probably the most prominent member of the American missionary community to speak out against the sending of a commission was Caleb Gates (President of Robert College) who arrived in Paris on 6 May. Gates argued that the commission would delay a settlement for too long and that decisions about the region's future, which in his opinion ought to include an American mandate for all of the predominantly Turkish-speaking parts of the Ottoman Empire, should be made in Paris. Such was Gates's prominence that Lybyer believed his strong opinion had 'spilled the beans' for the commission, meaning that he thought Gates had all but ended the commission's hope of going.[65] American Zionists, viewing the commission as a threat to their cause, continued to track events carefully and sought continued assurances of support for a Jewish national home in Palestine from Wilson. On 8 May, Felix Frankfurter wrote a letter to Wilson stating that the 'appointment of the Interallied Syrian commission and the assumed postponement for months [...] of the disposition of Near Eastern questions, have brought the deepest disquietude to the representatives of the Jewry of the world'. He further stated that the delay in finding a solution was 'bound to intensify the existing unrest by giving dangerous opportunities to Young Turk intrigue and to the stimulation of religious animosities', thus implicitly stating that the commission was not a wise undertaking. Wilson sent Frankfurter a brief note on 13 May acknowledging receipt of the letter in order to 'say how deeply I appreciate the importance and significance of the whole matter'. Frankfurter was not satisfied with the reply and immediately fired back a letter stating that this curt response 'has occasioned almost despair to the Jewish representatives now assembled in Paris'. These representatives, he continued in a mildly threatening tone, spoke 'not only for the Jews of Europe but also for the American Jewish Congress, the democratic voice of three million American Jews'. He reiterated his request for a 'reassuring word, written or spoken ... that you are purposing to have the Balfour Declaration written into the Treaty of Peace, and that you are aiming to see that Declaration translated into action'. Wilson quickly replied on 16 May that he was 'very much taken by surprise' that Frankfurter had found his previous letter 'discouraging' and stated that he saw 'every reason to hope that satisfactory guarantees [for the Zionists] can be secured'.[66]

As talks continued in Paris, events in the Ottoman lands appeared to be undermining the commission's reason for being. Italy, having temporarily walked out of the peace conference in late April over territory disputes in the northern Adriatic (particularly over Fiume), had been promised parts of Anatolia in exchange for their entrance into the war. Without consulting the Allies, they began landing troops on the southeast coast of Turkey in mid-March and showed no sign of leaving. When William Westermann learned about this, he sensed trouble, stating that it was 'another nail in the coffin which contains the corpse of a decent, objective settlement of the Turkish question'.[67] On 6 May, Wilson, Lloyd George and Clemenceau decided to support a landing of Greek troops at Smyrna (now Izmir) mainly to counter Italian designs on the eastern Mediterranean, but also to strengthen Greece's position in the region.[68] The Greek landing at Smyrna occurred on 15 May and the atrocities committed by the Greeks, both in Smyrna and during their march inland, caused outrage among many Turks.[69] As Lybyer wrote, 'things are very hot among the Turks since the Fergies [Greeks] landed at Smyrna and shot up the town more or less'.[70] The Italians, seeing this as an affront to their claims in Anatolia, landed troops at Kuşadası (Scala Nuova) and firmed up its military presence at Marmaris and Antalya under the pretence that there had been 'disorders' in these places and the Italians were needed to keep the peace.[71] As chunks of Anatolia were being taken by Greece and Italy, the commission members began to believe that their work was becoming irrelevant.

New proposals for settlements kept coming and Wilson continued to entertain them. On 13 May, Lloyd George proposed to divide Anatolia and Armenia between the United States (Armenia and Istanbul), France (Northern Anatolia), Greece (Smyrna and environs) and Italy (Southern Anatolia).[72] Wilson continued to reject the sending of American troops and restated that as much as he would like to commit the United States to a mandate in the region (preferably for Armenia or Istanbul), he could not do so without the consent of the US Senate.[73] On 17 May, an Indian Muslim delegation gave an impassioned plea for a continuation of the Caliphate and for Turkish sovereignty. They supported their plea, in part, by quoting Wilson's declaration that 'the Turkish Portions of the Ottoman Empire should be assured a secure sovereignty' in Point Twelve of his Fourteen Points.[74] This testimony left a major 'impression' on Wilson[75] and, on 19 May when negotiations about possible settlements for the region resumed, Wilson even admitted that he had 'forgotten he had used that word [sovereignty] in the 14 Points'. He also recalled that both 'he and Mr. Lloyd George had said they would not destroy Turkish sovereignty. He had forgotten this until reminded of it.' Lloyd George replied that he had also 'forgotten' committing to this, after which he proposed that the Caliphate should remain in place, with Wilson then suggesting that France could act in an advisory capacity over all of Anatolia. Clemenceau, who had become suspicious of just about everything his colleagues were proposing about the Ottoman lands at this point, only stated that 'the scheme should be written up and examined'. The Italians were left out entirely in this plan.[76]

The commission members' frustration and cynicism grew. Much to the ire of the Americans who were in Paris to support peace-making efforts, Wilson shared little of what was happening in the Supreme Council negotiations with them. Rumours about what was being proposed pertaining to the Ottoman lands led most of these Americans (including the commission members) to believe that decisions would be made without their input. On 13 May, for example, Sidney Mezes (the head of the Inquiry in Paris) called Westermann into his office and showed him a map of Anatolia on which were drawn the divisions proposed by Lloyd George earlier that day, stating 'the President wants to know if this map was acceptable'. In his diary, Westermann noted that this request matched a rumour he had heard that the Supreme Council was just about finished dividing the Ottoman lands.[77] Albert Lybyer, in hearing the rumours about the proposed settlement, lamented that 'the Europeans are disposed to carry out all the secret treaties, and even go beyond' them.[78] On 17 May, the Parisian newspapers began to carry stories stating that the settlement for the Ottoman lands was near completion, and Sydney Mezes confirmed to King and Lybyer that the plans as reported by the papers were 'probably nearly agreed upon'.[79]

By 18 May, King had concluded that the commission was superfluous, commenting that 'practically all the questions naturally referred to our commission' looked like they were going to be 'settled with the terms of the peace'.[80] Along these lines, George Montgomery wrote to his wife in mid-May that

> the Syrian commission seems to be about abandoned and every body is planning to go home. I hate to think of wasting my Turkish or French and German and my knowledge of Turkey but I shall not hesitate to chuck it all if nothing important turns up.[81]

Paris Peace Conference 2: Topsy-Turvydom 69

Lybyer's attitude about the commission shifted to one of resignation and he compared it to his time living in the region, stating 'it is here as it used to be in Constantinople – nothing is certain, nothing is impossible'. He did force himself to look on the bright side of the matter, stating 'we begin to think that our commission may yet be discarded, and that we may all be home for a summer vacation'.[82] All of this uncertainty appears to have spurred the commission into authoring a report containing their initial opinions about the reapportioning of the Ottoman lands. In an effort to ensure that their voice might be heard in some sense and that the work of the previous two months would not be entirely wasted, the commission produced a document in which they laid out their pre-journey views of the region (likely drafted by King on 15–17 May). Entitled 'The Dangers to the Allies of a Selfish Exploitation of the Turkish Empire', this document (which will be discussed at length in the next chapter) was signed by the five main commission members and was likely delivered to Wilson at some point after 19 May.[83]

Just when it appeared to the commission members that their endeavour was finished, the commission's fortunes shifted once again. The final episode that assured the commission's departure began on 20 May. King, having come to believe that 'the reason for the existence of the commission had ceased', called on House and told him he thought that 'the commission had better disband'. House told King to wait 'five or six days' longer and he promised to discuss the matter with President Wilson that same day.[84] The previous day, Rustem Haydar (Faysal's secretary) had visited Westermann and told him that 'Colonel House had given Faisal his personal word of honor, the day before Faisal left, that the commission would go to Syria and that [in] back of this word was the honor of the United States'. Westermann advised him to 'write to the Colonel and state this fact', which Haydar did on the same day.[85] The letter, which expressed severe disappointment that the United States (and House personally) had not honoured their commitment to send the commission, was sent to House immediately.[86] This, along with King's visit, prompted House to press Wilson on the matter of the commission.

House went to see Wilson on the afternoon of 20 May in order to discuss the commission. According to House, he bluntly told Wilson that 'it was something of a scandal that this commission had not already gone to Syria as promised the Arabs' to which Wilson replied that he had done all he could to get the other powers to name their commissioners. House then suggested that Wilson should tell the other leaders that the American portion of the commission would be leaving on 26 May 'regardless of the French and the English'. Wilson then 'adopted' this suggestion and said he would inform Clemenceau and Lloyd George of this the following day.[87] On the same night, King received word from Wilson that the commission was going. He immediately went to see Lybyer in the evening stating that Wilson wanted them to start the following week 'whether others go or not'. Lybyer was elated ('electrification!').[88]

King and Lybyer informed Crane the next morning (21 May) and Lybyer set about to hold discussions with members of the British, French and Italian delegations. He corresponded with British commissioner David Hogarth, who believed that the commission would not be a worthy undertaking unless President Wilson attempted to get the other leaders to agree to the 'suspension of the assignment of Turkish mandates, leaving us some honest purpose and character'. He also thought that the commission would serve little purpose without the French and so Wilson must 'insist' that the French appoint their commissioners 'without delay'.[89] Lybyer communicated Hogarth's concerns to King, who reiterated these in a letter to House. On this letter, in what is likely House's annotation, it was noted that Wilson replied that 'all mandates [were] provisional', indicating that he believed the regional questions were still open.[90] King put this issue more pointedly in another letter to House the next day, requesting that the:

> assigning of mandates, at least in the Arabic-speaking portions of the Turkish Empire, should be suspended in the meantime, in order that the commission may not be put in the false and intolerable position, in the view of the peoples of the Near East, of professedly examining a situation, with a view to recommendations, which has already been determined, or is in the process of being determined, by the Conference at Paris.[91]

Lybyer also spoke with Robert de Caix, who restated that the French would appoint commissioners only if all parties agreed that the mandate question was to be settled in Paris (nearly the opposite of King's request) and that the commission visit 'all areas' of the Ottoman lands. Lybyer held further discussions with one of the likely Italian representatives who stated that his delegation could be 'ready to go soon'.[92]

In the meantime, Lloyd George again tried to settle the matter of the Ottoman Empire on 21 May by offering yet another proposal for its division, with the Turks maintaining sovereignty over much of Anatolia and the Americans taking mandates for Constantinople, Armenia and (perhaps) over Turkish Anatolia. Any settlement reached pertaining to Greater Syria and Mesopotamia would remain provisional 'pending the report of the commission'. Wilson stated that he was largely agreeable to this plan and then announced that that the American portion of the commission would be departing soon, stating that 'the Delegates whom he had nominated were men of such standing that he could not keep them waiting any longer in Paris'. Wilson further stated he 'had instructed them to leave for Syria on Monday [26 May]' and to wait there for the rest of the commission to arrive. Lloyd George replied that 'he thought he would' give the 'same orders' to the British commissioners. Clemenceau, objecting to the 'provisional' nature of the Syria Mandate in Lloyd George's new proposal, immediately stated that he would 'drop out' because 'promises made to him had not been kept', after which he angrily accused Lloyd George of reneging on the promises he made to the French with respect to Greater Syria. Lloyd George vehemently rejected Clemenceau's charges and Wilson tried to calm the situation stating, in line with the pleas of King, that 'the consideration of this question be postponed for a time' and that the commission could find more information on the issue during this delay. Lloyd George replied that 'they ought to go to Syria', to which Clemenceau issued the following ultimatum: 'he was ready for the French representatives to go, as soon as the British troops in Syria had been replaced by the French'.[93]

The next morning, the argument continued. Clemenceau began with a well-planned rhetorical assault on Lloyd George's proposals and a defence of his claims to Syria, in which he again pointed out how Britain had been systematically lessening the territory that would be given to France. This incensed Lloyd George, who ranted against Clemenceau's portrayal of their past agreements and gave an ultimatum of his own, stating that 'unless the map he had presented was agreed to, he would have to await the report of the commission before withdrawing British troops'. Lloyd George had, of course, been informed that opinion would generally be against the French in the region and finished his retort with a likely insincere and rather Wilsonian pronouncement: 'If they [the commission] reported that the British were not wanted there, then the British had no right to stay, neither would the French if the report was against them.' Ignoring this point, Clemenceau and Lloyd George continued to argue about the validity of the Sykes–Picot Agreement, along with what was and was not agreed upon at their various subsequent meetings, prompting Lloyd George to once again threaten Clemenceau with sending the commission, stating 'now I shall send my commissioners, but I shall not withdraw the troops [from Syria]'. Clemenceau then attempted to gain the moral high ground in the argument, stating that Lloyd George was wrong but he 'would do no more' lest matters be pushed 'so far as to make trouble between the Entente'. 'It was for Great Britain to decide', he concluded, 'as to the withdrawal of her troops and to take the responsibility' for the consequences of this. Wilson chimed in with a comment no doubt intended to rankle them both, stating that he 'had never been able to see by what right France and Great Britain gave this country away to anyone'. Lloyd George, in an oddly quick reversal, stated that 'he could not send commissioners if the French would not send any', but that 'he was quite willing to abide by the decisions of the inhabitants as interpreted by' what was now a solely American commission. Wilson assured Clemenceau and Lloyd George that his 'commissioners were absolutely disinterested', further stating the 'one of them was Mr. Charles R. Craig [Crane], a very experienced and cosmopolitan man'. The meeting was then adjourned, with Clemenceau remaining conspicuously silent during these last exchanges.[94] Thus on 22 May, about two months after the idea was officially proposed by Wilson, the departure of the commission was finally assured.

After a more placid late morning Supreme Council session, Wilson had lunch with King, Crane and William Westermann, during which the president confirmed that the American Section of the International Commission on Mandates in Turkey (the official name they had adopted) would go regardless of whether or not the other powers joined them. He instructed them to 'see people and report to him'. In the meantime, it did not 'matter if mandates are temporarily assigned' (as King feared they would be) because Wilson would 'rely on their report' for a future, more permanent settlement.[95] In making the commission more of a personal advisory board on the Ottoman lands and taking this longer term view, Wilson's thinking about the commission had shifted and his expectations for it also appear to have been downgraded. He seems to have realised that, despite their assurances, the French and British were not likely to take its findings seriously especially if these findings undermined their claims to the region. Wilson also told King and Crane that the Zionist and Mesopotamian questions were 'virtually' closed but, in a moment fairly typical of Wilson's equivocation on these difficult issues, stated that the commission was not 'bound by any pre-conference or other agreement' or that there were no 'conference understandings that close any part of the question'.[96] This justifiably led King and Crane to believe that they had free reign when it came to the recommendations they could make.

Wilson further aired his evolving views on the reapportioning of the Ottoman lands to William Westermann and David Magie on 22 May. For the moment at least, the Arabic-speaking portions of the empire seemed to concern Wilson less than Anatolia, which he now referred to as the 'chief problem' of the Ottoman settlement likely because of the events of mid-May. Additionally, at this point, Wilson was sympathetic to leaving a politically powerless sultan in Istanbul, heeding the warnings of the Indian Muslim delegation received on 17 May. He was also ready to not allow the Italians to have any land in the region for 'they had no moral claim' to any of it. Importantly, Wilson was still resolute on the question of the allocation of mandates according to his ideals: 'Throughout the interview,' Westermann noted, 'the President declared himself as strongly opposed to the secret agreements. We think that he will still fight them.'[97]

As could have been expected, Felix Frankfurter and the Zionists were angered when they received word that the commission would go. As Frankfurter stated in a 25 May letter to Louis Brandeis, the Zionists 'had all settled down to the assumption that the commission was killed' and were thus surprised when, on 22 May 'at midnight' they 'heard that the President had ordered the American commission to proceed'. The next morning Frankfurter sprang into action, seeing Crane, Weizmann, House and other figures. When he saw House, he sought to gain further assurances that the Zionist question was settled in Wilson's mind, showing him the president's last letter. House advised him not to seek an audience with the president because he feared Frankfurter 'may run the risk of "irritating" him about matters on which he was already committed'.[98] In an attempt to make the commission aware of Wilson's promises, Frankfurter forwarded Wilson's most recent pro-Zionist letter to Crane on 23 May.[99] 'Of course', Frankfurter concluded to Brandeis, 'the whole commission is a sham' because the region's new political arrangements would be settled either in Paris or by the League of Nations. In any case, the matter would be concluded 'on a totally different basis than is contemplated by that commission.'[100]

Faysal and his representatives at the peace conference were afraid that the commission was becoming just such a 'sham' and that the delay in sending the commission meant that the reapportioning of the region was already occurring in Paris. With this in mind, the Hejaz Delegation sent Wilson a letter on 23 May requesting an assurance that he would 'await the results of the inquiry which the commission [...] will furnish before making the final decision on the problems of Arab Asia'.[101] Faysal, apparently not receiving much direct information from Paris, sent a cable to the Hejaz Delegation in early June stating that there was a 'rumour' in Syria that the commission might not come at all and that this 'evil rumour' had 'increasingly agitated' the people of the region. He further argued that if the people of Greater Syria had to 'consent to what is opposed to their wishes', then there would certainly be bloodshed and the 'civilised nations' of the peace conference would be to blame. This telegram was forwarded to the American delegation.[102]

The commission members generally seemed to ignore the controversy their undertaking was creating and went about making last-minute preparations for their journey. They bought more books, food and new outfits to make them look official, and also shipped many of their belongings back to the United States. The itinerary they drew up for their commission was, according to Montgomery, to leave on the evening of 29 May and go by train 'via Switzerland, Trieste, Bucharest, Constanza, boat on Black Sea to Constantinople arriving in about a week. Then we will go to Syria.'[103] The length of the trip was undetermined, with Lybyer stating to his wife, 'I have no idea when we shall return. It might of course be in time for the opening of college, but probably not. Mr. Crane does not wish to wander long.'[104] Westermann, who had initially supported the commission, then withdrew his support, then reluctantly supported it again in April after the Allenby telegram, was now back to believing that the commission was not a good idea. He wished the members well and privately instructed Yale and Montgomery 'not to let the commission propose a solution that was in contradiction to the plans drawn up' by the Inquiry. He also gave William Yale 'all the confidential documents bearing on the Syrian problem' and told him to use his 'discretion in showing them to the commissioners'.[105] Crane, wanting a few extra days in Istanbul, departed before his colleagues on 25 May.[106] The rest of the commission members left for Istanbul on 29 May. Westermann saw them off, telling Lybyer, in a statement typical of his conflicted views about the commission, that he was 'very glad you pushed this through' and that he had 'never expected to see' them leave.[107]

Any possibility of British, French or Italian participation in the commission ended shortly after the departure of the Americans. On 30 May, Allenby cabled Lloyd George, stating that unless the commission came soon, there would likely be an Arab uprising against the French and the British. On 31 May, Lloyd George brought this up in the Supreme Council and Clemenceau stated again that he would not send commissioners unless French troops began replacing British troops in Syria. Lloyd George, not yet ready to agree to this and also hoping not to further antagonise Clemenceau, stated he would not send his commissioners without the French. Italian Prime Minister Orlando stated that he would not send the Italian commissioners if the British and French did not go, and hence the 'Inter-Allied commission' formally became a solely American undertaking.[108] Though the commission members believed that there might be some advantages to the commission being solely American, such as simpler logistics and perhaps 'a franker expression of opinion' from the region's inhabitants,[109] the probability that the commission would become 'a great and influential body, with a real place in history', as Lybyer had once hoped, appeared to be significantly lessened by the withdrawal of America's allies.[110]

***

Despite the many obstacles placed in its way, the King–Crane Commission was finally departing for the Ottoman lands. The objections to the commission were many. Various diplomats in Paris argued that the uncertainty caused by any delay in finding a settlement for the region could do great harm and that all of the expertise needed to craft such a settlement was in Paris. Others stated that it would be difficult for the 'honest Americans' to learn the true feelings of the people because of the purported 'Oriental' propensity for dishonesty or because of the likely prevalence of British, French and Faysali propaganda in the region. Other people, like William Westermann, argued that a settlement along the lines of the Sykes–Picot Agreement was needed for the maintenance of 'international amity between France and England'.[111] It was not a secret that Lloyd George and Clemenceau were engaged in a deep dispute over this matter. As Lybyer noted in late May, the two were 'at swordspoints' and 'the sorest spot is Syria'.[112] He was nearly correct in a literal manner: Clemenceau reportedly challenged Lloyd George to a duel during the debates over the region.[113] The forces against the commission were strong, yet it still managed to make it to the region in a more diminutive form than was originally planned.

That the commission overcame these obstacles was attributable to Woodrow Wilson. Wilson favoured the idea of the commission because it fit into his vision for the world in the following ways: it was suggested by a representative of the region (Faysal), its mission was to ascertain the political desires of the region's people and it (potentially) countermanded secret treaties made during the war. The commission exemplified Wilson's general preference for 'processes over fixed terms' (in John Milton Cooper's words), meaning that major decisions needed to be arrived at only after lengthy deliberations that included numerous interested parties.[114] Wilson also understood that hopes had been raised by his lofty pronouncements made during the war and, more specifically, by his proposal of a fact-finding commission to the Ottoman lands. The question of honour (both personal and national) weighed heavily on his mind at this point: having promised that the commission would go, he did not want to break his word. His perseverance on the matter of the commission likely had a further personal dimension as well. Wilson had grown exasperated by the stances of Clemenceau and Lloyd George on the Ottoman lands. Having lost a number of battles at the peace conference concerning the disposition of other imperial lands, he decided to take a stand at this point. By the time he left Paris, however, it seems that Wilson realised that the commission would likely exert limited influence on any settlement for the region, agreeing in late June that the final apportioning of the Ottoman lands should not be delayed until the return of the commission.[115]

Within the commission, the roles of its members were already being defined. King and Lybyer were the commission's main champions and became its central figures. Without their persistence, the commission may have folded in Paris. Crane was the most eminent commission member but was also the least keen. Although he did consult an Orientalist friend on the matter and sat in on many of the sessions of expert testimony (discussed in the next chapter), Crane appeared to find little value in studying the region in an academic manner. Yale and Montgomery were both uncertain about the commission at first and were fairly peripheral figures during its time in Paris. Furthermore, the commission members were already forming their opinions about the reapportioning of the Ottoman lands while at the peace conference. Before recounting their time in the region, then, it is important to look at the early incarnations of commission members' opinions pertaining to the region they were about to tour.

CHAPTER 5

PRE-JOURNEY OPINIONS

The members of the King–Crane Commission possessed varying levels of knowledge about the Ottoman lands before the summer of 1919, and the 'knowledge' that they did possess was often firmly rooted in the prejudices of their time. Although the two commissioners were fairly prominent Americans who have left good-sized archival legacies, their backgrounds (and the rather meagre scholarly assessment of these backgrounds in existence) give little indication of what they believed about the Ottoman Empire. Henry Churchill King probably knew the least about the region and Charles Crane knew only what he had gleaned during his past visits. In contrast, the technical advisers (Lybyer, Yale and Montgomery) had all lived in the Ottoman lands and had studied about them to varying degrees. Yale and, to a lesser extent, Lybyer left lengthy writings pertaining to the region, making it easier to determine their thoughts prior to their time on the commission. Still, though, the fluid and unique postwar situation often rendered opinions held prior to the Paris Peace Conference at least somewhat obsolete. Although preconceptions about the region's people played a major role in the Commission members' beliefs about what could or should be done with the Ottoman lands, the parameters that the Allies constructed in the wartime agreements and the League of Nations Covenant (among other things) gave these preconceptions a new context in which to function. Furthermore, the region was going to be transformed and the commission members believed that their opinions could now possibly be turned into geopolitical reality. The gravity of the situation, along with the many competing political projects present at the peace conference, created a scenario in which the commission members were often rethinking their past opinions. Their preconceptions about the region's people, however, still provided the foundation of their beliefs.

Once appointed, King and Lybyer organised the commission's initial investigations, which included purchasing (and reading) a large amount of literature on the region, consulting with several delegations who had ties to the Ottoman lands and conferring with 'experts' who often gave them conflicting advice. Before they left Paris, the commission members laid out a number of their opinions about the region in their pre-journey writings, the most important of which was the document entitled 'The Dangers to the Allies from a Selfish Exploitation of the Turkish Empire' (signed by the five main commission members). This chapter is devoted to examining the tenor of the commission members' investigations about the region during their time in Paris and the general state of their opinions as they left for the Ottoman lands. Once established, this will help make it possible to gauge how their time in the region subsequently influenced their respective recommendations.

Books

Shortly after they were named to the commission, King and Lybyer began assembling a substantial reference library. The materials they collected included many of the contemporary English-language academic works on the region. The books they purchased to read 'for atmosphere', such as *The Arabian Nights* and the works of Herodotus and Plutarch, show the link they perceived between the region's ancient past and its present.[1] They also purchased travel literature on the region such as W.J. Childs's *Across Asia Minor on Foot* and *Travels and Politics in Armenia* by Noel Buxton (a British Member of Parliament) and Harold Buxton (a minister in England). The literature also included books by people who had lived in and studied the region for a long time, usually 'with bible in hand' in the words of one contemporary.[2] Examples of these works include missionary (and legendary beekeeper) P.J. Baldensperger's *The Immovable East* and William Ramsay's *Impressions of Turkey during Twelve Years' Wanderings*, with the latter of these being quoted extensively in their final report. They purchased basic geography books and primers on the region's religions, such as G.A. Smith's *Historical Geography of the Holy Land* and *The Religions of Modern Syria and*

Palestine by archaeologist F.J. Bliss. They also focused specifically on Islam, purchasing the Qu'ran and several biographies of the Prophet Muhammad. Finally, they bought numerous works of the era's Orientalists, including a number of C. Snouck Hurgronje's works and Samuel Zwemer's *Arabia: The Cradle of Islam.*

In general, the texts they selected show the state of European and American literature about the Middle East in this era and the transatlantic trends of scholarship regarding the Ottoman lands. These texts were primarily written by Western European and American scholars whose attachment to the region was usually of a missionary or an archaeological nature (with the archaeologists often being staunch Christians themselves). These texts also begin to show the conception of the Middle East harboured, or being learned, by the members of the commission. The region had an ancient and well-documented history that was still very much alive. It was the holiest part of the world and was inhabited by people who generally still lived in a similar manner to the characters in the Torah, the Bible and the Qu'ran. The Middle East, then, was stagnant in this way: archaeologists and historians of the ancient world were qualified to make assertions about the present partly because the present had hardly moved beyond the ancient past. Importantly, the authors of these books would have viewed the Middle East through approximately the same cultural lens as the King–Crane Commission members. Although this body of literature likely did help to inform the commission members who were less familiar with the region (like Henry Churchill King), they would mainly have served to reinforce their preconceptions about the Ottoman lands and its people.

Testimony from the Region in Paris

It was difficult for the commission to find people in Paris who could give legitimate insight into the 'desires' of the region's people for the simple reason that there were not many Ottoman subjects at the peace conference. They did, however, speak with a number of people from the Ottoman lands and were generally aware of the official testimony given by Ottoman groups, thus they were not entirely devoid of data from the people of the region before they left Paris.

Americans at the peace conference were particularly sympathetic to the Armenians, and the commission members were no exception.

The Armenian delegation frequently consulted with many prominent Americans and, as previously noted, William Westermann helped to sculpt the delegation's testimony before the Supreme Council. Arguably the commission's strongest advocate for the Armenians was George Montgomery, who was close to the Armenian delegation and dined with them on occasion. Lybyer also met with the Armenians frequently and appeared generally sympathetic to their cause. The Armenians also had detractors among the Americans at the Conference, the most prominent of whom was Caleb Gates. Gates believed that the creation of a large Armenia with ports on the Mediterranean and Black Seas was an overreach that would create more unnecessary acrimony in the region.[3] As the commission left for the Ottoman lands, its members were in agreement that there should be some sort of semi-independent Armenia and were aware of the Armenian testimony before the Supreme Council. The size and shape of this new country, however, would be the basis for discussion among the commission members in the ensuing months.

Beyond the Armenians, the commission members heard or would have been aware of the testimony of a few other delegations claiming to represent groups from the Ottoman lands, though these delegations were sometimes of questionable legitimacy. Interestingly, the legitimacy of Amir Faysal, the *de facto* spokesperson for Greater Syria, was rarely questioned at the peace conference even though he had lived in the Hejaz and Istanbul for most of his life and had been installed by the British as the leader of the Arab government in Damascus. The commission was fully aware of Faysal's public requests for a large, independent Arab state, though they were also aware that privately he seemed more agreeable to a British or American mandate. Along these lines, he told William Yale in private that he truly preferred the United States as mandatory power but dared not say so publicly, lest he upset the British. In his words, he was 'holding to Great Britain as a drowning man grasps at anything at hand'.[4] Yale later repeated this anecdote to the commission and added that Faysal 'may have told Brit. other things'.[5] The commission also believed that much of the pro-French testimony at the peace conference from people with ties to the region was of dubious merit because these people had been handpicked and perhaps bribed by the French. Information like this would only have served to reinforce the initial anti-French leanings of the commission members: not only had the French angered them by delaying the commission's departure, but the commission members were also starting to believe that the French had done this because most people in Greater Syria did not want French rule. Consequently, the commission entered the region expecting to find anti-French sentiment.

The King–Crane Commission was also familiar with the appeals of a group of Syrian-Americans who called themselves 'The New Syria National League'. This group, led by US citizen Abraham Mitrie Rihbany (a noted Presbyterian minister and author), sent the Americans at the peace conference a formal petition on 15 March 1919 which was later given to King. This petition called for a unified federal Syria with autonomous provinces. It further stated that 'because of ages of oppression, the people of Syria cannot at present assume the responsibilities of complete self-government' and thus needed a mandatory power. The mandate, they argued, should be held by the United States because it was 'free from colonial and imperialistic interests'.[6] Rihbany also arranged a 28 May meeting between the commission and a delegation of Palestinians and Syrians (who likely did not live in the region). The intent of this delegation was to voice opposition to a 'Zionistic state', arguing that the peace conference had 'heard' the Zionists but 'had not heard the Syrians'. The delegation emphasised that all Syrians were 'in full accord vs. [the] establishment of [a] Zionist regime' and the people of the region 'will never accept Zionist rule'. They further requested that 'no decision be taken by the peace conference before the people have been seen on the spot and consulted'.[7] With even Faysal acting in an ostensibly friendly manner towards the Zionists, such emphatic anti-Zionist testimony was fairly rare in Paris but it was a preview of what the commission would hear once they arrived in Palestine.

Other major interest groups either ignored or had no sway with the King–Crane Commission. The Zionists paid little direct attention to the commission, believing that it would likely not go and that, even if it did, American support for Zionism was already guaranteed. Once it was decided that the commission would go, many Zionists in Paris unsuccessfully tried to convince Felix Frankfurter to follow it to the region, fearing the commission's 'potentialities for mischief'.[8] Other groups from the Ottoman lands were even less well represented in front of the commission while in Paris. No one on the commission recorded any attempt by Ottoman representatives to contact them in Paris, and groups like the Kurds and Assyrians had no serious champions at the peace conference.[9] The Greeks, whose desires were well known, apparently did not feel it necessary to lobby the commission. In sum, the opinions of people from the region did not figure significantly in the commission's preparations for departure.

'Experts'

The commission members arranged briefings with the numerous American 'experts' on the Ottoman lands prior to their departure and received many different opinions about what should occur in the region's future. On 25 and 26 April, William Westermann briefed the commissioners on the agreements reached by the European powers during the war and how the main parties to these agreements now viewed them. On the first day of the briefing, Westermann discussed the emerging issue of oil, stating that the British were seeking to control 'the petroleum area [Mesopotamia]' and that this was 'not by accident'. Yale, having been attached to the British army during the war, then spoke at length about the details of the military campaign in the region. Westermann finished the first day of meetings by recounting his recommendations for the new split of the mainly Turkish-speaking portions of the Ottoman Empire, stating that there should be a 'Conspl. State, Greek Area, Anatolia, Armenia (No Kurd district)'. On the second day, Westermann argued for European or American occupation of the Ottoman lands because 'what has happened is [the] removal of the control which has held the country together for 500 years'. He feared that without strong mandatory oversight the 'natural relapse' would be 'into chaos, as in Russia'. 'Occupation', he argued, 'prevents anarchy'. The problem, Westermann continued, was that the United States was the only real power who could occupy these places selflessly, stating that 'if the U.S. does not take a mandate there, W. Asia will fall to imperialism of [the] sort dividing up Africa. Fr. [The French], Italians, and even British will never get out w.out [without] being kicked out.' He concluded that 'one result of the commission may be to show how much these people want America'.[10]

On 30 April, the commission continued its meetings with American experts on the region. Louis Heck, the new US Ambassador to the Ottoman Empire (and long-serving diplomat in the region), lectured them on the difficulties of any sort of American involvement in the Ottoman lands because the 'setting [was] dangerous'. He warned them against placing Christian minorities under the control of Muslim majorities lest 'Moslem fear be aroused'. Heck noted that the majority of Americans in the region believed that Constantinople should remain in the hands of the Turks and that the Sultan should remain in the city 'shorn of all political power'. Like Westermann, Heck thought that the commission would find a 'strong current of opinion among Turks for American control largely because America does not ask for it'. In the end (and unlike Westermann), Heck argued that it would be best to keep the empire together, at least in the short term, because division 'would increase racial antipathies and hatreds'.[11]

David Magie, the American author of an Inquiry report on the Kurds, discussed the generally overlooked Kurdish and Assyrian Christian situations before the commission on 2 May. The question of what to do with the region sometimes referred to as Kurdistan was generally of secondary concern to the powers at the conference, and employing Magie as an expert on the Kurds (a professor of classics who appeared to have no firsthand knowledge of this region) was a prime example of this. Magie compared the Kurds to the 'Highland Clans of Scotland', in that they had strong tribal leaders with no history of overall unity. He further asserted that the Kurds were serial 'brigands', having been 'taught by the Turks' in the art of raiding. Magie contended that it would be unwise to honour any requests for an independent Kurdistan because the Kurds had no history of governing themselves. The Assyrian Christians needed protection from the Kurds, and thus a mandatory power was necessary in the region. He concluded that it was necessary to 'divide' these dangerous Kurdish populations between several countries under strong mandatory powers in order to (euphemistically) 'settle' these people.[12]

On 5 May, the commission turned its attention to Greater Syria and heard testimony from William Yale about the region's political situation. Yale discussed Greater Syria in terms of confessional groups, stating that the Muslims had been oppressing the Christians for years. The only thing that had protected the region's Christians, according to Yale, were interventions by the European powers and the 'Capitulations' which had granted special rights to foreigners living in Ottoman lands. The 'Moslem Arabs', he argued, were 'far more religious and fanatical than the Turks'. Furthermore, a sense of Arab unity was emerging in the region but it was important to note that, according to Yale, the Arabs thought of their movement 'as not national but Moslem'. Yale preferred to keep the new Arab states small (should they come to exist) so that a new Arab/Islamic empire could not rise in place of the Ottomans. Small states also would allow for proper 'nationalism [to] be developed', implying, as the commission members often did, that a strong and mostly secular nationalism was the desired end to which these new mandates should aspire. Such Syrian nationalism, he noted, was currently being taught in the Syrian Protestant College and had the potential to help in the development of a modern nation. Yale concluded by describing what he believed the commission would hear from the region's people. The Muslims, he contended, would likely favour '(1) Independence (2) Amer. mandate (3) Brit. mandate', while some Christians in Lebanon would favour a French mandate. However, most of the people 'opposed [the] French' and 'France', he warned, 'does not wish the commission to see this'.[13]

Caleb Gates, being one of the longest serving and most respected missionary educators in the region, offered the commission yet another different opinion on the future of the Ottoman Empire on 8 May. As previously noted, Gates opposed the commission because he believed that the region was in 'need of [a] speedy decision', partly because the Turks did not yet 'realize that they are beaten' and were 'well organized, esp.[especially] in the interior'. On the matter of reapportioning the empire, he thought that there should be a single mandate over all of the Ottoman lands, without separating Istanbul, Armenia or the Arabic-speaking provinces. If the peace conference chose to split the empire, Gates argued that the United States (or Britain, if America refused) should take mandates for Anatolia and the Arabic-speaking provinces, while Armenia should be attached to Mesopotamia and placed under a British mandate.[14]

A number of further opinions came from varied people, perhaps the most credible of whom was Henry Morgenthau. At a dinner on 23 May, Morgenthau argued before the commission that the Sultan should be removed from Istanbul and that the Ottoman Empire should be split into a 'triple mandatory', by which he meant it should be divided between the United States, Britain and France, though he had little respect for the latter nation.[15] He believed that the United States should control the 'non-Arabic portions' of the empire and that this mandate should be split into 'distinct parts, the Consple [Constantinople] area, Turkish, Armenian, and Greek portions'.[16] More informally, Morgenthau discussed the politics of the nations hoping to get a piece of the Ottoman Empire as follows: 'France is weeping on our shoulder. In a year we will give her a kick and call her a dirty prostitute. Italy is a pup. Anglo-Saxons will rule the world.'[17]

Although they heard many more opinions in numerous settings, those noted here are indicative of the disparate voices helping to form the initial thoughts of the commission members. There were a number of commonalities in these opinions, with two of the most prominent being the assertions that the Turks had awfully mismanaged their empire and that the people of the region were not ready to govern themselves. Independence, according to the Americans they consulted, was not an option, but neither was old-style imperialism. The schemes they heard for splitting the Ottoman lands varied, with some people advocating the creation of as many as seven new mandates in the region, and others stating that the Ottoman Empire should remain unified. Some people argued that the United States should take substantial mandates in the region, though these people often acknowledged the unlikelihood of the US Senate accepting such a scheme. In sum, the commission had access to a diverse array of pre-journey opinions from these 'experts' which, in turn, helped to shape their own.

The Commission Members' Pre-Journey Opinions

Before departing for the region, the commission members expressed opinions about the people of the Ottoman lands and made broad recommendations for the possible territorial dispositions of the empire. As noted in the previous chapter, the commission members decided to write Wilson a statement summarising their pre-journey findings. The basic recommendations in this document, entitled 'The Dangers to the Allies from a Selfish Exploitation of the Turkish Empire', were as follows:

- The Ottoman Empire must be disbanded, with Constantinople being taken out of the hands of the Turks.
- The British should receive mandates for Mesopotamia and Palestine, and 'supervision' over the Hejaz.

- The French should receive a mandate for 'Syria liberally interpreted'. They argued that this was 'frankly based, not on the primary desires of the people, but on the international need of preserving friendly relations between France and Great Britain'.
- The United States should receive mandates for a 'Constantinopolan State', a large Armenia with ports on the Black and Mediterranean Seas, and possibly for the rest of Turkish Anatolia.
- There should also be 'an autonomous Greek region within Anatolia' based in Smyrna.

The commission members all signed this statement indicating that there was consensus on these points.

The members left further, if somewhat limited, evidence about their respective pre-journey stances towards the region in other documents as well, and from this evidence several themes that underpinned their thinking about the region emerge. More specifically, this evidence shows that the King–Crane Commission members arrived in the Ottoman lands instilled with particular opinions about the groups that inhabited the region. The members essentialised the region's groups, meaning that they assigned specific tendencies and potentials to them. According to the commission members, these groups had largely inherent potentials for a variety of things, the most important of which included propensities towards violence and religious fanaticism, the capacity (or lack thereof) to govern and, perhaps most importantly, the ability to become modern. The prominent themes in these writings are the subject of the rest of this chapter.

To begin with, the commission members' pre-journey writings offer a few windows into their perspectives on Muslims. Albert Lybyer left a large amount of evidence about his attitude towards Islam, being the only member of the commission who had published work that prominently featured the religion. Lybyer displayed a nominal respect for Islam in his book on the Ottoman Empire under Suleiman the Magnificent but the work contained a strong undertone of Christian superiority as well. At the beginning of the book, he noted that most people in the United States and Europe knew little about Islam, stating that the Western understanding of Islam had 'been shut off by a well-nigh impenetrable barrier' of 'prejudices' left over from the 'crusading days'. The 'main religious ideas of Mohammedanism', according to

Lybyer, were not 'inharmonious with those of Christianity'. Islam's 'most objectionable features, [which were] the seclusion of women, polygamy, and slavery', could be regarded as 'survivals from an older condition of mankind' that most Muslims were 'tending to abandon'. However, the 'real "tragedy of the Turk"' was that they 'remained Mohammedan', as opposed to converting to Christianity, or, perhaps, undertaking an Islamic reformation similar to that which so altered Europe. The 'deadening system' of Islam 'stilled their [the Ottomans'] active spirits, imprisoned their extraordinary adaptability, and held them at a stage of culture' that was quickly surpassed by 'the progressive West'.[18] Lybyer gave a similarly mixed appraisal of Islam in a 1917 speech to the City Club of Chicago entitled 'Turkey and the Great War', in which he stated that Islam had been 'a great source of power' for the Ottomans during their rise and had provided the 'intellectual talent of the empire' from 'perhaps the greatest educational system of its time'. Ultimately, though, Islam was too 'conservative' and stood 'in the way of political and social improvement'.[19] In general, Lybyer believed that Islam initially helped the Ottomans but eventually was a hindrance to modernisation and became one of the main causes of Ottoman decline.

William Yale's thoughts about Islam were less favourable than Lybyer's. Yale had not been impressed with the Muslim population of Greater Syria during his time in the region, and this was recorded in his writings. In a 1917 report to the State Department, for example, Yale noted that the local Muslims were 'ignorant and fanatical' (one of Yale's common refrains) and 'illiterate to an unbelievable degree'.[20] In two dispatches to the State Department in December 1918, Yale noted that the Arab 'upper classes' were developing a 'sullen hatred of Westerners and their civilization'. These 'upper classes' would soon be able to command the 'illiterate, fanatical, uncivilized and semi-savage' masses. Soon, a 'hatred of Western civilization, and the races of the West' would 'be burned deep in the hearts of all these teeming millions'. The cause of this hatred, in Yale's estimation, was at least partly the near-sighted imperialism of the British and the French, but it owed more to the fact that Muslim 'fanaticism' was a primary component of their being. Yale stated that if the Arabs had a more modern 'great Arab patriot' as a leader, he could, perhaps 'rouse his people from the mire of religious ignorance and fanaticism in which they are sunk' and 'wipe out the political conception of religious domination'. This, though, would take 'many years, and tireless efforts of great fearless men, in whose souls burns the fires of nationalism'. Sharif Hussein of Mecca, with whom the British had allied themselves, was not one of these men according to Yale. Hussein, Yale argued, was more concerned with creating a large Muslim state with an 'effective armed force [...] with all of the modern weapons of war'. In Yale's mind, Faysal was sent to Paris in order to 'solicit the consent of the Peace Congress' for such a state, 'under the disguise of Arab Independence'.[21] For Yale, the Muslim masses were an ignorant, subservient and fanatical lot who unthinkingly followed their often barbaric leaders. If the reapportioning of the Ottoman lands was not done carefully, Yale warned, another oppressive Muslim empire in the Middle East would rise, but this time it would be ruled by Arabs.

The other commission members left far less evidence of their attitudes towards Muslims before the summer of 1919. The 'Dangers' document mentions little about Islam, except to argue that there was minimal risk of pan-Islamic uprisings should the Caliphate be dissolved because the Muslims of the world were not 'truly unified'.[22] In his writings, Henry Churchill King mentioned little about Islam before his time on the commission though he certainly believed in the superiority of Christianity to all other religions.[23] He did, however, mention Turkey in a 1918 essay that largely parroted Wilson's rhetoric, stating 'the unspeakable Armenian massacre should be ample demonstration that the Turk should be driven absolutely out of Europe, and that Armenia and Syria should be entirely released from Turkish rule'. Throughout history, according to King, Turkey had 'demonstrated its utter unfitness to rule over other peoples'.[24] Charles Crane was interested in Islam and appeared to have had a mostly favourable opinion of it, though he did once denigrate Vladmir Lenin by stating that 'he was a supreme fanatic, with many of the qualities of a Muslim Mahdi'.[25] There is little in the records of George Montgomery and the other members of the commission to be able to assess their attitudes about Muslims before their 1919 journey. In general, however, Americans of this era would not have been predisposed to respect Islam as a religion, with Muslims mainly being described in English-language literature of the time as the sworn enemies of Christendom and the perpetrators of abhorrent massacres in the Middle East.[26]

In contrast to this, the commission members harboured more favourable opinions about the Christian groups of the Ottoman Empire, though the superiority of Christianity was something that was often inferred rather than stated explicitly. A telling example of this came in the 'Dangers' document, which referred to the Greeks and Armenians as 'the more able, industrious, and enterprising groups' of the Ottoman lands.[27] The fact that they saw no reason to justify this claim in the document, or similar claims in other documents, indicates that they, and their intended audience (Wilson and his advisors), would have seen the superiority of these two groups as self-evident. Furthermore, the occupations of the region's Christians, according to William Yale, proved that they were also largely at a different historical stage than their non-Christian neighbours. The Christians were usually 'merchants, manufacturers and are generally the professional class of the population', in contrast to the region's Muslims who occupied positions in a more feudal society (they were 'large land owners', 'tillers of the soil and tenders of the flocks'), thus pairing his conceptions of historical progress with religious classifications.[28] The commission members saw the massacres of the Armenians during the war, and other similar massacres throughout the region's history, through an almost exclusively confessional lens. In the Middle East, Christians were always in danger, which helped lead them to the conclusion that a Christian power was required to defend their co-religionists in the postwar Ottoman lands. On the whole, the commission members exhibited a pro-Christian bias ingrained in their social imaginary and mainly saw Christianity as a signifier that indicated a particular group's fitness for modernity.

The most debated aspect of the King–Crane Commission has been its members' views on Zionism. Numerous scholars, from Frank Manuel in 1949 to Michael Oren in 2007, have claimed that the commission was part of a missionary conspiracy conducted in an effort to undermine Zionist and European claims to the region. 'To the American missionaries in the Near East', Manuel claimed, 'the King–Crane Expedition was a triumph.'[29] This assertion appears to be inaccurate, partly because a number of prominent members of the missionary establishment opposed the commission, including Caleb Gates. Indeed, Wilson specifically suggested a relatively 'neutral' commission as a corrective to any such missionary bias, arguing that people like Howard Bliss may have been too 'involved' with the 'population'.[30] Moreover, much of the extant evidence indicates that the missionaries of the region were mainly concerned with being able to continue their work regardless of the politics surrounding the reapportioning of the Ottoman Empire.[31] The commission members, while perhaps being generally disinclined to support European imperial aims, claimed in their final report that they 'began their study of Zionism with minds predisposed in its favor', which was the standard viewpoint among Americans at the peace conference.[32] While some historians have insinuated that this statement was disingenuous, there does appear to be some evidence that it was, in fact, sincere.

Charles Crane's attitude towards Jews has been at the centre of a further accusation that antisemitism influenced the commission's recommendations on Zionism.[33] It is true that Crane harboured anti-Jewish feelings in 1919, but these feelings were complex and cannot be classified as general antisemitism. Crane did believe, at this point, that there were high-level international conspiracies involving wealthy Jews and Freemasons, and even went so far as to blame the Russian Revolution on such conspiracies. He further believed that many American Jews believed themselves to be 'first Jews then Americans'.[34] Additionally, Crane was often at political odds with influential Jewish-American banker Jacob Schiff and would highlight the largely Jewish identity of Schiff's inner-circle of friends when making disparaging comments about them.[35] This is tempered, though, by various other elements of his life, such as his wholehearted endorsement of Jewish Zionist Richard Gottheil for the post of Ambassador to the Ottoman Empire in 1913 and his staunch support of his friend Louis Brandeis (an ardent Zionist) during his bitterly contested nomination to the Supreme Court in 1916.[36] These political alliances and rivalries led Crane to distinguish between 'democratic Jews' (Gottheil and Brandeis) and 'German and Wall Street Jews' (Schiff). More to the point, Crane is on the record as being sympathetic to Zionism during World War I. Gottheil, for example, asked Crane to 'urge Brandeis not to forsake the Zionists' after he had been appointed to the Supreme Court, which is not something Gottheil would have asked if Crane were an avowed opponent of Zionism.[37] Furthermore, Crane is recorded as stating in 1916 that Jews 'could serve as a natural bridge between Europe and Asia'.[38] While it is true that Crane undoubtedly harboured more harshly antisemitic opinions later in his life, it appears that, in 1919 at least, Crane was not a staunch antisemite and likely still supported Zionism.[39]

Henry Churchill King, for his part, does not seem to have been overly interested in Zionism before his time on the commission, but his position as a well-known Christian leader with missionary connections has been used as implicit evidence that he was somehow part of an anti-Zionist conspiracy.[40] One problem with this assertion is that during this era, most prominent American Protestants had missionary connections and, despite this, most of these Protestant leaders in the United States were in fact supporters of Zionism. As Louis Brandeis stated in 1917, 'the vast mass of Christian opinion in this country, particularly of course the Protestant Churches, supports our idea [Zionism]'.[41] This, paired with the fact that there seems to be no evidence in King's past showing that he was anti-Zionist or antisemitic, indicates that it would have been unlikely for King to be predisposed against Zionism.

William Yale was the commission member who left the most evidence about his feelings toward the Zionist movement. Yale had been somewhat equivocal about Zionism during the war. Having travelled in Palestine extensively since 1913, Yale had firsthand experience with the Zionist colonies and, in an April 1918 memorandum, he displayed a somewhat nuanced view of what he saw as the different Zionist communities. He argued that there were 'the very Orthodox Zionists' who wanted only colonies and development based on 'strictly religious and orthodox lines'. There were also 'Nationalistic Zionists' who 'lay [the] greatest stress on Jewish nationality' and the 'Socialistic Zionists' who hoped 'to establish in Palestine a Socialistic Jewish Utopia'. Generally speaking, though, Yale believed that despite what they might be stating publicly, the 'ultimate aim' of the Zionists was the building of 'a Jewish State in Palestine' through gradual immigration and 'absorption of all industry and business of the Holy Land'. In this memorandum, Yale cited what he saw as the best argument for Zionism at length, which was, in essence, that the Zionists would come to the Middle East 'not as overlords and rulers' but as 'settlers and colonists bringing their civilization with them' and that in time 'they will accomplish the civilizing of the Oriental peoples as no Western Christian Power has been able to do'. Despite this, Yale stated that:

> Until the Jews prove to the world that their ideal of a Jewish country in Palestine is more than an ideal and a dream it would

seem as if it were an injustice to the present inhabitants of Palestine for the World Powers to create there an artificial Jewish State imposed upon an unwilling and hostile population.[42]

From this document, it seems that Yale distrusted Zionist motives. However, between April 1918 and January 1919, Yale became convinced that Zionism should move forward and he (along with George Montgomery) took part in the writing of concrete pro-Zionist recommendations with William Westermann at the start of the Paris Peace Conference. The spread of modernity was cited as a primary reason to support Zionism in these recommendations, with the establishment of a Jewish 'national home' constituting an 'integral part' of the 'future economic and political security of the entire region'.[43] Yale still appeared sceptical about Zionism at various points during the conference, but there is no evidence that he waivered from this general pro-Zionist stance.[44]

Overall, it appears that the commission members were conflicted about Zionism during their time in Paris. As they noted in the 'Dangers to the Allies' document, the commission members agreed that Palestine should be overseen by a mandatory power who would 'guard the holy places and the entire territory for the benefit of all peoples interested', meaning for the benefit of the indigenous population and the world religious communities with a stake in the region. They did not believe, however, that Palestine should be set aside 'simply for the Jews'.[45]

Beyond their opinions about the people of the Ottoman lands, the commission members harboured strong views about geopolitical issues as well. As the title of their pre-journey statement suggests ('The Dangers to the Allies from a Selfish Exploitation of the Turkish Empire'), the commission members had internalised Wilson's anti-imperialist rhetoric. In March 1918, for example, William Yale continually lamented both the escalating tensions between the British and the French in Greater Syria and the increasing suspicion of the locals about the intentions of these two powers. The British and the French, according to Yale, were 'creating an unfavourable impression among the Arabs' and causing them to 'doubt the sincerity of the Allies' avowals that they are not waging a war of annexation and of conquest'.[46] In December of the same year, Yale argued, similarly, that 'if Europe continues in the Near East the same policies it has followed in the past; if the same system of colonization, and subjection be followed; the Nations of the West will be but laying up trouble for the future'. Furthermore, according to Yale, conditions in Syria and Mesopotamia could become like Egypt, 'where a hatred of the West is burned deep in the Egyptian's soul' because of what he believed to be harsh British rule since 1882.[47] Similarly, George Montgomery summarised his take on the competition among the imperial powers in a March 1919 letter to his wife, though he was more sympathetic to the British: 'Italy and the French Foreign Office are out for loot and in time of distress England made secret treaties with them which sort of ties her hands.'[48]

These same ideas came out more emphatically in the 'Dangers' document. In this, the five main commission members argued that 'the Allies should bear in mind, that their fidelity to their announced aims in the war is here [in the division of the Ottoman lands] to be peculiarly tested'. If 'the division of the Turkish Empire by the Allies approaches a division primarily determined by the selfish national and corporate interests of the Allies', then the Allies likely would:

- 'call out the resentment' of many of their own citizens who believed that their respective countries had gone to war for lofty ideals and not imperial aggrandisement;
- sow 'dissension of the gravest kind' among themselves, 'threatening the moral unity of their cause and entailing serious world consequences';
- 'convince men of independent moral judgment all over the world' that 'the aims of the Allies had become as selfish and ruthless as those of the Germans'; and
- 'tend to encourage rebellious uprisings on the part of national groups, and to increase general sympathy with such uprisings'.[49]

Based on the evidence in this document, then, the five main commission members seemed to have believed that imperialism was both a national and international disease, one that caused moral degeneration at home and war abroad. They believed that imperialism was a major cause of World War I and feared that it would trigger future conflicts. They also feared both American and international disillusionment with the powers who had emerged victorious from World War I if old imperial ways continued. In the minds of the commission members, Wilsonian antiimperialism was the way out of this cycle of war and strife. Just and novel solutions, like internationalising the most strategic points in the Ottoman lands, also needed to be considered in the interest of international stability. In general, the members of the King–Crane Commission believed that they were emissaries of this new way of thinking; Wilson, in their minds, was something of a prophet and they were his disciples.

Also central to their thinking was Wilson's conception of the term 'self-determination'. In their pre-journey remarks about this concept, they generally accepted that self-determination was a guiding principle of Wilson's foreign policy and thus was something that should be a primary consideration in the postwar settlements. In December 1918, for instance, William Yale discussed the principle of self-determination as something only the United States cared about in the context of the Middle East. France and Britain, according to Yale, were going to do their best to 'persuade' Wilson that self-determination was 'being carried out' in the region while under their occupation, when in fact these countries cared little about this principle.[50] Albert Lybyer showed general support for self-determination before the journey, stating on 20 May 1919 that any settlement 'in regard to the Turkish situation' that involved granting portions of the empire to Britain, France, Greece and Italy would be 'the very negation of self-determination and the rights of the peoples'.[51] Charles Crane was a major proponent of self-determination but discussed it mainly in the context of the Balkans during his time in Paris. 'An essential condition for bringing about peace in the Balkans', according to Crane, was 'a sincere and full application of the doctrine of the self-determination of peoples'. The Balkans, he argued, did have distinct 'nations', large and small. He asserted, for example, that few groups had 'a stronger sense of nationality' or had 'fought for it longer or with more determination, than the Albanians', thus fulfilling Wilson's dictum of a 'well-defined' nationalism in Crane's mind. Before any settlement was reached, and if self-determination was to be made a reality, Crane believed that the world leaders gathered in Paris needed to consult both the people of the Balkans and the top experts in Balkan affairs. He perceived little effort by the powers to do either of these things at the peace conference.[52]

The 'Dangers' document also displayed general support for self-determination among the commission members. In these recommendations, the commission argued that, in the case of Turkey, 'if the principles of national unity and self-determination are to be applied at all to the Turkish people, at least a large central portion of Asia Minor, sufficient to provide for the bulk of the Turks' needed to be set aside under a mandatory power. Thus if peace was going to be kept, self-determination had to be the right even of the vanquished. The mandatory power would be given control of this new 'province' and would have a mission to give the Turks 'that good government that they have notoriously lacked'. In addition to this, they argued against the implementation of the British and French wartime agreements, stating that 'such a division would have to be forced upon the peoples concerned – not chosen by them', implying that this would go against Wilson's principles.[53] The concept of self-determination figured heavily in the commission members' thinking before their journey, and, in general, they concurred with Wilson that the people of the Middle East should be given a say in their future.

Finally, the commission members were contemplating what postwar role, if any, the United States might take in the Ottoman lands. Before their time in the region, the commission members had all internalised the belief that the United States, with Wilson leading the way, was the country that could cure the world's ills. The US, in their minds, was morally superior to the world's other powers and would have to play a more concrete role in global affairs if a more stable order was to be created. The commission members contended, furthermore, that the American people might become disillusioned if their government allowed the world to revert to the pre-war conditions that had made possible the occurrence of such a large-scale conflict. Importantly for the members of the commission, the people of the Middle East seemed to believe in the benevolence of the United States. William Yale, for example, believed that the strong reputation of the United States in the region was well-deserved, for reasons which included 'the disinterested devotion' of the Syrian Protestant College faculty, the 'splendid charitable and relief work carried on during the war by Americans' and the 'entrance of the United States into the War in the defence of the rights of small and oppressed nationalities'.[54] George Montgomery believed that the United States needed to be involved in the peace settlements and stated, in March of 1919, that it was 'up to us [the United States] if anything is done' about the damage that imperial wrangling had caused in the Ottoman Empire. Because of this, he believed that 'the U.S. ought to accept the mandate to look after the interests of some new country over there [in the Ottoman lands]'.[55] Perhaps most importantly, the commission members appear to have expressed agreement on this matter in the 'Dangers' document, in which they argued that any sort of 'selfish exploitation' of the region along traditional imperialist lines would anger 'the most solid portion of the American people'. Americans, the commission members contended, had consented to US participation in World War I only because they were convinced that their country's war aims were benevolent. Americans would therefore see any exploitation of the Ottoman lands 'as emphatically not illustrating the ends for which America came into the war'.[56] Thus before their journey, the five main members of the commission believed that the United States needed to play a substantive role in the future of the Ottoman lands or else Britain, France and Italy were likely to simply replace the Ottomans as the imperial rulers of the region.

***

Before their time in the region, the five main members of the commission harboured distinct ideas about the people of the Ottoman lands and had a broad sense of what should occur in this region's future. These preconceptions set the parameters of their investigation in the following manner: they had little faith in the ability of the indigenous populations of the region to guide themselves toward modernity and, because of this, the commission members agreed that independence was not an option. They believed that the victorious powers should be the ones to guide the people of the Ottoman lands towards modernity, and this guidance would come in the form of mandates. As shown in their anti-imperialist rhetoric, they genuinely believed that these mandates should not be colonies ripe for exploitation but instead should be benevolent projects to lead the region's people towards self-rule. Once they arrived in the Ottoman lands, the commission began to listen to representatives of the region, and this would serve to further sculpt their opinions within these basic parameters.

CHAPTER 6

ISTANBUL AND PALESTINE

The King–Crane Commission departed for the Ottoman lands with a distinct sense of purpose. They set and adhered to the following plan: they would briefly stop in Istanbul, followed by a long journey through Greater Syria, and then return to Istanbul. There they would consolidate their findings and, should circumstances permit, continue on to Anatolia, Armenia and Mesopotamia.[1] The commission members were arriving in a region brutalised by war, disease, famine and general deprivation. In addition to this, the centuries-old reign of the Ottoman Empire over these regions was now officially coming to an end, which, as historian Keith Watenpaugh has argued, led the people of the region to face a bevy of existential questions: 'what did it – the war, the occupation – all mean, but also, who are we and where do we belong, or rather, of which whole are we now part?'[2] With this in mind, it is not surprising that the end of the war was a catalyst for a period of great political activity in the region, and the news that a commission would be arriving in order to gauge the political desires of the people enhanced the intensity of this activity.[3] By late May 1919, Western diplomats and military personnel in the Ottoman lands were echoing General Edmund Allenby's sentiment that a commission on mandates must now travel to the region, if only to temporarily appease the local population. The King–Crane Commission was stepping into, and indeed heightening, a tense political moment.

Istanbul

The commission left Paris by train on 29 May, and the journey to Istanbul was relatively quick, especially considering that such a massive conflict had only recently ended. The commission members seemed content to be on such an adventure, with George Montgomery remarking that the 'whole party' was 'very congenial' during this portion of the journey.[4] On 4 June, they arrived in Istanbul on a ship that they had boarded at Constanza (Romania) the night before. Their visit overlapped with Ramadan (May 31–June 29) so the Muslim populations of the empire were fasting during the daylight hours.

Charles Crane, having left earlier than the main body of the commission, was awaiting them in Istanbul. Crane had made time to see a few sites in his beloved eastern Europe during his solo journey. In a letter to his wife, he described one such stop, a visit to a Jewish school in Ruse, Bulgaria, as follows:

> I had a delightful experience. I saw some beautiful children going along, evidently to school – one of them looking quite like our little Talmud reader of Jerusalem. At the school [...] there were perhaps one hundred children taught in old Spanish – their common language – Bulgarian, German and Hebrew. Yes, they knew of Justice Brandeis and the word had come throughout the 'Old Jewry' that they were to have a Jewish Republic and he was to be President of it. [...] There was a most charming little miss of five, Victoria, who took good care of me and I invited her to Constantinople College when she grows up.

Such sentiments support the contention that Crane was not patently antisemitic and anti-Zionist at this point in his life. Crane also exhibited a fair amount of sadness about change and modernisation in the region, which was a theme he returned to on a number of occasions during his time on the commission. In Ruse, for example, he stated that he had been excited to see the 'old Turkish town' but sadly a fire had destroyed much of it and 'most of the grace and beauty of the old Turkish life is gone'. He further noted seeing a 'peasant in the gorgeous old Balkan costume' that he lamented was 'unhappily fast disappearing in the "ready-made clothing" world'. Upon his arrival in Istanbul, he was particularly excited about attending commencement at Constantinople College before the commission started its business.[5]

When the commission convened in Istanbul, they found a city in distress. Istanbul, which had been occupied by the Allies in November 1918, was teeming with refugees and faced severe shortages of food and coal.[6] The Turks, angered by the fact that they were given all but no say in their own future at the Paris Peace Conference, had been further incensed by the Greek occupation of Smyrna and by the public calls of many of the city's Greeks for restored Hellenic rule over Istanbul.[7] Just before the commission arrived, American Consul General Gabriel Bie Ravndal stated in dispatches to the State Department that 'feelings' were 'running high' among the Turks. He hoped that the King–Crane Commission would 'have a tranquilizing tendency' on the population of the city and would 'contribute materially to allay public excitement at least for the time being'.[8]

In Istanbul, members of the commission were hosted by Americans who lived in the city, with Admiral Mark Bristol (Chief American Naval Officer in Istanbul) and Consul Ravndal meeting the main body of the commission when they arrived. Lybyer, Montgomery and Laurence Moore, who had extensive contacts in the city, spent most of the time socialising with old friends. Lybyer especially enjoyed his time in Istanbul catching up on the gossip among the American population, including one rather scandalous story about an American woman 'who ran away from Scutari College and married a Turk'. Additionally, he rather misguidedly tried to play matchmaker between Moore (an eligible bachelor) and a woman (Miss Sarah Anderson) who turned out to be deeply depressed because of the recent death of her mother. She was not interested in Moore. In addition to being rebuffed in this capacity, Moore fell and hurt his knee during his time in Istanbul. These were but the beginning of Moore's many awkward misfortunes during the journey.[9]

The commission members also began receiving opinions about the future of the region, both formally and informally. Montgomery waxed lyrical about the postwar mood of Istanbul in a letter to his sister, stating that he believed he now had insight into 'the atmosphere of the old ecclisiastical [sic] conferences; any number of parties, political parties, every one anxious to make his point of view prevail'. Lybyer noted that they met with many people, including Sir Edwin Pears, an Englishman who had lived in Istanbul for over 40 years, and with Halide Edip, the political activist and graduate of Constantinople College. In Istanbul, the people with whom they met often had strong opinions about the political future of the Ottoman Empire (as could be expected). Pears, for example, advocated a British mandate over Anatolia, while most of the city's Americans opposed the expulsion of Turks from Istanbul and condemned the behaviour of the Greeks at Smyrna. The commissioners received a few delegations while in Istanbul but decided to wait until their return for a full slate of interviews. These initial interviews included the following: a 'long conference' with the Grand Vezier (Damad Ferid Pasha) on 6 June in which he 'only asked that areas now occupied [by the Turks] should not be separated' from whatever new state they would receive; a short meeting with a group from Trabzon who requested to have American observers in their region in order to stop rampant 'brigandage'; and the reception of two Ottoman officials who offered a 'defence of their treatmt [treatment] of [the] Armenians' by stating that the 'Russians had stirred Armenians to revolt' and that 'traitors' had to be 'punished'. The normally placid Henry Churchill King, showing that American minds were very much closed on the Armenian massacres, 'was vexed' with this last group and 'said they did their cause no good'. On 6 June, the commission met and decided to leave for Syria as soon as possible. Two days later, they departed aboard an American destroyer with the intention of going to Beirut.[10] While on board, William Yale suggested they begin their work in Jaffa instead of Beirut because he believed it would save them time and that the element of surprise could undermine any British attempt to control the commission. King and Crane agreed to this proposal, so they steamed to Palestine, arriving in Jaffa on the morning of 10 June.[11]

The Political Setting in the Region

The political situation in the whole of Greater Syria was hopeful but contentious. The British occupied nearly the entire region and the French had a divisive presence on the Lebanese coast. Amir Faysal may have been accepted by most people at the Paris Peace Conference as the spokesman for Greater Syria, but he was viewed with scepticism by many of the region's elites for a number of understandable reasons: he was not from Greater Syria, had been installed as leader by force of British arms, was largely funded by the British government, and had an inner circle of advisers whose members were composed mainly of 'young, transnational elites', many of whom had little connection to Syria.[12] The notables of the region were angered by this and remained cool to Faysal. In addition, Faysal was far more amenable to having a mandatory power with substantial control over Syria than were the majority of politically active people in the region. He even had difficulty achieving any sort of consensus among the members of 'al-Fatat' (the 'secret society' of nationalists Faysal had joined during the war), who remained deeply divided between asking for independence, a British mandate, or an American mandate.[13]

Nationalism in Greater Syria, up until this point, was largely an idealistic discourse transplanted from Europe and meaningful mainly to the few who had been privileged enough to receive a European or American-style education. After the war, those espousing nationalism believed that they had an opportunity to implement their ideals, yet there was little consensus on what sort of new nation should emerge in the post-Ottoman Arab world. As James Gelvin has pointed out, nationalism calling for broader Arab unity was prevalent at the close of the war but soon gave way to the articulation of 'alternative visions for the nation and for the future of the region' by competing nationalist organisations, many of which (like al-Fatat and the Arab Club) began demanding some form of Syrian unity. Importantly though, and again according to Gelvin, 'no single, dominant nationalist discourse could be either coaxed or coerced' by Faysal or anyone else in postwar Greater Syria.[14]

Faysal, while looking and acting the part of the region's potential leader, was in a politically unforgiving position: on one side were nationalists, many of whom would accept nothing less than independence, and on the other were the Europeans and Americans who were set on dividing the region into mandates. Faysal also struggled to assure the religious minorities in the region (along with their self-proclaimed protectors in the West) that any new, largely Muslim government would respect their rights. Faysal's fortunes rested both on his ability to navigate the complex political currents in Greater Syria and on the effectiveness of the impending international commission.[15] The fact that the commission was coming to Greater Syria in order to ascertain the political desires of the people and that it was going to include members from the United States, a country that still had a strong reputation in the region, was enough to heighten expectations to near unreachable levels. Yet the delay in sending the commission, paired with the fact that the commission was no longer 'Inter-Allied' when it arrived, caused many people in the region to question Allied intentions, thus weakening Faysal who had invested so much of his political capital in the commission's legitimacy.[16] This led American officials in Greater Syria to note that the commission had taken on major importance. As J. B. Jackson, the American Consul in Aleppo, reported on 31 May, 'the attention of every person of note throughout this consular district is at present being directed toward the coming of the International commission'.[17] The same was true for Palestine.

The Zionists had a similarly difficult task on their hands partly because numerous local groups had already been formed with the intent of stopping Jewish immigration to Palestine. One set of groups were the Muslim-Christian Associations. Formed in late 1918 in the major cities of Palestine, these associations were generally comprised of wealthy and established notables who presented a united front in opposition to Zionism, though internally they often did not agree on other aspects of the region's political future. Other regional groups, such as al-Nadi al-'Arabi (the Arab Club) and al-Muntada al-Adabi (the Literary Club), were generally composed of 'the young Arab intelligentsia' and were similarly anti-Zionist, though they too were often not in total agreement about what to request besides the cessation of Zionism.[18] Despite their internal differences, opposition to Zionism provided these groups with a central organising principle and they voiced this opposition emphatically to the King–Crane Commission.

Despite being taken aback when it was announced that the commission was actually going to happen, the Zionists were well-prepared for its visit. As the commission arrived in the Ottoman lands, the local Zionists received instructions from their European and American leaders. Felix Frankfurter, for example, cabled on 13 June that the Zionists should 'make [a] full presentation of [the] achievements [of the Zionist] colonist[s] despite Turkish rule and almost insurmountable difficulties'. Furthermore, he stated that the Zionist project should not be judged 'merely by numbers in Palestine' but was instead based on a 'historical claim' which 'rested on [the] ardent desires [of] millions [of] Jews' who were 'ready to return from dispersion at the first opportunity'.[19] Chaim Weizmann repeated these arguments in a (rather belated) 21 June cable and added that the local Zionist Commission[20] should 'Inform them [the King–Crane Commission] [of] our cooperation with Feysal and our desire to work harmoniously with [the] Arab population for [the] good of Palestine'.[21] The Zionists in Palestine, however, required few instructions along these lines. They knew that their job was to get the commission to endorse Zionism and also knew that they had to accomplish two things in order for this to be a possibility: get all of the local Jews to back Zionism in front of the commission (in essence an attempt to collapse any distinction between Zionist and Jew) and try to minimise the anti-Zionist testimony (a challenging task by the summer of 1919).

The Commission's Method of Finding the Region's 'State of Opinion'

The commission began its work in Jaffa shortly after their arrival and the method they employed from the start continued in a fairly uniform manner thereafter. As mentioned previously, the first part of the King–Crane Commission's task was to learn the 'sentiments' or 'state of opinion' among the region's population concerning the 'divisions of territory' and 'assignments of mandates' to these territories.[22] The commission believed that they were already familiar with well-tested methods through which they could discover the 'state of opinion' in the region, to the point where it was never an object of discussion or debate among the commission members. They chose to 'meet in conference individuals and delegations who should represent all the significant groups in the various communities, and so to obtain as far as possible the opinions and desires of the whole people'. Put simply, they asked prominent members of the community to come before a panel of commission members to be questioned about their desires for the future.[23] This method fit loosely into the region's 'mazbata' tradition in which notables petitioned the government on a particular issue, usually in the form of a statement with signatures and official seals of the signatories.[24] Although the commission's approach to fact-finding may have had Western roots, it was a framework that would likely have appeared familiar to the people of the region.

At the suggestion of William Yale, the US State Department aided the commission in their task of finding these 'representative' leaders by asking their regional consuls to provide King and Crane with information indicating the people with whom they should speak at each location (which was to be written on index cards).[25] The instructions the consuls received were as follows:

> List important Syrians and Arabs, Christians, Moslems and Druzes, as well as Jews, among which should be included persons who are prominent in social, religious, commercial and political circles whom the commission should see. In regard to each person you should state on the card the name, religion, national grouping, age, languages spoken, their activities in the above mentioned circles, what present or past relations with the Government, their standing, and social or other influence in the community, and remarks on their character and ability, and what if any interest they are taking in the question. Like information should be given concerning prominent Turks, Armenians, Greeks, and Levantines.[26]

These were typically completed in a manner similar to the following card, written by Otis Glazebrook, the American Consul in Jerusalem:

Ramleh [location]
[1.] Tagi, Soliman
[2.] Moslem, Native
3. Age: 37
4. Languages: Arabic, Turkish & French
5. Lives on income from large properties. Blind. Poet. Philosopher.
6. No Government position.
7. Prominent. Of notable family.
8. Of influence as skilled writer.
9. Good character and exceptional ability.
10. For Arabic independence. Anti-zionist.[27]

The commission received this information from Glazebrook for Jerusalem and greater Palestine, as well as from consuls in Beirut (for greater Mount Lebanon), Aleppo and Aintab (now Gaziantep in Turkey), but they were not given this sort of guidance in Damascus because the United States did not reinstate a consul there until late June.

The interviews with these leaders were generally conducted in a single location (usually a private home, hotel, or municipal building) in each city or town, and the delegations would either arrive according to a pre-determined schedule (in the larger cities) or wait in line to be seen (in the smaller cities and towns). During the interviews, the only people allowed into the room were the members of the commission, an interpreter if needed, and the delegation being interviewed; no British, French, or Arab officials were permitted to oversee the proceedings.[28] Before each delegation gave its testimony, a member of the commission would read a prepared statement that gave the brief background of the commission. Henry Churchill King noted that the introduction to this statement of purpose went as follows:

> The commission are [sic] anxious to have the purpose of their mission clearly and accurately understood, so that both its significance on the one hand and its limitations on the other may be truly seen.[29]

The statement then described the mission thusly:

> The American Section of that [the International] commission is in the Near East simply and solely to get as accurate and definite information as possible concerning the conditions, the relations, and the desires of all the peoples and classes concerned in order that President Wilson and the American people may act with full knowledge of the facts.[30]

Later in the trip (26 June), as they faced increasing calls for independence, they added a reading of Article 22 of the League of Nations Covenant to their introduction, which stated that no such independence would be granted.[31] The commission also emphasised that the United States could not be depended upon to take a mandate, and that the commission itself had no power to make decisions.[32] After the explanation of the commission's purpose, a leader of the delegation would often give a speech explaining the views of the people they represented, which was sometimes accompanied by the handing over of a written petition to the commission. The commission members would then ask a somewhat scripted set of questions. They would also go off script at points if they believed a particular demand made by a delegation warranted more discussion. At first, the interviews were attended only by King and Crane, but on 16 June they decided that the technical advisers could also be present and this remained the case for the rest of the trip. After this, the two commissioners did not attend every hearing, and delegations were seen by different combinations of the five main commission members.[33] In hopes of maintaining the appearance of impartiality, the commission also decided to keep their acceptance of major acts of hospitality to a minimum: they accepted only a limited number of 'receptions, parties, and dinners' given by government officials and various other groups.[34]

The places where they received delegations were usually swarmed with crowds and the commission members often noted that people had travelled long distances to receive a hearing, all of which reflects how seriously the people of the region took the commission. The social positions of the people the commission interviewed during their time in Greater Syria were fairly similar at each stop and the list of interviewees at Jaffa provides a representative sample:

Rev. B.M. Nasir, Protestant Community
Moslem Christian Committee, President, Assem Bey Said (Moslem)
Mayor of Jaffa
Soulaiman Elle Tagi [on the above card], Elle Farougin, and Committee from Ludd, Ramleh and villages
Zionist Commission (Chairman, Mr. David Yellin)
Grand Rabbi Hakim Bashi
Greek Catholic Community (Did not come)
Grand Mufti of Jaffa, Tewfik Dejani Eff
The Arch-Mandarite of the Greek Orthodox Community (Largest Christian Community in Jaffa)
Committee of Protest against Moslem-Christian Committee
Arab Society "El Montada el Adabi Society"
Pere Andre (A Spaniard) President of the Latin Convent and Head of Latin Community
Pere Mamtullah, Head of Maronite Community and Committee.[35]

Although the commission interviewed representatives of other types of groups (such as labour unions and women's organisations), the vast majority of its interviewees were the leaders of religious groups, municipal councils, important families, or nationalist societies. It should be noted that the region's community ties were much more complex and fluid than the clearly demarcated confessional, familial and political divisions perceived by the commission. It is fair to assert, as Keith Watenpaugh has, that this 'breakdown of society' likely represented 'an American comprehension of late-Ottoman social structure'.[36] The King–Crane Commission's choice of sample, then, was skewed heavily to the elite members of society. It is clear that the commission members believed that these elites were representative (however imperfectly) of the region's 'state of opinion'. They were choosing to hear from leaders of groups who they believed were either conduits of the people they represented or had the ability to sway the opinions of their subjects. The commission members believed that this was the closest thing to a plebiscite that they could get in an area without a strong democratic history. This, in their minds, was a valid and even scientific way of testing 'the opinions and desires of the whole people'.

Jaffa

The commission arrived in Jaffa on the morning of 10 June, and they were greeted by the British commanders in residence there. They set up in a hotel that, coincidentally, was run by the man who had served as an interpreter for Charles Crane during his journey to the region a few years before the war. While the others were settling in, George Montgomery and the orderly Ross Lambing went to Beirut in order to collect Sami Haddad and rent cars from American organisations in the city, returning to Jaffa the following day. William Yale, knowing the city and its leading residents well, visited the people he believed to be the most prominent members of the community and set up interviews with them for the coming days. Yale would eventually perform this same task in Jerusalem, Beirut and Damascus, but British, French and American officials helped to arrange most of the interview schedules in the other places they visited. King, Crane and Lybyer spent their first day in Jaffa getting settled and then went to the 'Tennis Club' where they informally 'met a lot of natives' and discussed many matters not directly related to their work ('coins, agriculture (orange groves), and [the] architecture of Palestine').[37]

As in Istanbul, the commission members began to hear opinions about the region from the resident Europeans and Americans soon after they arrived. Lybyer wrote extensively about the views of one British officer ('Col. Gabriel') who stated that the British had been trying to stifle pro-independence sentiment in the region by telling 'people not to talk of indpdce [independence]' to the commission but instead to 'discuss different mandates'. Gabriel even told them that a 'meeting in favour of indpdce [was] broken up by [the] military govrnmt c.May 25.'[38] Gabriel also had a 'frank' discussion about Zionism with Lybyer, stating that the Zionists had 'overreached' and had 'aroused opposition in all quarters'. Jewish immigration to the region, he continued, could not be carried out in Palestine 'except by bayonet'.[39] Gabriel's opinion of Zionism was largely the norm among British officers in Palestine: regardless of its ideological merits, it was going to face much opposition in the region and hence make the job of the occupying British military immeasurably more difficult. Also on the day of their arrival (10 June), Consul Glazebrook came to Jaffa to meet the commission for dinner. As a long-time friend to Woodrow Wilson and a person who had lived in the region throughout the war, Glazebrook's opinion appeared to hold great sway with the commission. At dinner, Glazebrook briefed the commission members on the local situation and gave them his opinions about the reapportioning of the Ottoman lands, which Lybyer recorded as follows: 'unity of Ottoman Empire under U.S. as mandatory. Sultan to be removed fr. Consple. Each people to have a chance to develop [...] not complimentary to French'. Perhaps most importantly to the commission, Glazebrook, who was greatly sympathetic to the plight of the region's Jews during the war, had become 'Anti-Zionist'.[40]

On the following two days (11 and 12 June), the commissioners saw the Jaffa delegations noted on the list above, and three main issues dominated the proceedings: Zionism, the unity of Palestine and Syria, and the final political status of the region (independence versus mandates). The testimony given at Jaffa was fairly representative of subsequent testimony in Palestine and it is instructive to examine it in some detail.

The Zionists had prepared their testimony well and the speech of Siegfried Hoofien before the commission was fairly representative of the Zionist appeals in Palestine. Hoofien had arrived in Palestine in 1912 from the Netherlands and was the General Manager of the Anglo-

Palestine Company, a bank primarily devoted to the Zionist cause. On 11 June, Hoofien laid out the basic tenets of the prevailing justifications for Zionism in a rather blunt fashion. He began by stating emphatically that 'the question of Zionism cannot be studied "on the spot"', insinuating that the type of claims the Zionists were going to make were not necessarily going to be justified by what the King–Crane Commission saw or heard during their visit to Palestine. The first claim, Hoofien argued, was historical, with Jews having the strongest entitlement to Palestine of any group in the world:

> The historic title of the Jews to Palestine is clear. Palestine is the cradle of their race. In Palestine they have developed a national culture which in various forms has emanated through the whole world and the history of the last twenty centuries. [...] They were driven by [sic] the country by force and have never given up their claim to it. There is no other nation in the world, but the Jews, which considers Palestine as its national home. The Arab nation last of all.

According to Hoofien, not only was their claim just, but heeding such a claim would be beneficial to the region in a tangible way. The prosperous and modern Zionist colonies already in existence in Palestine gave 'only an idea on a very small scale and in a very incomplete way of what the Jews might be able to do and will do'. Beyond the material benefits the Zionists would bring to the region, Hoofien contended that the establishment of a Jewish national home in Palestine would aid the entire world in a less tangible way. The Zionists, he argued, were aiming to 'enrich humanity' and add to the 'spiritual life of the planet' by creating a land where Jews ('the most wronged of all' nations) could 'develop Jewish life at its purest and best'.

The remainder of Hoofien's speech consisted of responses to several known arguments against Zionism. The first common argument that he challenged was that the land could not produce enough food for a large influx of people. He emphatically denied this, stating that experts had found that the land could hold up to 'four million people'. He also contended that this particular anti-Zionist argument was misguided, employing a historical comparison that juxtaposed Zionism with the colonisation of North America: 'if the Pilgrim Fathers had been asked how many people can live in the United States or even in Pensylvania [sic]' they would have 'found some difficulty in giving any estimate'. Another argument he attempted to debunk was that the existence of Israel would give the world Jewry 'dual allegiance', meaning that they would have sympathies not just to their home country but to the new Jewish state as well. He discounted this suggestion by stating that being American, for example, was entirely different than being Jewish and thus it was easy to be both and have allegiances to both. Furthermore, he argued that this was not a problem for 'American-Irishmen or for Roman Catholics' who lived in the United States.

Hoofien also felt he had to defend Zionism against two other accusations: that the Jews could not be trusted to look after the 'holy places' and that establishing a Jewish national home would infringe on the rights of the region's people (thus being antithetical to self-determination). Hoofien brushed off the first of these in a comparative fashion, noting that 'if the Turks could during four centuries be trusted to possess and guard the Holy Spots, some measure of confidence might be vested in the Jewish People.' The second of these he took more seriously and addressed at length. Hoofien argued it was not possible for Jews to mistreat the inhabitants of the region because the 'Jewish national future cannot be built on a foundation of injustice [...] what is not just can not be Jewish'. Furthermore, British mandatory oversight (which every Jewish delegation requested) would ensure that no such violations would be made. In turning more specifically to self-determination, Hoofien presented his argument with numbers in mind. He began by stating what could be considered a direct refutation of self-determination:

> Theoretically the Zionists would fully uphold the Jewish claim to Palestine if there were not at present one single Jew in the country. Zionism is not a local Palestinian matter but a world problem and the question of the numerical proportion of the present Jewish population to the non-Jewish population is immaterial.

Moreover, he contended that the Jews constituted a 'nation' in the world, as did the Arabs. Hoofien concluded the following: 'The Arab inhabitants of Palestine who form only 2 per cent of the Arab nation have no right to speak in the name of that Nation, not even on a question mainly concerning Palestine.' If the Arabs of Palestine 'put up national claims' in the region, the question became 'one between the 30 million' Arabs and the '50 million' Jews, giving Jews the distinct numerical edge (though most world Jewish population estimates of the era put their number at approximately 14 million). Importantly to Hoofien, the matter was 'rightly discussed over the heads of the few people who chance to be on the spot'. The Arabs of Palestine would be respected, however, and once the Jews became a majority in the region, the Arabs 'should enjoy all the rights guaranteed to national minorities in other countries'.[41]

In sum, Hoofien's testimony was a rather undiplomatic version of the Zionist party line: Jews deserved a national home (or more) in Palestine because of Jewish history, Jewish ability to modernise the land, and the rather vague spiritual uplift the granting of such a home would bring to the world. The primary difficulty came in persuading the members of the commission that the Zionists would respect the rights of the non-Jewish inhabitants of the region. Importantly, this belittling of non-Jews in Palestine in the testimony of people like Hoofien led some of the commission members to question the sincerity of the more tactful defences of Zionism they heard.

Just as Hoofien's speech was fairly representative of the arguments put forth by Zionists, the petition of an organisation representing the 'Muslims of Jaffa' was also a fairly typical example of Muslim testimony received by the commission in Palestine. First, this group asked for the independence and unity of Syria 'in the North from Mount Taurus' to 'El-Arish and Rafa' in the South. They also emphasised that Palestine, which was 'an inseparable part of Syria', should have 'full internal autonomy', which meant that it could 'appoint its own Governors' and 'pass its own local laws'. On the matter of Zionism, they demanded that 'Jewish immigration into our country be absolutely prohibited'. They did add a caveat to this demand, stating that 'the original Jews residing in our country before the war we consider as native as ourselves'. This split was an important distinction throughout the region: the Jews who had been living in the region for years were noted as being part of the regional social fabric, whereas the (relatively) newly arrived, and largely European, Zionist Jews were seen as disruptive and threatening. Lastly, the delegation stated that if they were 'compelled to choose the guidance of any power', they would leave it 'to the decision of the Syrian Congress to take place at Damaskus [sic]'.[42] This congress, which Faysal had proposed on his return from Paris (1 May), was intended to be representative of the Syrian people and present a united front to the commission. Its delegates were gathering in Damascus by this point.[43] In general, the definite calls for independence and unity were prevalent among the delegations seen by the commission in Palestine but a number of these delegations requested that any decision about 'assistance' from a Western nation should be made by the Syrian Congress. Few asked for a mandate or assistance of any kind in Palestine and, intriguingly, few asked for Faysal to be the ruler, with some delegations even rejecting Faysal outright. Henry Churchill King noted, for example, that another Muslim delegation they received in Jaffa representing Ramleh, Ludd and '59 villages' demanded 'independence, but not under Faisal'.[44] In general, the testimony of the Muslims in Palestine was light on lengthy justifications but these delegations were fairly unequivocal and uniform in stating something akin to the above demands.

Generally speaking, the political atmosphere was tense but not toxic in Jaffa, and although the testimony the commission received was fairly uniform, they did hear some differences of opinion. The uneasy nature of the atmosphere was illustrated by an incident within the Jaffa Municipal Council. The council had been invited to speak before the commission, but its president neglected to notify its three Jewish members. The Jewish members, who had only heard about the council's testimony after it happened, protested to the president and received the following explanation, according to a report by the Zionist Commission: 'the President explained that he did not notify the Jewish members for the reason that he knew that the Moslems wanted to protest against Zionism, and he felt it might be uncomfortable for the Jewish members to be present'. Despite this rather partisan incident, the Jewish community in Jaffa was eventually 'quite satisfied with the hearing which they obtained' from the commission.[45] In Jaffa, the commission also received disparate testimony from Christian delegations with the Maronite and 'Greek Catholics' requesting France as their mandatory and the 'Latin Community' requesting that Palestine and Syria should become 'a constituent part of the Brit[ish] Empire'. The Christian delegations also differed on the matter of Zionism, with, for example, the Greek Orthodox being ardently anti-Zionist and the Maronites stating that 'Zionists [are] welcome, but not as citizens'.[46]

While in Jaffa, King and Crane, suspecting that negotiations about the disposition of the Ottoman Empire may well have been progressing in Paris, decided to send Wilson a brief communiqué delivering preliminary warnings on two matters. First, they informed Wilson that certain actions, like the 'careless descent of Greeks on Smyrna', had caused people to question the powers' commitment to the 'right of the people on self-determination'. Following from this, they also informed the president that the 'Moslem and Christian' population took a 'most hostile' attitude towards 'Jewish immigration' and 'any effort to establish Jewish sovereignty over them'. They ended the telegram by giving a pessimistic assessment of the prospects of Zionism in general: 'We doubt if any British Government or American official here believes that it is possible to carry out [the] Zionist program except through [the] support of [a] large army.'[47] It is clear that the commissioners' time in Paris, Istanbul and Jaffa confirmed their initial suspicions about both the justness of Greek actions in Smyrna and the viability of Zionism.

King also tasked Lybyer with detailing his impressions of the questions before them at the end of their rather intensive time in Jaffa, and Lybyer completed a major set of observations on 13 June. He began 'negatively', stating that the majority of people in Palestine were likely 'entirely opposed' to Zionism, that most of the 'non-Jewish population' opposed the separation of Palestine and Syria, and that 'many of the Moslems' were 'averse' to having Faysal as their ruler. He then stated 'positively' that many people in the region believed that they were indeed ready for independence and self-government with no help from a mandatory. He speculated that if the people were forced to ask for a mandatory, then the United States would likely be the choice of the majority, with the British being next and the French being the choice 'chiefly' of the Maronites. He went on to note that the British had been helpful thus far but had also tried to influence the testimony of a number of groups. Along these lines, he believed that the British military was acting 'under instructions, often contrary to the personal conviction of officers, from the British Foreign Office'. The Foreign Office, Lybyer believed, was quietly striving for Syria and Palestine to be placed under a British mandate which would be 'hardly distinguishable from ownership' and for Zionism to be carried out in some form. The Zionists, Lybyer continued, believed that 'their claims had been settled in their favour by the Balfour Declaration and President Wilson's statements, and that they need only make their plans for the political and economic management of the country'. By having to defend Zionist designs, Lybyer believed that the British authorities had put themselves 'in a very difficult position' and would have problems 'in their effort to keep the country quiet'.[48] The region, according to Lybyer, was heading for trouble if it remained on this path. Significantly, this document shows that Lybyer's ideas about the region seemed to be converging with those of King and Crane, and diverging from those set by William Westermann in Paris.

On the morning of 13 June, the commission set out for Jerusalem and, on the invitation of the Zionist Commission, they stopped at a number of Jewish colonies along the way.[49] They first called at Tel Aviv, then only a small agricultural settlement. The commission was duly impressed with the state of the colony, with Lybyer writing in his diary that in only ten years the Zionists had 'built a prosperous colony from desert'. The commission visited another Zionist agricultural school and then stopped at Rishon LeZion, a 37-year-old colony at the time, where they had lunch with the leaders of several Jewish settlements.[50] They were greeted with speeches imploring the commission to recognise what the Jews had accomplished in Palestine, namely that they had developed through their 'cleverness and infinite deep love for their land' several colonies that were 'like a Paradise' in places 'which were for a period of many hundreds of years a waste desert'.[51] The Zionists were again successful in impressing the commission, with Crane calling Rishon LeZion 'a very prosperous and well-conducted Jewish colony' and George Montgomery contributing that it was a 'nice place'.[52] Lybyer praised the 'excellent wines' and 'first-rate lunch' in the setting of vineyards and groves of orange, almond, and palm trees. He described the colonies as 'clearly industrious and prosperous' but concluded his assessment with an allusion to the grander political picture of the region: 'In the course of the day, we saw the best side of Zionism', insinuating his belief that there was another side as well.[53] They arrived in Jerusalem that evening.

Jerusalem

The political atmosphere in Jerusalem was edgier than in Jaffa. Faysal's allies in Palestine, usually members of the various nationalist clubs, had undertaken propaganda-related tasks such as spreading their various platforms via posters. A member of the Zionist Commission in Jerusalem, for example, noted that the following poster was placed near the Jaffa Gate outside the premises of the 'Arab Club' on 14 June:

Palestine is a part of Syria. We claim the complete autonomy of Syria, from the Taurus to Rafa. Syria is indivisible. We protest against Zionism and we refuse immigration into our country. Moslems, Christians and Jews are associated in the autonomy [of Syria]. Life to our Prince Feisal and Life to the Allies who protect Truth.[54]

Faysal's allies also attended meetings of local elites in hopes of persuading them to back Faysal's programme, but his agents had little success in doing this. According to a Zionist agent, there was a string of meetings on 13 and 14 June at the homes of prominent Jerusalem Muslims (like Kamil al-Husayni, the Mufti of Jerusalem). In these meetings, there were contentious discussions among the region's Muslim elite about which 'demands' they should 'hand over to the commission'. Suleiman Bey Nassif, a moderate nationalist who had strong contacts with the British and advocated Faysal's preferred position, 'tried to persuade them of the necessity of asking [for] a mandatory power', with Great Britain being the first choice and the United States being the second. There was resistance to this, especially from 'the delegates of Nablus and Acca [Acre]' who 'insisted very strongly in asking [for] the complete [sic] and absolute independence without any protection'. They 'insisted on this point of view' even though they were told that 'absolute independence is impossible' under the 'League of Nations treaty'. A compromise was reached, stating that all delegations should request 'unity and independence' but if pressed on declaring preference for a mandatory power, they should state that they defer to the decision of the upcoming 'National Assembly' in Damascus (the aforementioned Syrian Congress). Significantly, the Zionist agent who reported on this meeting also noted that the only non-controversial matter discussed was the 'request against Jewish immigration'.[55]

The commission members were deeply engaged in their work throughout their time in Jerusalem. On 14 June, the commission began informal meetings while Yale and their British liaison Colonel James Watson worked on the schedule of delegations. The commission members began, as they often did, by meeting with the Americans in the city, which in this case meant Otis Glazebrook and Major Edward Bliss Reed of the American Red Cross. Glazebrook warned the commission members that the rumour had spread around the city that the commission had no real power and was all 'camouflage'. It would be necessary, he argued, for the commission to 'affirm that there is reality' in the mission. Major Reed, who had been in the region for over a year doing relief work, gave the commission members his opinions, which Lybyer recorded in his diary as follows: 'R. [Reed] came here Zionistic, now is very much opposed. Zionists are unscrupulous, all Americans and British are opposed to them, all non-Jewish people of land also.' Divisions on Zionism within the commission surfaced as well: Lybyer had an 'argument on Zionism' with Montgomery, who contended that allowing Zionism to move forward would represent 'the greatest good for the greatest number', a utilitarian argument on which he would elaborate in his final recommendations for the region. When it was time to start seeing delegations in Jerusalem on 16 June, King and Crane had decided to allow the technical advisors into the meetings. They also decided that the commission needed to split up in order to be more efficient, which occurred the following day.[56]

The testimony they received while in Jerusalem was similar to that which they received in Jaffa, though the anti-Zionist rhetoric was ratcheted up by several groups. Perhaps the most prominent example of this was the 16 June testimony of the Muslim-Christian Association of Jerusalem whose demands were as follows:

> That Syria, which begins from the Taurus Mountains in the North up to Raffa in the South be absolutely independent.
>
> That Palestine (Southern Syria), which is an indivisible part of Syria be internally independent and that it should elect all its Governors from among the Nation, that it should frame its own laws according to the desires of the native population.
>
> We reject the Zionist immigration absolutely and protest very strongly against making Palestine a Jewish National Home and reject this as well and protest against Zionists with all the necessary strength. But as regards the native Jews who settled in our country long ago, we consider them as natives who have the same rights as we have [sic].

The Muslim-Christian Association's presentation to the commission sought to emphasise the rationale for these views. Arif Pasha al-Dajani, the leader of the group, presented the speech. He began by reminding the commission that Muslims and Christians made up the vast majority of Palestine's population, implicitly trying to establish these groups' 'self-determination' credentials. Furthermore, he argued that the Jews as a people had inhabited Palestine for only a small portion of Jewish history and that the era of 'Jewish reign in Palestine was but a time of strife, revolution, and misery' during which 'innocent prophets' were 'slain' (by which he meant, of course, Jesus). This proved the 'incapability of the Jews to govern themselves' and contrasted greatly with the Arab 'golden age' of 'independence' during which they 'were the center of education, politics, invention and civilization'. Al-Dajani continued in a harsher tone, stating that it was not possible for the Jews to be given a national home without prejudicing 'the civil and religious rights of the existing non-Jewish communities in Palestine'. The Jews, he continued, showed a 'love' of 'isolation and reluctance of mingling with others save their race' and (employing the antisemitic imagery so prominent in the era) had 'parasitic habits' and were 'sucking the very blood of the country through their seclusion and the various means of monopoly'. Like the Muslims of Jaffa, al-Dajani discerned between the 'native Jews', who had been 'Arabicised' and had 'lived smoothly' with the Arabs 'previous to the coming of the Zionists into the country', and the Zionists who had slowly 'seduced' these native Jews and 'poisoned' their minds. The Jews, according to al-Dajani, had no 'right' to create a national home in Palestine.[57]

Testimony in Jerusalem, the text for much of which was somehow obtained by the Zionist Commission, also showed Amir Faysal's lack of popularity in Palestine. On a few occasions, assessments of Faysal among those who testified to the commission in Jerusalem were favourable. On 19 June, for example, the 'Arabic Youth Association of Jerusalem' (al-Fatat) gave the commission the following effusive pro-Faysal testimony:

> Q. What are your relations with the Emir Feissal and what are the relations of the Emir to this Congress [the upcoming Syrian Congress]?
> R. Our relations with the Emir Feissal consiste [sic] in the fact that he is our representative at the peace conference of the Arab Nation. He is also the brain of the Nation and her active helper, her open eye and the source of our hope.[58]

The exaltation of Faysal in this testimony stands in stark contrast to testimony given by the 'Muslim Delegation' in Jerusalem (led by Jerusalem mayor Musa al-Husayni) who professed to know little about Faysal:

Q. What are your relations with the Hedjaz?
R. De relations religieuses seulement. [Only religious relations.]
Q. And your relations with the Emir Feissal?
R. We respect him as one who represented the Arabic Nation at the peace conference, but we have not [sic] private relations with him.[59]

The Muslim-Christian Association of Jerusalem had a similar reaction to this line of questioning. After being asked by a commission member whether or not they desired a 'Moslem Empire to replace the Ottoman Empire' with the 'Sultan of the Hedjaz' leading it, the interview went as follows:

R. We have no relations with the Hedjaz and we do not know the Hedjaz.
Q. And with Emir Feisal have you any relations with him?
R. Non.[60]

In Palestine overall, only two out of the 260 petitions the King–Crane Commission received requested to have 'Emir Faisal as King' and only 23 asked that decisions like this be left to the 'Damascus Conference'.[61] Upon acquiring pieces of information like these, the Zionist Commission in Jerusalem reported to their counterparts in Paris that serious efforts to reach a compromise with Faysal were unnecessary because 'we are convinced that he has little influence here'.[62]

The Zionist Commission in Jerusalem, which included two of the most committed American Zionists in Dr Harry Friedenwald and Robert Szold, gave a rather grand presentation and its testimony echoed Hoofien's speech in outline but was more diplomatic in tone. They opened by repeating the basic wishes of the Zionist Organisation, which were that the Jews wanted 'to reconstitute Palestine as their National Home' and that they should do this with Britain as the 'Mandatory or Trustee'. In justifying this, they laid out the historic and moral claims that the Jews had to Palestine and also recounted the approvals already given to the Zionist project by the Allied governments. The Zionist

Commission further reiterated the argument that there was 'ample room in the land for a large increase in the population' and that the ability of the land to provide for new immigrants was only going to increase with 'future scientific advances'. Lastly, the Zionists turned to the issue of 'prejudicing the interests of the local inhabitants', and on this they argued that Zionism, and its accompanying benefits (such as modern farming, hospitals and education) could only 'materially benefit' the people of the region, thus not infringing on their rights. In conclusion, they stated that once Zionism was allowed, there would be 'peace, harmony and progress in the land. And a great necessary step will have been taken in the securing of a better world.'[63]

The commission saw other delegations of Jews in Jerusalem as well, including a group of 'Native Jews' and a group of Sephardic Jews. These groups convinced the King–Crane Commission that the Jews of Jerusalem were united in their support for Zionism, which was something of a surprise because, as William Yale had informed the commission, there existed opposition to Zionism among the Jerusalem Jews only a few years before. Yale even sought out the Jews who he believed to be 'anti-Zionists' in Jerusalem, only to find that they had changed their minds and were now in favour of the project. The Zionists, working assiduously to make sure that the commission was presented with a united Jewish front, were angered by Yale's insistence on searching for the anti-Zionist Jews that he was so sure existed. The Zionists were also incensed that Yale 'would not consent' to 'have the representatives of the local Jewry selected by the [Zionist] commission'. One particular choice Yale made that angered the Zionists was to have Haham Bashi (Chief Rabbi of Jerusalem) Nissim Danon speak before the commission, with Yale having chosen him apparently because he thought the Danon might give the commission a dissenting Jewish view on Zionism. In protest, the Zionists claimed that he had been a Turkish appointment and represented no one.[64] Despite these protests, Danon spoke to the King–Crane Commission and seemed to surprise both Yale and the Zionists by endorsing the Zionist project.[65] Annoyed by Yale's behaviour, Harry Friedenwald protested to his superiors in Paris, claiming that Yale had 'acted with definite plans to injure us before the commission'. Despite this, Friedenwald proudly reported that among the 'Jewish deputations heard', there was 'practical unanimity in their demands, and not a single discordant note from any of the parties'. Friedenwald further stated that this was the result of the 'excellent labors' of certain members of the Zionist Commission.[66] The Zionists, then, were successful in homogenising opinion among Jews in Jerusalem. Along these lines, Albert Lybyer asked the Spaffords of the American Colony, who were long-time American residents of Jerusalem, about the disappearance of anti-Zionism among the Jews. The Spaffords replied to him that the 'Jerusalem Jews [were] now all for Zionism – much money spent'.[67]

Although the commission's work dominated their journey, its participants did find time to enjoy their surroundings by visiting Christian sites and wandering the streets of the cities in which they stopped. The commission members seemed generally impressed with what they observed, though their comments often reflected their pre-existing conceptions of the Middle East. Albert Lybyer stated, for example, that Jaffa 'stands up well' and was 'more oriental than Cons[tantino]ple in some ways. It has many flatroofed houses, narrow streets, sore-eyed children, lazy men sitting at coffee-houses, donkeys, little shops.'[68] Jerusalem inspired awe in the members of the commission, especially because it was the first trip there for most of the participants. Despite arriving late on 13 June, the members of the commission 'wandered for two hours through the heart of the city by moonlight'. They stayed in the city centre and spent a long time on their rooftop gazing at the sites, with Crane stating, 'it is of course the most inspiring picture in the world'.[69] Lybyer made it a point to see nearly all of the major sites in Jerusalem, being especially impressed with the Dome of the Rock, 'with its tiles, mosaics, and wonderful windows', and less impressed with Church of the Holy Sepulchre, which had 'beautiful elements' but 'was obviously in part based on false knowledge for it gathers an impossible number of sacred events within a small space'.[70] Montgomery was happy to be spending time in Jerusalem, which was something he had 'never expected to do'. He also was pleasantly surprised by the city, apparently having internalised the low expectations of Jerusalem cultivated by the steady stream of denigration in American accounts of the city, stating that 'the place is more interesting than I thought it would be'.[71]

On 17 and 18 June, the commission decided to travel to nearby cities in order to hear delegations. They first stopped in Bethlehem, visiting the Church of the Nativity and then setting up in the 'Town Hall' where 'about 60 notables presented addresses' to the commission. They then went to Hebron, where they had lunch with the military governor and saw more delegations.[72] In Hebron, a number of agents from the Arab

Figure 6.1 Members of the King–Crane Commission (in their car) and delegations in front of the Church of the Nativity in Bethlehem on 17 June 1919. (Source: Oberlin College Archives, Oberlin, Ohio).

nationalist societies in Jerusalem had shown up a few days before the arrival of the commission. The British military governor of Hebron, being under orders not to allow propaganda, 'did not permit the activity of the agents from Jerusalem to be too strong – he even retained several of this [sic] agitators for about three hours'.[73] The Jewish community in Hebron gave testimony that was similar to their counterparts in Jerusalem, stating the following:

> Today Southern Palestine is laid waste and unproductive through lack of population. There are no Jewish Colonies in the neighbourhood of Hebron and therefore the South is in a desolate state. We therefore desire to draw the attention of the Honourable commission to the fact of Jewish Immigration into Palestine. Southern Palestine, especially, needs a working and productive element and the Jews, by devotion and love to their land, are the very fit element to revive this country [sic].[74]

The message that modernity would be the product of Jewish immigration was perhaps the most consistent theme among pro-Zionist testimony in the region.

King, Crane, Yale and Haddad then carried on to Beersheeba while Lybyer, Brodie and Montgomery returned to Jerusalem to prepare for further delegations. Before they left Hebron, they saw some of the city's sights, including a 'real Jewish ghetto' and the 'Cave of the Patriarchs', where a bevy of figures sacred to Judaism, Christianity and Islam were said to be buried. They also climbed the minaret of a 'sacred mosque' where Lybyer viewed the landscape in terms of the Old Testament, 'seeing the site of David's city, and in the far distance, the place where David met Abigail'. On the way back to Jerusalem, they had car trouble (a frequent occurrence) which forced them to wait for hours to find other transport. They finally reached the city at 1:00 am.[75] On 18 June, the portion of the commission in Beersheba received delegations from the town and neighbouring area (including Gaza). The Bedouin populations of Beersheba gave a petition with the 'three demands' that were now becoming common (for independence and the unity of Palestine and Syria, and against Zionism) but they added that they delegated authority in these matters to 'our Emir the Emir Feissal'. The two Gazan delegations, one seemingly composed of community leaders and the other composed almost entirely of 'young people', uttered similar demands but were divided over whether or not to ask for British protection or complete independence. A Zionist agent reported that 'a quarrel was even engaged between the two delegations'.[76] This part of the commission then returned to Jerusalem that evening, stopping at a few sites along the way.

On the following day, the commission saw further Jerusalem delegations representing various societies and confessional communities, or the divisions therein ('Protestants', 'Maronites and Greek Catholics', 'Sephardic Jews of Jerusalem', delegations from 'Christian villages') and then heard from 17 different 'religious chiefs' of Jerusalem on 20 June. At that point, they had expected to receive Georges-Picot and General Allenby, but both of these officials changed their plans so the commission decided to leave Jerusalem earlier than they had originally intended. They departed for Damascus on 21 June with the intention of stopping at several towns along the way.[77]

Between 21 and 24 June, the commission saw delegations of the same general character in Ramallah, Nablus, Jenin, Acre and Nazareth, and there were several notable events at these places. In Ramallah, Lybyer reported that the British governor insisted on being present in one of the meetings, which was, of course, strictly against the commission's rules and made 'Yale cross'. They managed to keep this governor out of the rest of the meetings.[78] In Acre, the commission confronted a Jewish group about their claim that all of the people in Acre were for Jewish immigration, stating frankly that 'you have opponents here'. The Jewish delegation claimed that these 'opponents' had no legitimate reason to oppose them because they brought prosperity to the regions in which they settled. Following from this, they argued that those who opposed Jewish immigration actually 'were opponents of their own people'.[79] In Nazareth, the commission faced large crowds and the tension was high. The following is a description of Nazareth during the commission's visit, as reported by a Zionist delegate, and it illustrates the major political moment spawned by the commission:

> We went to Nazareth at night. The road was full of riders for the American commission; some faces looked friendly when we met, most of them showed open hatred or at least some embarrassment in our presence. We found Nazareth full of delegates. [...] The Nazareth Christian population, or at least the poor, greeted us Jews very heartily in the streets and shops; reproaches were addressed us *for not settling there*: the city is in despair, 'Should the Jews not come to revive its business, they will have to emigrate to Jerusalem, where a living can be made'. The Americans were very busy; they tried to be pleasant to every group, but it went in and out like with a cinema play. First came the Nazareth people: Arabs first and other Christians. The Orthodox were ordered by their Archbishop to claim for Jewish free immigration, and so they did. The Arab nationalists always presented signed protocols which were accepted almost without a word. They claimed: 1) No Jewish Homeland and no Jewish immigration. 2) No division of Palestine from Syria. 3) An Arab autonomy for the United Syria. 4) Should a trustee be unavoidable, an Arab general Congress in Damascus would decide upon it. When the Jews were let in, the commission begged us to consider their limited time and talk only English to avoid translations.[80]

In Tiberias, Zionist operatives ran into dissent among the Jewish population, having found a 'French Jewish subject' who 'claimed to be representative of some hundred French subjects' and was 'considering' asking the King–Crane Commission for a French mandate. They were able to change his mind 'after an explanation of the situation' and, on 23 June, this group gave the standard testimony suggested by the Zionist Commission.[81]

Towards the end of June, the Zionist Commission understood that the testimony was not going in their favour. In hopes of changing their fortunes, an unnamed Zionist wrote an internal memo that stated the author's concern about the anti-Zionist tenor of the testimony before the commission and laid out a plan to go forward. He stated that the emerging alliance between Muslims and Christians in the region was 'very artificial' and that the Zionists should try to make future 'quarrels [between them] as great as possible'. The document also suggested that the Zionists should exacerbate the split between the region's wealthy elites and the poor rural population, stating that they should 'continue to alienate the Fellahins from the Effendis by all available means – to put one against another'. In order to do these things, they needed to 'use all means of corruption and persuasion' they could muster. They also sensed that the anger and tension in the region had reached such a level that they needed to seek help from the British and be ready to defend themselves. If 'steps are not taken', the author of the report concluded ominously, 'I am afraid something might and will happen'.[82]

To these ends, the Zionist Commission sought to foment conflict among the Muslims and Christians, and to get as many Arab groups to speak in favour of Zionism as they could, though they achieved little success in both of these endeavours. One Zionist agent (likely agronomist Chaim Kalvarisky who had lived in Palestine since 1895) personally tried 'to make [a] real split and create a separation between the town people and the peasants (Fellahins)' around Jerusalem by showing the fellahin that 'their interests were opposed to those of the town people'. He succeeded, through 'arguments and persuasion with a little material means', in getting several groups to either not mention Zionism in their testimony to the commission or at least state that the chosen mandatory power could make the final decision about Jewish immigration. This agent also was able to cause confusion at Jaffa and Jerusalem because he convinced various fellahin to protest to the commission that notables claiming to speak for their village actually did not.[83] Another agent, who signed his documents as 'Reliable Informant', reported in an undated dispatch from Ramallah that an ally of Faysal's had arrived in the city in order to spread his recommended demands, organise elections for the Syrian Congress and 'obtain volunteers for the Sherifian army'. The agent suggested that 'an agitation' against these projects 'can be carried on by my friends among the villagers'.[84] The Zionists had some success in obtaining pro-Zionist petitions from several non-Jewish leaders. One such petition, from the mukhtar of a small village near Haifa, stated that 'we declare that there is no reason to forbid to the Jews the immigration into Palestine, especially if we take into consideration the benefits the art of agriculture and our estates will draw from their presence'.[85] Another 'Sheikh' from the village of Katrah wrote to the commission that they had 'learned from the colonists of the Jewish Katrah many things which improved our life, economically, personally and socially', though the petition did not specifically mention support for Jewish immigration.[86] Despite the efforts of the Zionists, the King–Crane Commission was flooded with anti-Zionist appeals (222 out of 260 petitions) in Palestine.[87] It seems that attitudes against Zionism in the region were too strong by 1919 for the Zionists to have much success in their endeavours, though their efforts along these lines were somewhat more successful in the 1920s.[88]

The commission members also continued their brief interludes of sightseeing on their journey to Damascus. George Montgomery informed his family that he had floated in the Dead Sea but refrained from bathing in the Jordan River because it was 'too absolutely dirty'. The theme of squalor echoed through the commission members' writings with Montgomery observing that the town of Jericho was 'a miserable village with a few mud hovels'[89] and King making the Biblical quip that 'wretched Magdala' was so awful that 'it was no wonder that Mary Magdalene left home'.[90] Montgomery also recounted a story about a minor incident at Acre to his son Giles:

> a little boy not more than 3 years old came up and wanted to shake hands with Dr. King. It was very pretty to see him reach up his hand but the brutal Arab officer who was showing us around whacked him over the mouth and sent him whimpering away.

He concluded his recounting of the episode with a moral: 'It is a rough world, and we must all get used to knocks.'[91] The commission members' respect for the people of the region was palpable, if patronising at times.

In Crane's words, 'All along we have been well welcomed by quaint little groups of humanity which we want so much not to disappoint in our work.'[92]

***

As the commission's time in Palestine drew to a close, the general tone of the testimony they were receiving was becoming clear to them. At first, the opinions of the Muslim and Christian groups that appeared before the commission were similar but not uniform. After two weeks in Palestine, though, Lybyer commented that 'the Arab program is taking shape' and that most delegations were showing 'careful orgztion [organisation]', noting that opinions had become more unified and adhered to the following three points:

- 'Unity of Palestine and Syria'.
- 'Opposed to Zionism and Jewish Immigration'.
- 'Complete independence', or at least the 'same protector for Syria and Palestine' (if one was necessary).[93]

If a 'same protector' was specified at all, Britain had received the most endorsements in Palestine. Crane also noted this emerging uniformity:

> So far the response of practically every one of the delegations has been the same: political union of Palestine and Syria based on history, language, traditions and economic necessity and great apprehension of any extensive Jewish immigration, always coupled with the statement that their relations with the old Jews who had lived here for years and for spiritual reasons were always satisfactory and friendly.[94]

Commission members generally attributed this growing uniformity to the influence of Faysal, though it seems that Faysal held far less sway than the commission and many subsequent historians have believed. This was especially true in Palestine, where many of the elites had little or no relationship with Faysal. Although Faysal and the politically active elites of the region appeared to agree that their overall case in front of the commission would be strengthened if they presented a unified view, reaching such a unified view was a contentious process in which

Amir Faysal and his associates were simply one of many parties, albeit one with British funding and support. The commission was aware of Faysal's pro-British position, later stating in the 'Confidential Appendix to the Report upon Syria' that 'evidence was presented that the Emir had tried immediately before the arrival of the commission in Damascus to secure the support of certain councils for a request for a British mandate, and that he had failed' and that Faysal likely preferred 'in his inmost heart the mandate of Great Britain'.[95] In addition, Faysal and other nationalists had sent out word that delegations in Palestine should request that decisions on the matter of which country should take a mandate for the region or provide 'technical assistance' to it would be left to the upcoming Syrian Congress. Only 8.9 per cent of the delegations in Palestine heeded this plea, which is further evidence of Faysal's political weakness. This backs James Gelvin's contention that 'local conditions were more important than directives from Damascus' even among Faysal's supposed allies.[96] It is also in line with historian Eugene Rogan's observation that Faysal's government had to work 'assiduously' to gain the support of notables in what was to become Transjordan, yet the support that Faysal was able to attain was tenuous and fleeting.[97] Although the commission members witnessed instances of his weakness, the increase in pro-Faysal testimony during later interviews appears to have made them overlook these instances. Most of Palestine's elites, however, appear to have remained sceptical about Faysal and were never quite convinced he was the right man to lead them.

Although the commission members did not comment much on Faysal's lack of popularity in Palestine, the groundswell of testimony against Zionism certainly caught their attention. The commission members did display sympathy towards the principles embodied in Zionism during their time in Palestine. In the interview with the 'Native Jews' of Jerusalem, for example, the Zionists noted that King addressed the delegation in the following manner:

> Mr. King assured the delegation that the commission is convinced of the rightfulness of the Jewish claims 'and that the delegation has not to convert the commission on that point' But [sic] he would like to know the opinion of the delegation concerning the possibilities of carrying out the Zionist schemes in Palestine in a pacific manner towards the Arabs who are against it [...][98]

The Zionists typically responded to this by stating that, once implemented, the Arabs would see that Zionism would benefit everyone in Palestine. This contention convinced some of the members of the commission (like George Montgomery) but the nearly unanimous opposition to Zionism among the Arab populations in Palestine caused King, Crane and Lybyer to doubt the feasibility of the project. William Yale mentioned little about his personal take on Zionism at this point, but never appears to have waivered from the pro-Zionist position he had developed while working with Westermann. It is also important to note that the commission had, according to the Zionists, listened to the Zionist case in an honest and fair manner. The only complaint that the Zionists made was, ironically, against Yale, a supporter of Zionism.

As they left Palestine, the commission members believed that they had started their mission successfully and that they were receiving a true picture of the sentiments of the region's population. The commission members noted a few British and Arab attempts to shape the opinions of the delegations they received but believed that the impact of these efforts were minor. Although the commission did not seem to realise that the Zionists were sending their agents to create uniformity among the Jewish populations, the lack of anti-Zionism among any of the 'native' Jews appeared to cause some suspicion among the commission members. Despite the efforts of the Zionists, the three most prominent demands in Palestine were independence (85 per cent of the petitions), unity of Palestine and Syria (67 per cent), and 'against the Zionist program' (85 per cent).[99] Although the commission was instructed not to consider complete independence as an option for the region, the overwhelming nature of the demands for unity and against Zionism would certainly have made these demands impossible for the commission members to ignore.

CHAPTER 7

SYRIA AND LEBANON

For the commission, Damascus offered a contrast to the contentious but somewhat disorganised political atmosphere of Palestine: it was a grand city in which a (somewhat) local leader seemed to have control, and it was also the scene of the Syrian Congress, a more comprehendible and organised political event than they had yet witnessed. The testimony of the Muslims and Christians in what is now Syria was similar to that given in Palestine but became more uniform and more emphatic as it went along. Lebanon was a different matter, with calls for a French mandatory gaining substantial support for the first time. In general, testimony in these parts of Greater Syria made the commission members believe that there were fairly strong regional and confessional divisions of opinion. This, in turn, helped to sharpen the emerging divides within the commission itself.

Damascus

The main portion of the commission arrived in Damascus on 25 June (near the end of Ramadan) and remained there until 4 July. Charles Crane went a day early because he wanted to ensure that he arrived in time to see the 'Night of Power' ceremony, which was an evening of extensive prayer commemorating the revelation of the first verses of the Qu'ran to Muhammad. As could be expected, political operatives were aware of Crane's location at all times. Crane, who had hoped to slip into Damascus unnoticed, noted to his wife that he failed in this regard:

Although every effort had been made for me to enter quietly, and practically incognito, there was a most ardent group of young Arabs at the train who made most impassioned speeches for independence. They want[ed] also to take [me] at once to their club but I was rescued by a magnificent British officer [...] The ardent Arabs, however, were not to be disposed of so easily and came to the hotel to keep up their demonstrations and sang fine Arab songs under my window.[1]

Yale, having also arrived early to set the commission's schedule, visited Faysal and told him that he must spread the word that the commission 'did not want demonstrations and receptions' while they were in the city. Faysal told Yale that the people were quite excited about the commission's visit and that he could do little to stifle peoples' desire to host and influence the commission. Faysal also insisted that the commission should attend one 'gala dinner' in their honour, which Yale accepted. Yale then called at many of the 'Arab clubs' and met with leaders of various groups, alerting them to the times they would be seen by the commission and maintaining that no attempts to influence the commission outside of the standard petitions would be tolerated.[2]

The Zionists were nervously watching the situation in Damascus unfold. Abraham Elmaleh, a Sephardi journalist and educator from Jerusalem who likely served as one of the unnamed Zionist agents in Palestine, had followed the commission to Damascus and reported that the atmosphere was emphatically anti-Zionist. He stated that the newspapers of the region were grooming the opinions of the region's people in the following manner:

A few days before the coming of the American commission these newspapers began to prepare the minds of their readers for it by violently agitating against the Leaders of Zionism and the Zionist movement. The opposition to the immigration of Jews into Palestine was chiefly apparent. [...] All papers without distinction of party or sect published minute details of the Palestine Arabs' commendable attitude against Jews, of their violent opposition to Jewish immigration into this country and against a National Home for the people of Israel in its land; they lauded the 'heroes' who stood up against the joint enemy and published long communications from their special correspondents on the fraternal feelings between the Christians and Moslems in reference to the future of Palestine and their opposition to the Zionists.[3]

The newspapers published what they claimed were transcripts of the testimony of Palestinian Muslims and Christians; perhaps predictably, the accuracy of these newspaper accounts appears to have been suspect. For example, an account of the Jerusalem Muslim-Christian Association's testimony, although similar in sentiment, bore little resemblance to another transcript of this testimony and, importantly, left out their ambivalence about Faysal.[4] The newspapers also displayed the general demands of the region's people (independence, unity) and chastised the few Arabs who had supported Zionism in nationalistic terms, claiming 'The curse of God and the Arab people fell upon the heads of these men, – betrayers of their people and their birthplace.'[5]

Elmaleh generally characterised Damascus at this point as being in a state of political 'chaos' and assessed the political divisions within the city as follows:

1) [The] party desiring complete autonomy without protection or trusteeship, at the head of which is 'The Arabic Club'; 2) Party desiring internal autonomy under protection of England, at the head of which is the Emir Feisal [...]; 3) Party desiring autonomy under the protection America [...] 4) Party desiring protection of France. This is the smallest party of the four...

Elmaleh further noted that there was great 'hatred between the various parties'. He reiterated the weakness of Amir Faysal's position in the region and the antipathy to his British sympathies, stating that 'the Arab Club in Damascus vilified the Emir Feisal personally using such abusing language as "Traitor to his birthplace", bribed, sold to the British etc.' The 'Arab Club' appeared to be the most well-organised and active group according to Elmaleh, with its members posting 'large bills in Arabic and English' stating things like 'We demand absolute independence'. They also gave speeches 'at all corners directed naturally against the Zionists and Jewish immigration'. 'Pamphlets', Elmaleh continued, 'were published to an unlimited degree' stating similar demands, though not all mentioned Zionism. One such pamphlet, entitled 'Autonomy or Death', implored 'Arabs, Moslems, Christians and Jews' to request unity and independence, with no mention of Zionism, perhaps in an attempt to get the local Jews to speak out against, or at least not mention, Jewish immigration to Palestine. Ominously, however, Elmaleh noted that 'some speakers were not afraid to use the following words' at a 'largely attended' meeting of the Club: 'We shall assuredly deal with the Jews as the Crusaders did, as Spain did, as Russia treated them and as Poland is treating them now, that is, slaughter them.'[6] As will be further discussed below, the Jews of Damascus were understandably nervous about their position in the city.

The commission also took notice of the tense political atmosphere and the existence of varied propaganda in Damascus. As they arrived in the city, Lybyer noted in a letter to his wife that 'there is great excitement in Damascus over us, – in fact in all of Syria'.[7] Similarly, Yale would later recall that the 'Damascenes were seething with emotions which might easily blow off the safety valve.' The fact that the 'stimulus of politics' and the 'enthusiasm over self-determination' brought on by their visit coincided with the end of Ramadan only added to the volatile atmosphere, in Yale's opinion.[8] The commission also collected a number of the leaflets circulated during their time in the city. One such leaflet, distributed 'in the Bazaars of Damascus' on 25 June, laid out the 'demands of the people of the Coast now found in Damascus'. The demands in the document were as follows: complete independence of a unified Syria, protest against Article 22 of the League of Nations Covenant, rejection of all French and Zionist claims, and acceptance of help from the United States (Britain and Faysal were not mentioned).[9] Lybyer attributed, or perhaps over-attributed, the spread of this propaganda to 'agents of Emir Faisal', stating that 'differences of opinion have been skilfully accommodated, certain formulas have been distributed in manuscript and print and taught orally'.[10] The commission was well aware of the propaganda in their midst.

One of the events that left the greatest impression on the commission in Damascus (and which Crane had been so eager to see) was the 'Night of Power' ceremony that occurred on the day the main body of the commission arrived. The commission members were invited to the ceremony at the storied Ummayad Mosque, but William Yale counselled them to 'politely refuse' because he believed that the 'Christians of Damascus would receive a very unfavorable impression if we accepted such an invitation'. The rest of the commission 'overruled' Yale on this matter and Yale even decided to join them because he 'did not want to miss so unusual a show'.[11] Lybyer described the event as follows:

> The service was held in the great courtyard. Probably three or four thousand people were there. In the center was a raised platform on which the Emir Faisal and four officers were going through the prayers. We were taken up to that platform and actually given seats on cushions at the sides. I was about four feet from the Emir. The Moslems whom we saw were mostly very earnest. After prayers everybody closed up kneeling, and priests recited from the high stand, while at intervals all chanted in chorus a beautiful refrain beginning Ihsan Allah.[12]

The commission members who attended were awed by the 'greatness of the occasion', with Yale referring to it as a 'thrilling experience'.[13] It is likely that such an event helped to solidify the commission members' sense of Faysal's political prominence among the people of Syria as well.

The commission started receiving delegations the following afternoon (26 June) and began by briefly seeing Faysal and his advisors in an unofficial interview. Faysal told the commissioners that the 'people [were] asking for indepdce – Asked 100% and expected 90%'. After Faysal left, they had what Lybyer characterised as a 'very interesting' interview with the 'Ulemma' of Damascus (the most prominent Muslim leaders in the city).[14] The Ulemma, Lybyer recorded, placed 'vigorous emphasis on three points'. The leaders repeated the expected anti-Zionist testimony of their predecessors in Palestine and then, in a slight departure from the testimony the commission had come to expect, they requested that the United States be their mandatory power and vehemently rejected any French involvement in the region.[15] On 27 and 28 June, the commission saw many more delegations, which followed a pattern similar to the past: a 'Council' of city notables; the leaders of the Greek Orthodox, Greek Catholic, Druze and Jewish communities; the municipal council; and a number of political clubs including the Arab Club.[16] The testimony again went along familiar lines, with the exception of the Greek Orthodox patriarch, who claimed that he was 'not interested' in the Zionist question and 'could not express an opinion on the matter'.[17] Additionally, several of the delegations began asking for an American mandate for the entirety of Greater Syria and emphatically praised the United States. Although such praise had occasionally occurred in Palestine, the surge in its frequency and the request for the American mandate was 'somewhat startling' to Lybyer.[18] Testimony from many of the delegations was being printed in newspapers quickly, sometimes even the day after it was given. Lybyer labelled a 27 June newspaper transcript of the commission's interview with the city's Muslim leaders (on 26 June) as the 'Alleged Conversation at Interview of Mufti, etc. with commission', indicating that it may not have been entirely accurate. The general sentiment, though, did match a summary of the same testimony written by Lybyer.[19]

On occasion, the commission would hear testimony from a native of the region who was also well-versed in the language of modernity. The commission members valued the opinion of these people because they bridged the divide between the 'backwards' Ottoman lands and the 'modern world'. One such person was the Chief of Police in Damascus, Gabriel Haddad Pasha. Haddad had been born in Tripoli (Lebanon) and was educated at the Syrian Protestant College, with this education largely providing said 'bridge' to the modern world in the commission members' minds. Haddad was an experienced police officer, having initially served for many years in the Ottoman gendarmerie, though he was forced to flee Syria for Egypt after advocating a bit too vigorously for Ottoman governmental reform. In Egypt, he had worked for the British government and enlisted in the British army at the beginning of World War I. After the occupation of Syria, the British charged Haddad with the task of building up a 'reliable' police force in and around Damascus. Haddad claimed that once he took over the force, he gave his 'principal attention to personnel' and dismissed 'all persons known to be bad' then 'tried out the rest'. He then had to 'organize the finances and [the] health regime of his forces', claiming that all of this had been 'rotten' before he arrived. The manner in which Haddad discussed reforming the police force would certainly have been in line with the commission's vision of the future for the region, with his focus on merit-based promotion, ending corruption, financial reform, and general attention to health. Furthermore, Haddad claimed that the 'people' of Greater Syria, 'both Moslem and Christian' had 'excellent stuff', by which he meant they had the 'capability, reliability, morality, etc.' to be moulded into an excellent gendarmerie, further arguing that the 'best officers' were 'quite equal to

Europeans of the same age'. The current state of the region's government was, however, 'still very bad' and 'corrupt'. Because of this, a mandate was needed 'until the new generation can be trained up in better ways', but he noted that the mandatory power 'should be one that would not colonize the country'.[20] Greater Syria, for Haddad, was a land of unfulfilled potential that had been held back by the Ottomans, which is a perspective that was also held by most of the commission members.

The Zionists, for their part, again tried to ensure that the testimony of the local Jews was in line with their goals. The Damascene Jews, fearing for their own safety in a city that was rife with anti-Zionist sentiment, were nervous about their testimony before the commission. Elmaleh, despite having little respect for this group of Jews (stating that they 'by nature are not great men'), understood that they were 'between a hammer and an anvil' in their current situation. He noted that one of the leaders of the Jewish community suggested that they needed to keep their safety in mind and tell the commission that 'the question of Palestine does not affect them'. This alarmed Elmaleh and he engaged in an ultimately successful struggle to convince them that giving pro-Zionist responses was the only way to 'answer the commission as true Jews'. His job was made easier when a member of the commission (likely William Yale) arrived and guaranteed the Damascus Jews that their answers to the commission would be 'held in complete secrecy'. Just as the various contingents of Arab nationalists were attempting to dictate the testimony of as many people as possible, Elmaleh 'drew up all questions which the American commission might ask the Jews and the answers which the community should make'. This element of Elmaleh's work was particularly noteworthy because he had written derisively about Arab attempts to 'prepare the opinions' of their people, and then went on to perform this same task among the Jews as if it was somehow different when he did it. The Damascus Jewish delegation answered the questions in the same manner as the other Jewish delegations had, and the triumphant Elmaleh continued to Beirut in order to galvanise Jewish opinion before the commission arrived there.[21]

On 28 June (the last night of Ramadan), the commission had perhaps their most memorable (and touristic) night of their journey. Faysal invited the commission to his residence for the grand, Bedouin-style 'gala dinner' that the commission had agreed to attend. Lybyer described the beginning of the dinner in the following manner:

We were taken into a reception room and dressed in Bedouin costume, which was afterward given us. I had a salmon-pink kimono sort of thing – silk, and a large white silk square over my head bound with blue and gold fillet. Those of us who wore no mustaches or beards had a somewhat feminine look.[22]

Similarly, Montgomery referred to their attire as brightly coloured 'Bedouin kimonos'.[23] Before dinner, there was a long programme of often didactic entertainment, beginning with a performance from what Lybyer described as 'naturally eloquent' boys and girls. The show began with song and 'simple Bedouin' dance by the 'Daughters of the Arab Martyrs' who were 'girls of 7–14 years of age' (the martyrs being the men who were hanged in Greater Syria by Turkish governor Jamal Pasha). Following this, there were further nationalist songs of 'war and independence' sung by 'boy scouts brought from Jerusalem'. These songs had a particularly nationalist bent with undertones of anti-Zionism, with one stanza being 'The land is ours; we will live for it; we will die for it'. 'Contests with swords and sticks followed' the performance of the boys and girls, and then came 'a Bedouin dance by real and desert men. Musicians kept wild music going.' Dinner was a stereotypically Bedouin affair during which Lybyer appeared to feel happily out of his element:

We sat by fours on the terrace on costly rugs. Each group had a tray [...] heaped with a mound of food. The basics was [sic] pilaff with plenty of mutton scattered through in large and small pieces, a covering of almond and pistachio nuts, and a final covering of papery bread: each tray had food enough for twelve or fifteen people. Bowls of youghourt with chopped cucumber provided a salad. The best way to eat it was to put a few spoonfuls of the youghourt at some place near the edge and mix up a little pool. The Druse Sheikhs ate it with their fingers making skilful use of the bread. Later [we] were brought small individual bowls of custard with almond and pistachio nuts ground on top.

After dinner, there was a Karagöz show (Lybyer: 'Curious little puppets fought and bled and died') and an interestingly gendered nationalist play:

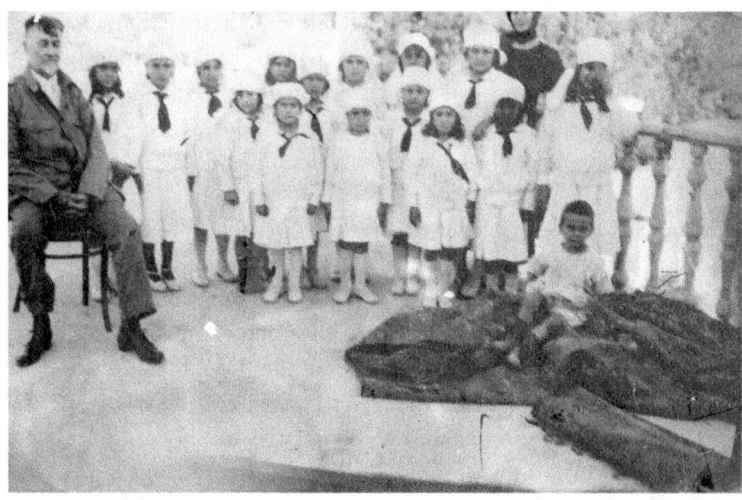

Figure 7.1 Charles Crane with the 'Daughters of the Arab Martyrs'. (Source: World War I Photograph Album, 1918–19, American University of Beirut/Library Archives).

Then some of the 'Martyr's daughters' gave a little play – 'Syria Enchained.' A girl lay chained to a rock, and recited with great fervor and fire the woes of Syria including the execution of her father. Then one came with a long shining sword (borrowed from the Emir's aid Yussef Bey) and cut the bonds – she represented Faisal. Then others came to the stage and they sang a song of joy.

According to Yale, a 'current of political intrigue' undergirded the party that 'added much to the excitement of the evening'. Throughout the night, the commission members were having conversations with Faysali partisans, with Lybyer being told by Amir Faysal's physician 'why his people do not like' the French. Lybyer also noted that the British and French officers present were watching each other with 'suspicious eyes'. After being served 'large dishes of ice cream', the commission returned to the hotel still in costume. Although the commission members would have been cognisant that much of the party was well-organised propaganda, they would certainly have gotten Faysal's message and been impressed by the manner in which it was presented.[24]

After resting on 29 June, the commission saw an eclectic mix of petitioners the following day. This list included General Allenby (who recommended that the United States should take the mandate for a united Syria), a number of people brought in solely to 'give views on the present administration [of Amir Faysal]' at the request of the British and the French, along with a number of 'picturesque Sheikhs from Kerak' who had travelled '30 hours through great dangers' to see the commission. Of the many delegations they received in Damascus, perhaps the one that elicited the most surprise among the commission members was a group of 12 Muslim women who (in the same nationalist vein as the dinner entertainment) were said to have been 'relatives of the martyrs'. These women astonished the commission members by lifting their veils while giving the interview, revealing, in Lybyer's words, that 'two or three [were] very good looking'. Lybyer also noted that the women were 'eloquent' and pleaded for 'absolute independence' with 'no help whatsoever' because they believed such help would 'make their men lazy'.[25] According to historian Elizabeth Thompson, this unveiling was a calculated political move by the women, who were allied with Faysal and sought to 'emphasize the enlightened political ambitions of Faysal's Arab government'.[26]

The following morning, 1 July, the commission (minus Yale and a sick Crane) embarked on a day-long train journey to hear testimony in Amman and Dera'a. The highlight of the trip was, however, their mode of transportation between the Amman train station and the city centre, which was three miles away. In King's words:

> We had a great time at Amman too, because they met us with riding horses at the station [...] We found when we got on our horses that they were not tourists [sic] hacks but really spirited Arab horses. The one I got on was the sort that does not like to be left behind by anybody, and simply rushed ahead of most of the crowd and brought me to the village three or four minutes before the rest of them appeared. I was thankful to be able to stay on and keep alive. One of our group [the luckless Laurence Moore] was thrown from his horse and it was a mercy that he and others were not injured.[27]

George Montgomery was happy to have had such a diversion and found the whole incident 'very funny'.[28] While in Amman they saw '19

Figure 7.2 Delegations awaiting their audience with the commission in Amman. (Source: Oberlin College Archives, Oberlin, Ohio).

delegations in $2\frac{1}{2}$ hours, about 200 persons', with the makeup of these delegations being similar in character to those they had seen previously.[29] The uniformity of testimony seemed to be creeping in a bit more: the three surviving petitions from Amman are practically identical in their wording, handwriting, ink colour and paper. All three of these groups asked for independence, repudiated French claims to Syria, and sought technical assistance from the United States or Great Britain (should the United States refuse).[30] After they were finished hearing the delegations in Amman, they decided that it would be wiser not to attempt to ride horses back to the train and instead 'returned in carriages'.[31] On the way back to Damascus, they stopped at Dera'a and heard one delegation of '9 splendid orators'. They also fit in some souvenir shopping, purchasing some 'Bedouin girl-trappings, ornaments, etc.' As they left Dera'a, Lybyer noted that the local Bedouins 'galloped' alongside them and had a 'race w. train'. They returned to Damascus that night.[32]

On 2 July, they continued to hear testimony from prominent Damascenes, as arranged by William Yale. Yale had not gone to Amman because he felt he needed to stay behind to investigate the lack of support for the French, support which he was certain had existed 'among some groups, both Christian and Moslem' during the war. Because the 'situation had changed so radically', Yale 'called on a variety of Arabs' to ask about this and learned that there had indeed been a large amount of anti-French agitation in the preceding months. He then discussed the matter with the British political officer Colonel Kinahan Cornwallis, asking him how much the British had to do with this campaign. Cornwallis replied that there had indeed been much agitation but that the British 'had nothing to do with it', yet Yale noted that allowing such a campaign to go on against 'their principal ally' would have legitimately angered the French.[33] Yale then told the commission that pro-French testimony had been suppressed, which the rest of the commission had difficulty believing perhaps because they had seen no evidence for this. This caused some members of the commission to begin to doubt Yale's impartiality. Lybyer, for example, seemed to lose his trust in Yale, noting the following later in the journey: 'Captain Yale is very pro-French, and uses some of their tricks, apparently endeavoring to keep the commission more under one influence than the other.'[34] In general, most of the commission members came to Greater Syria with prejudice against French aspirations in the region because of their perceived obstruction of the commission in Paris, though it must be noted that Yale and Montgomery were far less influenced by this sentiment. The vehemence of the anti-French testimony in Syria would only have served to confirm King, Crane and Lybyer's suspicions that the French obstructed the commission because it had little support in the region.

On their final day in Damascus (3 July), the commission again saw many important delegations, including a delegation of recently returned Syrian exiles from Cairo (which included prominent nationalists Michel Lutfallah and Dr 'Abd al Rahman Shahbandar) and a group representing various trade organisations. The two most important delegations, however, were the official representatives of the Syrian Congress and Amir Faysal himself. Faysal had formally convened the Syrian Congress on 1 July, though meetings involving many of its members had been taking place in Damascus throughout June. The congress was supposed to be comprised of 85 indirectly elected officials (controversially employing the old Ottoman electoral system for expediency's sake) and 35 invited religious leaders, though fewer than this actually attended.[35] Faysal tasked the congress with crafting a unified resolution to present to the King–Crane Commission. The wording of this resolution was debated, though judging by the growing uniformity of the testimony to the commission in Damascus, it is likely that the framework for this resolution was in place before the congress convened. After two days of wrangling, the so-called 'Damascus Program' was approved. In this document, the congress protested Article 22 of the League of Nations Covenant and called for 'complete political independence' of a unified Greater Syria. If the powers insisted, the new state would accept 'technical and economic assistance' (not a mandate) from the United States as long as it did not impinge on this independence. Britain was named the second choice to give such assistance if the United States would not, and both French and Zionist claims to the land were repudiated entirely. The congress further mentioned its expectation that 'President Wilson and the free American people will be our supporters for the realization of our hopes.' A delegation from the congress presented their programme to the commission, and the commission took it very seriously, later stating that 'it is the most substantial document presented to the commission, and deserves to be treated with great respect'. The full text of the Damascus Program was included in the commission's final report.[36]

Amir Faysal, who claimed to be speaking as the 'political representative and defender of the rights of Syria', gave the final speech to the commission in Damascus and effusively endorsed the Damascus Program. The speech also represented perhaps the most emphatic denunciation of French rule in Syria heard by the commission. Faysal listed and explained the reasons he rejected French rule in the following manner:

- 'Economical reasons': The 'commercial class' of Syria believed 'that the French nation is known for its commercial exclusiveness and keen competition with the natives in their resources, notwithstanding the fact that the support of the French authorities is totally given to the French tradesmen, and France does not adopt the policy of the "open door"'. Furthermore, the French colonies were characterised by the 'stagnation of industry', the 'prevention of the natives to develop' their economy, and the 'suppression' of the land's 'agricultural capacity'.
- 'Social reasons': France 'applies her own systems to the countries brought under her control, and disregards the national feeling, and disrespecting [sic] the traditions of those particular countries. That would mean certain death to Syrians as a distinctive people.'
- 'Political reasons': France removes 'manliness and boldness from the people and prevents it [sic] from progress and development as a

political body [...] Every one who opposes her political views is persecuted officially while those adhering to her are left in peace to prosecute their own aims. The French follow the policy of favouring their partisans, appointing them, though worthless, to the high offices at the expense of those who are more competent but not amenable to their intrigues'.[37]

According to Lybyer, the speech was a fitting end to their time in Damascus, as Faysal 'made a splendid impression' with a 'statesman'-like understanding of the situation.[38]

Lebanon and the End of the Greater Syrian Journey

The commission left Damascus for Baalbek the next morning (4 July) where they were planning to conduct more interviews before moving on to Beirut. Along the way, Lybyer remarked on the beauty of the region, noting the 'red coloring of the hills' and calling the Beqa'a Valley a 'wonderful long trough'.[39] Upon reaching Baalbek, they spent the afternoon wandering the famed Roman ruins before settling in for the night. In Baalbek, William Yale again was in control of organising the interviews. Yale had come to believe that the growing uniformity of the petitions being given to the commission was the result of a successful propaganda campaign by Faysal's Arab government. Therefore, in choosing the groups who would testify before the commission in Baalbek, he sought to ensure that the commission received testimony from 'those elements in the villages not in accord' with the 'hand-picked Arab government delegations'. He had hoped to do this himself but his car broke down so he sent an 'energetic' and 'bold looking Arab' to 'deliver invitations in the commission's name' to groups in the villages likely not in agreement with the Damascus Program.[40] This angered Lybyer, who believed that Yale had been deliberately choosing groups with pro-French leanings and, indeed, they saw delegations that voiced 'strong opposition' to the Damascus Program in Baalbek, along with those who endorsed it. Lybyer came to believe that pro-French testimony was being overrepresented and wrote to his wife that these activities worked 'in the long run against his [Yale's] purposes, and is one of the reasons why it is hard to be fair to the French'.[41] After the interviews in Baalbek, the main body of the commission drove to the town of Aley, in the mountains above Beirut, where they had decided to lodge in an effort to stay out of the summer heat of the coast. Yale and Montgomery continued on to Beirut in order to organise the delegations the commission would receive.

On 6 July, Crane decided that the commission should send another dispatch to President Wilson in order to update him on their progress. The cable was 'worked on' by only Crane, King and Lybyer, likely because their opinions had become more or less congruous.[42] The cable wound up being about 600 words long and cost 'about $300 to send', which was quite a sum in 1919.[43] In this cable, which was sent on 10 July, they argued that 'certain points' in their investigation had become 'unmistakable', which included:

> Intense desire for unity of all Syria and Palestine and for as early independence as possible. Unexpected[ly] strong expressions of national feeling. Singular[ly] determined repulsion to becoming a mere colony of any power and against any kind of French mandate. Only marked exceptions to this statement are found in strong parties of Lebanese who demand complete separation of Lebanon with French collaboration. In our judgement proclamation of French mandate for all Syria would precipitate warfare between Arabs and French, and force Great Britain to dangerous alternative. [...] Both British Government and French officers share conviction that unity of whole of Syria and Palestine is most desirable. They feel that constant friction and danger to peace are otherwise inevitable between British subjects, French and Arabs. But there is little clear evidence that either British Government or French Government are willing entirely to withdraw.

They mentioned little about Zionism, stating only that 'subsequent experience only confirms earlier dispatch on Zionism'. They also stated that 'America genuinely first choice of most for mandatary because [it is] believed [Americans] have no territorial ambition'. King, Crane and Lybyer went on to describe the desires of the Syrian Congress and then praised Faysal as being the man who could ably lead a new Syrian state. The three were thus aligned in their thoughts and the observations noted here presaged some of the conclusions in the commission's final report.[44]

Yale and Montgomery, who were staying in Beirut, only learned about the contents of the cable after it had been written, and they both found it 'hysterical, exaggerated, and unnecessarily alarming'.[45] Yale immediately wrote a letter to William Westermann that countered the views in the telegram to Wilson, stating that he still harboured opinions that fell 'along the lines of the decisions we arrived at at [sic] Paris'. While King, Crane and Lybyer were more trusting of what they were observing, Yale was far more sceptical. He believed that the region's Muslims were dangerously 'fanatical' and sought to 'dominate' the other minorities. He also believed that promises made to the Zionists and the French needed to be kept for both international political reasons and in order to guarantee the safety of the region's minorities. Yale concluded that to 'misjudge the present situation', as he believed King, Crane and Lybyer had done, could 'cost the lives of thousands of Christians in Syria'.[46] Just as the commissioners, it seems, had nearly made up their minds about Greater Syria at this point, Yale's letter to Westermann also foreshadowed his eventual conclusions. The dissent within the commission, which had never been hidden, was now entirely on the surface but, aside from Lybyer's occasional scathing comments about Yale, the dissent did not seem to affect the generally cordial relationship between the commission members.

After completing their respective memoranda, the commission began its work in Beirut, a city whose population had been ravaged by the war. Impressions of the political state of Beirut differed among various observers. The Zionist agent Abraham Elmaleh noted that Beirut was relatively 'quiet' compared with the 'political chaos that reigned in Damascus'. He also noted that newspaper censorship was much lighter in Beirut and views on Zionism were much more reasonable in his reckoning.[47] In contrast to this, Lybyer believed that there was more political intrigue in Beirut than in Damascus and that the city was a 'nest of propaganda'. He noted that his prejudice against the French continued to grow because they had 'spent large sums' to sway local opinion in their favour. In a candid assessment of the region's propaganda, Lybyer informed his wife that 'the French methods are sometimes puerile, such as petty persecutions, heavy hand on the press, etc. The British are far more subtle – they pay a lump sum monthly to the Emir Faisal's government, and it attends to the rest.'[48] Having been so harshly denounced in Damascus, the French worked hard on two primary

Figure 7.3 The King–Crane Commission at the Hotel Royal in Beirut. In the back row (left to right) are Dr. Sami Haddad, Yale, Lybyer, Montgomery, Captain Donald Brodie and Laurence Moore. In the front are King (left) and Crane (right). (Source: Oberlin College Archives, Oberlin, Ohio).

tasks in Lebanon: secure as many calls as possible for a French mandate over the region and limit the influence of the Syrian nationalists. Word of the Damascus Program was widespread by the time the commission arrived in Lebanon, with 16 notables from the vicinity having been present at the Syrian Congress and numerous nationalists combing the countryside trying to garner support for their cause.[49] For Lybyer, as for King and Crane, these competing propaganda machines were not equivalent: anti-French sentiment, in their minds, may have been sculpted by propaganda but was essentially real, while pro-French attitudes were manufactured to a larger degree than other viewpoints.

For Abraham Elmaleh, Beirut provided another challenging task. He arrived in the city a few days before the commission (2 July) and first went to see Zionist sympathiser Joseph Farhi, the influential businessman who was vice-president of the Jewish 'communal council' ('Vaad Ha'ir'). Elmaleh then went with Farhi to see Selim Dana, 'Chief Director of the French Bank of Syria', who he believed to be the most influential member of the Jewish community, stating 'his words receive attention everywhere and his opinion is accepted on every question'. Much to Elmaleh's dismay, Dana demurred on the topic of Zionism. 'His views on the National Movement', according to Elmaleh, 'are those of an assimilationist', with Dana further stating that he believed there to be 'nothing between the Jews of Palestine and Syria'. A 'long discussion of 2 hours in duration' ensued and Dana was eventually convinced to 'sign any memorandum that we [the Zionists] desire on the question of Palestine and to present it to the American commission on the condition that the question of choice of the Protecting Power be left open'. After this, Elmaleh met Beirut's Vaad Ha'ir and was able to convince them to allow himself and Joseph Farhi to craft the pro-Zionist 'memorandum' that they would present to the King–Crane Commission, though the Council insisted on asking for a French mandate over Lebanon.[50]

After the pro-Zionist memorandum was crafted by Elmaleh and Farhi, Selim Dana showed it to the French Military Governor. In regards to the mandatory power, the memo stated that it was 'France that we desire to see guarding our country towards Progress and Prosperity'. In response to this, the military governor stated that he 'was very glad to know of the decision of the Jews in relation to France and promised that all Political Parties of Syria that supported France, would endorse the demands of the Jews in Palestine'. The next day, François Georges-Picot, now the French High Commissioner in Beirut, thanked Dana for his support for France and stated the following:

> I may inform you that I have printed 50 copies of the Memorandum which you handed to Mr. Coupen and distributed them to all the Political parties that support France, with a request that they should support the demands of the Jews in reference to Palestine, and you will see [for] yourself the results.[51]

It is difficult to tell how much this impromptu alliance actually helped the Zionist cause. On the one hand, only two groups (0.45 per cent) in Lebanon eventually supported the 'Zionist Program' so it did not seem to help much. On the other hand, only 19.7 per cent of the petitions the commission received during their time in Lebanon were 'Against the Zionist Program' so it is possible that it lessened outward resistance to Zionism.[52] In sum, Zionism was still a nearly impossible sell in Lebanon but it did not mobilise as much opposition as it had in Palestine and around Damascus.

In Beirut, Yale had been going about his normal routine of organising the delegations, this time with the help of Montgomery. According to Yale, he called on Georges-Picot when he arrived in the city and was handed 'a dossier of many closely typed pages listing an innumerable number of delegations from Beirut and many villages of the Lebanon, which he said had arranged to present their views to the American commissioners'. Yale, as he had done elsewhere, 'diplomatically' refused such a pre-fabricated list and insisted that the commission do this portion of the work itself. Georges-Picot was not happy but remained 'polite and diplomatic'.[53]

On 7 July, the commission began seeing delegations on the balcony of a hotel, with Muslims and Christians dominating the first day of testimony.[54] The opening three delegations were Muslims of various ilks, with the first being the 'Kadi, Mufti, Ulemas'.[55] The testimony of this group adhered to the Damascus Program and emphasised Greater Syria's fitness for self-rule, especially relative to other eastern European peoples who had already been granted independence. More specifically, they stated 'We cannot believe that the Powers which recognised the justice of the demands of the inhabitants of the new nationalities such as Poland, for liberation should regard us as unfit for absolute autonomy.' The commission launched into a set of questions, and the discussion went as follows:

> Q: If the peace conference should decide to give a mandate for Syria to France, what would be your attitude?
> A: We have explained our attitude in our memorandum and no power on earth will make us alter it.
> Q: Why are you not favourably disposed to France?
> A: We have explained our reasons for our opposition to which we shall adhere with all our force (here the reasons were detailed).
> Q: Do you desire that Emir Feisal should be Governor or King.
> A: A King shall reign over us.
> Q: What form of Government do you desire.
> A: A Decentralised Government that would protect minority rights.
> Q: If Emir Feisal should be King in Damascus, what would be the attitude of Beirut to the inland cities.
> A: Beirut would be connected with Damascus politically and economically.

Q: What is your relation to the Hedjaz Kingdom?
A: A religious and not a political relationship. [sic][56]

The other Muslim delegations appear to have responded in a similar manner. The delegations of Greek Orthodox who followed the Muslims were split between asking for French and American/British assistance for their new country. Lybyer stated that there was a 'heavy fight' over this matter within the Greek Orthodox community, with both sides claiming to have 'a great majority'. Two days later, Lybyer went to see the ailing Greek Orthodox Archbishop who confirmed that his congregation was divided, though he personally was 'vs. French control'. Following the Greek Orthodox delegations, the Maronite Archbishop gave emphatically pro-French testimony and the Greek Catholics testified in favour of the French as well.[57]

The following day, the commission saw a more diverse set of delegations. They started with additional confessional representatives in the morning (Protestants, Jews, Syrian Catholics, Druzes and Roman Catholics). The Jews, as a group, gave the commission the promised testimony, with the Chief Rabbi welcoming the commission with a pro-Zionist speech 'composed' by Elmaleh.[58] After these religious groups, the commission interviewed a delegation of bankers who were asked for opinions on the 'financial and commercial' issues of the region.[59] During an afternoon break, they visited a trade school for women set up during the war by '5 wealthy Moslem women'.[60] Later, some 'veiled women' from the school appeared before the commission in an official manner and read 'an excellent paper' in which they stated that they were 'for the independence of [a] united Syria, with limited assistance from the Anglo-Saxon nations'. Lybyer further noted that they seemed 'more determined' on this matter 'even than the Moslem men'.[61] Yale later remarked that this group of women 'sought principally to impress upon' the commission 'the danger threatening the chastity of Islamic womanhood, if the French were given a mandate for Syria or any part thereof'. Yale, having lived in the region since 1913, had apparently been unimpressed with the morality of the region's people, quipping 'my knowledge of the morals of the Islamic world led me to suspect that they would not suffer any precipitous decline from contact with the French'.[62]

On a personal level, the members of the commission were exhausted by the end of their time in Beirut. George Montgomery wrote to his wife that he was 'fed up with wandering' and was 'anxious to get home'.[63] King, Crane and Brodie had each been sick, with Crane's illness keeping him out of many of the interviews in Damascus.[64] Crane was ill in Beirut as well, with Lybyer writing to his wife that, 'We are all well except that Mr. Crane's digestion has been upset for a week, and he eats little but youghourt.'[65] Crane also appeared to start to lose interest in the commission by the time they reached Beirut, and his lack of interest rankled Lybyer, who observed that Crane's attendance at meetings was no longer 'very prompt or certain'. 'Mr. Crane does not like rules', he continued, 'he leaves when he is tired, and decides hastily sometimes.'[66] Crane was always the least interested member of the commission but because he was the most revered of its members, he remained influential when he wanted to be, though these moments occurred less and less as their time in the region wore on. William Yale, for his part, entertained himself in Beirut by engaging in the 'ungodly' behaviour of which he was so fond. He later recounted the following story:

> A Syrian lady of some distinction occupied a room second beyond mine. We had, at idle moments, flirted with one another from our respective balconies, which were not adjoining. In a moment of boldness and on the day of the commission's departure, I entered the vacant room adjoining mine and, stepping on the balcony, proceeded to enter the fair lady's room. While we were engaged in idle chatter, a newly arrived guest was ushered into the adjoining room, cutting off my line of retreat. In the hallway I could hear the members of the commission stacking their baggage and asking where I might be. Despite the embarrassment to myself and the possibility of compromising the fair lady, I, of necessity, broke off our brief acquaintance by leaving her room through the door instead of the window, much to the astonishment and scandal of my colleagues.[67]

The commission then moved on to towns in the vicinity of Beirut.

Outside Beirut, French propaganda seemed even more blatant to the commission members. On the morning of 10 July, King and Lybyer travelled south, passing through a 'small demonstration' at Sidon, on their way to Tyre, where Lybyer noted that the French governor 'had everything thoroughly arranged'. This governor was 'a wily man' who acted as interpreter in order to 'see that each group spoke as arranged'. Despite his presence, 'the Shiite Ulema spoke out strongly for Damascus progr'. King and Lybyer were told that five days before the French had appointed 'an ignorant Cadi [sic] and Mufti who would declare for France' although this was not the wish of the community, and also had 'two very seedy "Protestant Delegates" sent in' who apparently lacked any legitimacy. In the afternoon, they went to Sidon and met Montgomery and Yale in order to hear further delegations. Lybyer noted that the governor here 'had not been able to hold people' in Sidon, with the delegations giving testimony 'mostly for Dam[ascus]-Program', though they did see a delegation of 'Christian ladies' who 'spoke for France'. Lybyer also noted that the small delegation of local Jews in Sidon, which Elmaleh had apparently not seen, were 'very fearful', though he did not elaborate on this. They returned to Beirut that evening.[68]

On 11 July, the delegation split again, with King and Lybyer going to Ainab and Baabda, while Montgomery and Yale went back into the Beqa'a Valley, visiting Zahleh and Mu'allaqa. At Ainab, there was a 'demonstration of 400 to 500' outside the hall in which they were going to hear testimony and 'shouts for America and Wilson' emanated from this group. At Baabda, Lybyer again complained that French officials had 'picked delegates' and noted that a 'brave boy' who had 'declared for the U.S.' had been 'browbeaten' prompting the commission to ask the French governor to protect him.[69] While Lybyer was noting coercion by the French, Montgomery witnessed a case that showed 'the oppression of the Sherifian government' in Mu'allaqa, where the elected president of the 'Municipal Council' had been 'dismissed for going to Beirut' to consult with the French authorities, and other members of the council had similarly lost their positions 'for putting into the minutes a pro-French resolution'. The new council was appointed by the government in Damascus and was predictably anti-French. Things were calmer in Zahleh, with the only item of note being that the Orthodox delegations were split in the same manner as their Beirut counterparts (one group asking for France as mandatory power and the other asking for 'America or Great Britain'). Unsurprisingly, both claimed to represent the majority of the Orthodox population of the town.[70] At the end of their interviews, the commission members returned to their respective hotels (in Beirut and Aley) and prepared to leave the following morning.

Figure 7.4 The reception of the commission at Tripoli, 12 July, 1919. (Source: Oberlin College Archives, Oberlin, Ohio).

From 12 to 14 July, the commission was granted the use of General Allenby's rather luxurious yacht to motor up the coast to Tripoli, Alexandretta and Latakia, again seeing delegations at each. According to Lybyer, Tripoli was especially tense, and the French soldiers had orders for their bayonets to remain 'fixed'. The delegations were again 'slated carefully' by the French but this did not stop their opinions from being mixed. Many of the Christians, including the 'Maronites and Latins', advocated for some form of French mandate, while the 'Ulema were brave' and 'declared for the Damascus Program'. The bishop of the Greek Orthodox contingent in the city, who the commission's normally mild-mannered translator Sami Haddad declared to be a 'great rascal', admitted that his congregation was divided, which remained consistent with the Orthodox opinions elsewhere in Greater Syria.[71] Lybyer's antipathy towards the French and their style of propaganda became more and more palpable as the commission's journey continued. At Tripoli, for example, Lybyer noted:

> The military governor is the worst French man we have seen – had a lot of opponents to French mandate in prison – others were exiled, many browbeaten and bought. I shall have great stories of the South American type of politics used by the French. They

damage seriously the case they have – they do not deceive us – we hear practically everything from one source or another.[72]

Is it important to note that Lybyer, for some reason, continually reserved such vitriol for the French almost exclusively; in Lybyer's mind it seemed that propaganda by the Arabs (as funded by the British) was to be expected while propaganda by the French and their allies was somehow an egregious intrusion into the process. Although the French propaganda does appear to have been less subtle than that of most of its counterparts, the scorn of Lybyer (and by extension King and Crane) was too pronounced to have simply been influenced by what the commission witnessed in Greater Syria. The French, in Lybyer's mind, seemed somehow prone to such brazen behaviour whereas the British did not.

In Alexandretta and Latakia (on 13 and 14 July, respectively), the commission had a more pleasant experience. In Alexandretta, Lybyer declared that the French military governor was 'a very decent, hard-working fellow – the best we have seen'.[73] The commission saw, in Alexandretta, a 'fairly free expression of opinion',[74] though some of the Greek Orthodox population (who were again divided) claimed that the 'greater majority signed the French program under compulsion' of 'agents'.[75] The commission also saw, for the first time, a number of groups who self-identified as Turks, and their aspirations were mixed. The group labelled by Lybyer as the 'Turks of Alexandretta and Antioch', for example, asked to 'remain under Ottoman rule' whereas a group of 'Turkish Notables' stated that they were 'satisfied with France with special recognition for Turks'. A delegation of local Jews (not seen by Elmaleh) gave testimony to the commission as well, with the only note taken about this testimony being that they 'wish security'.[76] The following day the commission moved on to Latakia by boat, where there were 'hundreds of people lining the shore' in anticipation of their arrival and 'great crowds in the streets', including 'large numbers of women'. Lybyer stated that there was 'great excitement' and evidence of an 'intense political struggle', though the French had 'not been able to swing things' entirely in their favour. With Latakia not being accessible by a good road, the commission returned to Tripoli by ship in order to take cars inland to Aleppo.[77]

In personal terms, the commission members continued to have mixed fortunes during their time in Lebanon. Montgomery was dealing with personal financial troubles at this point in their journey, knowing that his wife would not have enough money to pay his son's private school tuition because he had not yet been paid for his work on the commission.[78] Crane was still sick and had remained on the boat while the others saw delegations in Alexandretta and Latakia.[79] Yale seemed to be enjoying his time, especially on the yacht, which he declared to be 'delightful'.[80] Lybyer was quite happy with his position of prominence on the commission, writing to his wife that he was meeting all of the region's 'prominent people, French, English and native'.[81] He also enjoyed recording stories of some of the more quirky characters he met, such as the French doctor with whom he had lunch in Alexandretta. This doctor told him about the terrible conditions in the region, stating that '2 French die of malaria every day'. He also noted that this same doctor got 'drunk easily' and wound up telling him about his '4 legit sons and 2 illegitimate'.[82] Lybyer was continually impressed by the beauty of the region and recorded this in his writings on various occasions, such as the following description of dusk at Tripoli: 'Full moon rose over mountains as we left Tripoli. Moon pale, Mtns. pink above, olive below; dark cloud on one hill, lighter cloud half way down under the moon.'[83]

The commission returned to land transport on 15 July, though Crane and Donald Brodie stayed aboard Allenby's yacht and carried on to Beirut, likely to allow Crane to further convalesce. The rest of the commission rode in cars from Tripoli to Homs. Immediately, they came across more evidence of French malfeasance as they were confronted by 'a great crowd of people, on horse and foot' on the way to Homs. They stopped the commission in order to protest 'against the way the French governor of Tripoli prevented people from seeing us [the commission] on [the previous] Saturday'. A second group making similar claims confronted them a few miles further down the road. The commission made it to Homs that afternoon.[84] On their first afternoon in Homs, the commission members chose to explore the city with the Australian major who was in charge of the town. They wandered the 'rather barren bazaars' and bought silk (a famed Homs product).[85] The commission saw delegations the next morning, and the demands were back to 'mostly straight Damascus Program' with a '12th article added – protest vs. behaviour of French on W. [West] coast'. The only notable dissent, according to Lybyer, came from a Circassian delegation that was 'unhappy' with the Arab government in Damascus and sought a British mandate. The commission left Homs that evening and went to Hama, where they again saw

Figure 7.5 The reception of the commission at Latakia, 14 July 1919 (Source: World War I Photograph Album, 1918–19, American University of Beirut/Library Archives).

delegations of a similar nature on 16 July, with Lybyer noting that the Greek Orthodox population of the city, which had been fractious in other towns, seemed to be 'mainly for France'. They then went to the train station to catch a 7:00 p.m. train to Aleppo, hoping to arrive later that night. The train, however, did not reach the station until about 11:00 p.m., which meant that the journey would take place overnight. Although they did get a 'special car' with 'comfortable sofas', there was not enough space for proper sleeping.[86] Montgomery and Laurence Moore took advantage of the cool night weather and rode on the roof for some of the journey, while the others did their best to get some sleep on the sofas.[87] They arrived at the Aleppo train station at 5:00 a.m. and were greeted by 'a lot of people', including US Consul Jesse B. Jackson, who had apparently been at the station since 11:45 p.m. (their expected time of arrival). The commission decided to take this day (17 July) off and began seeing the Aleppo delegations on the following morning.[88]

Like in the other cities, the residents of Aleppo were subject to intense lobbying before the commission's arrival. As usual, William Yale had

Figure 7.6 The commission stopping at a village north of Homs. (Source: World War I Photograph Album, 1918–19, American University of Beirut/Library Archives).

reached Aleppo a few days before the main body of the commission (14 July) and crafted a programme of delegations with the help of Consul Jackson. In a letter to the State Department, Jackson noted that there was 'strong evidence' of outside interference in the city but that 'every effort was made to induce the local government to prevent anything of the kind'.[89] One agent of such 'outside interference' was, once again, Abraham Elmaleh, who noted that his task of getting the Jews of Aleppo to present 'a unified front' for Zionism was 'more difficult than in Damascus and in Beirut'. The problems were several: the local Jews, he stated, were not interested in political matters, especially after witnessing the 'massacres of the Armenians by the Arabs immediately after the conquest of Syria' in February 1919.[90] Elmaleh believed that the Jews in Aleppo were more 'keenly watched' by the 'Moslem Arabs' than their more anonymous counterparts in the other cities and, indeed, local policemen had 'visited the houses of the Jews forcing them to sign their consent to all decisions of the Syrian Congress'. Despite their apprehensions, Elmaleh was able to organise a gathering of the Jewish 'notables' of Aleppo to whom he 'fully related all the happenings' in Greater Syria thus far and 'requested them to unite with their brethren so that the American commission should gain the impression that on the question of Palestine there was no division of opinion among scattered Jewry'. Elmaleh was pleased when 'his words were favourably received', stating that 'assimilation had not entered the Aleppo Community as for instance at Beirut'. Aleppo's Jews decided to support Zionism and leave the question of the mandatory power for Syria 'to the League of Nations'. Elmaleh's apparent victory took a dramatic turn when the forces in the city agitating for the Damascus Program somehow learned of the testimony that was to be given by the Jews and 'warned' the leaders of the Jewish community 'that as a result of such a statement to the commission they would be in danger'. This 'made the Jews afraid', according to Elmaleh, and a second meeting was held in which they decided to adhere more closely to the Damascus Program on the question of mandates but still to 'utterly oppose' the Damascus Program 'in relation to Palestine'. Elmaleh and two others were appointed to write the official memorandum to the commission.[91]

After recovering from their largely sleepless night on the train, the commission members set out to see Aleppo on 17 July. George Montgomery and Albert Lybyer decided to visit one of the elements of this more northerly city that concerned them the most: Aleppo's Armenian refugee camps. There were thousands of Armenians in these camps being cared for by the British, local Armenians and 'about 20 Americans' from the American Committee for Relief in the Near East (formerly known as ACASR).[92] Lybyer noted that these camps were 'crowded' and were inhabited by 'an unprepossessing lot' with many medical issues ('sore eyes and skin diseases').[93] Judging from this group, Lybyer began to believe that the Armenians as a race would require a great deal of time to recover from the traumas of the war.

On 18 and 19 July, the commission returned to its regular routine of seeing delegations. Lybyer reported that there was the 'appearance of great freedom' in Aleppo but that there was also 'evidence of both Arab and French influence'. Just as they had in Damascus, the nationalist newspapers both advertised what they believed people should say to the commission and then summarised what had been said to the commission after testimony was given.[94] The influence of those backing the Damascus Program became even more noticeable in the written petitions received by the commission, with a number of them identically rehashing its demands. Conversely, the Catholic population of the city advocated for a French mandate in all of Greater Syria and claimed that the 'great majority would be for France except for governmental

Figure 7.7 Representatives of the 'wards of the city of Aleppo'. (Source: Oberlin College Archives, Oberlin, Ohio).

pressure'. The commission heard further testimony from a large number of women in Aleppo, with delegations of Muslim and Protestant women backing the Damascus Program. They also received a 'pro-French group' of 'nuns' and women wearing 'cosmetics and frills'.[95] Beyond these groups, the commission interviewed the only delegation from Mesopotamia they would see during their journey. The group backed the Damascus Program and asked that the commission tour their region.[96] The Jewish members of the Aleppo Municipal Council signed a statement that backed the Damascus Program but they also wrote an addendum stating their support for Zionism that, as noted previously, was likely penned by Elmaleh.[97] Perhaps the most notable episode in Aleppo occurred when a group of Bedouin sheikhs from the 'Aniza tribes 'expressed a strong desire' for France as mandatory power. This angered many of those advocating the Damascus Program in Aleppo, and these sheikhs were 'caught by the local Arabs, possibly through British influence'. They were then 'threatened, and forced to sign a petition' for the commission that essentially endorsed the Damascus Program.[98] In sum, Aleppo fell into the same broad patterns as the commission's other stops: there was propaganda, there were difficult and divisive decisions being made by the region's groups, and there was controversy.

On 19 July, George Montgomery left for Adana in order to take over Yale's job of organising delegations for the commission because they were now entering the primarily Turkish-speaking zones of their inquiry. He noted that his train had seven boxcars 'filled with Armenian refugees being repatriated to various station [sic] north and west of Konia', with some expecting to be in the cars for as long as four days.[99] On 20 July, the rest of the commission boarded a train to Adana to continue their work. The still ailing Charles Crane had only arrived in Aleppo at 2:00 a.m. that morning, apparently having decided that he needed to stay near the coast in hopes of getting well. They had another 'special train' that consisted of '4 cars' but Lybyer complained that it was 'too shaky for writing, and too noisy for conversation'. Lybyer further remarked on the high quality of the workmanship along the German-designed railway. They reached Adana at 6:00 p.m.[100]

In Adana, a city under French and Turkish control, the commission again saw numerous delegations from the region, with Turkish and Armenian groups having more representation than they had in other locations. Before seeing delegations on 21 July, however, the commission stopped at the site where two American missionaries were killed during the 1909 massacre of Armenians in the city, an event that was well publicised in the United States. The large number of Armenians in Adana ('20–25,000') came as something of a surprise to the commission, and the Armenian leaders asked for a large, independent Armenian state under an American mandate. The Turks, in contrast, generally asked to remain under Ottoman rule.[101] The French presence was strong in Adana and Montgomery noted that the French were 'going ahead as if they expected to stay'. Their purpose, Montgomery believed, was 'to establish a fait accompli, in case that the United States does not take a mandate for Armenia', with Armenia rightfully including Adana in Montgomery's mind.[102] In the early afternoon, they took a train to Mersin where the American destroyer *Hazelwood* was waiting for them. They boarded the ship that evening and set sail for Istanbul. After 'six strenuous weeks', the Syrian adventure was finished.[103]

The Results from Greater Syria

The tabulation of the large amount of data the commission received in Greater Syria was accomplished in a meticulous fashion, with the

Figure 7.8 The commission's 'special train' to Adana. (Source: World War I Photograph Album, 1918–19, American University of Beirut/Library Archives).

commission members compiling the demands of the petitioners and then converting these into precise numbers and percentages. The commission admitted in its final report that problems existed with their sample such as the number of petitions being 'not proportional to the numerical strength' of the region's various groups and the fact that many petitions showed the 'influence of organised propaganda' (yet acknowledging that such propaganda was 'natural and inevitable'). Nevertheless, they believed that the petitions displayed 'a fairly accurate analysis of present political opinion in Syria'.[104] In the words of Charles Crane, their journey 'looked very hopeless and dishevelled [sic]' at the beginning 'but unravelled as we moved along, leaving a fairly clear picture of the longings and apprehensions' of the people.[105] The following points, generally in line with the Damascus Program, were unmistakable to the commission members:

- The majority of the petitioners (80.4 per cent) received by the commission believed that Greater Syria, often defined by the delegations as existing from the 'Taurus to Rafah' (including what is now Syria, Lebanon, Israel/Palestine and Jordan) must remain unified.

- The majority of the delegates backed the full independence of Syria and wanted no mandate (73.5 per cent). The compromise between Faysal and those advocating complete independence was to accept 'technical and economic assistance' from the United States (57 per cent) or Great Britain should the United States not accept (55.3 per cent). A majority (60.5 per cent) also made 'General Anti-French Statements'.
- The majority supported the establishment of a 'Democratic Kingdom' with Faysal as king (59 per cent).
- The majority of the delegates were anti-Zionist (72.3 per cent), with many fervently so.[106]

However, the commission members acknowledged that the testimony varied in different parts of Greater Syria. The testimony they received in the OETA East (what is now Syria and Jordan for the most part) could hardly have been more emphatic. Of the 1,157 petitions they received, 94.3 per cent asked for a united Greater Syria, 92.3 per cent were for the 'Absolute Independence of Syria', and 87 per cent asked for a 'Democratic Kingdom' with nearly all of these requesting 'Emir Feisal as king'. Furthermore, 86.1 per cent asked for the United States as 'First Choice' for assistance, 85 per cent made 'General Anti-French Statements', and 90 per cent were against the 'Zionist Program'. In Lebanon (OETA West), the testimony was different. The population was about evenly divided over whether 'Greater Lebanon' should be independent or united with Syria (43.9 per cent for independence versus 41.9 per cent for unity). Nearly 50 per cent of the population asked for a French mandate, whereas 25.5 per cent made anti-French statements.[107] The results from the OETA South, or Palestine (recounted in Chapter 6), were more in line with those of the OETA East, though distinct differences did exist on issues such as Faysal becoming king, mandates, and the involvement of the French in the region. As questionable as these statistics may seem to a modern day critic, they would likely have appeared more convincing and even 'scientific' to an observer of this era. To the commission members, the opinions of the 'people' of this region were clear but they disagreed about how much weight such opinions should be given in their final recommendations.

***

The summer of 1919 was a vibrant and contentious political moment in Greater Syria. The varied political groups, thinking that the King–Crane Commission was going to be an influential body, expended huge amounts of energy trying to ensure that their political projects were advocated in the testimony given to the commission. The region's people transformed the traditional Ottoman practice of petitioning (previously a relational device useful to both subject and sovereign) into a 'modern political tool, used to recruit and generate public opinion and foster a modern political collective discourse'.[108] The Syrian nationalists were ultimately successful in convincing the majority of the people who testified before the commission (approximately 60 per cent) to largely adhere to the demands embodied in the Damascus Program. The fact that it was not difficult to get people to support this position likely indicates that the general parameters of the political project represented by the Damascus Program had a fairly broad resonance in the region.

Abraham Elmaleh almost singlehandedly carried the Zionist cause to the often sceptical Jews in the larger cities of Syria and Lebanon and proved adept at this job. 'All the Jews without any distinction', he noted, 'even those who appear to be assimilationists, are united with us in our demands, and are ready at all times to declare this.' Though this may have been an overstatement, his accomplishment was impressive. His assessment of the state of opinion among the non-Jews, however, would not have been encouraging to the Zionists: 'All the Arabs in Syria under the government of the Sheriff [sic] are opposed to the Zionists, to Jewish immigration and to a National Home for the people of Israel in the land of Israel.'[109] Generally speaking, Elmaleh and the Zionists exerted little energy to attempt to convert non-Jews to their cause, which was perhaps an acknowledgement that any such attempt along these lines would have been largely fruitless. The situation in Lebanon appears to have been different from elsewhere: the vast majority of the delegations interviewed by the King–Crane Commission (just under 80 per cent) offered no opinion on Zionism.[110] Though Elmaleh did not have access to these numbers, he concluded optimistically in his final report to the Zionist Commission that: 'All the Lebanon together with the parties which support France in the coastal cities of Syria, favour Jewish immigration and do not place obstacles in its way.'[111] While the former conclusion ('favour Jewish immigration') was not supported by the testimony given to the commission, the latter conclusion ('do not place obstacles in its way') was more in line with what the commission observed. It seems that few of the people questioned by the commission in Lebanon considered Palestine's future relevant to their political situation.

The British and the French, as the commission noted, employed different kinds of influence in the region. The British, being the monetary backer of Faysal's government, conducted their occupation with a relatively light hand and were successful in keeping anti-British sentiment to a minimum. Although the commission noted occasional interference by British officers in the region, this work was rarely seen as blatant by commission members. The French had larger troubles: anti-French sentiment was widespread by the time the commission arrived, and this sentiment was emphatically voiced to the commission members. While it is true that the commission did not look favourably upon the French presence in the region, they read the anti-French sentiment they witnessed as legitimate and overwhelming. After seeing a large number of delegations in Lebanon, for example, Lybyer declared that despite having spent 'large sums', the French had 'won practically no Moslems and only part of the Christians'.[112] It was an inauspicious beginning for a country that hoped to occupy the region for the foreseeable future.

Many historians commenting on this era have focused almost exclusively on the presence of propaganda and coercion by Faysal and the various nationalist groups throughout Greater Syria. Based on the evidence reviewed here, the Syrian nationalists (themselves far from monolithic) did appear to be the largest but were far from the only group conducting propaganda in the region during the visit of the King–Crane Commission. Interestingly, agents of the many competing political projects in the region often protested each other's actions as being somehow dishonest and contemptible despite engaging in similar activities themselves. Such posturing is a normal part of a moment of political upheaval (indeed it would have been more unusual had it not occurred), yet it is wrong to say that it was either the exclusive domain of the various nationalists of the region or that the opinions that were produced by it were somehow less genuine than they would have otherwise been (with the occasional moments of physical coercion excepted). The people, or at least the elites of the region, made calculated political decisions in 1919: they had to decide whom to support in the politically charged postwar atmosphere and take a stand that they believed would positively influence their respective futures. These were decisions made at a particularly contentious moment by people well-versed in the complex political structures of the late Ottoman Empire and need to be taken seriously in this context.

The commission's time in Greater Syria was certainly the most intensive part of their trip but it was also only one segment of their expected itinerary. They headed to Istanbul to regroup, begin writing their 'Report upon Syria' and figure out the best way to learn 'the desires of the people' in the other parts of the Ottoman lands.

CHAPTER 8

ISTANBUL, PARIS AND THE RECOMMENDATIONS

The commission departed for Istanbul exhausted and a scene from the ship gives insight into their rare moments of relaxation: 'In the cabin here Dr. King and Brodie and Moore are reading, Mr. Crane and Captain Yale are playing solitaire, Dr. Haddad, our Arabic interpreter from Beirut is dozing, and Montgomery is feeding a victrola [record player].'[1] The commission arrived in Istanbul on 23 July and settled into Constantinople College to continue their work.

In general, it is hard to disagree with William Yale's later assessment of the commission's work in Istanbul as 'quite unimportant' relative to its work in Syria.[2] Many factors combined to lessen their desire and ability to travel beyond Istanbul, so the commission attempted to find residents of the city who represented the interests of Anatolia's different regions and groups. While the commission could be accused of seeing an imperfect sample of Greater Syria's population, the Anatolian delegations were certainly far less 'representative'. This was apparent in their final report: in relation to their Syria findings, the commission's recommendations for Turkey (not to mention Mesopotamia) were based on relatively little data. After a couple weeks in Istanbul, they had all but decided that they would not continue their travels in the region. This left them with the final task of finishing their report and then delivering it to Paris and Washington.

Istanbul

After their arrival in Istanbul, many of the commission members were engaged in the writing of their final report on Greater Syria, though they also spent much time consulting with the city's Americans and interviewed numerous local delegations. According to King, they worked on the 'Syria' portion of their report from 23 July to 8 August, taking breaks to see delegations within that period. This was followed by the writing of the 'Mesopotamia' report (9 to 14 August) and the 'Turkey' report (14 to 21 August).[3] King, Lybyer, Brodie, Haddad and Toren worked together to compile the data from Greater Syria (recounted in the previous chapter) and write the report, with King and Lybyer doing most of the writing. In Lybyer's words, 'Brodie prepared summary tables and comments, I wrote a brief history, and Dr. King wrote the recommendations. With these also I have helped, by frequent consultations en route.' Crane seemed to have had little patience for this portion of the commission's work and went 'to town a great deal' rather than working on the report. When he was with King and Lybyer, he 'approved and advised at various junctures' and made 'additions and improvements'.[4] After they had nearly finished writing the report, Lybyer noted at a dinner that 'King contributes the morality, and I the territoriality of the report'. King chimed in that Crane had added the 'geniality'.[5] Yale, being largely in disagreement with the recommendations that were being written, was given little work to do on the report but did attend a number of the interviews the commission conducted in Istanbul.[6] According to George Montgomery, Lybyer was the most influential adviser: '[I] didn't do very much work on the writing. Lybyer did a lot and the reports are more according to his view of things that [sic] according to Yale's or mine.'[7] After the recommendations on Syria were finished, King and Lybyer collaborated on the Turkey report and the Mesopotamia report (which was initially envisioned as 'a short appendix to the report on Syria').[8]

When they arrived in Istanbul, further travel was a distinct possibility and most members of the commission expected that they still had another couple months of wandering ahead of them. There was discussion about going to Mesopotamia and into the interior of Anatolia, but this increasingly became half-hearted talk for a number of reasons. These included fatigue and illness among the commission members, family issues (Lybyer learned upon arriving in Istanbul that his wife had serious health problems) and the commission's dwindling funds (they would need to be reauthorised to spend more if they wished to travel further). By early August, the commission had all but given up on the possibility of more travel, with Lybyer stating 'Crane averse to further travel – wishes to go to Paris soon. Kg. no longer talks of going to Mesopotamia – doubtful about interior of Asia Minor.'[9] King cabled the leadership in Paris on 6 August that the commission intended 'to finish their task within the current month' (a timeline that just about precluded further travel) and the American commissioners at the peace conference approved this plan.[10] Unbeknown to the commission members, the American leadership in Paris had decided, on 2 August, that it was time to recall nearly all 'field missions', including the King–Crane Commission.[11] On 15 August, they sent a cable to Istanbul asking the commission to leave for Paris 'not later than September first'.[12] Although the commission knew that returning to Paris without further travel in the Ottoman lands would handicap their ability to write solid reports about Turkey and Mesopotamia, both their dwindling enthusiasm and the decisions made by the American leadership in Paris truncated their time in the region.

After about a week of work on the 'Report upon Syria', the commission began seeing delegations again and continued to do this intermittently throughout their time in Istanbul. The individuals and groups interviewed in Istanbul were diverse and had a somewhat different character than those of Greater Syria. Like in Greater Syria, they interviewed many religious leaders. Primarily though, the list of interviewees consisted mostly of the following: Ottoman governors and officials; leaders of numerous political parties; newspaper editors; groups of Kurds, Georgians, Armenians and Greeks; and other people thought to be somehow representative of different portions of Anatolia.[13] Throughout their time in Istanbul, the full commission was usually not involved in interviewing these delegations. Crane and Montgomery conducted many of the interviews, with Montgomery doing 'most of the questioning' and 'Crane often inattentive'.[14] While most of the commission members were exhausted and ready to leave Istanbul, Crane seemed to be the leader in this domain.

On 31 July, the commission members interviewed many prominent Turks and 'surprised' a number of the delegates by questioning them about the 'Armenian massacres' instead of asking about their political desires. Reflecting the deep impression that the events surrounding the Armenians made on Americans during the war, the commissioners were fixated on learning the answers to the following questions:

- What had been done to 'punish those most responsible' for the massacres?
- What was being done to 'help to restore the Armenians (or other deported populations) to their home and property'?
- Could the Turks guarantee 'the safety and rights of Armenians' in the future?[15]

King explained to one of the Turkish delegations that the commission 'does not wish to set apart an area in which [a] minority of Armenians shall rule [a] majority of others – but an area must be set aside in which Armenians will not be under [the] rule of the Turks'. 'It seems to us', he continued, 'that all of the other problems of the Turkish Empire are obscured by this, and this must be cleared up.'[16] To the list of concerns about the Armenians, the commission would often add that 'the world' needed to be sure that 'the straits will be kept open', thus insinuating that the Dardanelles and the Bosphorus would likely need to be placed under the control of some international guarantor.[17]

In response, the Turkish elites interviewed by the commission almost uniformly contended that the Turkish people should not be punished for what happened to the Armenians during the war. Some Turks acknowledged that they were ultimately to blame for what had happened to the Armenians, with one Turkish university professor, for example, telling Lybyer that Turks were 'tolerant' but 'had been provoked' and then 'made mistakes'.[18] Most Turks, however, did not admit to this level of culpability. For example, a group of Ottoman officials argued before the commission that:

> The question of the Armenian massacres is very complicated; the Armenian side only has been heard. They have had the ears of the world and have conducted great propaganda. It is true that massacres of Armenians took place, but were all in the nature of reprisals, and more Turkish lives than Armenian were sacrificed in this feud. Neither we nor the Turkish nation are responsible for the

deportations. It was the C.U.P. organization, a group of ten or twenty men. The Turkish people were unable to prevent this. They were paralyzed by martial law, dying of cold and illness, not aware of what was going on, and deceived about it afterwards.[19]

Furthermore, according to many Turkish delegations, Wilsonian principles dictated that Turks should be allowed to remain in control of their own fate and not be controlled by an Armenian minority anywhere in Anatolia. One group, for example, noted that there did not exist 'in the territory of the Empire, any region where the Armenians were in the majority, either at the present time, before the war, or even since the founding of the Ottoman State'. Thus, according to President Wilson's principles, they could not (and the world should not) accept a state in which the Armenians ruled over Turks because it would mean 'the domination of a minority over a majority' that would 'inevitably provoke the continuation of disturbances'.[20] Along these same lines, prominent Young Turk Ahmet Riza Pasha argued to the commission that Wilson's principles had to be applied universally or no one was obliged to abide by them. 'We do not wish to be more Catholic than the Pope', he pointedly quipped, and continued by arguing that 'the majority has a right to rule in any country'. King, probably incensed, 'asked how the majority came to exist' insinuating that the massacres had created some of these majorities. Lybyer reported that Riza Pasha gave 'no direct answer' to this.[21]

The Turks rarely mentioned the topic of which country should take a mandatory for Anatolia but when pressed, a few delegations requested that the United States take this mandatory. Such was the general tenor of the testimony by the selected Turkish elites in Istanbul: they argued that they should not be punished for anything that happened during the war because the war was conducted by unpopular and incompetent leaders who were now out of power. Knowing that they were in front of Americans, they also prominently employed Wilsonian rhetoric to support their contention that Turkey should remain independent. One major miscalculation they made, however, was underestimating the 'deep and painful impression' that the Armenian massacres had made on the American populace and hence the Americans in front of them.[22] Although the commission members were still debating how exactly Anatolia should be split, it was clear to them that the Turks were not fit to govern any of it in the near future. Turkish testimony to the contrary played little role in the commission's final recommendations.

The commission also saw a number of Armenian delegations in Istanbul and these delegations knew that they had allies among this group of Americans. The Armenians interviewed were unanimous in their anger towards the Turks and did not think that there was a chance of living together peacefully with them. 'Under no pretext whatever', one Armenian petitioner stated, 'must our fate be associated with that of the Turks.'[23] Most of them believed that they needed protection from the Turks: 'The only way to prevent more bloodshed', stated members of the Armenian Hunchak party (a group advocating Armenian independence), 'is military occupation' by a foreign power. This power needed only to 'add a few troops', they argued, and then the Armenians could begin to form their new country without fear from the Turks.[24] Many of the Armenians interviewed were confident that an Armenian state could easily govern itself after such protection was afforded, but some were not so confident about this. The 'Gregorian Patriarch' of Istanbul, for example, stated that 'the Armenian nation had been under the Turk for six hundred years and is not now in a position to take up the art of government'. 'The Mandatory Power', he continued, 'should get them together and teach them the art of government. They are advanced and educated and it might not take long.'[25] Many of these delegations noted that the makeup of the new country would likely be problematic, with issues such as the blending of competing political ideologies, the mixing of Russian and Turkish Armenians, and the presence of other non-Turkish people such as the Kurds all adding to the complexity of the new state.[26] Throughout this testimony, both the commission and the Armenians were unwavering in support for the creation of a substantial new Armenian state in eastern Anatolia but were also cognisant of the fact that it would be a difficult undertaking.

The commission also saw a varied array of people representing other groups in the Ottoman lands. The Kurds interviewed by the commission uniformly sought greater autonomy, with two Kurdish leaders from Kirkuk and Sulaymaniyah stating that the Kurds were 'hurt' by 'much talk of Armenia and little talk of Kurdistan'.[27] The 'Kurdish Democratic Party' rather grandly requested 'a Kurdish government in the districts where Kurds are in a great majority', which meant 'Kharput, Diarbekir, Van, Bitlis, part of Erzerum (Bayazid), and all of Mosul, together with an outlet to the sea'. Temporarily, however, they were happy to have a mandatory power and requested 'autonomy' within 'a British mandate as a part of Irak'. They further stated that they 'would like to exchange' any Armenians within the new borders of Kurdistan 'for the Kurds in Armenia' and also denied that Kurds had anything to do with the Armenian massacres.[28] A number of Greek delegations argued that the coast of Turkey should belong to Greece ('the whole coast is truly Greek') and that the Greek populations of Turkey could no longer get along with the Turks.[29] A 'Greek Smyrna Committee' claimed that the Greeks were not to blame for the problems after the Greek troops had landed in Smyrna in May; it was instead the culmination of 'trouble' that had been in existence 'for six hundred years'.[30] A Greek lawyer told the commission that if the Sultan was removed, the Greeks would take a larger role in society and act as 'a means for the diffusion of American civilization and ideals' in Anatolia.[31] The commission also saw Georgian, Chaldean and Assyrian delegations who each asked for protection and varying levels of autonomy, with there being palpable enmity between the Kurds and the Assyrians. Based on the fact that they were vying for the same lands, the Assyrians asked that they be 'kept as a separate nation', whereas the Kurdish delegation stated that the Assyrians were 'not entitled to separate territory because they are nowhere in the majority'.[32] In all of this testimony, the degree to which conceptions of ethnic nationalism had gained prominence among the elites of the Ottoman Empire at this point is striking. People who were part of an Ottoman whole for centuries now decreed that their ethnic identities made them deserving of an autonomous state.

Beyond the delegations from the Ottoman Empire, the commission members also sought advice from prominent Americans and Europeans living in Istanbul. Most Americans in the city seemed to be supportive of the United States taking 'absolutely the whole of Turkey under a single mandate'.[33] Admiral Mark Bristol appears to have been quite influential in the writing of the Turkish section of the commission's final report and his views on the Turks were more favourable than many of the other ex-patriots in Istanbul. Bristol originally advocated 'the unity of whole [Ottoman Empire], w. Syr. and Mesopot'. Later, however, Lybyer reported that he and King were 'trying to reach common ground' with Bristol, even allowing Bristol to comment on drafts of the Turkey report. He negotiated with Lybyer and King as to what would be written, yielding to a partition of the empire (the cleaving off of a 'small Armenia' and Syria) but holding firm 'for Turks [to remain in power] in Consple.'[34] Mary Mills Patrick (head of the Constantinople College) composed a document in January 1919 that contained her views about the reapportioning of the Ottoman lands and had sent it to her College's main benefactor, Charles Crane. Her opinion, which appears to have remained the same six months on, was that there should be 'an American Mandatory over all the Turkish Empire', though 'with the possible exception of Mesopotamia and Southern Palestine'. The people of the Ottoman Empire, she believed, trusted the United States 'to retire and leave them their independence' after 'having taught the people how to govern themselves'.[35] Mary Graffam, a missionary at Sivas who had remained at her station throughout the war, gave the commission a heart-wrenching account of what she had witnessed during the Armenian massacres and expounded on the poor state of the Armenians who remained in Sivas. Repatriation was impossible, according to Graffam, because if an Armenian man were to return to his city, he would find that 'his women are in one Turkish house, his rugs are in another, and the Turks hold his land'. She insisted that the only solution was to separate the Turks and Armenians. 'It is past human imagination', she continued, 'to leave them together.'[36] George White, President of Anatolia College in Marsovan, told the commission that a settlement needed to be reached quickly because Mustafa Kemal had been 'inflaming all the Turks to a campaign of bloodshed, spoliation, and warfare with all Christians'.[37] Sir Edwin Pears, who they had spoken with on their previous stop in Istanbul, told the commission rather bluntly that 'the sooner the Turks become a governed race, or even become extinct as a race[,] the better'. 'The best means to do this', he continued, 'is to establish Christian States within the confines of Anatolia', citing the Greeks of Istanbul and the Anatolian coast (rather than the 'Hellenes' from Greece) as the most capable of doing this.[38] The mixture of opinions among expatriates, as indicated by these five, was diverse, but few were sympathetic to the Turks.

The commission members' time in Istanbul was comfortable and without major incidents. Laurence Moore's run of bad luck continued when he was hit by a car on 6 August. He was badly 'bruised-head, shoulder, hand, and especially [in the] neighborhood of the knee', and also suffered 'temporary aphasia'. He remained on bed rest throughout most of their time in Istanbul.[39] The commission was treated well by Mary Mills

Patrick, and the staff of Constantinople College was under instructions to 'do everything possible to please' their main benefactor Charles Crane.[40] Crane, only somewhat interested in the toil of report writing at this point, travelled to Bursa on 16 August in order to see Sheikh Ahmad Sharif as-Senussi, a prominent Sufi sheikh from northern Africa (Egypt/Libya) who had come for the coronation of Sultan Mehmed VI the previous year and had not yet left. Crane came back apparently enthused by his interview with the Sheikh and insisted on adding a paragraph in the final report about the success of the Senussi desert kingdom.[41] As noted earlier, William Yale was not given much to do in the final writing of the report and was 'beg[g]ing to live in [a] hotel at Prinkipo [Buyukada, an island close to Istanbul]'.[42] Yale did later protest that the report should include 'more discussion' of the 'possible division of Syria', in line with his opinions, though he knew the report was not going to recommend this.[43] In general, their time wound down amicably and they were all happy to move on from the commission by the time they left.

On 21 August, the commission boarded an American destroyer (the USS *Dupont*) and headed back to Paris. At Crane's request, they stopped at a monastery near Mount Athos in Greece that he had previously visited in 1911. They went ashore, toured the monastery, and were enchanted by the monk choir.[44] Lybyer noted, with some surprise, that the monks did not even allow 'female animals' in the monastery. Also on board the ship was an executive from Standard Oil who discussed the impending battle for oil rights in the region with them, and the attractive niece of the Russian White Army General Anton Denikin. Yale immediately gravitated towards her. The ever-diligent Henry Churchill King isolated himself in the captain's cabin and took primary responsibility for putting the finishing touches on the reports, consulting with the rest of the commission on various drafts. They landed in Venice on 24 August and visited with King's son, who was a chaplain on an American ship moored there. From Venice, they took a train to Paris on 26 August, arriving the following day.[45]

Paris

When the commission reached Paris, American influence at the conference had waned. President Wilson was back in the United States facing a stiff political battle to get Senate approval of the Versailles

Treaty and hence American entry into the League of Nations. King and Crane presented the 'Report upon Syria' to the American delegation at the Paris Peace Conference on 28 August, and later cabled a summary of their findings to Wilson (31 August).[46] The other sections of the report were finalised shortly thereafter and Joseph Grew had 20 copies of the final document made for the State Department.[47] The commissioners also gave an interview to a *New York Times* reporter in Paris during which they hinted at but did not explicitly reveal their findings.[48] Although the British and the French were not given copies of the report, the British were allowed to read it and take 'copious notes' and the French were at least aware of its content.[49] The commission knew that their report had the potential to cause controversy, with Charles Crane stating that he believed their efforts were 'worthwhile' but that the report would 'not make us any friends'.[50]

The commission members remained on good terms with each other despite enduring such an arduous journey and being in fairly strong disagreement about their recommendations. They continued to dine together and spoke frequently while in Paris. Crane decided to go to Prague to visit his good friend Thomas Masaryk, who had recently been elected as the first President of Czechoslovakia, and his son Richard, who had been named the first American minister to the new country. Yale, who was still busy 'entertaining' General Denikin's niece, stayed on to do further work at the peace conference. King, Lybyer, Montgomery and Brodie sailed for the United States together on 6 September, and Brodie delivered the report to the White House on 27 September.[51] President Wilson, however, had shown signs of extreme fatigue in Colorado two days earlier and returned to Washington to rest. He suffered a stroke on 2 October.[52] Although Wilson may never have read the King–Crane Commission Report, he would likely have been aware of the commission's general conclusions from the several earlier telegrams the commissioners had sent. The report remained in bureaucratic limbo for over three years and was not publicised or published until December 1922.

Three Sets of Recommendations

As has been noted, the five most important commission members did not agree about the recommendations they should make to Wilson, and the commission produced three sets of recommendations in total: one official and two internal. The two internal documents came from Yale and Montgomery, whose differences of opinion with King, Crane and Lybyer had surfaced on a number of occasions during their trip. After they left Greater Syria, William Yale and George Montgomery each wrote a memorandum to the commissioners that gave their opinions about the future divisions of Greater Syria. They submitted these on 26 July.

As will be further analysed in Chapters 9 and 10, William Yale believed that the unity of opinion in the region was an illusion manufactured by a small cadre of 'Young Arabs' who sought to create an intolerant regime in which Muslims would dominate all minorities. Yale argued that promises made to the Jews and the French during the war should be kept and that this could be done without much trouble. He recommended the following:

- Greater Syria should not remain unified because 'Syrian nationalism' was very weak.
- Faysal, being an outsider and 'not a strong enough personality', had little ability to rule the region and would need a strong mandatory power to keep him in office. For lack of better options, inland Syria should be an Arab state under Faysal with the League of Nations holding the mandate.
- Palestine should 'be separated from Syria and constituted as a National Home for the Jewish People under the Mandate of Great Britain'.
- Lebanon should be separated politically and placed under a French mandate.
- Though Greater Syria should be split politically, there should be no economic barriers between these new countries.[53]

Similarly, George Montgomery did not believe that the Muslims of Greater Syria could form a tolerant, modern government. He also thought that many other factors needed to be taken into consideration when making decisions about the region, such as grander geopolitical concerns and the ability of the Jews to modernise Palestine. In his 'Report on Syria', Montgomery stated the following:

- Greater Syria could not and should not be unified because a Syrian national character did not exist and religious antagonisms were too strong in the region.

- The commission should not recommend that the United States become a mandatory power in Greater Syria because it was highly unlikely that the United States would accept such a mandate.
- Britain should be given the mandate for an independent Palestine and the French should be given the mandate for an independent Lebanon.
- The Zionist programme should be supported because of the benefit it would bring to the region.
- Syria should be 'administered with Prince Feisal as Amir under a joint mandate to France and Great Britain'.[54]

At some point during his time in Istanbul, Montgomery also wrote a report for Anatolia and Armenia, though the only copy in his papers is unfinished. In this, he recommended that a large Armenia should be established in eastern Anatolia and the Caucasus under an American mandate with ports on both the Mediterranean and the Black Sea. He also recommended that the League of Nations should decide who would receive the mandate for a Constantinopolan state and a much reduced Turkish state in Anatolia.[55] These memoranda were read and lightly annotated by King and Lybyer, but had little bearing on the commission's final report.

The King–Crane Commission Report (officially the *Report of the American Section of the International Commission on Mandates in Turkey*) expressed the opinions of Henry Churchill King, Charles Crane and Albert Lybyer. The three sections of the report were very different. The Syria section contained statistical analysis of the petitions they received while visiting the region. The Turkey section, for which they saw a number of delegations in Istanbul, had nothing of the sort. They admittedly had very little data for the Mesopotamia section so it was relatively short and gave little context for its recommendations. They also added a more candid appendix 'For Use of Americans Only' in which they placed information that they thought might cause diplomatic discomfort in Paris. The following is a brief summary of their recommendations, the justifications for which will be analysed in the following chapters.

Syria
- A single mandatory power should be assigned to a unified Greater Syria and, as per petitioners' requests, the United States should be the first choice to help steward the country towards democracy and

independence. Great Britain should be given the mandate if the United States did not accept the responsibility. Lebanon should be given 'a large measure of local autonomy' within this new country.
- Amir Faysal should be the head of this new state, which should be a 'constitutional monarchy along democratic lines'.
- France should not be granted a mandate in the region, though if it was politically necessary, a French mandate in Lebanon would be the best compromise.
- The Zionist programme should be significantly curtailed because of strong sentiment against it.[56]

Turkey and Armenia
- The United States should receive the mandate for the newly created 'International Constantinopolitan State' that would remain an independent international territory under the jurisdiction of the League of Nations.
- The United States should also receive mandates for a Turkish state in Anatolia and an Armenian state with an outlet on the Black Sea. Greece should be given no territory in Anatolia but Smyrna should be given a measure of autonomy within the new Turkish state.[57]

Mesopotamia
- Mesopotamia should remain unified and should be constituted of (at least) the Ottoman vilayets of Basra, Baghdad and Mosul. Further territory to the north of Mosul could also be included.
- Great Britain should receive the Mesopotamia mandate, and the government should be a constitutional monarchy under one of Sharif Hussein's sons.[58]

In all three sections, the commissioners emphatically argued that a mandate should not be treated as a colony. The mandatory power's duty was to 'educate' the people of these regions in 'self-government' and help them create 'a democratic state' that protected its minorities. The mandates would help to develop an 'intelligent' citizenry with a 'strong national feeling' whose overarching goal was 'the progress of the country'.[59] The appendix of the report summarised the 'interference' with their work by the French, British and Arabs, along with summarising many of the main arguments for and against the more contentious issues they tackled, such as Zionism and French claims in Syria.[60]

Aftermath

With the submission of the report, the commission's work was finished. It seems that the only place that the existence of the King–Crane Commission had any tangible impact was in Greater Syria. As has been noted by James Gelvin, the commission had the effect of raising hopes in Greater Syria, with Faysal and the 'Westernised nationalist elites' who sided with him staking their credibility on its outcome. When it appeared that the commission was going to have little impact on decisions made in Paris, the people of the region's confidence in Faysal and his allies waned significantly and a more populist nationalism emerged.[61] The commission had even less impact in Paris, where the report was all but ignored, and the United States had little say in either of the subsequent settlements for the Ottoman Lands (the Treaties of Sevres and Lausanne). American influence in the region, which seemed to be on the rise with the advent of the King–Crane Commission, remained relatively minimal in the years immediately following the war. By the end of 1919, the British withdrew from the parts of Greater Syria most coveted by the French, and the French occupied Damascus in July 1920, marking the beginning of a bitter occupation. The British Mandate in Palestine fared little better, with violence involving Arabs, Zionists and occupying forces escalating throughout the 1920s and 1930s. In Anatolia, the showdown between the resurgent Turks and the advancing Greek army escalated into a vicious war. The Turks eventually defeated the Greeks and established the new nation of Turkey.[62] The commission members watched these developments with great dismay.[63]

The members of the commission folded back into their normal civilian lives, though requests by people who wished to discuss their time on the commission forced them to revisit it on occasion. In November 1919, King received a request to give testimony in the Senate 'on the question of mandates' but he stated that he could not do this without the consent of President Wilson, having given an unsolicited pledge to Wilson (along with Crane) not to discuss the commission's findings.⁶⁴ There were occasional clamours from the public too: on 6 December 1919, for example, historian and prominent Zionist Richard Gottheil wrote a letter to *The New York Times* wondering why the report 'should lie upon some table or in some drawer in the State Department and not be made public'.⁶⁵ In 1921, historian Stephen Duggan sent an official request to the State Department to see the report but the request was denied.⁶⁶ The findings of the commission did manage to seep into the public sphere to a small degree. For example, the report's general conclusions were mentioned in an article from *The New York Times* on 5 April 1920 entitled 'Only America can save Armenia' and in a 1 August 1920 letter to the editor in the same paper from scholar H.I. Katibah.⁶⁷ Additionally, in the April 1921 *Journal of International Relations*, historian Stephen Duggan wrote that although the commission's findings had never been published, 'the newspaper accounts and the reports of eyewitnesses of the Mission's work enable one to arrive at a conclusion that is probably not far removed from that of the official report'. He also discussed the rise of Arab animosity towards the presence of the Zionists and the French in Greater Syria.⁶⁸ King and Crane were exasperated that their findings were not public knowledge but they kept their pledge to stay quiet.

In 1922, Ray Stannard Baker was in the midst of organising Wilson's papers for a book when he realised that Wilson did not have the copy of the King–Crane Commission Report turned in by Brodie.⁶⁹ Baker requested a copy of the report from Crane, who passed the request on to King (who apparently had the only copies). King still insisted that they get Wilson's permission to forward a copy of the report to Baker and, on 6 July 1922, Crane made this request to Wilson. Wilson immediately consented stating 'I have no objection to Baker's making public the Report on Syria. Indeed I think this is a very timely moment for its publication.'⁷⁰ Baker used the report as the basis for a chapter in his book about the peace conference, and this chapter was serialised in *The New York Times* on 20 August 1922 with an accompanying article briefly summarising the report's findings. This article caught the eye of James W. Brown, the editor of the trade publication *Editor and Publisher*. Brown, a self-proclaimed advocate of Wilsonian ideals, decided to publish the full report in his newspaper, believing that it would 'render a service to American editorial writers'. Brown received permission to publish the report from Wilson and he commissioned William T. Ellis, a journalist with experience in the Middle East, to write an introduction. Crane was first made aware that this was going to happen on 21 November, after which he shared the news with King.[71] It was published in *Editor and Publisher* on 2 December 1922 and then in *The New York Times* on 3 and 4 December. Donald Brodie, who had become Crane's personal secretary, immediately ordered 20,000 copies of the *Editor and Publisher* edition to be distributed to universities worldwide.[72]

The King–Crane Commission Report stirred controversy immediately after its publication, with a number of newspaper editors and other commentators debating the merits of its recommendations. On the same day that Ray Stannard Baker's article appeared in *The New York Times* (20 August 1922), the paper's editorial page declared that earlier publication of the 'exhumed' report 'might have helped to prevent' the trouble that seemed to be engulfing Greater Syria.[73] Shortly after this, the *New York Evening Post* published an editorial about the commission that expressed admiration for the commission's work but noted that it had 'not considered whether the folks at home [...] were in the frame of mind to accept their recommendations' and also had not given sufficient weight to the various wartime agreements when writing the report. Additionally, the editorial stated that 'for fuller light on the whole problem [...] it might be desirable to give to the public the minority report by Captain William Yale'. Donald Brodie replied to this assertion in a letter to the editor of the *Evening Post*, stating that Yale's report was not a 'minority report' but merely a memorandum written 'in order to assist the commissioners' in writing their final recommendations.[74] Albert Lybyer eventually sent the editor of the *Post* copies of both Yale's and Montgomery's reports for publication, though the editor never published them.[75] Lybyer also provided these two reports to several historians who requested them, including William Westermann who, in a January 1923 letter, curtly informed Lybyer that he believed the commission's recommendations to be irrelevant because they failed to take into account the 'existent political desires [of Britain and France] which could not be conjured away'.[76] Prominent American Zionist Samuel Untermyer also wrote an article in the influential current events journal *The Forum* shortly after the report's publication in which he called the commission's conclusions 'without value' and 'biased'.[77] The commission members decided not to be drawn into public debate about their recommendations, with Lybyer stating in 1923 that the report 'was now a historical document'.[78] The controversy about the commission's recommendations, however, had only just begun.

CHAPTER 9

ACCOUNTING FOR THE DIFFERENCES 1: THE ABILITY TO BECOME MODERN

Beginning in the immediate aftermath of its report being made public, scholars have drawn many different and often partisan conclusions about the King–Crane Commission. Few of these scholars, however, have taken the time to consult the archival materials of the commission members and even fewer have focused on the disagreement within the commission. The following two chapters constitute a comprehensive assessment of the rationales behind the commission members' recommendations and are based on an extensive examination of their archival materials. These chapters aim to analyse why the five main members of the commission came to their respective and disparate conclusions. More specifically, these chapters will attempt to determine what accounted for the differences of opinion between the commission members who were primarily responsible for the report (King, Crane and Lybyer, with some sympathetic additional writings by Donald Brodie) and for the dissent expressed within the commission (Yale and Montgomery). Although these chapters will compare the commission members' opinions on a number of different topics, the two primary areas of disagreement between the commission members were as follows:

- They disagreed on the respective abilities of various groups in the Ottoman lands to become modern.

- They disagreed on the best way to implement Wilsonian ideals in the Ottoman lands and, in some cases, differed on the applicability of these ideals to the region.

Chapter 9 will primarily cover the first of these two areas and Chapter 10 will cover the second, as well as a few other significant factors in their decision making.

***

As noted in Chapter 2, the King–Crane Commission members arrived in the Middle East instilled with a particularly Americanised Western social imaginary in which issues pertaining to modernity, race and religion factored heavily. As part of this social imaginary, the commission members had internalised the following three conceptions of the world:

- The United States (and, to a slightly lesser extent, certain European nations) represented the zenith of modernity and should be seen as the model towards which the rest of the world should progress.
- The world's population could be organised into a hierarchy of races, with 'Anglo-Saxons' occupying the top slot.
- Protestant Christianity represented the world's highest form of religion.

It is hardly surprising, as this chapter will argue, that these three conceptions played a major role in determining the commission members' recommendations about the future of a region occupied largely by Turkish and Arab Muslims living 'traditional' lifestyles. Yet the region was home to many different groups that the commission members saw as having different inherent abilities, whether this came from their racial background or from the religion they practised (or a combination of the two). Importantly, the commission members were not entirely in accord about the relative potentials of these groups, which was one of the main causes of disagreement within the commission. The point of departure for this chapter, then, is an analysis of the commission members' agreements and disagreements about the ability of the region's various groups to become modern.

The Commission Members' Definition of Modernity

All of the King–Crane Commission members defined modernity in a similar fashion and this shared definition is largely summarised in a passage from the King–Crane Commission Report. As part of their general argument in favour of an American mandate for Anatolia, the authors of the report offered the following summary of modernity's components:

> This general statement, indeed, may be said to include the specific reasons why Turkey should have a mandate: to secure genuinely good government, without oppression, bribery, or corruption, for the Turks themselves; to guarantee the rights of all minorities – racial or religious; to deliver Turkey from the demoralization of the incessant intrigue from outside; to secure, without selfish exploitation by the Mandatary or any other outside Power, Turkey's economic development and economic independence, for there is not the slightest doubt that she has been living far below her material possibilities; in line with the Allied settlement with Germany, to disband most of the Turkish Army and do away with military conscription, depending upon a well-organized gendarmerie for the larger police duties of the State,–all this for the better good of the common people and to break the power of intriguing imperialists over them; to put beneath all Turkish life a national system of universal education, that should lift her entire people; to train the various peoples of the State steadily into self-government; in a word, to make Turkey a state of high order on a modern basis of equal rights to all before the law, and of religious liberty. This would inevitably result in a state not purely (though predominantly) Turkish in race and in control, a cosmopolitan state in which various racial stocks were contained and in whose government all representatively share.[1]

In this definition, modernity was a system of both ideas (democracy, equality, pluralism) and institutions that established and reproduced these ideas. These institutions would include a 'system of universal education', which would implant liberal values into the population, and a 'gendarmerie' that would enforce the laws of a 'good government'.

Having these, and other, institutions in place would 'do much to assure that the abuses of the old time would not return'.[2] Donald Brodie expanded on this, noting that Faysal and his allies were 'already planning for the right kind of democratic institutions, for hospitals, schools, colleges and orphanages, as well as for purely political organizations'.[3] These organisations were necessary for the implantation, spread, and maintenance of this liberal, democratic modernity. In the minds of the commission members, the missionaries had done the region a great service by beginning to establish some of these institutions, but many more were needed.

The commission members also discussed pluralism extensively, noting that it was perhaps the most necessary feature of modernity in this diverse region. In their minds, it was possible for different groups to live together in a modern secular society, and such religious and racial diversity could even serve to strengthen a society. In the Ottoman lands, a region with a complex mix of groups, some sort of pluralistic arrangement was unavoidable. The authors of the report stated the following:

> The war and the consequent breaking up of the Turkish Empire, moreover, give a great opportunity – not likely to return – to build now in Syria a Near East State on the modern basis of full religious liberty, deliberately including Various [sic] religious faiths, and especially guarding the rights of minorities [...] The mixed and varied populations have lived together with a fair degree of unity under Turkish domination, and in spite of the divisive Turkish policy. They ought to do far better under a state on modern lines and with an enlightened mandatory.[4]

The United States, with its various sects of Christianity and its Jews, along with its various 'races' from Europe, was tacit proof that pluralism could work.[5] Universal education, no doubt in the Western style, was required to breed such a tolerant society. According to William Yale, the 'fanaticism' in the region (serving as the antithesis of tolerance) could only be 'abated by education'.[6] Although the commission members did not always agree on the people of the region's capacity for religious and ethnic tolerance (which led to some of their contrasting recommendations), they did believe that tolerance of diversity was a hallmark of any successful modern society.

Beyond these features of modernity, the commission members also elaborated on other more specific characteristics that they saw as necessary components of a modern society. In line with Marshall Hodgson's observation that advocates of modernity always pushed 'the most modern features of Western ways',[7] the authors of the report argued that the modernisation of the region's economy had to begin via improvements to the land. To do this, up-to-date methods, such as 'afforestation, modern methods of agriculture, utilization of waterpower, reclamation of wastelands, scientific irrigation, and the like', would have to be employed.[8] George Montgomery also discussed the economic shift that the region must undertake and, when arguing in favour of Zionism, contributed that the Zionists would provide 'advantage to the entire country from the increase in land values' and 'from the opportunity given to the fellaheen of earning wages'.[9] In addition, William Yale argued for more individual property rights in the region, stating that the land needed to be owned by individual farmers and not rented from 'large land holding Arab families'.[10] The suggested transplantation of an American-style society to the Middle East was near total.

In general, commission members argued that the current, seemingly feudal economic and governmental system of the region needed to be replaced by what amounted to a capitalist, agrarian economy based on the latest agricultural techniques, all backed by a 'good government'. The general characteristics of a modern society agreed upon by the commission members can be summarised as follows:

- A trustworthy, representative, and, by implication, secular government that protected the rights of minorities and women.
- A strong code of inviolable laws with a strong police force to implement and enforce these laws.
- An economic system that helped the region utilise its 'material possibilities'.
- A national education system for both general education and to ready the people for self-government.
- National sovereignty (eventually) without external interference.

Underlying their shared understanding of what constituted a modern society was a belief more central and implicit in their writings: the commission members believed that the establishment of Western-style states in the Middle East was compulsory for the region's future prosperity. The commission members were both defining modern society as superior and arguing for a major rupture with what they saw as the traditional life of the region. This move towards modernity was necessary, according to the members of the commission, even if the path to it was going to be challenging. As Charles Crane stated 'it is a very difficult matter to reconstitute the Turkish Empire in an American way.'[11]

The Move to Modernity

Members of the King–Crane Commission agreed that the Middle East was a region that still existed very much as it had in the Bible, or at least as it had since the beginning of the Islamic era, yet modernity had already found its way to the region in some significant ways that variously surprised, encouraged, and disturbed them. Within their social imaginary, history was progressive and unilinear. All societies were moving towards the future and that future was represented, in its highest form, by the United States. Most importantly though, the commission members agreed that the wholesale arrival of modernity was both necessary and inevitable; planning the best way to abet its arrival was one of the most prominent themes in their writings.

For this small group of Americans, and for most of their contemporaries with experience in the Ottoman lands, the region had been temporally stagnant for millennia and mostly still existed in an earlier historical epoch than the United States. Commission members continually referred to the people, places and general occurrences they observed as having remained unchanged for centuries. Donald Brodie, for example, emphasised the seemingly archaic farming techniques of the 'true fellahin' who farmed 'just as their fathers have done for three thousand years'.[12] Antipathies between Muslims and Christians, according to William Yale, had remained unchanged since 'the time of the Moslem conquests'.[13] 'Palestine', he stated while selectively choosing eras in support of his analysis, 'is still to them the battleground taken from the Christians by Saladin'.[14] Yale also described the 'Sheiks of Hebron' as being 'old men with flowing white beards, like characters out of the Old Testament'.[15] Charles Crane underscored his belief in the stagnation of the local way of life by referring to their mission as 'much

Figure 9.1 Delegates at Quneitra led by the mayor (centre) with commission members Laurence Moore (fifth from the left) and Montgomery (centre), 25 June, 1919. The varied styles of clothing were indicative of what the commission saw in the region. (Source: World War I Photograph Album, 1918–19, American University of Beirut/Library Archives).

like studying "human geology," if there is such a thing'[16] and to the people of Greater Syria as an 'interesting mosaic of humanity left there through the drift of ages'.[17] He wrote to his wife that Bedouin 'processes of life and actual appearances had changed little in thousands of years and Abraham himself undoubtedly looked upon similar bodies and talked with them in much the same way that we did'. In Beersheba, Crane also noted that 'the folk came in from long distances by caravan and probably that picture and the processes of barter were very old'.[18] Members of the commission seemed to believe that visiting the Middle East was as close as they could get to time travel; the vast majority of the region still existed in a previous stage of history and most of them felt privileged to be able to encounter it before it was gone.

As much as the commission members saw the movement towards modernity as inevitable, their fascination with the 'old' world was noteworthy. Charles Crane, who romanticised the Middle East more than any other commission member, observed in Jerusalem that the dignified 'turbanned men' in the city had the 'the best man's walk in the world'.[19] In Hebron, Lybyer wrote in the same vein that the many 'native delegations from all around were waiting in groups under trees, and very picturesque they were'. More specifically, he noted that the 'faces and costumes' of 'the Mufti, the chief Rabbi, the nobles and the sheikhs of the villages, etc.' would 'make a wonderful picture'.[20] He repeated this sentiment later in their journey, mentioning the 'picturesque sheikhs from Kerak' and describing the Druze delegation at Damascus as '18 splendid men'.[21] This veneration of the nobility and seeming timelessness of the region's people, and the urge to document it in photos, came from the commission members' romantic conceptions of the region but also from their general belief that this pre-modern era was passing. Photography was a way of preserving what would inevitably be gone.

This fascination with the 'old' Middle East produced a sort of antimodern longing that lingered among these Americans. Donald Brodie, for example, disapprovingly contrasted what he saw as the more authentic lifestyles of the 'true fellahin' with the 'smartly attired, French-speaking merchants' of the coastal cities who were war-profiteers and 'were frankly imitating the culture of Paris and London in their homes, their dress, and their general manner of life'.[22] Charles Crane voiced the most concern along these lines and still saw much to admire in the 'old ways' of the region. Having first visited the Middle East in 1878, Crane was disturbed at the changes he had witnessed, stating that 'the Palestine of trains and automobiles and Jews distresses me. I prefer the horses, tents and Russian pilgrims. The old color and glory have gone.'[23] Crane later wrote that 'one of the most distressing' encounters he had during his time on the commission was a conversation with a group of Damascus 'handworkers' who told him that they had not been able to find any young apprentices willing to take up their trade. Crane noted, with regret, that they were the last of the old Middle Eastern craftsmen and that their arts were now 'gone forever'. In a bazaar in Damascus, Crane further recorded that elements of the modern West were replacing vestiges of the old Middle East, with examples being a 'steamroller going up and down' a street and 'a corrugated sheet iron roof being put up'. 'The old, beautiful handmade things', Crane observed, had 'nearly vanished' from the bazaar; the shops now had modern 'glass windows exposing only western aniline dyed things looking very much like the Bowery [a déclassé New York City neighbourhood]'. He bemoaned the fact that 'Western modes and manners have put a pressure on the Near East that has been irresistible' and that 'the power of Paris has, in the matter of styles, been felt by the women and the power of London has ruled the men'.[24] The old Middle East was disappearing, according to Crane, and while he believed much of the transformation was for the best, he longed for the parts of it that had made it so different from the West.

However he may have romanticised the region, Crane (perhaps reluctantly) concurred with his fellow commission members' contention that the move to modernity was the only way for the region to achieve future prosperity. The commission members believed that modernity was not just arriving, but that it was necessarily arriving in a single package that would soon envelop the Ottoman lands. This was born out by their astonishment at observing what they would characterise as elements of modernity (such as industry or Western clothes) among seemingly ancient surroundings. Donald Brodie, for example, noted that they observed many 'startling contrasts' between what they saw as the old and the new in the region, such as 'the excellent drill in an ancient garden of an ultra-modern troop of Arab Boy Scouts'.[25] William Yale, in seeking to explicate what he saw as the confusing social nature of the region, argued that Syria was a mix of numerous types of organisations and different stages of history: 'One finds co-existent in Syria, tribal life, feudal life (religious and political feudalism), and the beginnings of modern industrial social life.' According to Yale, if the region was going to compete in the modern world, they would need to move rapidly to this latter stage of history.[26] George Montgomery predicted a homogenisation of the Middle East and lamented in a letter to his wife that 'I suppose that the time will come when visiting these places will not be very different from visiting Buffalo, Detroit and Chicago.'[27] Modernity was arriving and it was arriving in the only form with which the commission members were familiar. The singularity of modernity was firmly ingrained in their minds and recommending some different, hybrid form of modernity perhaps more suitable to the region's conditions barely seemed to have occurred to them. Having a strong mandatory power to push the people and governmental structures of the region towards modernity was, according to the authors of the report, the only conceivable recommendation they could make. 'It is in fact impossible', their final report noted, 'to discern any other method of setting Western Asia in order.'[28]

Seen in this light, the task given to the mandatory power would be arduous but the potential, or at least the possibility, of advancement

THE ABILITY TO BECOME MODERN 191

Figure 9.2 The 'ultra modern' Boy Scouts in Damascus. (Source: World War I Photograph Album, 1918–19, American University of Beirut/ Library Archives).

existed in the region. According to commission members, one of the most convincing examples that the people of the Ottoman lands were willing to accept modernity was the apparent change in the treatment of the region's Muslim women. As noted in the previous chapters, the commission saw several women's groups and were impressed by the fact that they were allowed to testify and even felt liberated enough to lift their veils in some cases. In Hebron, Lybyer also showed great surprise at the way in which a group of Muslim women were being treated:

> In the mosque were groups of veiled *women* [Lybyer's emphasis] seated receiving instruction, and men studying and praying nearby. We wonder if this is a new monument in Mohammedanism – we never saw the like before. And this is perhaps the most fanatical group of Moslems in the world.[29]

As Lybyer insinuated in this quote, the liberalisation of Islam was, perhaps, imminent if women were beginning to be treated with some degree of equality. Similarly, Donald Brodie was impressed by an incident in Damascus where 'a Moslem lady, the wife of one of the distinguished citizens of the state, stepped up on the running board [of a commission car], threw back her veil, and made several short impassioned appeals in Arabic regarding independence that were loudly cheered'.[30] Amir Faysal's attitude towards women also impressed the commission members, and the best indication of this was Crane's recounting of Faysal's stated desire 'to one day see an American women's college at Mecca. So the world is moving...'[31] Crane saw this idea as so significant that he relayed it to Woodrow Wilson as evidence of Faysal's liberal intentions, stating in the 10 July telegram to the president that Faysal 'even talks seriously of American College for women at Mecca'.[32] These indications of increasingly liberal attitudes towards women were, for many commission members, a powerful sign of the region's shift towards modernity.

Modernity in the Testimony of the Region's Groups

That the commission members were going to recommend this shift towards modernity was perhaps all but pre-ordained, but this recommendation was reinforced by some of the testimony they heard while in the region. Many of the delegations received by the commission in Greater Syria had either already internalised various discourses of modernity or employed them simply to impress the commission members. Although elements of modernity appeared sporadically in the testimony of the region's Arab delegations (both Muslim and Christian), it featured more centrally in the testimony of the Zionists.

The region's Arab delegations placed their hopes mainly on arguments based on the moralistic and anti-colonial terms laid out, in part, by Woodrow Wilson. Within this discourse, many elements of the commission's general conception of modernity were employed, like those having to do with nationalism and sovereignty. These same delegations rarely discussed the more technical aspects of modernisation like industrial development, agricultural techniques and education. Perhaps the best example of this was Amir Faysal's speech to the King–Crane Commission on 3 July. In this statement, he spoke in the modern governmental terms that the commission members wanted to hear, with statements like the following: 'The Syrians desire a Democratic Government on the decentralization principle, safeguarding the rights of minorities and maintaining local traditions.' Yet Faysal's discussion of economic modernisation was far vaguer than his discussion of government. One of the main reasons that the people of Syria did not want the French as a mandatory power, he stated (as noted in Chapter 7), was that there was a 'stagnation of industry' in other French colonies and that natives were prevented from developing their 'agricultural capacity'. Faysal also argued that the future development of the land required the continuation of free trade within the Ottoman Empire's previous borders (with free trade being both a tenet of modernity and something that had existed from 'time immemorial'). Although Faysal showed that he understood the necessity of economic development, his lack of specific testimony to this effect seemed to show that he knew little of what was required to bring this about.[33] In the existing records of testimony from other Muslim and Christian groups, little more was said about the economic aspect of modernity. The Muslim-Christian Association of Jerusalem, for example, provided what was perhaps the norm in this testimony, stating only that they would require 'specialists for everything' in the development of their country but that they could 'get them from Europe and America for our money'.[34] In the minds of the commission members, such testimony hardly showed that this group, and other groups like it, had any clear conception of what it took to become an economically developed, modern nation, which made the guidance of a mandatory power all the more necessary.

This unconvincing testimony contrasted sharply with the testimony of the Zionists. In their statements to the commission, the Zionists employed the language of modernity as one of the primary justifications of their cause. Although the Zionists largely sidestepped the issue of modern governance by asking for the British as mandatory power, they did state that they would ensure pluralism in any sort of Zionist commonwealth. 'The political rights of the Jews in Palestine', declared the Zionist delegation in Jerusalem, 'shall in no way prejudice the civil rights of the other inhabitants of the land. All the inhabitants of the land without distinction of race or religion, shall enjoy equal rights.'[35] Primarily, though, the Zionists discussed the improvements they had already made, and would continue to make, to the region's land via both their expertise in modern farming techniques and access to agricultural technology. In discussing, for example, how the region could handle the influx of a large number of Jewish immigrants, Sigfried Hoofien of the Anglo-Palestine Company told the commission that 'we assume that Palestine would be able to support on a basis of horticulture, intensive agriculture and small industries based thereon, a population of three to four million. That is what experts tell us since many years [sic].'[36] Similarly, the Zionist delegation at Jerusalem stated that 'a well planned colonisation using modern methods and instruments, could multiply many times over the number of inhabitants, and could make it possible for the settlement of even millions of new settlers'.[37] According to David Yellin, a long-time educator in Palestine and head of a Jerusalem Zionist delegation, it was almost as if the land had been waiting for them to help it reach its potential, telling the commission that 'Palestine is very sparsely populated, the land is for the most part uncultivated, and waits for cultivation and development.'[38] Indeed, the Zionists portrayed themselves and their modern ways as the saviours of the land, with a member of the Zionist delegation at Jaffa stating that 'there is no other element who will be able to return and build the country other than the Jews', which implied that the population currently inhabiting the region did not have the ability to do this.[39]

The Zionists also sought to point out that the region's Arabs had greatly benefited from the Zionist colonies, and they discussed this benefit using the vocabulary of modernity. 'The economic condition of the Arabs in the cities', the Jerusalem Zionists argued, 'has improved in a very high degree because of the growth of the Jewish settlement with its high development of industry and commerce, export and import, and the investment of valuable capital in the land'. The Arabs had also profited from the schools built by the Zionists, as 'many of the Arabs with modern education have received their schooling' in Jewish schools. The Jews had selflessly lent their medical skills 'unremittingly' to the Arabs too, with 'Jewish ophthalmic physicians' providing eye care, and several Jewish institutions treating issues as wide-ranging as rabies, cholera, and mental illness among Arabs. The Zionists expanded on this in a 'Report on the Sanitary Condition of Palestine and the part played by the Jews', which gave a short but technical description of the decline in the incidence of disease in the region since the arrival of the Zionists. Furthermore, the Jerusalem Zionists gave an example of the improvement of an Arab village in the vicinity of a Jewish colony: it was becoming modern in the 'type of its buildings, its viticulture, orchards and other agricultural activities, the use of newly imported seeds and plants, the introduction of modern agricultural instuments [sic] and machines, etc.' This village had also benefitted greatly from the 'good roads' constructed by the Jews, and some of its 'unemployed Arabs' had been able to find work in the Jewish colonies. Those villages that were not near Jewish colonies, according to the Zionists, were making no such progress.[40]

Taken as a whole, this testimony showed that the Zionists knew they had an edge when it came to economic modernity and also knew that the commission would be impressed by their work, which, as previously noted, they were. In less than 50 years, the Zionists had brought modern agriculture and medicine to the region, things that the Ottomans had struggled to do for the Arabs and the Arabs had not done in any large-scale manner for themselves. The Arab delegations could not boast of similar achievements. The Zionists portrayed themselves as modernisers and as people who would bring modernity to the region without costing a mandatory power anything. The Arabs and other people in the region would need Europeans or Americans to make the land modern for them whereas the Jews could make the land modern for themselves. Neither group, however, uniformly convinced the commission members of their intent or ability to form a modern, liberal government, which became one of the main elements of disagreement within the commission.

Middle Eastern Groups and their Fitness for Modernity

One of the most salient points in the commission members' writings is that the inherent characteristics of the region's groups would play a major role in the progression of the Ottoman lands towards modernity. Discourses pertaining to the ability of the region's various groups to form modern societies appear overtly in a number of instances and seem to be lurking just below the surface in others. In writing about the people of the Middle East, the members of the commission shared similar attitudes toward Turks and the various sects of Christians, but their opinions were more divergent when they wrote about Muslim Arabs and Jews. It should also be noted that the commission members employed religion in two ways with respect to race. Religion was usually portrayed as signifying the potential of a specific (often racial) group, with the acceptance of a particular religion (usually Christianity) being an outward sign of a group's fitness for modernity. Sometimes though, religion existed outside of race as a remedy for the inherent ills of a racial population. This section begins by recounting the commission members' fairly rare discussions about how they categorised the region's groups and then moves to a lengthy analysis of the commission members' conceptions of the various Middle Eastern groups, focusing on their beliefs about the readiness of these groups for modernity.

The commission members almost never found it necessary to explicitly explain the rationale behind their categorisation of Middle Eastern people, apparently taking many of these divisions as self-evident. For the commission members and for other Americans of the era, the Middle East was a land of many groups and the primary markers of these groups were usually listed (when they were listed at all) as 'blood', religion, language and place of origin. For example, in the Inquiry's January 1919 'Report upon Just and Practical Boundaries for Subdivisions of the Turkish Empire', William Westermann and his co-authors (which included Yale and Montgomery) provided perhaps the only overt pre-journey definition of the region's groups by Americans studying the Ottoman question, and this definition was arguably representative of the dominant American viewpoint. In this report, the authors argued that a 'nation', in its truest form, could be defined as 'peoples of one blood, fairly pure from radical [possibly meant racial] intermixture, who are massed in one given area'. The Turks, who despite being 'ethnographical hybrids', displayed the characteristics of a cohesive 'nation', as did 'the desert Arabs of the great Arabian peninsula, a people practically untouched by infiltration of foreign blood'. In acknowledging, then, that 'blood' only provided the basis for the categorisation of two groups in the region, the report's authors delved into language and religion in categorising the others, stating that:

> A Turk is a man of Mohammedan religion who speaks the Turkish language. An Arab is, generally speaking, a man of Mohammedan religion who [sic] native tongue is Arabic. Yet the Syrian Arabs are ethnographically distinct from the desert Arabs and have totally different political ambitions. An Armenian is a man who is a

member of either the Gregorian, the Catholic, or the Protestant Armenian religious organizations and speaks the Armenian tongue, whether he lives in Cilician Adana or in Erivan beyond the old Russia border.[41]

Hence, for Westermann and his co-authors, 'blood' was a primary marker of their groupings (when it had not been 'infiltrated'), but religion, language, and sometimes even living situation or 'ambitions' played major roles in separating the groups of the region.

The commission members discussed the region's groups in a similar manner. William Yale, for example, focused on the role of religion and race in his analysis of Greater Syria. He argued that the people differed 'religiously' in that there was a '"crazy quilt" of religions and sects' in the region, 'each jealous of one another, each more fanatically [sic] than the other and intolerant of all others.' He also argued that there was little 'racial' unity in Greater Syria:

> There is the pure type of Bedouin Arab, there are the town dwelling Syrians, the Lebanese who are far from Arabs, along the Hedjaz Railroad there are scattered colonies of Circassians, in Damascus there is a colony of Algerians, in the Lebanon there are Shiites of Persian origins, in the Alexandretta Region there are Turks and Armenians, and in Palestine there are Jews.'[42]

Thus Yale rarely discussed language in his categorisation of the region's groups. Instead, he alluded to the idea of 'blood' in his mention of the 'pure type of Bedouin Arab' but seemed to privilege both religion ('Shiites', 'Jews' and, more obviously, Christians and other Muslims) and a seemingly self-evident grouping of peoples based on their place of origin (Persians, Circassians, Algerians). King, Crane and Lybyer also spoke in similar terms about the groups of the region. At points, they mimicked the religio-linguistic view of the region's social divisions, reserving the term Turk for 'those persons whose mother-tongue is Turkish and who profess the Mohammedan religion'. At other points, however, language played a lesser and somewhat confusing role in their classification. In Cilicia, for example, they stated that the Arabs were 'mainly Turkish-speaking, but are chiefly Nusairiyeh or Alouites' and the Armenians were also 'chiefly Turkish-speaking'.[43] In general, specifically defining the groups they were observing was not a major concern for the commission members. It was obvious to them that there were religious, linguistic and somewhat muddled racial divisions in the region. The commission members tended to give primacy to the grander religious labels (Muslims, Christians and Jews), unless a different classification suited a particular recommendation they wanted to make.

Christians

Before they left for the Middle East, the commission members all appeared to harbour strong pro-Christian beliefs. By the end of their time in the region this had not changed: the commission members agreed about the general qualities of Middle Eastern Christians even as they disagreed on the future disposition of the regions in which these Christians formed a large portion of the population. In numerous documents, the commission members portrayed Christians as a minority who were past and potential victims of Muslims (either Arab or Turk), placing the duty of protecting the region's vulnerable Christians in the hands of the Western (Christian) nations. The commission members also generally depicted Christians as more Western and as somehow more able to spread modernity to the Ottoman lands, despite often voicing disappointment with the Christians they observed while in the region. This general agreement, however, did not lead to homogeneous recommendations. Although they all believed that a new, rather large Armenian state should be formed, they disagreed about issues pertaining to the Greeks and whether or not Lebanon should be separated from Greater Syria.

The manner in which the commission members discussed Christians was fairly uniform and was similar to the way that they discussed Muslims. The word 'Christian' was used as a blanket term for all sects of Christianity in the region and, in their recommendations, the specific confessional differences were seldom mentioned as being important. Christianity was usually taken as a primary and somewhat inherent factor behind the relative prosperity of the region's Christian groups and the areas in which these Christians formed a large portion of the population, such as Lebanon and coastal Anatolian cities. The religious complexities of Lebanon offered one telling context for discussion of the region's Christians and provided perhaps the best proof of the superiority of Christianity in the minds of the commission members. William Yale, for example, seemed to believe that Lebanon was more modern because of its Christianity. He argued that separating largely Christian Lebanon from Syria would keep Lebanon on its modernising trajectory and that 'a self-respecting, self-governing Christian Arab state may tend to bring civilizing influences on the Moslem Arabs'. The success of a Christian-dominated (but 'secular') Lebanon could also 'create in the mind of the Moslem a respect and admiration for the Syrian Christian whom today he despises as an inferior'.[44] The authors of the King–Crane Commission Report also saw Lebanon as a largely Christian area that had gained prosperity after leaving 'the jurisdiction of the Porte' in 1861, stating 'roads have been built, trees planted, and a large number of stone houses erected'. Yet according to the report's authors, having become prosperous and more modern was the very reason to keep Lebanon unified with Syria. They contended that Lebanon, as a more prosperous region and a 'predominantly Christian country', would 'be in a position to exert a stronger and more helpful influence' on the newly unified Syrian (predominantly Muslim) state.[45] Regardless of this difference in their recommendations, the Christians of Lebanon remained the superior, civilising group in both of these accounts.

The Greeks were also exalted by the commission members as paragons of modernity in an otherwise backwards region, though they generally believed that the 'results' of the recent events at Smyrna, along with other Greek claims they saw as unjustified, 'did not seem to indicate' that the Greeks were worthy of any sort of grander empire in the region. King, Crane and Lybyer stated in the report that 'the ability of the Greeks is not in question, nor is their enthusiasm for education', and that their timeless 'special gifts' had made them 'particularly successful as colonists', in an apparent reference to the colonies of ancient Greece.[46] Despite this, Charles Crane and Albert Lybyer noted in a telegram to President Wilson that the Greeks had not yet proven 'very successful in self-government', and they could not recommend that the Greeks be granted 'imperialistic rule' over parts of the Turkish Empire.[47] In fact, their special qualities were needed in the new Turkish state because they had virtues that the Turks lacked or, as the authors of the commission report noted, 'the two races supplement each other'.[48]

When discussing a new Armenian state, the commission members generally contended that the Armenians were far superior to their neighbouring races. King, Crane and Lybyer exalted the Armenians as being worthy of having their own state partly because of their 'sufferings' and 'endurance', but mainly because of 'their loyalty to principles, their unbroken spirit and ambition, and their demonstrated industry, ability, and self-reliance', all of which were decidedly Anglo-Saxon qualities.[49] Donald Brodie similarly noted that the Armenians were 'capable and efficient' and displayed 'thrift and industry'. The Armenian 'loyalty to the Allies and to his Christian faith', Brodie continued, 'must never be forgotten'.[50] In George Montgomery's report on the future of Turkey, the superiority of the Armenians was largely taken as self-evident and their attributes, while not clearly defined, could be seen in the fact that they had been able to 'maintain' their religion against Muslims 'through many hundred years'. Their superiority was sufficient for Montgomery to recommend the creation of a massive Armenian state spanning from the Black Sea to the Mediterranean. He recommended Armenian leadership over this state even though they would only constitute 26 per cent of its population (using somewhat massaged pre-war figures).[51]

Despite this praise for Armenians and sympathy for their plight, what the commission members observed in the Middle East did not always match their preconceived notions of the Armenians. After seeing many Armenian refugees in Greater Syria, Albert Lybyer wrote that 'the remnant', meaning those who had survived the massacres, were 'indeed an unpromising lot of seed [...] for the future Armenian nation, – ugly, stupid, diseased, lazy, ragged and wretched – many of these qualities are not their fault – but at best the outlook is discouraging'.[52] Lybyer also noted that the Armenian leadership they encountered could be 'cocky and difficult'.[53] Likewise, Donald Brodie stated that while on their journey, he had learned that 'the Armenian is not quite such a worthy fellow after all'. He stated that the Armenians were capable of 'treachery' and were often not 'genuinely likeable', with some having 'unfortunate' personalities and 'unpleasant personal qualities'. He claimed that American relief workers had been 'antagonized by the ingratitude and the seeming shiftlessness of many refugees'. Brodie also stated that the generosity of the American people in relief efforts, a generosity not matched by the 'wealthier Armenians', had made the Armenians 'complacent'.[54] Despite these reservations, the commission members' belief in the Armenians as a Christian (hence capable) race allowed them to overlook what they perceived as inherent flaws and to recommend a strong new Armenia overseen by the United States.

Another major element of agreement among the commission members was the belief that the Christians of the Ottoman lands were vulnerable to mass slaughter by the region's other groups. The discourse of Christian victimhood is strong throughout the writings of the commission members, with the spectre of the mass removal and killing of Armenians during the war, crimes that were 'black as any in human history', underpinning much of commission members' writings.[55] The authors of the King–Crane Commission Report, for example, stated that the Christian people in Lebanon 'naturally fear' Muslim domination and argued that it would be necessary to establish numerous safeguards in order to protect all Christians within Greater Syria.[56] They also stated that there was still 'implicit threatening of massacre' against the Armenians in Turkey and that the world owed the Armenians an 'adequate guarantee of safety'.[57] Furthermore, the 'Syrian Chaldeans and Nestorian Christians' in the Kurdish lands would also need to be provided guarantees of 'full security', and the Greeks who were to remain in the new Turkish state would have to be 'fully guarded'.[58] Additionally, William Yale argued that Lebanon should be separated from Greater Syria in order to 'put an end to Christian intimidation and domination by the Moslems', and that many of the Christian Syrian exiles advocating Syrian nationalism no longer understood 'the danger to the Christian minorities' posed by the Muslim majority. The region's 'terrified' Christians, according to Yale, had 'given their support to the [Damascus] program' not because they believed in it, but 'out of fear for the Jews and in concession to the Moslems'.[59] Similarly, George Montgomery stated that there was 'much real terror of the Moslems among the Christians' and that if the two were brought together into one state, the Muslims would likely be put 'on the defensive' and would (euphemistically) 'become reactionary'.[60] On the whole, the portrayal of Christians as a persecuted minority was accepted by the commission members as an unquestioned fact throughout the region.

In sum, the commission members argued that Christians exhibited characteristics more in line with the superior races of Europe and the United States. They were 'civilising', able to tutor their Muslim neighbours, and could bring the region along towards the modern ideal largely agreed upon by the commission members. In all of these discussions, the Christians of the region are portrayed as a defenceless and less developed version of their Western relatives and hence the Western powers had a responsibility to protect them. This served as one of the main justifications for the establishment of mandates in the region, just as it had done for the involvement of European powers in the Middle East during the preceding century.

Muslims

The commission members deeply disagreed about the ability of Muslims to become modern. As previously noted, all of the commission members agreed that modernity required a strong secular government so that every citizen could freely practise their chosen religion. Modern governments, the commission members believed, had to stand above the religious fray. King, Crane and Lybyer argued that Muslims could keep their religion out of government to the same extent that Christians had done in the United States. They even believed that there were elements within Islam that could help the society transform from traditional to modern. Conversely, Montgomery and Yale argued that Muslims had little chance of becoming secular and would oppress the religious minorities in their midst as soon as they had the chance. It is important to note that commission members usually singled out Turks as a separate race, though they were often also included in general discussions about Muslims. The term 'Arab', while frequently being used to denote a race, was also commonly used synonymously with the term 'Muslim'. This analysis follows the lead of the King–Crane Commission members by discussing Turks and Arabs as separate races at points, and as Muslims at others.

The views of the King–Crane Commission members concerning the Turks were fairly typical for Europeans and Americans of the era. For years, Turks had been disparaged as violent and barbaric, and the commission members reproduced a discourse that nearly every elite in American society would have internalised. Although many people who had met Turks (including many of the commission members) admitted that individually they had redeeming features, these features did not outweigh their centuries of savagery and misrule as a race. During the late nineteenth and early twentieth centuries, actions taken by the Turks against various Christian groups in their empire had been widely publicised in the United States and fit nicely into American conceptions of the Turks, as did their treatment of Armenians during the war.[61] Despite hearing testimony from a few missionaries to the contrary, members of the King–Crane Commission unanimously believed that the Turks did not deserve to be left in a position of power after the war.

The attractive qualities of Turks made a token appearance in the writings of King–Crane Commission members. They often felt obliged to preface diatribes against Turks with a few positive statements. In the King–Crane Commission Report, for example, the authors stated that the 'agreeable and attractive personal qualities of the Turks' commonly made them 'the best liked, probably, of all the peoples in the Empire' and that these qualities 'turn most foreigners who stay long in the country into pro-Turks'.[62] Donald Brodie agreed with this point, stating that the urban Turk was 'an agreeable surprise' to 'the American who is making his first acquaintance with the peoples of the Near East', as Brodie himself was doing during his time on the commission. The Turk, he continued, was very European in look and manners, which stood in great contrast to the American stereotype of 'a blood-thirsty bandit with a black beard, picturesque costume and swaggering sword'. The 'country' Turk was 'almost as pleasing' too, according to Brodie, in that 'he is ignorant and poor and dirty' but usually 'friendly'. In general, Brodie believed that the 'average Turk' made a 'friendly agreeable impression' and appeared more 'cultured' than the other races of the region.[63] This is where any favourable discussion of the Turks stopped.

Despite occasional complimentary statements, the authors of the King–Crane Commission Report were mostly unsympathetic in their assessment of the Turks. They declared that the Turks were a 'wretched failure' at governing with a 'superlatively bad record of misrule'. They had run 'a government of simple exploitation' which was 'characterized by incessant corruption, plunder and bribery', and were 'simply not conceivably equal' to ruling such a strategically important part of the world. They had failed despite having 'generally good laws', implying that their downfall was not attributable to the Western-oriented modernisation projects of the late-Ottoman era, but instead was a product of some other unnamed flaw. King, Crane and Lybyer acknowledged that the Turks had been tolerant of other groups in the Ottoman Empire, but that this had been a 'negative, indolent tolerance'. So while they may have given other groups a loose autonomy within the empire, these groups were 'constantly despised, robbed, oppressed' by the Turks as well. For these oppressed groups, the report continued, 'nothing has been secure – whether property, lives, wives, or children'. The Turks had oppressed Greeks and Armenians mainly because these two 'races' were 'abler, more industrious, enterprising, and prosperous than the Turks'. And although the government had been responsible for most of these policies, the Turkish people had been 'all too willing to share' in the oppression. These were not 'crimes of passion' but were the product of the character of a race and a religion. The Armenian massacres, according to the report's authors, were simply a manifestation of this character.[64] When discussing these massacres, King, Crane and Lybyer noted that they did not feel the need to recount these 'hideous atrocities', citing James Bryce's well-known report for this, but wrote that there was no doubt that the Turks were responsible.[65] More importantly they noted that the Turks were 'unrepentant' on the whole about the 'horrible massacre' of the Armenians, and there was only 'the slightest evidence that the Turkish Government or the people as a whole have recognized or repudiated the crime of the Armenian massacres, or done anything appreciable to set them right'. Additionally, there was little in what they saw during their time in the region that gave them 'reasonable hope that the massacres might not be repeated'. Still, the authors of the report believed that a return to Islam (having, by implication, been lost by the Ottoman leaders at some point) could bring the Turks back to respectability, just as it had to other 'backward and degenerated' populations of the region.[66]

The other commission members said less about the Turks. William Yale was rather quiet on the subject, there being no question as to whether or not the Ottomans would remain in power in Greater Syria (his area of expertise). George Montgomery appeared to hold an even bleaker view of the Turks than King, Crane and Lybyer. For Montgomery, the Turks were prone to 'cruelty' and 'misrule', and still represented a threat 'to wipe out the remaining fragments of the Christian races' in the Ottoman lands.[67] Donald Brodie, despite having some kind words to say about the general character of the Turks, believed that they had been 'guilty of misrule and exploitation' and that 'corruption, intrigue and oppression' had been 'all too prevalent' in their government. The Turks, according to Brodie, had shown 'indifference' rather than tolerance to the minorities of their empire and were 'capable of the greatest intolerance at times of religious or emotional excitement'.

Brodie concluded that 'the average Turk is an untrained, temperamental child in the larger affairs of men and of nations, and must be treated as such'.[68] In general, there was no question in the minds of the commission members that the Turks had proven that they could not handle the pressures of the modern world, though the authors of the report believed that there was a chance for them to improve. Montgomery and Brodie showed few signs of harbouring such a belief.

Although Islam figured prominently in the commission members' discussion of the Turks, it played an even more conspicuous role when they discussed the Arabs. In their characterisation of the Arabs, the commission members often conflated the terms 'Arabs' with 'Moslems' and quietly emphasised Arab/Muslim inferiority to Christians. In the report, for example, statements such as 'the Moslem and Christian population was unanimously against Zionism' and 'as Christians and Moslems they can honor all of the Holy Places' contrasted with statements like 'the intense opposition of Arabs and Christians to the Zionist Programme' and 'the native Arabs and Christians, who so unitedly oppose Zionism', yet the intended meaning of the usage was the same.[69] While the commission members acknowledged in places that the Christians of the region could be classified as Arabs, it seemed that the ones who most deserved to be called Arabs in their minds were those who had accepted Islam as their religion.

One of the major points of contention among the commission members concerned the role of Islam in the future of the region. King, Crane and Lybyer believed that there was much of value in Islam. They argued that the Muslim Arabs and Turks could and should maintain their faith while moving towards modernity. For example, they argued that although the Ottomans had horribly mismanaged their empire, there was still much in the 'Oriental spirit' that could be preserved on the path to modernity and that some religious elements of Islam would complement modernity well:

> Is there not something far greater to be looked for, than that gradual driving out of the 'Oriental Spirit' in Turkey? In one sense, doubtless, that spirit is doomed and must go. [...] [But] are there not priceless Oriental values, gratefully to be recognized and sedulously to be preserved? And may not Turkey [...] become in some rich and high sense mediating land as well between the

Occident and the Orient, teaching the nations how to combine the quietism of the East, and the pragmatism of the West; the religious dependence of the East, and the scientific mastery of the West; the mental and spiritual fellowship of the East, and the mental and spiritual independence of the West?[70]

Donald Brodie was also impressed with the devotion inspired by Islam in the region, stating that the 'sense of religious awe and veneration of the Deity' made a 'profound impression' on him. Islam, for Brodie, gave a society potential: 'If something of the spirit of brotherhood inherent in Christianity can be infused with the passionate devotion of Islam, religion may yet be a powerful factor for progress in the Near East.'[71] In short, the religious element, in perhaps some modified form, was something that was salvageable about the Middle East. Just as the American people had been guided by strong Christian beliefs throughout their modernising journey, the Turks and the Arabs could be aided by Islam throughout theirs. Yet the separation was clear: Islam could only act as a helpful companion to true modernisation; science and secularity brought progress.

In extolling the virtues of Islam, King, Crane and Lybyer implicitly countered the common belief that Islam was not compatible with Western, liberal ways. Crane, for example, argued in a 10 July letter to Wilson that 'the every-day people [in Greater Syria] are sober, industrious, and intelligent', which provided promising 'raw material' for a new state.[72] In the report, they went so far as to say that there were already examples of good governance in the Muslim Arab world, with the most specific example of this (included at the behest of Crane) being the Senussis in northern Africa, who had organised the Bedouin tribes in large parts of what is now Libya and Egypt.[73] The report's authors argued that 'under influences purely Moslem', the Senussis had been able to establish 'a vast state in a most barren and unpromising land'. They had succeeded in 'up-lifting, organizing, and harmonizing a most backward and degenerated population in the heart of Africa within a comparatively few years'. The success of the Senussis was proof for King, Crane and Lybyer that Muslims could govern themselves: 'It rather affords ample warrant for expecting that under new democratic processes and in due time Moslems will prove themselves able to build up and manage their own states in the Arabian and Anatolian Peninsulas.'[74]

Thus the authors were arguing that not only was it possible for Muslim societies to produce effective governments, but that they currently were doing so in part of the Muslim world; in a sense, some Muslims were already moving towards the next stage of history and had done so on their own. The Senussis, according to the authors of the report, were proof that modernity was not the exclusive domain of Christians.

King, Crane and Lybyer also argued that the Muslim admiration of the United States they observed during their time in the region constituted further proof of Islam's compatibility with modernity. The fact that the region's Muslims were able to recognise America's superiority over other modern states suggested that they too could strive to attain American-style modernity. To illustrate this, the authors of the report cited the petitioners' oft-repeated esteem for America's 'genuinely democratic spirit', its lack of 'colonial ambitions', and the 'unselfish aims with which she had come into the war'.[75] Amir Faysal himself was especially fit for managing this move towards modernity because he was 'a confirmed believer in the Anglo-Saxon race', thus showing that he acknowledged the hierarchy of races in some form. This proved that he was both modern and rational.[76] The authors of the report also argued that the Arabs judged the United States as more likely than the European powers to 'treat men of all races with a genuine respect born of some insight into their own individual gifts'.[77] The implication here was clear: Arab recognition and admiration of America's modern and secular qualities indicated the sincerity of their intent to become modern in the American sense. Yet this belief in the capabilities of Arabs was accompanied by apprehension in the report. King, Crane and Lybyer did acknowledge that the soon-to-be-assigned mandatory power needed to watch the new country 'closely' in order to ensure the protection of 'Christians and other non-Muslim groups', thus acknowledging but downplaying the common view that Muslim Arabs had a tendency towards sectarian violence.[78]

Interestingly, King, Crane and Lybyer did not propose the formation of an American-style democracy in Greater Syria but rather chose to recommend 'a constitutional monarchy along democratic lines', which would have been a somewhat antiquated mode of governance in their minds. A constitutional monarchy was a traditional government with modern elements and the authors of the report believed that it would be less jarring to people who were still largely mired in a traditional lifestyle. This government, according to the report, was 'naturally adapted to the Arabs, with their long training under tribal conditions, and their traditional respect for their chiefs'. 'They seem to need', the report continued, 'more than most people, a King as the personal symbol of the power of the State.'[79] In general, though, the authors of the report believed that Muslim religiosity, when harnessed by the secular spirit they judged to be present in the Arabs, could be a helpful companion along the road to modernity. The fact that Americans had already taken a similar road while accompanied by Christianity made them the most qualified tutors.

George Montgomery and William Yale had far less faith in the ability of Muslims to become modern. These two displayed what Maxime Rodinson has called a belief in the existence of 'homo Islamicus', meaning that the characteristics of Islam determined the essence of the people in a Muslim society, having a far greater impact than religions in other societies.[80] Montgomery exemplified this in the following quote:

> I have little expectation that a Moslem Arab government in Syria can develop any importance. Mohommedan empires grew and prospered only as long as there was loot to be looted and divided. Islam contains no nucleus of unselfishness which may hold out a hope of a Mohommedan reformation. At best there can be only a weak eclecticism like Bahism, or a mysticism like some of the sects. Mohommedanism is vigorous, not as it serves but only as it conquers. There is in it no heart to meet the needs of modern society.

According to Montgomery, Islam defined the Arabs and he expressed little, if any, hope that Muslims could be taught, or even had a desire to learn, the ways of modernity.

Montgomery went so far as to partially denigrate the past achievements of Islamic civilisation as products of a bygone era of semi-enlightened despotism and not as something that could be cited as proof of the civilisation's potential: 'One should not be misled by the ancient importance in arts and sciences of an Arab nation. As despotisms, the Moslem governments provided brief periods of tranquillity and prosperity in which arts and sciences could grow.' But this era had passed, according to Montgomery, and 'no such despotism is possible to a Moslem government under the new system.' Instead, Muslims had turned violent and cared only about asserting their dominance in the region:

> I anticipate that most of the efforts of the Moslem Arabs will be spent in a fight against Christians and Christianity. The prophecy may seem pessimistic, but it is hard for those who have not lived here to realize that religious allegiances and antipathy are the primary social energies.

Furthermore, Muslims were seeking a new empire, in Montgomery's mind, and sought unity with Lebanon 'perhaps because of the greater power thus accruing to them'. For Montgomery, a 'non-Moslem block' in the form of a Jewish state was needed because 'it will be an announcement to the Arabs of Syria that their national development is not in the direction of Egypt', thus lessening the possibility of a new Arab empire. For Montgomery, the Muslims of the region could not be trusted. If given independence, they would seek a new empire that would be perhaps worse than the Ottomans. These people, according to Montgomery, needed to be protected from themselves, their violent impulses, and their religion. The best way to do this was to make them British or French imperial subjects. Modern programmes, like the capitalist agricultural expansion of the Zionists, could introduce them to things like wage labour and be the source of a general re-education of the Arab Muslims.[81]

Though William Yale's views on the Muslim ability to adopt modernity were not as openly harsh as Montgomery's, he did come to similar conclusions. Yale believed that the region's Muslims were wealthy, self-interested and manipulative, or poor, ignorant and easily whipped into a violent frenzy. Although he sometimes showed a nuanced understanding of the region's varied groups in his writings (at least in comparison to Montgomery), Yale wavered between expressing hope for the region's Muslims to become modern after a long period of tutelage, and conveying a profound pessimism that this could ever happen. The latter seemed to take precedence in his final recommendations.

Yale wrote extensively about the flaws of Muslims/Arabs in the justifications for his recommendations. Along the same lines as his pre-commission writings, Yale claimed that poor Muslims were 'docile and easily manageable' as well as 'ignorant and fanatical', and could easily 'be swayed by their religious leaders'. Furthermore, the subservient Muslim masses only supported the Damascus Program 'because they believe that it means Moslem supremacy and independence, and because they are ordered to'. The wealthy Muslims were also 'profoundly fanatical, profoundly Islamic' and had only just realised the 'power they possess over the mass of the ignorant Moslems'.[82] Hence, Yale characterised the Muslim Arab as ignorant and submissive if poor, and tyrannical (or potentially so) if wealthy. During the war, Yale argued that the fanatical attitudes of the Arabs partly stemmed from their fear of British and French imperialism, though this sort of analysis did not make it into his recommendations. In an analytical shift, Yale argued that the region's Muslims, being determined to dominate the minorities in their midst, became the would-be imperialists, while the imperial powers (whose aims Yale had constantly derided during the war) were now recommended to oversee the mandates because they were the only thing that could stop Muslim domination. The threat of an Islamic empire, in Yale's mind, was worse than the expansion of the British or French Empires.

According to Yale, this hunger for power among the notables did not lend itself well to the acquisition of modern traits like secularism. He continued to believe that these powerful Muslims were seeking a 'Moslem Arab State, not a liberal Syrian State'.[83] This liberal state under the leadership of Amir Faysal, the same one that King, Crane and Lybyer believed could eventually succeed, was not a legitimate possibility any time in the near future because 'among the Moslems there are but a few, a very few educated men, and among these educated Moslems, but very few are hearty supporters of the liberal policy of the Emir'.[84] These powerful men, which Yale ominously labelled the 'Young Arabs' in direct comparison to the vilified Young Turks, had no intention of creating a modern nation and if the United States got involved in the mandate 'our aims would not be the aims of the Young Arabs, our ideals would not be their ideals'.[85] Instead, he continually raised the spectre of a new Muslim Arab empire under Sharif Hussein, juxtaposing this as the antithesis of the modern, secular state. Faysal, and those behind his regime, could not be trusted.

In addition, Yale believed that the Muslim Arabs would even have a deleterious effect on the groups of the region with a chance to move towards modernity, arguing that the Christians of Lebanon needed to be separated from Syria so that they could 'have the opportunity to develop without lot or hindrance from the Moslems'. Attempting to help foster a 'united, national and secular state' in Greater Syria would be a 'dangerous, troublesome and uncertain experiment' in Yale's reckoning.[86] In general, Yale set up a number of dichotomies in his recommendations: the developing Christians versus the stagnating (or regressing) Muslims; the liberal state versus the 'Moslem Arab State'; the ideals of the United States versus the ideals of the 'Young Arabs'. The Muslim Arabs, in William Yale's construction, had little ability or desire to create a modern society at any time in the near future.

In their characterisations of the ability of Muslims to become modern, the members of the King–Crane Commission attributed different essences to Muslims. Montgomery and Yale discounted the ability of Muslims to become modern, largely because their religion led them to be violent, fanatical and tyrannical. For these two, secular tolerance in the Middle East, along with allegiance to the secular nation over religion (a main tenet of modernity), was not possible in the foreseeable future. King, Crane and Lybyer argued that Islam (and its practitioners) had much to offer the modern world and did not preclude the formation of a new secular, modern society. In keeping with Maxime Rodinson's observations about scholars of the Middle East, the authors of the report eschewed Yale and Montgomery's religious/racial determinism and instead saw the region as 'societies in transition', though they argued that future change should only go in a very specific direction.[87]

Jews

The lines of disagreement within the commission on the matter of Zionism were clearly drawn at the end of their time in the Ottoman lands: King, Crane and Lybyer believed that Zionism was unjust and a violation of self-determination, while Montgomery and Yale believed that Zionism was the best available way to modernise Palestine. The disagreement stemmed more from their views about modernity than from perceived Jewish racial traits. The commission members all believed that Jews had a number of inherent strengths, which gave them the unquestioned ability to develop Palestine, and flaws, which would need to be overcome if they were to be the effective stewards of modernity in the region. The era's common refrain of Jews as 'exclusive', 'materialistic' and scheming was part of the commission members' shared social imaginary, being both explicitly mentioned on a number of occasions and appearing to underlie various comments on others. In the King–Crane Commission Report, these flaws partly overshadowed the benefits that Zionism could bring to the region, while in the memorandums of Montgomery and Yale these were flaws that could be overlooked because of the prosperity Zionism would deliver to Palestine. Montgomery even believed that Zionism could shift Jews away from their flaws, hence representing an opportunity for general Jewish improvement.

The terminology used by the commission members to discuss the Jews of Greater Syria shifted during their time in the region: in June, the commission members usually distinguished between the 'native' Jews and the Zionists, but they generally conflated the two terms in their final reports. While they were in Greater Syria, the King–Crane Commission received testimony from many (if not most) of the major Jewish delegations in the region. The heritage of these delegations was mixed, with many of them coming from families who had lived in the region for centuries, and others being recent Zionist immigrants from Europe. William Yale employed this classificatory split when determining the delegations the commission would receive in Greater Syria, making sure that the commission would get testimony from the 'Native Jews' as well as the 'Zionists'.[88] This perceived split between these two groups of Jews was often part of the discourse of the region's non-Jewish delegations as well, with many of the Arab delegations (both Christian and Muslim) stating that they had excellent relations with the 'native' Jews but poor relations with the Zionists. That the region's non-Jewish delegations employed this same terminology fit particularly well into Charles Crane's attitudes towards Jews. In summarising the testimony that the commission had received, Crane wrote that many of the non-Jewish delegations had stated that 'their relations with the old Jews who had lived here for years [...] were always satisfactory and friendly. But [there was] a clear feeling of menace about the modern pushing Jew.'[89] This statement exemplifies Crane's attitude about Jews: he did not feel antipathy towards Jews as a whole at this point in his life but singled out the 'menace' of the 'modern pushing' Jew, which to him usually came in the form of wealthy and influential European or American businessmen. The Zionists, to Crane, appeared to be an arm of this type of Jew. That the nuance of this terminology largely disappeared towards the end of the commission members' time in the region can mainly be attributed to the fact that the Jewish delegations in Greater Syria uniformly testified in favour of Zionism. In their final recommendations, the members of the King–Crane Commission flattened the diversity of the Jewish populations of the region and employed the terms 'Jews' or 'Zionists' to include both the 'native Jews' and the new Zionist immigrants.

In the King–Crane Commission Report, the three authors recommended that the Zionist programme be 'greatly reduced' and justified this in a number of ways. Although they claimed to have been 'predisposed' in favour of Zionism before they arrived in Jaffa, 'the actual facts in Palestine, coupled with the force of the general principles proclaimed by the allies' had led them to modify their opinions. The 'actual facts' of Palestine for King, Crane and Lybyer consisted of the following: the Zionists looked 'forward to practically the complete dispossession of the present non-Jewish inhabitants of Palestine' despite their assurances otherwise; Jews were unreliable custodians of the 'Holy Places'; the historical claims of the Jews, as 'based on an occupation of two thousand years ago', were illegitimate; and, perhaps most importantly, Zionism was a violation of the principle of self-determination (to be discussed in the next chapter).[90] Their conceptions of both race and modernity lay behind their formulation of these 'facts'.

To King, Crane and Lybyer, Jews had distinct characteristics as a race that served to undermine their credibility as colonists of Palestine. While the three authors of the report did not discuss the racial characteristics of Jews extensively in their writings, the available evidence indicates that they believed Jews, as a race, were often 'exclusive' and 'materialistic', and this was born out in their colonisation methods in Palestine. Albert Lybyer, for example, praised the qualities of a Jewish colony in his diary but also noted in a tellingly terse sentence fragment that it was also 'self-contained', thus indicating a perception of the Jewish propensity towards exclusivity.[91] In addition, King, Crane and Lybyer did not believe Zionist claims that Jewish immigration was bringing great benefit to all of the region's people. When a Zionist delegation made this claim before the commission in Jaffa, the commissioners questioned them extensively on this matter, asking why they had not integrated into local communities, but instead chose to create 'exclusive' colonies. They also asked how the Zionists could guarantee that the Arabs would not be 'under oppression' in a state that was to become more and more dominated by Jews.[92] Instead of accepting that the Zionists were beneficent in their ambitions, King, Crane and Lybyer came to believe that they were aiming to dominate Palestine and take it as their own. The Zionists were, to this extent, untrustworthy in the opinion of these commission members.

The authors of the report went so far as to raise the spectre of a Jewish lack of respect for (at best) or destruction of (at worst) Muslim and Christian holy sites in Palestine. The ostensible rationale behind this argument was that the world's Christians and Muslims would not be comfortable with Jews as custodians of their 'Holy Places'. This logic may have been borrowed from testimony they received while in the region. The 'Ulema of Damascus', for example, stated on 26 June that: There are in Palestine places holy to Christians and Moslems and not to Jews, and places holy to Moslems and not to Christians; all places are holy to Moslems; therefore the Moslems should control the land.[93] King, Crane and Lybyer escalated the severity of this rhetoric by claiming that the Christian and Muslim holy sites were 'abhorrent' to the Jews because they had no religious connection to them. In fact, according to the authors of the report, handing these sites over to the Jews could even add to the strength of anti-Jewish sentiment throughout the world. If Christians and Muslims would fear for the security of these places, it would 'intensify, with a certainty like fate, the anti-Jewish feeling both in Palestine and in all other portions of the world which look to Palestine as the "Holy Land"'.[94] The Jews, then, could not be trusted to occupy Palestine and would even worsen their world position if they did.

The report's authors did acknowledge the possible benefits of Zionism, having been impressed by the colonies that they visited. These colonies displayed what the Jews could bring to the Middle East, which was, in essence, modernity. The praise of the Zionist colonies (as previously mentioned) showed that King, Crane and Lybyer did not simply write Zionism off because it was a Jewish project. Lybyer's comment after visiting these colonies ('in the course of the day, we saw the best side of Zionism') is significant: the promise of modernity being brought to the region by the Zionists was enticing but the cost, that is the 'dispossession' of the local populations, was too high.[95] Modernity would have to be brought to the region in a more just manner, and, according to King, Crane and Lybyer, the United States was capable of doing this without the potential drawbacks of Zionism.

Although George Montgomery's conception of the racial strengths and weaknesses of Jews was similar to that of King, Crane and Lybyer, he was the most ardent advocate for Zionism on the commission throughout its time in the Ottoman lands. Montgomery was arguing in favour of Zionism as early as 12 June, with Lybyer noting in his diary that 'M. [Montgomery] talked for Zionism' during a walk through the streets of Jaffa. The topic came up between Lybyer and Montgomery again on 14 June in Jerusalem, with Montgomery stating more specifically that it was right to back Zionism because it represented 'the greatest good for the greatest number' of people in the region, an argument he placed in opposition to self-determination (which will be discussed in the next chapter).[96] While Montgomery backed his advocacy of Zionism with claims of numerous sorts, all of which he believed to support this utilitarian argument, discussions of Jewish racial superiority and their ability to modernise the region were the most prominent justifications he offered.

The formal articulation of Montgomery's views on Zionism came in three places: his 'Report on Syria' and two other documents written during the commission's time in the Ottoman lands entitled 'Questions on Zionism' and 'The Attitude toward Zionism'. These documents were similar in argument and presented a favourable racial portrait of the Jews. In arguing that the Jews were a gifted people, Montgomery stated that important figures at the Paris Peace Conference (including Wilson and House) had shown 'admiration for the achievements of the Jewish race'. They had also been 'impressed by what appears to be the miracle of the Jewish race through the centuries' and 'by the theories [of Jewish racial vigour] which this remarkable history suggests'. As a race, they were the 'reverse of warlike', a claim that Montgomery used to dismiss the anti-Zionist views of 'warlike' (by implication) British military officials in the region who appeared to 'naturally feel an antagonism' towards the 'peaceful' Jews. The protests of the Arabs, Montgomery noted, came from 'jealousy and rivalry' rather than principled, rational opposition. Montgomery also argued that the Jews were both wealthy and generous, and this made them well equipped to modernise Palestine which was going to be an expensive project. Many of the leaders of the

Zionist movement had grown up in the West, thus making them more likely to remake the Ottoman lands in a Western manner and generally contribute to the 'development' of the metonymical 'country' or 'land'. They had 'beneficent' aims and sought not to 'dispossess the fellah' but to instead change the unjust feudal nature of the current landholding system in the region. This would make it possible for the fellahin either 'to buy their farms from the large landholders' or to earn 'wages' from the Zionists that would give them 'a certain independence in contrast with the serfdom under the landlords'. Either way, the 'fellahs' would be 'more benefited under the Zionists than under the Arab regime' and their 'situation' would be 'greatly improved by the coming of the Zionists'. In this characterisation, Montgomery argued that allowing the Zionists to go ahead with their programme would improve the situation of the entire population of Palestine, with the exception of the 'feudal' Arab landowners who, in his opinion, were the ones behind both what he saw as the economic stagnation of the region and the protests against Zionism.[97]

Montgomery felt that he did have to acknowledge the generally accepted flaws of the Jewish race. He wrote that the Jews 'with all their remarkable qualities seem to have certain char[acter]istics which have made them disliked' such as 'materialism' and 'exclusivity'. Montgomery went so far as to say the 'experiment in nationalism' that Zionism represented would give the Jews a 'refuge from persecution' and confidence that 'their race is assured'. This, in turn, could cure them of their tendency to be 'exclusive and separate' and stop them from 'keeping so exclusively to the customs of antiquity', hence becoming more modern as a race. Interestingly, Montgomery argued that there would be 'little ground for fear as to the Christian and Moslem holy places' (as had been expressed by delegations on occasion), not because the Jews could be trusted to protect these places, but because the League of Nations would be in the region to ensure that nothing would happen to them. Indeed, Montgomery essentially recognised these concerns as valid by recommending that 'proper reservations be made for the safe-guarding of the Christian and Moslem Holy Places'. Although Montgomery generally spoke in glowing terms about the 'Jewish race', statements like these showed that he either did not entirely trust the Zionists or at least was acknowledging that others likely saw this as a major problem with the Zionist programme.[98]

When taken as a whole, Montgomery's belief in the superiority of the Zionists and the 'Jewish race' seems to have been drawn from the fact that they were far more modern than their Arab counterparts, and that they had the ability and financial means to spread modernity to the region. While he did harbour a few reservations about the Jews (which were fairly common in his day), he felt that Zionism could indeed improve the Jews as a race, and could also improve the quality of life for the majority of the inhabitants of Palestine. According to Montgomery, modernity was unquestionably the best destination for this region and the Western powers were lucky that a group as astute as the Zionists was offering their modernising services at no cost to the victorious powers.

Despite being inclined to support Zionism, William Yale angered the Zionists during the commission's time in the region, with the Zionists claiming that he was working against their cause (as recounted in Chapter 6). In contrast to the aspersions cast on Yale by the Zionists, he appears to have been growing more convinced that Zionism was indeed a good way to improve the region during his time on the commission. Yale's definitive statement of support for Zionism came in his 'Report on Syria'. Interestingly, he felt the need to begin his defence of Zionism with a major caveat, stating at the beginning of his conclusions on Palestine that his pro-Zionist recommendations were 'entirely contrary to the wishes of the people of Palestine and those of most of the inhabitants of Syria'. He believed that the Zionists, with all of their excellent racial traits, represented an opportunity to move Palestine towards an American version of modernity, which was by far the best type:

> Jewish energy, Jewish genius and Jewish finances will bring many advantages to Palestine and perhaps to all of the East. Modern western methods and civilisation will be brought to Palestine by the Jews, the country will be developed along modern western lines as it could not hope to be even under the most enlightened mandatory Power. With the immigration of the Jews into Palestine a new element will be introduced in to the Orient. An Eastern race well-versed in western culture and profoundly in sympathy with western ideals will be established in the Orient. Furthermore, a Jewish State will inevitably fall under the control of American Jews who will work out along Jewish lines American ideals and American

civilization, and a Jewish Commonwealth in Palestine will develop into an out-post in the Orient, of Americanism.

Yale acknowledged, though, that the feeling against Zionism was 'intense' throughout the region and he predicted that the mandatory power who took control of Palestine would likely have to deal with 'disturbances and demonstrations against the Jews'. Like the Christians, Jews were also potential victims of the Muslims, and hence the Western powers needed to protect them 'with a strong hand'. He concluded that 'The Arabs may never become reconciled to Jewish immigration, but they will become reconciled to the fact that they must accept it as inevitable.'[99]

Yale and Montgomery's position here is clear: they believed that bringing modernity to the Middle East was the way forward for the region, yet they thought that it could only be done by moving able people into the region. The Zionists, already wanting to undertake such an endeavour, were the best available stewards of modernity and thus were presented as a capable, modern race who could even improve themselves by undertaking such a project. In Yale and Montgomery's racial construction, the fitness of the Jews to create a modern society was proven; the ability of Arabs or Turks to move towards modernity was suspect at best.

***

In looking at the writings of the King–Crane Commission members, it is clear that discourses pertaining to modernity, race and religion were extremely influential in their thinking. It is also clear that these discourses played a central role in shaping the commission members' attitudes towards the region and, eventually, in determining their final recommendations. In taking this approach to the King–Crane Commission, it is possible to draw two major conclusions on both the degree to which these discourses pre-determined the commission member's recommendations, and on the relative strength and malleability of the contending discourses of modernity, race and religion that surfaced in their writings.

First, this analysis shows that the King–Crane Commission members did seem to share a social imaginary and this, at least in part, helped to determine their recommendations. This can be seen in their writings mainly through what they did not propose: certain recommendations either hardly occurred to them (leaving the region to develop towards something not resembling modernity) or were impossible to justify within the accepted logic of this shared social imaginary (Greater Syrian independence). This is particularly true in their discussions of modernity. Although the commission members disagreed about the ability of the Ottoman subjects to become modern, they agreed (and did not even find it necessary to debate) that modernity was the best and only possible destination for the Ottoman lands.[100]

This shared social imaginary played a further role in the commission members' attitudes towards the region's groups. Broad conceptions of race and religion were ingrained in the minds of the commission members and within this social imaginary it was widely accepted that Middle Eastern races were inferior to their Western counterparts. For example, if a commission member endorsed a position backing Muslims (be they Turk or Arab), a plan had to be put in place to allay common fears about their 'known' tendency towards violence. If Zionism was endorsed, the 'fact' that there was a Jewish tendency towards 'exclusivity' and 'materialism' had to be acknowledged as an obstacle to the plan. A particularly revealing hallmark of this social imaginary was the absence of anyone taking Arab calls for independence and self-government very seriously. It was obvious to everyone involved in the commission that Arabs were not modern enough or competent enough to run their own nation state without extensive tutelage. With respect to both modernity and race, the social imaginary of the commission members did appear to be delimiting to a significant degree.

Second, while the social imaginary of the era may have delimited the possible recommendations of commission members, there were numerous contending discourses not wholly incorporated into this social imaginary that provided space for disagreement among the commission members and gave them numerous discursive tools to deploy in their opposing arguments. This played out to an extent in their disagreements over the region's future path to modernity and more strongly in the role that race and religion played in their recommendations.

The differences in their views on modernity were apparent mainly in their disagreement over how the region was to be modernised. The unspoken question among commission members was this: what was the best way to spread modernity to the Middle East? According to Yale and Montgomery, the British, French and Jews were modern and could make the region more so; the Muslim Arabs and Turks could not. Yet they did suggest that the Arabs and Turks could possibly make progress if they were slotted into a French/British/Zionist-created economic system with things like private land and wage labour. In short, other people would be doing the modernising and the Arabs and Turks would provide the necessary manpower, which was not far removed from some of the existing imperial arrangements in other parts of the British and French Empires. In the view of King, Crane and Lybyer, Muslim Arabs and Turks were capable of eventually achieving modernity under the far less intrusive tutelage of the United States (or, if need be, Britain). Yet in this framework, the Arabs and Turks would be taught how to modernise themselves and would not have it done for them. In the minds of King, Crane and Lybyer, this made their recommendations distinctly anti-imperial and far more beneficent. Though these conclusions can be partly attributed to differences of opinion about the correct path to modernity, race and religion stand out even more strongly as a cause of the disagreement.

It is not surprising that race and religion played prominent roles in the commission members' determinations about the relative fitness of Middle Eastern inhabitants for modernity. Race and religion, being such essentialising concepts in this era, could be employed to justify many different recommendations within the space delimited by the commission members' shared social imaginary; beyond the generally agreed-upon racial characteristics lay much room for contestation. Did Muslim Arabs and Turks have the 'heart' to eventually run a modern state? Was it possible for Muslim Arabs and Turks to live in the same state as Christians without persecuting them? Could Jews be counted on to look after the non-Jewish residents of Palestine, or would their 'exclusivity' lead them to look after only Jews and dispossess all others? The underlying conceptions of the commission members did not dictate their answers to these questions. The internal logic and terminology of the era's discourses pertaining to religion and race could be used to justify either 'yes' or 'no' answers to any of the above questions. Race and religion served as convenient and malleable justificatory tools for Americans debating their government's policy towards the rest of the world, which is what made (and makes) them such powerful concepts.[101]

Modernity, race and religion played perhaps the most powerful role in shaping the commission members' attitudes towards the region but the complexity of their decision-making processes incorporated more elements than this. Questions of self-determination, imperialism, nationalism and reparations for massacres also figured prominently in their recommendations and this is the subject of the next chapter.

CHAPTER 10

ACCOUNTING FOR THE DIFFERENCES 2: THE KING-CRANE COMMISSION AND WILSONIAN IDEALS

The commission members' pre-existing conceptions about modernity, race and religion strongly influenced their respective recommendations but other factors played a major role in the formation of their opinions as well. In their recommendations, the commission members addressed many concerns that were fairly unique to the post-World War I era and these concerns were, arguably, both more debatable in the context of their time and less rooted in their social imaginaries. Although the commission members cited a large variety of such factors as justifications for their recommendations, this chapter focuses on the themes that appear to have played the largest roles in determining their opinions. The most influential of these themes was centred on the role that Wilsonian ideals should play in the reformation of the Ottoman lands. In the immediate aftermath of World War I, Wilson's concept of self-determination (which he used synonymously with terms such as 'the consent of the governed' and 'the desires of the people') was seen by many as a novel and rhetorically powerful principle on which to base state creation. It was also a point that Wilson had emphatically backed and thus became something that every commission member had to address. The Ottoman lands, however, provided a confusing laboratory for the application of Wilsonian ideals and highlighted how difficult it was to translate these ideals into reality. Another such theme in the commission members' divergent recommendations was their attitude towards imperialism, with a focus on what they saw as the dangers of allowing the British and the French (along with, to a lesser extent, the Greeks and the Italians) to divide the region for their own imperial gain. A third major issue was the future role of the United States in the Ottoman lands: although the commission members concurred on the favourable national characteristics of their own country relative to the other powers, they disagreed about whether or not the United States should assume mandatory responsibilities in the region. A fourth issue the commission members discussed at length, and one that was closely associated with self-determination, was the region's apparently blooming nationalisms. The authenticity and potentials of these various nationalisms, along with the ability of Amir Faysal to harness the nationalist aspirations in Greater Syria, were major points of contention among the commission members. Each of these four issues will be discussed in its own section below.

Applying Wilsonian Ideals

The concept of self-determination had taken on a life of its own by 1919. As previously stated, Wilson rather inconveniently did not specifically define self-determination and, as a result, different people took it to mean different things. The Ottoman Empire was home to a variety of communities whose interpretations of self-determination were often in conflict with both the other groups of the region and with the Allied powers. Prominent figures in the Ottoman lands believed that the words of Wilson supported their right to establish self-governing states. This came out in many petitions to both the Paris Peace Conference and the King–Crane Commission. Amir Faysal, for example, cited Wilson in his testimony before the Supreme Council on 6 February 1919, arguing that Arab independence was 'in accord with the principles laid down by President Wilson and accepted by all of the Allies'.[1] Moreover, the Syrian Congress in the summer of 1919 also placed Wilson prominently in the Damascus Program, stating 'the noble principles enunciated by President Wilson strengthen our confidence that our desires from the depths of our hearts, shall be the decisive factor in determining our future'.[2] Some Turkish intellectuals went so far as to form a 'Wilsonian League', which, in a letter to the American delegation at the peace conference, praised Wilson's ideals as 'the solution to the problems of the present war'.[3] Additionally, representatives of the 'Kurdish Democratic Party', in appealing for 'the establishment of a Kurdish Government in the districts where the Kurds are in a great majority' justified their request by stating that their right to self-government 'was not invented by them but by the Americans themselves through President Wilson'.[4] In short, the dissemination and interpretation of Wilson's pronouncements provided politically prominent figures in the Ottoman lands with what was in their minds a legitimate basis for the establishment of independent, self-governing states.

The King–Crane Commission's interpretation of Wilson's pronouncements was more in line with the president's intentions. The basic framework of the commission's recommendations was already established by Wilson before its time in the Ottoman lands: the commission was going to recommend the most appropriate division of the region into new states and then propose mandatory powers to guide these new states towards self-government. A mandatory power, as was written in the commission's final report, 'should come in not at all as a colonizing power in the old sense of that term' but as a 'Mandatary under the League of Nations'. This was differentiated from a colonial power and justified as in line with the principle of self-determination based on the following characteristics:

- The term of the mandate would not be open-ended but 'limited', though it would have to be long enough 'to ensure the success of the new state'.
- The 'Mandatory Administration' would be characterised by 'a strong and vital educational emphasis' helping to cultivate a 'democratic state' and 'sound national spirit'.
- The foreign power chosen would ensure 'religious liberty' and the country would be moved towards 'economic independence'.

In short, the commission members believed that recommending mandatory powers seemed to be a perfectly legitimate application of self-determination because these 'powers' would be readying the new countries of the region for self-government and independence, and because the people of the Ottoman lands had been consulted about which 'power' they desired.[5]

The King-Crane Commission and Wilsonian Ideals 225

The gulf between this 'Wilsonian' vision of the region's future and the visions of the Ottoman subjects was sometimes visible in the interactions between the commission and the petitioners they received. After hearing a request for independence, for example, the commission would politely insist that the delegation name their favoured mandatory power in the following manner: 'Which is the Power you choose as a Mandatory Power for this country in case Complete Independence [sic] will not be granted?'[6] This disconnect is further exemplified by a story about a meeting with delegations in Hebron recounted by William Yale:

> Mr. Crane opened the meeting in a business-like way, telling Dr. Haddad to inform the Sheiks that we had been sent out for the peace conference by President Wilson to ascertain their wishes as to whom they desired to rule over them. One arose to reply saying they wished to govern themselves. Mr. Crane then asked Dr. Haddad to explain that the peace conference had decided they must have some mandatory power to rule them. Whom did they prefer? Again an old Sheik arose and said, 'We wish to govern ourselves.' Over and over again Dr. Haddad explained about the Mandatory Power, and over and over again the Sheiks responded that they wished to govern themselves. Finally Mr. Crane grew impatient, his voice betrayed a trace of anger. Turning to Dr. Haddad he said: 'I have had enough of this, they must declare whom they prefer as a Mandatory Power.' Dr. Haddad pressed the question once more. All the Sheiks arose and filed past the commission, giving us a profound salaam. The last to go said with the greatest dignity, 'If the peace conference insists that someone rule over us, inform President Wilson we choose that Allah shall be our ruler.' Then silently they left the room.[7]

As mentioned in Chapter 6, about three weeks into their time in Greater Syria the commission began opening their interviews with a reading of Article 22 of the League of Nations Covenant in order to inform the delegations that independence would not be granted. Despite the fact that the commission was generally upfront about their (and, essentially, Wilson's) vision for the Ottoman lands, the region's people viewed their future political possibilities differently, often because of their different interpretations of Wilson's pronouncements. It is plain to see how this laid the groundwork for future disillusionment among these Ottoman subjects.

Even though the Commission members seemed to have the same basic understanding of Wilson's ideals, their attempt to apply self-determination to the Ottoman lands highlighted how difficult it would be to implement this concept in the real world. Perhaps the most troubling issue for the commission members was how to apply self-determination to a region that, in their minds, was teeming with many intermingled groups that had difficulty living with each other. Although creating new states around homogenous racial and cultural 'nations' was not Wilson's primary vision for self-determination, it was an element that, when present, could make for the more logical crafting of new boundaries. Consequently, the racial and religious makeup of the various new states the commission members were proposing was a constant point of discussion. Although this may have been their main quandary, there were other, even more vexing issues. For example, they had to decide whether or not diasporic communities should have a say in the political reapportionment of their 'homeland', especially if these communities had been forced to leave this homeland, as was the case, according to certain members of the commission, with the Lebanese and the Jews. In a more drastic example, they had to decide how to count populations that had been the victims of massacres during the war, as was the case with the Armenians. Depopulation due to massacre and deportation was certainly not something for which the Armenians should be penalised, but it did not change the fact that their numbers were greatly depleted in the region, thus making it harder for the commission to base any recommendation that favoured the Armenians on the 'desires of the people'.

The members of the commission were among the first people to attempt to apply Wilsonian ideals and hence grapple with these difficult questions. As could be expected, the answers they produced were convoluted and controversial. More specifically, the commission members came to different conclusions about issues related to self-determination: primarily, they disagreed on many of the quandaries raised by self-determination and this disagreement, which again followed the familiar lines documented above (King, Crane and Lybyer on one side; Montgomery and Yale on the other), revolved around two main issues. First, they disagreed over which groups of people in the region constituted nations suitable for statehood and, further, how the populations of these groups should be counted. Second, they disagreed about the circumstances under which self-determination could be overridden as the primary consideration for recommending the creation of a state, which mainly surfaced in their discussions of Armenia and Palestine.

King, Crane and Lybyer

King, Crane and Lybyer based large portions of their recommendations in the 'Report upon Syria' on a literal, ostensibly demographic reading of self-determination. They felt that their method of obtaining 'the opinions and desires of the whole people' had yielded a reliable, though not perfectly accurate, representation of these desires. They described their attempt to get a cross-section of opinions as follows:

> The endeavour was made to ascertain the opinions and desires of every important group, sect and organization, of a few well-informed representative individuals, and of significant minorities or sub-divisions, especially in cases where there seemed to be disposition, for any reason, to suppress these.

The authors of the report acknowledged that their opinion-gathering techniques were flawed in some ways, with the main problems being:

- the number of petitions in each region was not proportionate to the population of the regions;
- the number of petitions received from each religious group was not proportionate to the respective populations of these religious groups;
- the number of signatures on each petition varied widely yet they tabulated their main statistics from the number of overall petitions regardless of the number of signatures;
- some petitions appeared to have been heavily influence by 'propaganda'; and
- there was reason to suspect that a small amount of petitions had fraudulent signatures.

In light of their imperfect data gathering and analytical methods, they acknowledged that their report could not 'be regarded as a mathematically accurate analysis of the real desires of the peoples of

Syria', yet they did believe that it presented 'a fairly accurate analysis of present political opinion' and that 'no vital interest or element of the population' had 'been omitted in the inquiry'. They added, rather expressively, that 'as in a composite photograph, certain great, common emphases are unmistakable'. Thus after seeing 442 groups and receiving 1,863 petitions ('written or oral or both') in Greater Syria, the authors of the report believed that they could safely state that they had a solid understanding of the political desires of the estimated '3,247,500' people of the region. 'The petitions', they concluded, 'are certainly representative'.[8]

In general, King, Crane and Lybyer split self-determination into two main levels. The first, and primary, level provided them with a basis for state creation: they believed that if a discernible group of people constituted a popular majority (or plurality, at least) in a particular region, then this group deserved to form a state. The authors of the report realised, however, that it was not practical to give states to all of the diverse and intermixed groups of Greater Syria and Anatolia, and therefore, as the second level of self-determination, they recommended some sort of ill-defined autonomy or League of Nations/mandatory power protection for the minority groups within these new self-determined states. The minorities would also have the opportunity to serve in any new government and this government would protect their rights. They expanded on these two levels at length.

King, Crane and Lybyer primarily defined self-determination as 'the desires of the people', which they interpreted in the context of their investigation as the majority of the opinions they received. For example, they continually cited the majority opinions in various portions of Greater Syria, and in Greater Syria as a whole, as the primary rationales for their recommendations. In recommending that Syria remain unified, King, Crane and Lybyer stated that their recommendation was 'in accordance with the great majority of the people of Syria'. The report's authors also stated that the choice of 'Mandatary' for the region needed to be 'freely desired by the people' and, subsequently, because 'more than 60 per cent' of the petitions presented asked for the United States as mandatory power, they were compelled to recommend that 'from the point of view of the desires of the "people concerned", the Mandate should clearly go to America'. They argued, along these same lines, that because 'nearly nine-tenths' of the population of Palestine was 'emphatically against the entire Zionist program' and '72 per cent – 1350 in all – of all the petitions in the whole of Syria were directed against the Zionist program', they had to recommend that Zionist objectives be 'greatly modified'. In the face of such overwhelming popular opposition, other oft-cited rationales for Zionism, such as staking a claim to the region based either on the potential improvements they could bring to the land or on 'an occupation of two thousand years ago', could, in the rather curt words of the report, 'hardly be seriously considered'.[9] This specific reckoning of self-determination was the most decisive rationale on which King, Crane and Lybyer believed they needed to base their recommendations.

In the regions where they had not been able to travel as extensively as they had in Greater Syria, the authors of the report would often cite expert testimony or vague population figures to justify their claims, but they continued to cling to some semblance of the 'majority' definition of self-determination. In the case of Armenia, they argued it was 'universally recognised that the Armenians themselves desire an American mandate', and therefore they were compelled to recommend that the United States take the mandate. Furthermore, in recommending against a large Armenian state with ports on the Black and Mediterranean Seas, King, Crane and Lybyer argued that Armenians represented only a small minority in much of the region proposed for this state. With this being the case, the 'majority populations would be injured' if they were forced to live in an Armenian-ruled state, which in turn would constitute a 'violation of all "Wilsonian principles"'.[10] When they discussed Turkey, the report's authors similarly argued that there needed to be a Turkish state in Anatolia because 'there remains a large mass of territory, in which the greatest single element of the population is Turkish'. The authors of the report also thought they had consulted many people who knew 'Turkish public opinion' well. Specifically, they noted that 'on the whole, it is highly probable that a large majority of the Turkish people, wishing a mandate at all, would favour the American Mandate', citing the opinions of various journalists and prominent Turks to this effect.[11] Hence, in the parts of the Middle East where they had not consulted the opinions of the people as much as they had in Greater Syria, King, Crane and Lybyer still maintained a view of self-determination that focused on the likely opinions of a region's majority population.

In addition to the prominent reliance on majority opinions in justifying their recommendations, the report's authors also added cultural and linguistic elements to their argument. The best example of this came in their recommendations in favour of the unity of Syria. Despite the fact that substantial groups in Lebanon and Palestine had requested independence from Greater Syria, King, Crane and Lybyer justified their recommendation for unity by arguing that 'the country is very largely Arab in language, culture, traditions, and customs' and that the 'racial and language unity' of Syria was 'too manifest' to make 'the setting up of independent states within its boundaries desirable'.[12] For these commission members, then, the setting up of new, self-determined states could only come in relatively large culturally unified regions in which a majority of the people agreed on the basic framework of their state. The dominant racial group in such a region, like the Arabs in Syria, would lead its (eventual) democratic government but, as was a key factor in this particular take on self-determination, the dominant group also needed to earnestly respect the rights of all minorities in their midst.

In the next, lesser level of self-determination, King, Crane and Lybyer recommended 'autonomy' for prominent minority groups whose population was not large enough to warrant them being granted a state of their own. The region around Mount Lebanon and Beirut, according to the report's authors, was a 'predominantly Christian country' but it was too small and diverse for them to recommend that it be separated from Syria. They argued, instead, that Lebanon should be granted 'reasonable local autonomy' (the details of which were never expanded upon) and its Christian population should be watched over by the League of Nations. Indeed, King, Crane and Lybyer believed that the creation of such a pluralistic state would help to reconcile the differences between all of the groups involved and be part of a process of re-education that would improve the 'unpleasant relations' between these groups. These three commission members also discussed the granting of autonomy to a number of other groups, though exactly how large these groups had to be in order to be considered for autonomy was unclear. The Greeks of Smyrna were recommended for autonomy 'in a territory strictly confined to a district in which they were in a decided majority', while the Greeks of 'Pontus' (the Black Sea Region), who would be split between the new Armenian state and the Turkish state, 'would seem to be too small a minority' to be granted autonomy. King, Crane and Lybyer also argued 'in the interests of a reasonable self-determination' that autonomy should be granted in the new Turkish State 'for some of the smaller racial groups'. They stated, for example, that there should be some sort of autonomous Kurdistan in the Turkish state (which was one of their few mentions of the Kurds).[13] While the details of these recommendations were never made clear, recommending autonomy for certain groups did give the authors of the report a way to argue that self-determination had been granted to the minorities in these new states to some degree.

Conversely, King, Crane and Lybyer argued that favouring any minority group at the expense of other groups in the region would be decidedly against self-determination. The primary example of this came in their argument against what they saw as the privileging of Jews through support for Zionism. They believed that Zionism represented an affront to the 'general principles proclaimed by the Allies' for two main reasons. First, the Jews who would primarily benefit from Zionism were currently living mostly in Europe. Therefore, making pro-Zionist recommendations would violate Wilson's pronouncement that no settlement for a particular region should be made for the advantage of people other than those living in that region. Second, they argued that Zionism would inevitably infringe upon the rights of the people of Palestine. They expanded on this point in a critique of the Balfour Declaration, arguing that there was no way that the 'civil and religious rights of the existing non-Jewish communities in Palestine' could not be 'prejudiced' by the Zionist programme, hence making the programme directly at odds with self-determination in their minds. The Jews, they insisted, did not deserve special treatment and would be a well-protected minority (like all of the other minorities) in the newly unified Syrian state.[14]

In their recommendations, King, Crane and Lybyer did argue that there were two 'special reasons' that overrode self-determination or at least legitimised a different interpretation of it. The first, as will be discussed later in the chapter, had to do with the geopolitical issues raised by the dissolution of the Ottoman Empire or, in their words, 'vexing world-questions' such as the future disposition of the 'Turkish Straits'. Despite the fact that the area around the Bosphorus and the Dardanelles was largely Turkish, the strategic importance of the Straits dictated that they recommend international, rather than Turkish, control over the new state.

The second 'special reason' was oppression on the scale experienced by the Armenians. Despite the fact that they did not travel to the more Armenian-populated portions of the Ottoman lands, they recommended the establishment of a rather large Armenian state spanning an area in which the Armenians formed only a relatively small percentage of the population. In framing their justification for this recommendation, King, Crane and Lybyer argued that the establishment of an Armenian state was 'in a sense penal for the Turkish people', meaning that because the Turks continued not to take responsibility or make amends for the Armenian massacres, they deserved to lose land in Eastern Anatolia. More importantly, though, the report's authors argued that because of their suffering and strong racial qualities, the Armenians had 'earned the right' to 'look forward to a national life of their own'. In this new state, which would at first contain a small percentage of Armenians, the mandatory power could create a situation (through repatriation and immigration) in which an Armenian majority (or at least large plurality) could eventually be established. This state, perhaps more than others, needed a strong mandatory power: they proposed an Armenia 'from which the Mandatory should not withdraw, until the Armenians constituted an actual majority of the entire population, or at least until the Turks were fewer than the Armenians'.[15] In general, King, Crane and Lybyer believed that the Armenian massacres justified sidestepping self-determination in the short term in order to right what was, in their opinions, one of the worst wrongs in the history of the world. This was their answer to the quandary of how to apply self-determination to regions that had been ethnically cleansed of a particular population: give power to the remnants of the group that had been victimised (especially one with as much 'potential' as the Armenians) and then work to create a situation in which the group would become the majority in the new state. In this case, they were arguing that there were specific conditions under which self-determination could and should be manufactured.

There were two caveats to this point. The first was that the report's authors were careful not to advocate for the creation of self-determination by compulsory exchange of populations. On several occasions, they noted that voluntary population exchanges may take place and could even be facilitated by a mandatory power, but exchanges, in their view, should never be forced. Turks, they figured, 'might tend to increasingly withdraw' from the Armenian state, though they stated explicitly that 'no compulsion should be put on any people' to move. Similarly, Kurdistan could be populated with 'nearly all Kurds' by a 'shift' of the 'comparatively small numbers of both Turks and Armenians out of this area by voluntary exchange of population', and some of the 'smaller racial groups' remaining in the cities of the new Turkish state could be 'allowed' to 'transfer' to other new states 'if they so choose'. Hence the homogenisation of new states, in their minds, could be coaxed but should never be forced.[16]

The second caveat was that while oppression could be a justification for sidestepping self-determination, the oppression of the Jews in Europe had not yet reached the level that could justify taking the drastic step of helping them move from Europe to Palestine. Henry Churchill King even briefly discussed the matter of Jewish oppression in Poland (the site of numerous anti-Jewish pogroms at the end of World War I) with the Jerusalem Zionist delegation. The Zionist delegation claimed that 'millions of Jews' needed to 'emigrate from their countries in Europe' because of the oppression they were experiencing, and that their 'only road leads to Palestine'. King, however, was under the impression that Jews were 'obtaining their rights in Poland and in other countries' and thus there would be 'no more need for such emigration for them'.[17] Although King, Crane and Lybyer acknowledged the existence of Jewish oppression in Europe, they did not believe that it was on par with Armenian suffering in the Ottoman Empire, and they also did not believe that bringing 'millions' of European Jews to Palestine was an appropriate way to make amends for whatever oppression that the Jews had suffered.

Yale and Montgomery

While King, Crane and Lybyer gave self-determination primacy in their recommendations, William Yale and George Montgomery believed that self-determination was only one of many considerations that needed to be taken into account when determining the future of the Ottoman lands. They did, however, realise that they needed to address self-determination at length likely because Wilson had made it a significant part of his rhetoric. Yale and Montgomery both engaged in selective use of 'the desires of the people' as a factor in their recommendations and often employed rather creative demographic justifications for their opinions in order to show that these opinions were in line with self-determination.

In his recommendations, William Yale often recounted the stated desires of the people that the commission had interviewed, yet he continually inferred that most of these attitudes were spurious or that their origins were recent and likely fleeting. Because Yale doubted the genuineness of the testimony that the delegations had been giving to the commission, he believed that neither he nor the commission should base their recommendations solely on this testimony. This view, paired with his assessment of the respective qualities of the region's various groups, often led him to make recommendations that were directly opposed to the opinions that the commission heard while in the region. This came out most emphatically in his recommendations for Palestine, in which he argued that the region should be separated from Syria and that Zionism should continue despite this being 'entirely contrary to the wishes of the people of Palestine and those of most of the inhabitants of Syria'. Unsurprisingly, the one local 'desire' to which he chose to adhere was recommending Great Britain as mandatory power for Palestine partly because 'the Jews all desire the British'. Yale added a worldly dimension to his usage of self-determination in the justification of his support for Zionism by claiming that 'the wishes and desires of 14,000,000 Jews who have a national history, national traditions, and a strong national feeling must be taken into consideration'.[18] These points, when taken with his opinion that the Zionists would be able to modernise the region more effectively than its current inhabitants, gave Yale what he believed was a strong foundation to override the wishes of the majority of the Palestine delegations.

In turning to Lebanon, Yale employed 'the desires of the people' as a justification for the separation of Lebanon from Syria, pointing out that such a separation:

> would meet with the desires of the great majority of the inhabitants of Mount Lebanon, with the desires of about fifty per cent. of the inhabitants of Greater Mount Lebanon, and with the desires of more than a fifth of the total population of United Syria.[19]

In addition to this, Yale stretched his usage of self-determination in arguing that about '300,000 to 400,000' Lebanese Christians had emigrated during the 'last half century' after suffering from 'Moslem oppression'. Because these 'emigrants still took an intense interest in their mountain and in the welfare of their Christian brethren there', they (like the world Jewry) also deserved some sort of consideration in determining the future of the region.[20] Yale further employed the language of self-determination when discussing Syria by recommending a general League of Nations mandate partly because the 'vast majority of the inhabitants have flatly refused the assistance of France'.[21] Thus, self-determination for Yale was something that could be used for legitimating recommendations but could be cast off when there were other overriding factors. It was also something, in Yale's mind, that was not necessarily bound by a contiguous piece of land, as shown by the inclusion of diaspora communities in his justifications.

George Montgomery was the commission member with the least enthusiasm for self-determination, though he still employed it in his justifications at some points and felt compelled to address it when he was recommending against the apparent desires of the people. In advocating the formation of a large Armenia, for example, Montgomery manipulated population figures in order to suit his political project, illustrating that he felt the need to at least attempt to address demographic self-determination in justifying his recommendations. His main argument for the formation of an Armenia with ports on both the Mediterranean and the Black Seas was that the Armenians had gained the 'right to an opportunity of national life' because of the 'terrible ordeal of blood and massacre through which they have been put at the hands of the Turks'. Yet he felt it necessary to statistically create an Armenian plurality in this region by using pre-war population estimates and dividing the population of the region's Muslims into Turks, 'Lazes', and 'Kizil-bash Shiites'. In this new territory, the Armenians would be (or would have been before the war) 26 per cent of the population, while the Turks would be 25 per cent.[22]

In discussing his support for Zionism, however, Montgomery diminished the importance of the 'desires of the people' and discarded self-determination as a major factor in his recommendations. He believed that the Zionists deserved the region partly because of the oppression they had experienced, stating that 'the Jews are still being persecuted in Poland, Russia, and Roumania' and that Palestine could become 'a refuge from persecution' for them.[23] Along with this oppression, Montgomery also felt that the question of Zionism was bigger than Palestine:

> Zionism can not be considered from the standpoint of Palestine alone. It must be considered also from the standpoint of history, of racial achievements, of Jewish persecution and of anti-semitism. There must be no narrow interpretation and application of the word rights, but the greatest benefit to the greatest number must be considered.[24]

The 'rights' to which he was referring were the 'rights of the existing [majority] non-Jewish communities in Palestine' that the Balfour Declaration pledged could not be 'prejudiced' if Zionism were to go forward. According to Montgomery, demographic self-determination was secondary to his utilitarian argument in this special case and Zionism, as noted above, 'should be encouraged for the benefit which it will bring to the country'.[25] Although Montgomery did appear to back Zionism before his time in the region, his contention that the Jews could bring benefit to all of the region's people mirrored arguments given to the commission by the numerous Zionist delegations they saw while in Palestine.[26]

In general, Montgomery staked his pro-Zionist opinions on a decidedly anti-self-determination platform, claiming that Palestine was 'not the place for one to make up his mind whether to be a pro-Zionist or an anti-Zionist' because 'most of the points of view in Palestine give an anti-Zionist vista'. His feelings about the 'desires of the people' came out even more emphatically in the following statement:

> Now with regard to the desires of the people, it seems to me that the report (if it is to deal only with desires) should look beyond the desires as expressed and should try to grasp what the desires would be if the people could see what Zionism is likely to do for the land in the coming years. Such a forecast involves the beneficent interest of wealthy men and the whole hearted interest of experts. In considering such interest of wealthy men and experts, it is not fair to pay too much heed to the words of a few zealots but there should be considered the official program where the benefit foreseen is not that solely of the Jews but of the Arab population as well, and we

may remember that the mandatary will be present to insure [sic] justice.

The people of the region, in Montgomery's paternalistic estimation, did not realise that the Zionists could greatly help them. The modernisation of the land by the Jews would bring the 'greatest good for the greatest number' and that 'number' included the Arabs. This, according to Montgomery, was a more benevolent basis for state creation, in that it would help the population far more than simply abiding by the wishes of the majority of Palestine. More specifically, Montgomery argued that 'if one comes to Palestine without appreciating this, let us say newer conception of social economy, the point of view which he accepts will be quite different from those who believe in values as determining policies.'[27] Zionism was in the best interest of the land and its people, according to Montgomery, and this trumped all other considerations.

In general, the members of the King–Crane Commission grappled with self-determination in different ways. King, Crane and Lybyer were fairly confident they knew what self-determination meant and were also fairly confident that their methods had given them an understanding of what the 'desires of the people' in Greater Syria were at this point in time. Their understanding of self-determination was such that they realised that it should be used as the basis for state creation, but they also acknowledged that it needed to be adapted to protect the minorities of the region, hence their discussion of autonomy. The report's authors chose to bend the concept slightly in the case of extreme oppression (as represented by the Armenians) in order to craft a situation in which self-determination could eventually be created. Both Montgomery and Yale found ways to sculpt population numbers to fit their recommendations and, if this effort appeared weak or could not be done, they drew on many other arguments in an attempt to rhetorically override the 'desires of the people'. For all of the commission members, there existed a gulf between the regions that they had toured and the regions that they had not. While they could specifically utilise the testimony of the people of Greater Syria in their recommendations, they fell back upon general population numbers and 'expert' testimony for the regions they did not visit. These parts of their recommendations generally worked from the assumption that the region's groups were largely monolithic. All of the commission members assumed, for example, that 'Armenians' were a cohesive unit with similar political desires whether they lived in Erivan or Adana. Their evidence for such assertions was thin and it was sometimes acknowledged as such, yet the assumption of the monolithic Middle Eastern racial/religious group was pervasive among the commission members.

As one of the first tests of self-determination in application, the King–Crane Commission showed that the concept was malleable, ill-defined, and debatable when being used as the justification for state creation or minority protection. In this sense, this application was in line with many of the other attempts at applying the concept in postwar Europe and elsewhere. Wilson's advocacy of self-determination meant that it could not be ignored by the diplomats who were grappling with the major questions of postwar territory redistribution, but as the experience of the King–Crane Commission showed, the practical application of the concept was fraught with complications.

Imperialism and Geopolitics

By the end of World War I, geopolitical anti-imperialism (to borrow Frank Ninkovich's term) had become an important part of American foreign policy. According to Woodrow Wilson and many others, imperialism had been one of the major causes of World War I. If the world was going to avoid such pointless conflagration in the future, Wilson argued that imperialism and the international rivalries it spawned needed to be done away with or, at a minimum, revamped in a manner more favourable to the imperial subjects of the world. If imperialism was archaic, then the feudal political system that spawned it (monarchy) was even more so, according to Wilson. He believed that democracies could transform the world into a more fair and benevolent place, while autocracies would only spread more imperialism and war. Democracy, therefore, needed to be embraced by ex-imperial powers like Germany, Austria and Turkey, but it also needed to be taught to the new countries formed in the wake of the disintegration of these empires. These new countries, or at least the non-European ones, would be tutored towards self-government by 'mandatory powers' which were distinctly not imperial in Wilson's mind.[28] The Paris Peace Conference was full of incidents that pitted more traditional imperialist aspirations against Wilson's rhetoric of self-determination.[29] Britain and France were, rather awkwardly, Wilson's two closest wartime allies and also the world's two largest remaining empires for which this anti-imperialist rhetoric would have been most pertinent. They were also the two powers most interested in the Ottoman lands, which led to numerous confrontations between Wilson, Clemenceau and Lloyd George, as well as, on a smaller scale, between the King–Crane Commission and the British and French military occupiers of Greater Syria.

The recommendations of the King–Crane Commission members reflected Wilson's anti-imperialism to varying degrees, with the contours of disagreement drawn along familiar lines: King, Crane and Lybyer were staunch defenders of Wilson's vision while Yale and Montgomery were less convinced that the president's ideals were the best basis for the reconstitution of the Middle East. All of the five main commission members recognised that British and French designs on the Ottoman lands were problematic, but their conclusions differed with regards to the future role of these imperial powers in the region. Furthermore, debates about imperialism necessarily included extensive consideration of the region's geopolitical importance, the focus of which was usually the question of Constantinople and the 'Turkish Straits'. The idea that the Ottomans had controlled highly strategic lands that were prone to imperial intrigue was pervasive among the commission members, and this consideration often provided them with a justification for their respective recommendations. Taken together, their opinions about anti-imperialism and geopolitics show that, at very least, the commission members agreed that the world needed to move away from traditional imperialism. The question of the most effective way to do this was where they differed.

Before the summer of 1919, the members of the King–Crane Commission left a fair amount of evidence indicating that they generally agreed with Wilson's brand of anti-imperialism and his belief in the geopolitical importance of the Ottoman lands. After their time in the region, the ideas of King, Crane and Lybyer about imperialism in the Ottoman lands changed little, while Yale and Montgomery recorded opinions that were not entirely in line with the 'Dangers to the Allies of a Selfish Exploitation' document they had signed before their journey. King, Crane and Lybyer often spoke in unmistakable Wilsonian terms about the purpose of their mission, arguing, for example, that their recommendations were made for 'the establishment of progressively righteous relations among men, not for sowing the seeds of endless and bitter discord'. These 'seeds' of 'discord', the authors of the report argued, were beginning to be sown by the 'occupation of the Smyrna region by the Greeks' because there was no way that 'such seizure of territory' could be 'harmonized with the professed principles of the Allies in the war'. They also believed, in the case of Turkey, that a 'selfish division and exploitation of territory' would 'naturally provoke violent retaliation' upon both its 'immediate transgressors' and 'the Christian population generally'. The Turks, they argued, might 'take the occasion to rid themselves entirely of those whom they look upon as internal enemies', thus provoking further atrocities against Armenians or other Christians. 'In that case', they continued, 'the Allies would have to share the guilt of the Turks'.[30]

In their report, King, Crane and Lybyer also asserted that carrying on with an externally imposed division of Turkey would simply continue the flawed system of imperialism that had caused the war, beckoning 'moral dissension among the world's leaders and deliberately inviting the moral shipwreck of the world'. They concluded this emphatically Wilsonian point with a rhetorical question that professed their lofty ideals:

> Is it not high time, then, in this crisis of the world's history, and after the immeasurable sacrifices of the Great War, that intelligent men should recognize the stupid futility of the old method of incessant political and commercial national strife, and face this age-long Eastern Question in a totally new spirit?

This reformulation of the 'Eastern Question' was central to their reasoning. King, Crane and Lybyer were seeking to 'change this age-old "Eastern Question" from one of selfish scramble among nations to one of recognizing here a great and distinctly international or world interest'. For these three commission members, the problems of the Turks certainly came from the fact that they had all of the flaws inherent in being Turkish and Muslim, but it also arose from the fact that the powers of the 'Occident' had, for at least the last century, been coveting the region inhabited by the Turks. This region, according to the authors of the report, needed 'to be freed from Occidental domination'.[31]

At the heart of the 'Eastern Question', for King, Crane and Lybyer, was the 'scramble' for Istanbul because of its strategic importance.

President Wilson had given the commission a clear mandate for coming up with a solution to the problem posed by the city and its adjacent waterways by mentioning it in Point Twelve of his Fourteen Points speech ('The Dardanelles should be permanently opened as a free passage to the ships and commerce of all nations under international guarantees'). With this in mind, the authors of the report argued (citing extensively from English author Leonard Woolf's 1917 book *The Future of Constantinople*) that Istanbul had to be under League of Nations administration because 'this perpetual centre of intrigue and endless cause of trouble must be done away with'. This 'intrigue' had continued following the war with 'the Greeks' having 'already declared their ambition to have Constantinople in their hands'. The authors of the report also continually referred to Istanbul in terms of metaphorical illness: it was 'a great plague spot of the world', something that needed to be removed from Turkey via 'surgery which would sever from their State such a seat of infection'.[32] Donald Brodie concurred with this in his assessment of the region written shortly after their journey, stating that Turkey had been 'seriously handicapped' by 'Occidental' desires for Istanbul:

> The empires of the world have always cast covetous eyes on the Bosphorus and the Dardanelles as the key of the treasure-houses of the Orient. Constantinople has ever been a nest of the most corrupt and insidious intrigue. The lobby of the Pera Palace is still filled with the secret agents of the great powers scheming to get advantage of the Turk and all other powers. [...] With their capital a center of the worst kind of international intrigue, it is little wonder that the Turk has been corrupted partly, perhaps, in self-defense.[33]

Thus Brodie joined King, Crane and Lybyer in believing that by creating an international 'Constantinopolan State' run by the League of Nations, a major cause of regional rivalries would be removed. A similar sentiment was voiced about Syria in the King–Crane Commission Report:

> As a portion of the bridge-land uniting Europe, Asia, and Africa, too – where in a peculiar degree the East and the West meet – Syria has a place of such strategic importance, politically and

commercially, and from the point of view of world civilization, as also to make it imperative that the settlement here brought about should be so just as to give promise of permanently good results for the whole cause of the development of a righteous civilization in the world. Every part of the former Turkish Empire must be given a new life and opportunity under thoroughly changed political conditions.[34]

The 'strategic importance' of Ottoman lands made a peaceful and just dissolution of the empire all the more important. This issue was therefore 'a great world responsibility' and it was clear to these commission members that 'larger world interests must prevail', especially in the question of Istanbul and the Straits.[35]

The authors of the report also noted that the French and the British were still acting in an 'old' imperialist manner in Greater Syria, with the French being the guiltier of the two parties. As they had expected, French and British actions were angering both each other and the local populations, thus creating the basis for future conflict. The French, according to King, Crane and Lybyer, 'worked with varying energy and success to obtain the reality or at least the appearance of a desire for a French mandate'. They employed numerous forms of propaganda to this end, including 'inspired articles in newspapers, attempts at browbeating and espionage, [and] the hindrance by French soldiers of the attempts of individuals and groups to reach the commission'. The French had also removed local officials 'because they had declined to support a French mandate' and used tactics like 'threats and bribes and even imprisonment and banishment for the same purpose'. The British, for their part, 'were proceeding as though expecting that Britain will remain permanently in control of Palestine', by which they meant they were 'planning for the growth of cities, the building of roads and railways, and the construction of harbors'.[36] King, Crane and Lybyer found little evidence that the French and British were changing their imperialist ways. In their Wilsonian way of thinking, then, the region was bound for major trouble if the United States did not step in, which led them to recommend extensive American mandates in the Ottoman lands.

William Yale agreed with the authors of the report that the British and French were intent on imperial domination of the region, yet he chose to recommend that these two powers take mandates for the region anyway. The British, according to Yale, were not 'disinterested', had not 'played the game fair' with the French, and had been behind 'much propaganda, despite their protestations to the contrary'. Based on his observations during the war and during his time on the commission, Yale believed that the British intended 'if possible, to keep Palestine' and 'control Syria', though they would be willing to cede Mount Lebanon to France so that there would not be an 'open break' between the two countries. This imperialist policy, according to Yale, was 'so evident that it cannot be mistaken'. Yale held similar beliefs about the French, stating that they had 'looked upon Syria as the booty which they would secure on a successful conclusion of the hostilities'. He asserted that French claims to the region were 'commercial, imperialistic, and sentimental', yet they had been outwitted by the British, who had cleverly 'secured partial control' of Faysal and his allies. The French, Yale argued, believed they had little ability to get any support from the Muslims, so they directed propaganda efforts at Christians, with partial success. This policy, paired with Britain's attainment of Muslim support in the region, had helped to 'deepen hatreds between Moslem and Christian'. The policies of France and Britain, Yale concluded, were 'a curse to the country and if persisted in will eventually result in massacres' because they had 'done everything possible to make union and co-operation [between Muslims and Christians] impossible'.[37] These two imperial powers had helped to create a noxious political atmosphere in the region, yet, for reasons discussed in the next two sections of this chapter, Yale saw no other alternative to recommending that Britain and France play a major role in the region's future. (George Montgomery commented little on imperialism).

Carving up the Ottoman Empire, according to the commission members, was fraught with danger. This danger came from the strategic world position of the Ottoman lands and the questionable intentions of the actors who were seeking to play a major role in creating the new mandates. In the minds of the commission members, the British and French had never stopped being two of the world's foremost imperial powers during the war and showed little inclination to change in its aftermath. The alternative to British and French mandates (besides the disregarded request for independence) was to have the United States take control of parts of the region, and this possibility proved contentious among the commission members.

The United States and the Ottoman Lands

As has been noted in previous chapters, the commission members unanimously believed that the United States was the paragon of modernity and the most benevolent country on earth. This was partly evidenced by what they saw as their country's well-intentioned stewardship of the Philippines and Cuba, and its selfless entrance into World War I. The fact that most of the petitioners asked for the United States as their mandatory power only reinforced these ideas among the commission members. Yet in their final recommendations, they did not concur about the role that the United States should play in the future of the region. King, Crane and Lybyer argued that the people of the region could move towards modernity with the help of the right tutor, and that tutor, as overwhelmingly requested by these people, should be the United States. They further argued that the choice of the United States as mandatory power in Syria was based on the local 'knowledge of America's record', the centrepiece of which was America's lack of 'territorial and colonial ambitions' that 'her treatment both of Cuba and the Philippines seemed to them to illustrate'. Additional reasons given by the delegations for choosing an American mandate, according to the report, included the 'genuinely democratic spirit of the United States', the country's 'ample resources', and its 'unselfish war aims'.[38] The commission members no doubt enjoyed the affirmation such statements gave to their national pride; as Charles Crane noted to a friend, the 'trust' of the region's people 'in America and in President Wilson is touching'. 'It would be most inspiring', he continued, 'to assist in founding a new state on Wilsonian principles to be presided over by a lineal descendant of Mohammed.'[39] This was put even more emphatically by Donald Brodie, who stated that 'America to the Arab was a magic word' and that the commission found the 'earnest faith in America and American ideals' on display before for them to be 'startling'.[40]

Using the evidence that the commission gathered, the report's authors argued that the United States should take extensive mandates in the Ottoman lands. America, rather than Britain or France, was the logical choice for such mandates because it was 'disinterested' and had 'no rival imperial interests to press' in the region, thus being likely to cause 'less friction' than the other powers. It also was not 'a colonizing power' and 'could be relied upon to withdraw from the country as soon as her work is done'. Furthermore, the United States was a 'rich' country with 'abundant resources for the development of the sound prosperity of Syria' and could easily provide the 'large amount of capital' that was 'so necessitous in a thousand ways' for the modernisation of Turkey. In exchange for their investment, the American people could expect 'before the mandate ended a fair return on capital' but should not anticipate 'large financial profits'. The United States also had the required 'experts' who could train the locals in 'science, industry, administration, and above all education'.[41] For King, Crane and Lybyer, these specific stipulations served as major points of differentiation between the United States and unreformed imperial powers like France and Britain. The United States, in their minds, was not a colonial power and did not want to occupy or profit from the region. The members of the commission, like many Americans of their day, were unanimous on this point: they continually classified American forays into places like the Philippines and Cuba, not to mention the American West (all of which were either annexed or still occupied), as somehow not colonial or imperial. In addition to this, the United States had 'capital' and 'experts' whereas these other powers were left with a paucity of these things as a result of the war. From the standpoint of both a lack of imperial ambitions and an abundance of resources, then, the United States was easily the best candidate for mandates in the region.

America's ideals, in the minds of King, Crane and Lybyer, were its strongest assets and its most important qualifications for the undertaking of mandates over Anatolia, Armenia and Greater Syria. These 'great dominant convictions' at the 'foundation of the common life of America' included:

- a 'passion for peace';
- a 'passion for democracy' and respect 'for the common man everywhere';
- a 'passion for universal education, as possible for the rank and file of every nation';
- a 'passion for the development of a national spirit in every people, not as narrow conceit, but as faith in a divine individuality, to which the people must be true'; and
- a 'belief in the principle of the separation of Church and State in government administration, for the highest good both of religion and of state' which would ensure 'complete religious liberty'.

The United States was, in the minds of King, Crane and Lybyer, uniquely suited to become a mandatory power in the Middle East. Although they admitted that they did not know 'whether America is now willing to accept the general single mandate for Turkey', they believed that consideration of these domestic issues was not 'part of the task of the commission'.[42] They did, however, contend that the United States had a new global role to fill. The Ottoman lands, these three believed, showed promise and modernisation was a real possibility under the United States. As Crane wrote to President Wilson on 10 July 1919, 'there is raw material here for a much more promising state than we had in the Philippines'.[43]

Although William Yale and George Montgomery seemed to back the idea of the United States playing a major role in the region before their time on the commission, they grew more sceptical about this idea while visiting the Ottoman lands. In his 8 July letter to William Westermann, Yale wrote that America should be left 'out of the mandate question' for Greater Syria primarily because the other powers had already laid claim to the region, and, in the case of Palestine, that 'America had made very definite promises to the Jews' that were going to be difficult to fulfil. He believed that Britain, with its lengthy imperial history, was far better suited for the implementation of these promises. Yale did not preclude the United States from playing a role in the portions of the Ottoman Empire for which he was not making recommendations (Istanbul, Anatolia, Armenia) and, in fact, noted the potential of American involvement in these places as one further reason he could not recommend that the United States take a role in Greater Syria.[44] Later in the journey Yale seemed to back off his expectation that the United States would play a future role in the region, with Albert Lybyer noting in late July that Yale had become 'very pessimistic' in writing his report and now believed that there was 'no chance what[so]ever [that] America [would] accept any mandate'.[45]

In his final recommendations, Yale further elaborated on his belief that the United States should not take a mandate in Greater Syria, noting that America was not suited for this role because the region had a complicated and perhaps dangerous future. His fear of some form of new 'Arab Moslem Confederation' taking shape led him to believe that the Muslim majority in a pluralistic, united Syria would only be a force of oppression. Attempting to develop Greater Syria 'as a united, national and secular state' would be a 'dangerous, troublesome and uncertain experiment for the United States', unless 'the rest of the Arab provinces of the former Ottoman Empire were under our control'. Such a suggestion, for Yale, seemed to be impossible for a few reasons: the other powers involved in the settlement would not accept it, the American people would not consent to it and it was likely an impossible and thankless task to begin with. According to Yale, it was better to divide these former Ottoman provinces and give them different mandatory powers in order to protect the region, and the world, from another despotic Muslim empire (which is a theme that will be revisited in the next section).[46]

George Montgomery, for his part, acknowledged that the United States was the preferred mandatory power throughout the region yet he did not include the United States in his recommendations outside of Armenia. 'The preference for America', he argued, 'was to be expected', yet he downplayed this preference as not being 'as hearty as might have been expected'. This 'preference' was explainable by what he saw as the benign imperial past of the United States 'which had handled Cuba and the Philippines gently'. Conversely, Great Britain had 'handled Egypt roughly', which contributed to its mixed reputation in the region. Despite this, Montgomery did not advocate that the United States assume any role in Greater Syria because he believed that there was no 'chance of the United States accepting' a mandate for this region. He also believed that there was no possibility of America 'being allowed to accept' such a mandate by Britain and France. The United States, if it were to take 'any mandate at all', was already 'committed to Armenia', according to Montgomery. Furthermore, he argued that 'if America is to assume or to be allowed to assume any added responsibility, this ought to be in mandates such as that over Kurdistan, or in Transcaucasia, or in Anatolia which will contribute to the success of the Armenian experiment'. 'Europe', he concluded, would not 'consent at one and the same time to such mandates and also to a Mandate over Syria', thus he was not recommending that the United States take any mandate in Greater Syria despite it being the choice of the majority of the delegations they received.[47]

The United States, in the minds of the commission members, was morally superior to Britain and France, and had the ability to become a successful mandatory power. King, Crane and Lybyer employed these beliefs as the main justifications for their recommendation that the United States take mandates for huge parts of the Ottoman lands. However, issues related to US domestic politics (Americans perhaps not wanting major mandates), global politics (the British and French not allowing the United States to take control of the region), and the potential of future trouble in the region were all issues that helped to justify the dissenting opinions of Montgomery and Yale. King, Crane and Lybyer believed they were shaping a new internationalist destiny for the United States, whereas Montgomery and Yale felt they were being realistic.

Regional Nationalisms, Amir Faysal, and the Threat of Arab-Muslim Imperialism

The members of the King–Crane Commission offered different views on the nature of the region's nationalisms, particularly disputing both the goals of these various nationalisms and Amir Faysal's ability to harness Syrian nationalist sentiment. For the commission members, nationalism was a modern and desirable trait, yet they disagreed upon the type of nationalism that was possible in the region. William Yale was the commission member who was most sceptical about nationalism among Arabs, believing that a Faysal-led, unified Syria was merely a cover for the building of a new empire dominated by an oppressive Arab-Muslim ethnic nationalism. George Montgomery was also sceptical of both Arab nationalism and Faysal along these same lines. He instead saw Zionism as the true nationalism set to bloom in the region. Conversely, Henry Churchill King, Charles Crane and Albert Lybyer believed that a form of tolerant civic nationalism could mature in the region under the right tutelage and that the threat of a new Arab/Muslim empire was largely overstated. Faysal, in their minds, was an ideal leader for a unified Syria.[48]

William Yale, the commission member who displayed the most emphatic views on these issues, had developed a deep distrust of Arab nationalism during his wartime deployment in Syria. Any Arab movement, he believed, was merely a front for something more insidious. In a December 1918 despatch to the State Department, for example, Yale argued that 'today there has arisen among the Arabs a vague consciousness of their nationality; and the present movement among the Arabs is called an Arab movement; but it is essentially a

Moslem Movement.' Those who did not know the Middle East, he continued, were going to hear the nationalist terms in which Amir Faysal's entourage would speak at the Paris Peace Conference ('Arab nationality; Arabic language; Arab independence, Arab greatness') and would likely conclude that there existed a 'viril [sic] and profound nationalism' in the region. 'The contrary is the case', Yale argued, because the primary devotion of the Arabs was religious and not nationalist: 'The entire life of the Moslem Arabs is bound up with religious traditions and customs, rites and ceremonies; the basis of their laws is the Koran; their educational institutions are Islamic Seminaries, their language and literature are that of Mohammed.' Yale believed that the Arabs clearly had an ulterior motive for posing in this pseudo-nationalist fashion, stating that 'an Arab Empire means a Moslem Empire; the fact of it being Arab is but secondary'. Faysal, Yale concluded, had gone to Paris 'under the disguise of Arab Independence' but what he and his 'nationalists' truly desired was an oppressive, anti-modern, and Arab-ruled Islamic empire.[49]

During his time on the commission, Yale's opinion on these matters became more pronounced. In his 8 July letter to William Westermann, Yale reiterated his distrust of nationalism in the region and inferred that a grander Islamic conspiracy existed:

> In my judgment the expression of national feeling which we have heard is not evidence of a strong national feeling. Through it all from Beersheba in the south to Damascus and Baalbeck I have felt a distant note of Pan-Arabism and Pan-Islamism. By a clever, well organized and thorough propaganda [campaign] the Moslems of Palestine and Syria have been united on a program which superficially has every sign of being Syrian Nationalism, but which is basically Islamic.

The commission, he believed, was being duped. He went on to unfavourably compare Faysal and his inner circle to the Young Turks, stating 'Among the Young Turks in 1908 there were more well meaning, more intelligent, patriotic men, and more sincere and honest men, than there are in the present Arab movement.' The Young Turk movement, he continued, soon turned to 'chauvinistic nationalism and pro-Islamism, and so to a greater degree, it is almost certain that the present Arab movement, or Syrian national movement will turn into fanatical Islam'. Christians, Yale argued, had joined the 'Arab movement' only because, in Palestine, they had a 'fear of Zionism' and, in Syria, because 'they dare not do otherwise'. Independence was the goal of the Young Arabs, which was 'quite natural' in Yale's mind, because if they were constrained by a mandatory power, they might not be able to 'dominate' the Christians.[50]

Yale furthered this critique of the 'Young Arabs' in his recommendations, highlighting their deceptive civic-sounding nationalism and their lack of true 'liberal' credentials. These 'Young Arabs' were skilful politicians, according to Yale, and had been able to manipulate the people of the region to their own illiberal ends. The façade they had built, however, could easily 'be mistaken for Nationalism':

> The Young Arab Party is controlled by just such spirits as dominated the Committee of Union and Progress [...] their aim and ideal is not the building of a Syrian State in which the Christians and Moslems would be on terms of equality. They are not nationalists and have no desire to see such a liberal state develop. The ideal of the Young Arab is the resurrection of a Moslem Arab State and eventually a Moslem Arab Empire somewhat along the lines of the empires of the Ommayads and the Abbasids. They have used most skillfully every means of winning the support of all the different groups, and they have very carefully and skillfully covered with a cloak of Nationalism their real aims and purposes. [...] But their cloak of Nationalism is so thin and so torn at spots that one occasionally gets a glimpse of the real fabric underneath.

Yale did believe that there was a fledgling 'Liberal Movement' among the 'Moslems in Syria', but that it was 'too feeble, too weak in numbers and in conviction to resist the vigorous, energetic group of Young Arabs'. The ambitious Sharif Hussein was the man behind these 'Young Arabs' and their pan-Islamic movement, according to Yale, and Hussein was merely using his more liberal son Faysal to gain control of Syria. In general, the region's 'liberals', though they did exist, had little chance to make any impact on a new state. The 'strength of fanaticism' far outweighed any 'liberal movement' among the Muslims and a strong mandatory power was needed to protect the region's minorities against these 'fanatics'.[51] Yale did not believe that a tolerant, civic nationalism in Greater Syria was possible in the postwar environment and, judging by the tone of his writing, he doubted that such a thing would ever be possible.

Amir Faysal, in Yale's assessment (which had become more positive since December 1918), did have many attractive personal qualities: he was 'liberal and open-minded and wishes to see Christians, Druzes and Moslems working together for the best interests of the State'. His prestige, however, was 'temporary and had already lost much of its éclat'. 'His personality', according to Yale, was 'not a powerful one; he is loved but not feared, he is courted but not obeyed', thus rehashing the pervasive idea that powerful and perhaps violent leadership was the only kind that the people of the region responded to. By the summer of 1919, Yale argued that much of Faysal's clout rested solely on the fact that he had a 'princely income from the British' and he was 'the dispenser of favors and lucrative posts'. Once this was gone, he would 'no longer be able to win supporters by lavishly bestowing honors and appointments' on them. His 'ideas', concluded Yale, could not 'prevail' over the illiberal 'Young Arabs' without 'the support of a foreign power'. Faysal's grip on power in Syria was tenuous and the basis of his prestige was fleeting. Although Yale did recommend that Faysal remain the leader of Syria under a League of Nations mandate in his final report, he did not hold out much hope that he would remain so for long.[52]

George Montgomery also believed that Muslims were poised to dominate the region and needed to be stopped. Granting independence to a unified Syria, he argued, would leave the region's minorities dangerously exposed. Montgomery further believed that backing a Zionist state in Palestine was in fact a safeguard against Arab-Muslim ambitions. Not only would a Zionist state thwart expansionist Muslim intentions, it would also provide Jews 'a place for trying out an experiment in [Jewish] nationalism' and, as previously noted, the project could 'do much to overcome the materialism so often connected with the name of the Jew'. For Montgomery, the establishment of a Zionist state and the cultivation of this emerging Jewish nationalism provided a dual benefit for the world: the reining in of dangerous Muslims and the betterment of the international Jewry.[53]

King, Crane and Lybyer were far more convinced that a form of inclusive civic nationalism could be established in Greater Syria. They argued that it was a 'matter of justice to the Arabs, in recognition of the Arab people and their desire for national expression, and of deep lasting concern to the world, that an Arab State along modern political lines should be formed'. Nationalism was young in Syria, however, and they noted that whichever mandatory power took control of Syria would be charged with educating this new Arab state in matters of nationhood; as they stated in the report, 'this systematic cultivation of national spirit is particularly required in a country like Syria, which has only recently come to self-consciousness'.[54] King, Crane and Lybyer, then, believed that the Arab nationalism they observed was both nascent and genuine. They also believed that this was a desirable development and one that could help further the Arabs as a people. Unlike Yale and Montgomery, they did not question the veracity of this movement.

Furthermore, King, Crane and Lybyer did not question Faysal's ability to lead such a state. The region needed a strong ruler as a 'personal symbol of power' and Faysal was the only person qualified to fill this role. The reasons for this, according to the authors of the report, were fivefold. First, Faysal had 'led the Arabs in cooperation with the Allies against the Turks, and entered Damascus in triumph' thus elevating his position among the people of Syria. Second, King, Crane and Lybyer continually emphasised Faysal's Hashemite cachet to prove his legitimacy as a leader among Muslims. Being 'the son of the Sherif of Mecca, and as such honored throughout the Moslem world' gave him a 'great advantage' because the people would, they believed, automatically respect this. This assertion is emblematic of the commission members' propensity to give primacy to Faysal's religious position and overestimate the stature that this lent him in Greater Syria, as was shown by his lack of support in Palestine. Third, the authors of the report believed that Faysal had the attributes of a leader, like being 'tolerant and wise, skilful in dealing with men, winning in manner, a man of sincerity, insight, and power'. He was also, as noted above, a man of pro-Western liberal leanings holding 'broad sympathies with the best in the Occident'. Fourth, he had already obtained 'an excellent political education' developed 'during the past two years in the desert and at Damascus and Paris'. He was willing to compromise when he needed to and 'promises well as a constitutional monarch, who could work amicably in coordination with a mandatory power'. And fifth, the majority of the delegations asked for Faysal to be their leader, thus the commission was in some sense obliged to recommend him to become the head of the new state. Although they never overtly mentioned the threat of an Arab or Muslim empire, King, Crane and Lybyer did briefly acknowledge this concern by stating that once Faysal took the role as the head of the Syrian state, he should 'renounce all rights of inheritance of the crown of the Hejaz'. They argued that this would be necessary because 'otherwise serious complications might arise in the future', though what these complications might be went unsaid.[55]

The King–Crane Commission members all witnessed the same displays of nationalism while they were in the Ottoman lands but they assessed what they witnessed in different ways. King, Crane and Lybyer did not doubt the veracity of the Arab nationalism they witnessed, nor did they question Amir Faysal's ability to lead the people of Greater Syria towards a tolerant civic nationalism. William Yale and George Montgomery believed that they were able to see this Faysal-led Arab nationalism for what it was: a thinly veiled attempt to allow Arab-Muslims to dominate the region in an exclusive ethno-nationalist fashion. The commission members' disagreement on this matter predictably mirrored their general attitudes towards Islam.

***

The King–Crane Commission members' respective recommendations may have been rooted in their social imaginaries, but the members also grappled with the more immediate concerns of their day and their respective beliefs about these concerns played a major role in their recommendations. In general, all of the five main commission members believed, along with Wilson, that imperial wrangling was one of the main causes of World War I and, if such a war was to be avoided in the future, the imperialist system would have to change. Wilson believed that this would take a major adjustment on the part of the remaining imperial powers, as well as a reformulation of the rights of the world's people based on democratic ideals. The commission members took this message to heart in various ways and the degree to which they agreed with Wilson's reformulation of the world order had major implications on their recommendations in two main ways.

First, the commission members agreed with Wilson that the British and the French had indeed been part of the imperial problem before the war. In the postwar world, and particularly in the Ottoman lands, the commission members believed (to varying degrees) that the imperialist impulses of the British and French could be tempered by the new League of Nations mandatory system. The United States, possessing no such imperialist impulse in the minds of the commission members, made an excellent candidate to oversee the new states of the region, though the commission members disagreed on whether or not the United States would or should take these mandates. The general split on the commission went as follows: King, Crane and Lybyer believed that the United States needed to take a more active role in world affairs in order to change the world order. Taking a mandate or mandates in the Ottoman lands was, in their minds, an excellent opportunity to perform such a role. Yale and Montgomery, however, did not believe that the United States had enough international experience or national will to take on mandates in the region except, perhaps, in Armenia. One further concern about imperialism, voiced mainly by William Yale, was that a new and troublesome Arab-Muslim empire might rise in place of the Ottoman Empire and this possibility needed to be guarded against. In general, however, the commission members were in agreement that the establishment of paternalistic mandates instead of colonies was a step forward for the world and a break with the imperialist system.

Second, self-determination was a concept that was both potent and malleable in this era, and because Woodrow Wilson gave it such rhetorical prominence in its various iterations, the members of the King–Crane Commission were obliged to grapple with its ambiguity. Self-determination forced commission members to try to disentangle the 'groups' of the Ottoman lands and then determine which of these groups were prominent enough to deserve consideration for statehood and which were destined to become protected minorities. Inevitably, difficult questions arose for which self-determination provided no simple solution. The concept probably raised more questions than it answered, which made it possible for the commission members to adapt it to most of their arguments. The demographic realities of regions like Palestine, Lebanon and the various proposed Armenian states forced members of the commission to attempt to craft justifications that overrode the minority status of the group or groups they championed. In the end, all the commission members believed that the Western powers would control the immediate future of the region but King, Crane and Lybyer incorporated more of what they saw as the 'desires of the people' into their recommendations, making them more in line with Wilson's ideals than Yale and Montgomery.

CHAPTER 11

CONCLUSION

The King–Crane Commission is becoming an increasingly forgotten moment in history. This is partly because the United States chose not to play a role in the reapportioning of the Ottoman lands and therefore the policy that the commission was meant to influence never came into being. Despite its lack of implications in the policy arena, the commission (as a historical artefact) became embroiled in the partisan battles surrounding the Israeli–Palestinian conflict. In instances when the commission has been mentioned in academic works, scholars have variously labelled it as prescient or prejudiced, knowledgeable or naïve. The interpretive gulf between these positions is so wide that these scholars hardly seem to be talking about the same thing. In light of this, a reappraisal of the King–Crane Commission like the one undertaken in this volume is long overdue. Although its historical impact might not have been as significant as some of its participants had hoped, the King–Crane Commission provides an excellent window into American thinking about the Middle East at the dawn of more substantial American involvement in the region. Few Americans had been thinking analytically about the Middle East in 1919, thus it is a rare opportunity to closely study a group of American elites who were asked to do just this. The question employed to guide this study has been 'Why did the King–Crane Commission members arrive at their respective conclusions?' The primary goal of this final section is to answer this question; however, it is first necessary to discuss what this study has added to the history of Greater Syria, which was the commission's focus.

Greater Syria

A fair amount of work has been done on the history of 1919 Greater Syria in recent years, and this study adds to this growing body of work in a number of ways. A few historians have contended that the testimony given to the King–Crane Commission was more the product of Arab nationalist propaganda than a genuine outpouring of political desires.[1] Although it is certainly true that people were attempting to marshal opinion in Greater Syria during the summer of 1919, this was to be expected in the context of a perceived political watershed like the King–Crane Commission; indeed, it would have been odd if this had not happened. Furthermore, much (if not most) of this propaganda was not centrally directed from the government of Amir Faysal. In 1919, Faysal and his allies were only one of many factions attempting to shape Greater Syria's future. Within this context, the Damascus Program, having been agreed upon by representatives of many of these contending and somewhat fluid blocs at the Syrian Congress, represents a rather impressive political achievement and provides a window into the shifting nationalist currents in Greater Syria.[2] It is also important to note that the people of the region were not mindless drones blindly mouthing statements given to them, as many histories of this era have insinuated. Greater Syria had been a hotbed of political activity while it was part of the Ottoman Empire and the leaders of the region's various communities had experience making decisions that would land them on one side or the other of thorny political issues. Although it is important to recognise the varying pressures that these leaders may have faced in making their decisions, it is also important to recognise that many people in places like Palestine and Lebanon did dissent from the majority, demonstrating that dissent was possible in this setting. The people of the Greater Syria were well-practised in the political wrangling of their own region and made informed decisions based on their assessment of the situation. To belittle these decisions is to ignore the complex political history of the region.

This study also sheds new light on Zionist attempts to marshal opinion in 1919 Greater Syria, which appear to be unknown to most historians of the era. As discussed in Chapters 6 and 7, the Zionist Commission sent out agents to ensure that (at the very least) no Jew spoke against Zionism, and the agents were successful in this endeavour.

A large number of Jews in the region seemed to show a genuine concern about publicly endorsing Zionism. This was mainly because they did not want to poison their relationships with the growing number of vehemently anti-Zionist people in the region, many of whom were their neighbours and long-time associates in various capacities. Additionally, the Zionists attempted, with very limited success, to gather pro-Zionist testimony from Arabs who lived in the vicinity of their colonies in hopes of bolstering their position with the commission. Evidence indicates that the summer of 1919 was a moment when the Zionists were able to substantially consolidate support for their cause among the non-Zionist Jewish leadership of the region. When paired with the swell of anti-Zionist sentiment among non-Jews during this same moment, it appears that the visit of the King–Crane Commission, by forcing people to take sides in this dispute, played a role in decreasing the future likelihood of peaceful co-existence between the Jews and the other populations of the region. It was a moment that accelerated a broad communal realignment in Greater Syria.[3]

The King–Crane Commission

In the analysis of decisions made by historical actors, historians often pay little attention to the limited list of alternatives conceivable to a particular person; statements like a person was 'of their time' are often substituted for historical analysis of how 'their time' delimited the person's conception of the world and hence the possible decisions he or she might make. Understanding the limitations placed on an historical actor by their social imaginary is part of understanding the complexity of the human decision-making process. More generally, comprehending the multitude of discourses that shaped decisions made by historical actors is imperative in any comprehensive and fair historical account. By analysing these discourses in order to better gauge the full spectrum of concepts influencing a person in a given era, a historian can deeply contextualise an individual and more fully understand why particular decisions have been made. Without a detailed understanding of the discourses governing a person's thinking (both internal and external to their social imaginary), historians run the risk of viewing evidence selectively and drawing conclusions that fall in line with their pre-existing political beliefs. If scholars choose to limit themselves to one or even a few such discourses (which is almost always a politically motivated choice), they are at risk of substituting 'classificatory categories' for 'real human beings'.[4] While it is true that the analysis of decisions is limited in that one cannot fully delve into the mind of an historical actor, certain analyses are more comprehensive and likely more accurate than others. To date, most accounts of the King–Crane Commission have fallen into this trap: they have been selective, superficial and partisan. A comprehensive historical analysis of the decisions made by the commission members has never really been attempted, which underlines the contribution of this study.

An analysis of the discourses present in the writings of the commission members supports the general argument that they shared a social imaginary. The fact that they were in near total agreement about several topics helps to lay out a portion of the social imaginary's framework. What the commission members did not recommend is just as telling about American thinking pertaining to the Middle East in this era as their actual recommendations. Perhaps the best example of this was their refusal to recommend independence for any part of the region despite it being requested by a large majority of the delegations they interviewed. Had the King–Crane Commission returned from their journey to the Middle East advocating independence for the region, they would have been viewed as naïfs. It was obvious to American and European experts at the time that such a conclusion was not only wrong but also ridiculous, irresponsible and dangerous. The commission members did harbour competing visions for the future of the region, however, and the analysis of their respective justifications for these visions has provided the main findings of this study.

King, Crane and Lybyer

In a general sense, this study has found that although the recommendations of King, Crane and Lybyer in the commission's final report were delimited by discourses of race, religion and modernity, the decisive factor in their decision making was their perception of what constituted an equitable solution for the majority of the people living in the Ottoman lands. Their recommendations pertaining to the Muslims of the region exemplify this. Before their tour of the region, King knew little of Islam, Crane had shown an interest in it, and Lybyer had often denigrated it in his past writings. During and after their time in the region, these three commission members continued to disparage the Muslims of the region by doing things like deriding the Turkish ability to govern and generally infantilising the Arabs. Yet based on the fact that the King–Crane Commission Report discussed Islam in a far better light than was typical of American writing in this era, it appears that their time in the Middle East may have improved their perception of Islam and its adherents. That these three men viewed the Muslim majority of the Ottoman lands as both able and noble was certainly a factor in their recommending a unified, Muslim-dominated Greater Syria. Despite their qualified faith in Arab Muslims and general disparagement of Turkish Muslims, King, Crane and Lybyer's conception of self-determination, along with the demographic realities of the region, led them to recommend the formation of states in which Muslims comprised large majorities and hence would (eventually) have the primary role in governance. Self-determination also meant that Christians and other minority groups needed to be granted an undefined 'autonomy' within these new states. They decided, however, that international politics and penalties for the commitment of atrocities could override self-determination in the cases of Istanbul and Armenia. The dominating belief of the King–Crane Commission Report was, however, that the region's Muslims had both the potential to build and govern modern states and that they had the right to do this because they constituted the majority of the population.

One of the major accusations against the King–Crane Commission is that its anti-Zionist recommendations had roots in the authors' antisemitism and pro-missionary stance. More specifically, the anti-Jewish tendencies of Charles Crane have been used on various occasions to insinuate that the King–Crane Commission was antisemitic as a whole. This study has found that anti-Jewish sentiment did not play a major role in the recommendations of the King–Crane Commission. Based on the evidence reviewed here, Crane's opposition to Zionism stemmed less from his dislike of what he saw as certain 'types' of Jews and more from his belief that the Zionists were poised to do what, in his mind, was in direct opposition to the principle of self-determination and hence morally wrong. Following from this, and underpinned by the fact that King and Lybyer (the report's primary authors) showed no sign of anti-Jewish tendencies, this study has found no empirical basis for the argument that the anti-Zionism in the King–Crane Commission Report had its roots in antisemitism.

This study has also found no evidence to back the contention that the King–Crane Commission was a mouthpiece for anti-Zionist 'missionary designs' in Greater Syria. Some missionaries from the region supported the sending of the commission to the Ottoman lands while others did not. Missionaries, it seemed, were more worried about being able to continue their work in the region no matter what future lay in store for the Ottoman lands. According to the evidence examined here, there is simply no proof that King, Crane or Lybyer were predisposed to recommend against Zionism. The evidence in existence shows that King, Crane and Lybyer did, however, have difficulty understanding how mass Jewish immigration to Palestine would not infringe on the rights of the region's existing non-Jewish inhabitants. Their time in the region and the opinions of the delegations they interviewed confirmed this doubt.

While this study does not back the argument that King, Crane and Lybyer were predisposed for or against any particular position beyond those precluded by their social imaginary and orders from Wilson, it also does not endorse the viewpoint that the King–Crane Commission Report accurately reflected the wishes of the region's people. The commission's method of collecting data is not convincing from the perspective of modern academia. The commission received opinions from local leaders who claimed to represent larger populations, though the degree to which most of these people did actually represent the opinions of their respective groups is not knowable. Although it is true that the report's authors were among the chorus of voices in 1919 who accurately predicted that taking a pro-Zionist and imperialist path in the region would only lead to violence, this does not mean that their writings and the data that they gathered should be employed uncritically.

Yale and Montgomery

Race and religion played a larger role in the recommendations of George Montgomery and William Yale. They both believed that Muslims (in general) could not be trusted and, when it came to governing, the Arabs would likely be worse than the Turks. The region, they contended, needed to be ruled by external powers for the foreseeable future. On the question of Zionism, both Yale and Montgomery had supported the creation of a Jewish homeland in Palestine before the journey and became more emphatic in their support afterwards. Despite the lack of support for Zionism in Greater Syria, they believed that the best qualities of the Jews would help bring modernity to the region and improve the life of everyone in Palestine. Although they acknowledged the 'flaws' of the Jews as a group, Montgomery and Yale believed that the largely anti-Zionist population of the region would eventually be convinced that Zionism was best for them. These reasons, along with their sympathy for the persecuted Jews of Europe, made Montgomery and Yale believe that the establishment of a Jewish homeland in Palestine was just. It is interesting and perhaps telling to note that while many academics have accused the King–Crane Commission of having antisemitic undertones, few have remarked about Yale or Montgomery being anti-Arab, anti-Turk or anti-Muslim, which they clearly were. If any prejudices had a major effect on the recommendations of the commission members, these were certainly the most influential.

As Yale and Montgomery realised that their beliefs about the region's future did not always conform to the 'consent of the governed', they drifted further from Wilsonian ideals and even felt the need to employ arguments at odds with these ideals in order to justify their recommendations. Although they did consider the United States as superior to the other powers, they did not believe that their country should get involved in what were likely going to be difficult territories to administer. Yale and Montgomery did not preclude the United States from taking any role in the region but they believed that their country should stay away from major commitments in Muslim lands.

***

The King–Crane Commission has come to mean many different things to many different people. In 1919, most elites in the region saw it as an intervention by a benevolent world power on their behalf. When their statements to the commission were largely ignored, these people were greatly disappointed. The British and French, however, remained the major villains in most of these peoples' narratives, with the reputation of the United States going into precipitous decline only after it supported the establishment of the state of Israel in 1948. For Zionists, on the other hand, the King–Crane Commission represented (and still, to a certain extent, represents) a threat to their project. Supporters of Zionism tried to stop the commission at its inception and have, in the ensuing years, consistently tried to disparage and defame some of its members.

The King–Crane Commission also revealed a rift within American elite thinking about their country's role in the postwar world. King, Crane and Lybyer's emphatically interventionist reading of Wilson's pronouncements pertaining to foreign policy showed that they felt that the United States should play a more active and benevolent role in the wider world. Yale, Montgomery and others saw such a vision for America's global role as unrealistic, especially in the context of the Ottoman Empire's largely Muslim lands. Furthermore, these two camps disagreed on the role that the world's people should have in decisions regarding their own futures. King, Crane and Lybyer's recommendations aligned more closely with what the majority of their interviewees believed was best for themselves, while Yale and Montgomery based their recommendations more on what they believed was best for the region and its people. It is important to note that these debates have morphed but have never entirely gone away.

When writing about the King–Crane Commission during a time in which the United States is deeply linked to the Middle East and devotes considerable diplomatic and military resources to the region, it is instructive to return to an era when this was less so. American conceptions of the region were fairly well-formed long before the United States started playing a major role in the Middle East, and the policies crafted thereafter were shaped by the discourses already in existence. As this study has shown, the writings of the King–Crane Commission are probably most fruitfully and compellingly employed as a resource in the study of the evolving American discourses pertaining to the Middle East and the influence of these discourses on American policy in the region. The disagreement within the commission illustrates disparate strands of American thought about the Middle East during the World War I era, though these are strands that might appear familiar to a modern observer of this often-fraught relationship. The fact that these attitudes are recognisable nearly a century later leads to the rather uncomfortable conclusion that perhaps there has been little appreciable change in American conceptions of the Middle East since 1919.

NOTES

Chapter 1 Introduction

1. Champaign, Illinois, University of Illinois Archives, MS Albert Lybyer Papers, Box 3, fol. 'Howard, Harry N.', Howard to Lybyer, 4 August 1943. Hereafter referred to as MS Lybyer.
2. This number comes from the author's extensive survey of the library holdings at the University of Manchester and other UK repositories, along with a lengthy search of academic journal databases and the internet.
3. George Antonius, *The Arab Awakening: The Story of the Arab National Movement* (Beirut: Librairie du Liban, 1969, originally published 1937), pp. 296, 351, 397. It should be noted that Antonius's book was funded by, and dedicated to, commission member Charles Crane.
4. Ussama Makdisi, *Faith Misplaced: The Broken Promise of U.S. Arab Relations: 1820–2001* (New York: Public Affairs, 2010), pp. 137–43.
5. Other proponents of this viewpoint include Harry N. Howard, *The King–Crane Commission: An American Inquiry into the Middle East* (Beirut: Khayats, 1963), pp. 320–7; A. L. Tibawi, *Anglo-Arab Relations and the Question of Palestine 1914–1921* (London: Luzac & Company, 1978), pp. 361–3; Benny Morris, *Righteous Victims: A History of the Zionist-Arab Conflict, 1881–2001* (New York: Vintage, 2001), pp. 88–92; Rashid Khalidi, *Resurrecting Empire: Western Footprints and America's Perilous Path in the Middle East* (London: I.B.Tauris, 2004), pp. 32–3, 120–1; Eugene Rogan, *The Arabs: A History* (New York: Basic Books, 2009), pp. 158–62; and Ali A. Allawi, *Faisal I of Iraq* (New Haven: Yale University Press, 2014), pp. 243–5.
6. Frank Manuel, *The Realities of American-Palestine Relations* (New York: Public Affairs Press, 1949), pp. 223–52.
7. Michael Oren, *Power, Faith, and Fantasy: America in the Middle East 1776 to the Present* (New York: W. W. Norton & Company, 2007), pp. 386–90.

8. See also Frank Brecher, 'Woodrow Wilson and the "King–Crane Commission" to the Near East' in his book *Reluctant Ally: United States Foreign Policy toward the Jews from Wilson to Roosevelt* (New York: Greenwood, 1991), pp. 13–24; Peter Grose, *Israel in the Mind of America* (New York: Alfred A. Knopf, 1984), pp. 86–92; Stuart Knee, *The Concept of Zionist Dissent in the American Mind 1917–1941* (New York: Robert Speller & Sons, 1979), pp. 11–39; and Robert D. Kaplan, *The Arabists: The Romance of an American Elite* (New York: The Free Press, 1993), pp. 68–72. Two final perspectives on the commission come from Elie Kedourie and James Gelvin. Kedourie has argued that the commission provoked an injurious political firestorm in the region and that its recommendations merely parroted the propaganda of aspiring leader Amir Faysal (Elie Kedourie, *England and the Middle East: The Destruction of the Ottoman Empire, 1914–1921* (London: Bowes & Bowes, 1956), pp. 139–47). James Gelvin has similarly noted that the commission caused a major upheaval in the region but he instead focused his analysis on the ramifications of its failure to influence the region's future, with many of the elites who sided with Faysal losing credibility after the commission's report had no impact on the new political makeup of Greater Syria (James Gelvin, 'The Ironic Legacy of the King–Crane Commission', in *The Middle East and the United States: A Historical and Political Reassessment* ed. by David W. Lesch, 3rd edn (Boulder, CO: Westview Press, 2003), pp. 13–29).
9. According to Taylor, people from a group, in any given era, generally share a similar social imaginary that is filled with broad concepts that both dictate what they perceive as being the normal functioning of reality and mediate their perceptions of social phenomena in this reality. Importantly, the social imaginary delimits human perceptual capacity, meaning that it 'constitutes a horizon that we are virtually incapable of thinking beyond'. See Charles Taylor, *Modern Social Imaginaries* (Durham N.C.: Duke University Press, 2004), pp. 23–30, 69–100, 109–42. Quote on p. 185.
10. Discourses are defined here as historically specific and partially fixed (at any given moment) systems of meaning within and from which subjects form their understanding of reality. It is important to note that this is largely a discursive study, meaning that it focuses on an analysis of the discourses present in the writings of the commission members more so than on the commission members themselves. The broader contention here is that these discourses had more influence on the commission members' recommendations than did their personalities or other aspects of their lives. This definition of discourse is amalgamated from Ernesto Laclau and Chantal Mouffe, *Hegemony and Socialist Strategy: Towards a Radical Democratic Politics*, (London: Verso, 1985), pp. 105–42; Michel Foucault, *The Archeology of Knowledge* (London: Tavistok, 1972 [1969]), pp. 3–76; Norman Fairclough, *Discourse and Social Change* (Cambridge: Polity Press, 1992); David Howarth, *Discourse* (Buckingham: Open University Press, 2000), Miguel Cabrera, *Postsocial History: An Introduction* (Lanham, Maryland: Lexington Books, 2004), pp. 19–60; and Charles Taylor, *Modern Social Imaginaries* (Durham N.C.: Duke University Press, 2004), pp. 176–8.

11. Timothy Mitchell, *Colonising Egypt* (Berkeley: University of California Press, 1991), p. 166.
12. Michael Shapiro, *Reading the Postmodern Polity: Political Theory as Textual Practice* (Minneapolis: University of Minnesota Press, 1991), p. 3.
13. It has recently been treated as such in Matthew Jacobs, *Imagining the Middle East: The Building of an American Foreign Policy, 1918–1967* (Chapel Hill: University of North Carolina Press, 2011).

Chapter 2 Backdrop of the King–Crane Commission

1. See Gerrit Gong, *The Standard of 'Civilization' in International Society* (Oxford: Clarendon Press, 1984), pp. 3–23; Emily Rosenberg, *Spreading the American Dream: American Economic and Cultural Expansion 1890–1945* (New York: Hill and Wang, 1982), pp. 7–13; and Walter L. Hixson, *The Myth of American Diplomacy* (New Haven: Yale University Press, 2008), pp. 6–7.
2. Frank Ninkovich, *The United States and Imperialism* (Malden: Blackwell Publishers, 2001), pp. 91–2. The italics are in the original text.
3. Raymond Williams, *Keywords: A Vocabulary of Culture and Society* (London: Flamingo, 1983), pp. 208–9.
4. Rosenberg, pp. 3–86, quotes on p. 9.
5. Carl Degler, *In Search of Human Nature: The Decline and Revivalism of Darwinism in American Social Thought* (Oxford: Oxford University Press, 1991), p. 41.
6. The term 'scavenger ideology' is used by George Mosse in *Towards a Final Solution: A History of European Racism* (Madison: University of Wisconsin Press, 1985), p. 234, while Walter LaFeber uses the term 'rubbery' in *The Cambridge History of American Foreign Relations Volume II: The American Search for Opportunity, 1865–1913* (Cambridge: Cambridge University Press, 1995), p. 51. For a general discussion of this point, see Michael Omi and Howard Winant, *Racial Formation in the United States: From the 1960s to the 1990s*, 2nd edn (New York: Routledge, 1994), pp. 53–76, and Howard Winant, *Racial Conditions: Politics, Theory, Comparisons* (Minneapolis: University of Minnesota Press, 1994), pp. 13–22.
7. Vasant Kaiwar and Sucheta Mazumdar, 'Race, Orient, Nation in the Time-Space of Modernity', in *Antimonies of Modernity: Essays on Race, Orient, Nation*, ed. by Vasant Kaiwar et al. (Durham: Duke University Press, 2003), p. 265, and Ann Stoler, 'Racial Histories and Their Regimes of Truth', in *Political Power and Social Theory*, 11 (1997), pp. 183–206.
8. Eric Hobsbawm, *The Age of Empire 1875–1914* (New York: Vintage, 1989), pp. 56–83.
9. See Reginald Horsman, *Race and Manifest Destiny: The Origins of American Racial Anglo-Saxonism* (Cambridge: Harvard University Press, 1981).
10. David Roediger, *Working Toward Whiteness: How America's Immigrants Became White* (New York: Basic Books, 2005), pp. 3–34.

11. On these points, see Matthew Frye Jacobson's works *Barbarian Virtues: The United States Encounters Foreign People at Home and Abroad, 1876–1917* (New York: Hill and Wang, 2000) and *Whiteness of a Different Color: European Immigrants and the Alchemy of Race* (Cambridge: Harvard University Press, 1998). On difference in the temporal condition of different races, see also Howard Winant, 'Racial Formation and Hegemony: Global and Local Developments' in *Racism, Modernity and Identity on the Western Front*, ed. by Ali Rattansi and Sallie Westwood (Cambridge, MA: Polity Press, 1994), pp. 270–2.
12. See Jacobson, *Barbarian Virtues*, pp. 221–34, and Eric T. Love, *Race over Empire: Racism and U.S. Imperialism 1865–1900* (Chapel Hill: University of North Carolina Press, 2004).
13. Rosenberg, p. 8.
14. Makdisi, *Faith Misplaced*, pp. 48, 157.
15. Jacobson, *Barbarian Virtues*, p. 159.
16. Degler, pp. 59–83.
17. Jacobson, *Barbarian Virtues*, p. 108.
18. 'An Address to a Joint Session of Congress', 11 February 1918, in *Papers of Woodrow Wilson* ed. by Arthur Link, 69 vols (Princeton: Princeton University Press, 1986), 46, pp. 318–24. Hereafter referred to as *PWW*.
19. For similar assessments, see Trygve Throntveit, 'The Fable of the Fourteen Points: Woodrow Wilson and National Self-Determination', *Diplomatic History*, 35 No. 3 (June, 2011), pp. 445–81, and Erez Manela, *The Wilsonian Moment: Self-Determination and the International Origins of Anti-Colonial Nationalism* (Oxford: Oxford University Press, 2007), pp. 37–45.
20. This section is the synthesis of many works. In order to avoid excessive footnoting, the most salient of these works will be listed here. They include, but are not limited to, Mustafa Aksakal, *The Ottoman Road to War in 1914* (Cambridge: Cambridge University Press, 2008); Selim Deringil, *The Well-Protected Domains: Ideology and the Legitimation of Power in the Ottoman Empire 1876–1909* (London: I.B.Tauris, 1999); Gwynne Dyer, 'The Turkish Armistice of 1918: 1—The Turkish Decision for a Separate Peace, Autumn, 1918', *International Journal of Middle Eastern Studies*, 8, no. 2 (May, 1972), pp. 143–52; Gwynne Dyer, 'The Turkish Armistice of 1918: 2: A Lost Opportunity: The Armistice Negotiations at Mudros', *International Journal of Middle Eastern Studies*, 8, no. 3 (October, 1972); David Fromkin, *A Peace to End All Peace: The Fall of the Ottoman Empire and the Creation of the Modern Middle East* (New York: Henry Holt, 1989); Paul Helmreich, *From Paris to Sevres: The Partition of the Ottoman Empire at the peace conference of 1919–1920* (Columbus: Ohio State University Press, 1974); Margaret MacMillan, *Peacemakers: Six Months that changed the World* (London: John Murray, 2001); Fawwaz Traboulsi, *A History of Modern Lebanon* (New York: Pluto Press, 2007); Donald Quataert, *The Ottoman Empire 1700–1922*, 2nd edn (Cambridge: Cambridge University Press, 2005); James Renton, *The Zionist Masquerade: The Birth of the Anglo-Zionist Alliance 1914–1918* (London: Palgrave Macmillan, 2007); Bruce

Westrate, *The Arab Bureau: British Policy in the Middle East 1916–1920* (University Park, Pennsylvania: Pennsylvania State University Press, 1992); Meir Zamir, 'Faisal and the Lebanese Question, 1918–1920', *Middle Eastern Studies*, 27, no. 3 (July, 1991), pp. 405–7; Meir Zamir, *The Formation of Modern Lebanon* (Ithaca: Cornell University Press, 1985); and Erik J. Zürcher, *Turkey: A Modern History* (London: I.B.Tauris, 2007).

21. John Denovo, *American Interests and Policies in the Middle East 1900–1939* (Minneapolis: University of Minnesota Press, 1963), pp. 39–42, 169.
22. 'From the Diary of Colonel House', 3 January 1919, *PWW*, 40, p. 404.
23. 'An Address' in Baltimore, Maryland, 6 April 1918, *PWW*, 47, p. 269.
24. 'An Annual Message on the State of the Union', 4 December 1917, *PWW*, 45, pp. 197–200.
25. See John Milton Cooper, 'A Friend in Power? Woodrow Wilson and Armenia' and Lloyd Ambrosius, 'Wilsonian Diplomacy and Armenia' both in *America and the Armenian Genocide of 1915* ed. by Jay Winter (Cambridge: Cambridge University Press, 2003), pp. 103–12, 113–45.
26. 'From Cleveland Hoadley Dodge', 2 December 1917, *PWW*, 45, p. 185.
27. 'From the Diary of Colonel House', 19 May 1918, *PWW*, 48, p. 69.
28. 'Sir William Wiseman to Sir Eric Drummond', 27 August 1918, *PWW*, 49, p. 365.
29. See Frank Brecher, 'Revisiting Ambassador Morgenthau's Turkish Peace Mission of 1917', *Middle Eastern Studies*, 24, no. 3 (July, 1988), pp. 357–63, William Yale, 'Henry Morgenthau's Special Mission of 1917', *World Politics*, 1, no. 3 (April, 1949), pp. 308–20, and Jehuda Reinharz, *Chaim Weizmann: The Making of a Statesman* (Oxford: Oxford University Press, 1993), pp. 153–71.
30. John Milton Cooper, *Woodrow Wilson: A Biography* (New York: Vintage Books, 2009), p. 387.
31. For a similar analysis, see Manela, pp. 40–2.
32. Melvin Urofsky, *American Zionism: From Herzl to the Holocaust* (Lincoln: University of Nebraska Press, 1975), pp. 81–116, and Naomi Cohen, *The Americanization of Zionism, 1897–1948* (Hanover and London: Brandeis University Press, 2003), pp. 4–7.
33. 'A Memorandum by Jacob Judah Aaron de Haas', 6 May 1917, *PWW*, 42, pp. 234–5.
34. 'From the Diary of Colonel House', 10 September 1917, *PWW*, 44, p. 186.
35. 'Wilson to Stephen Samuel Wise', 31 August 1918, *PWW*, 49, p. 403.
36. 'From Robert Lansing', 13 December 1917, *PWW*, 45, p. 286. For a more full discussion of this, see Renton, *Zionist Masquerade*, pp. 130–48, and Urofsky, *American Zionism*, pp. 202–20.
37. See Manela, pp. 19–21.
38. Thomas J. Knock, *To End All Wars: Woodrow Wilson and the Quest for a New World Order* (Princeton: Princeton University Press, 1992), pp. 194–201.

Chapter 3 Paris Peace Conference 1: The Idea of a Commission

1. For the best general overview of this topic, see Arthur Walworth, *Wilson and His Peacemakers: American Diplomacy at the Paris Peace Conference, 1919* (New York: W. W. Norton & Co., 1986), especially pp. 1–5.
2. 'Inquiry Document No. 882 *Report on the Inquiry, May 10 1918*' in *Papers Relating to the Foreign Relations of the United States, The Paris Peace Conference, 1919*, 13 vols (Washington: Government Printing Office, 1942), I, pp. 86–7. Hereafter referred to as *FRUS PPC*.
3. Lawrence E. Gelfand, *The Inquiry: American Preparations for Peace, 1917–1919* (New Haven: Yale University Press, 1963), pp. 50, 60–1, 239–58. For the report, see New Haven, Yale University Library, MS William Yale Papers, Record Group 658, Box 7, fol. 6, 'Report upon Just and Practical Boundaries for Subdivisions of the Turkish Empire by W. L. Westermann and Others'. Hereafter referred to as MS Yale-Yale.
4. The Supreme Council, also known as the Council of Ten in the first two months of the conference, was the main deliberative body and consisted of the heads of state and foreign ministers of Britain, France, the United States, Italy, and Japan. This was slimmed down to the Council of Four in March, with only the leaders of Britain, France, the United States, and Italy participating. See MacMillan, p. 61.
5. See MacMillan, pp. 107–16.
6. 'Council of Four', 17 May 1919, *FRUS PPC*, V, p. 700.
7. 'Draft Resolutions in Reference to Mandates', *FRUS PPC*, III, pp. 795–6.
8. MacMillan, pp. 20, 227–31, 262–4. Plebiscites included those in Klagenfurt, East Prussia, and Upper Silesia.
9. See ibid., pp. 357–437.
10. College Park, Maryland, United States National Archives, State Department, Microfilm M820 (General Records of the American Commission to Negotiate Peace, 1918–1931), 'Committees and Commissions, Mandates in Turkey', various correspondence between Isaiah Bowman, Joseph Grew, and others, December 1918 and January 1919. Hereafter referred to as NA-ACNP.
11. New York, Columbia University Rare Book and Manuscript Library, William Linn Westermann Papers 'Personal Diary of William Westermann at the Paris Peace Conference', 23 March 1919. Hereafter referred to as MS Westermann.
12. As quoted in Harold Nicolson, *Peacemaking 1919* (London: Constable & Co., 1933), p. 116.
13. For more detail on Faysal's background, see Allawi, pp. 3–39.
14. MS Westermann, 'Diary', 12 January 1919.
15. MS Westermann, 'Diary', 20 January 1919.
16. Malcolm Russell, *The First Modern Arab State: Syria under Faysal, 1918–1920* (Minneapolis: Bibliotheca Islamica, 1985), pp. 18, 30.
17. MS Yale-Yale, Box 6 fol. 6, 'Memorandum by the Emir Feisal'.

18. MS Yale-Yale, Box 6, fol. 9, 'Conversation with Emir Faisal [...] January 20th, 1919' and MS Westermann, 'Diary', 20 January 1919.
19. MS Yale-Yale, Box 6, fol. 17, 'Memorandum on Syria', 26 March 1919.
20. Allawi, p. 197.
21. MS Westermann, 'Diary', 27 January 1919.
22. MS Yale-Yale, Box 6, fol. 10 '"Territorial Claims of the Hedjas Government" copy of Feisal Memorandum' 29 January 1919.
23. 'Minutes of the Daily Meetings of the commissioners Plenipotentiary', 1 February and 10 February 1919, in *FRUS-PPC*, XI, pp. 8, 27.
24. 'Secretary's Notes of a Conversation Held in M. Pichon's Room at the Quai d'Orsay, Paris, on Thursday, 4 February, 1919', *FRUS PPC*, III, p. 872.
25. Library of Congress, Washington, D.C., Manuscript Division, Henry White Papers, Box 53 fol. 'Turkey (March–May 1919)', Memorandum by William Westermann, 28 May 1919.
26. See MacMillan, pp. 357–67 and Michael Llewellyn Smith, *Ionian Vision: Greece in Asia Minor 1919–1922* (New York: St. Martin's Press, 1973), pp. 75–6.
27. 'Secretary's Notes [...] Thursday, 6 February, 1919', *FRUS PPC*, III, pp. 889–91.
28. Ibid., p. 891.
29. Ibid., pp. 891–2.
30. Library of Congress, Washington, D.C., Manuscript Division, Robert Lansing Papers, 'Diary', Microfilm Reel 2, 6 February 1919. Hereafter referred to as MS Lansing.
31. 'A Memorandum by Tasker Howard Bliss', 8 February 1919, *PWW*, 55, p. 4.
32. Christopher M. Andrew, and Alexander Sydney Kanya-Forstner, *France Overseas: The Climax of French Imperial Expansion* (London: Thames and Hudson, 1981), pp. 188–9. Quote on p. 189.
33. MS Westermann, 'Diary', 20 January 1919.
34. Howard S. Bliss to Wilson, 7 February 1919, *PWW*, 54, p. 551.
35. Bliss to Wilson, 11 February 1919, *PWW*, 55, p. 86.
36. 'Hankey's Notes of a Meeting of the Council of Ten' Quai d'Orsay, Paris, 13 February 1919, *PWW*, 55, pp. 141–5. Quote on p. 142.
37. 'Secretary's Notes [...] Thursday, 13 February, 1919', *FRUS PPC*, III, p. 1018.
38. 'Secretary's Notes [...] Thursday, 15 February, 1919', *FRUS PPC*, IV, pp. 2–4, MS Westermann, 'Diary', 12 and 13/14 February 1919, and Andrew and Kanya-Forstner, pp. 187–8.
39. Frederic C. Howe, *The Confessions of a Reformer* (New York: Charles Scribner's Sons, 1925), pp. 283–306. Quote on p. 301.
40. Joseph Grabill, *Protestant Diplomacy in the Near East: Missionary Influence on American Policy, 1810–1927* (Minneapolis: University of Minnesota Press, 1971), pp. 159–61.
41. 'Minutes of the Daily Meetings of the commissioners Plenipotentiary', 20 February and 22 February 1919, *FRUS PPC*, XI, pp. 61, 66–7.
42. NA-ACNP, Reel 183, 'Committees and Commissions, Mandates in Turkey', various correspondence, February and March 1919.

43. 'Secretary's Notes [...] Thursday, 15 February, 1919', *FRUS PPC*, IV, pp. 147–57; and MS Westermann, 'Diary', 25 and 28 February.
44. New Haven, Yale University Library, MS Colonel E. M. House Papers, MS 466, Box 202, fol. 2/586, 'Brief Statement of Armenian National Claims'. Hereafter referred to as MS House.
45. 'Minutes of the Daily Meetings of the commissioners Plenipotentiary', 26 February 1919, *FRUS PPC*, XI, pp. 76–7.
46. Howard S. Bliss to Woodrow Wilson, 10 March 1919, *PWW*, 55, pp. 472–3.
47. 'Secretary's Notes [...] Thursday, 27 February, 1919', *FRUS PPC*, IV, pp. 161–70.
48. Walworth, pp. 480–1.
49. Edward M. House, *The Intimate Papers of Colonel House: Volume IV, The Ending of the War June 1918–November 1919*, ed. by Charles Seymour (London: Ernest Benn Limited, 1926), p. 369.
50. This was now the Council of Four, which included only the British, French, American, and Italian heads of state.
51. 'Council of Four: Minutes of Meeting', 20 March 1919, *FRUS PPC*, V, pp. 1–8.
52. Ibid., pp. 8–10.
53. Ibid., p. 12.
54. Andrew and Kanya-Forstner, p. 193.
55. 'Council of Four', 20 March 1919, *FRUS PPC*, V, pp. 12–13.
56. Ibid., pp. 13–14.
57. 'Future Administration of Certain Portions of the Turkish Empire under the Mandatory System', *PWW*, 56, pp. 272–5.
58. 'A Translation of a Letter from Prince Faisal' 24 March 1919, *PWW*, 56, pp. 243–4.
59. MS House, Box 201, fol. 2/569, 'Notes of a conversation between Colonel House and Emir Faisal', 29 March 1919.
60. MS Westermann, 'Diary', 4 April 1919.
61. 'A Memorandum by Arthur James Balfour', 23 March 1919, *PWW*, 56, pp. 203–4.
62. Andrew and Kanya-Forstner, pp. 193–5.
63. MS Westermann, 'Diary', 23 March 1919.
64. See Allawi, pp. 214–17. Faysal later denied writing this letter and disowned it.
65. Washington, D.C., Library of Congress, Manuscript Division, Felix Frankfurter Papers, Reel 103, Faysal to Frankfurter 1 March 1919, and Frankfurter to Faysal, 3 March 1919. Hereafter referred to as MS Frankfurter.
66. MS Frankfurter, Reel 15, Frankfurter to Brandeis, 3 March 1919.
67. 'From the Diary of Colonel House', 26 March 1919, *PWW*, 56, pp. 309–10.
68. Henry Wickham Steed, *Through Thirty Years 1892–1922: A Personal Narrative*, 2 vols (London: William Heinemann, 1924), II, p. 300.
69. MS Yale-Yale, Box 6, fol. 17, 'Memorandum on Syria' 26 March 1919. See also Elisabeth Burgoyne, *Gertrude Bell: From her Personal Papers*, 2 vols (London: Ernest Benn, 1961), 2, p. 110.

70. Paul Mantoux, *Paris Peace Conference 1919: Proceedings of the Council of Four (March 24–April 18)*, trans. by John Boardman Whitton (Geneva: Librairie Droz, 1964), p. 30.
71. 'A Memorandum by Arthur James Balfour', 23 March 1919, *PWW*, 56, pp. 203–4.
72. MS Westermann, 'Diary', 23 March 1919.

Chapter 4   Paris Peace Conference 2: Topsy-Turvydom

1. New York, Columbia University Rare Book and Manuscript Library, Bakhmeteff Archive, MS Crane Family Papers, Box 13, fol. 18, 'Charles R. Crane to Cornelia W. Smith Crane', 28 April 1919. Hereafter referred to as MS Crane.
2. NA-ACNP, 'Committees and Commissions, Mandates in Turkey', various correspondence, March and April 1919.
3. 'Minutes of the Daily Meetings of the commissioners Plenipotentiary', 20 March 1919, *FRUS PPC*, XI, p. 128, and 'From the Diary of Ray Stannard Baker', 20 March 1919', *PWW*, 56, pp. 103–4. Note that he did state 'American' in the singular either because it was not certain at this point how many commissioners each country would name or because he already had Charles Crane in mind.
4. 'Ray Stannard Baker to Woodrow Wilson', 21 March 1919, *PWW*, 56, pp. 155–6.
5. Oberlin, Ohio, Oberlin College Archives, MS Henry Churchill King, RG 2/6, King–Crane Commission Microfilm Reel Section A, 'Diary to Wife', 25 March 1919. Hereafter referred to as MS King.
6. 'From the Diary of Colonel House', 26 March 1919, *PWW*, 56, pp. 309–10. 'Syrian commission' was the most common term used for the commission during these initial stages, despite the instructions including Anatolia, Armenia, and Mesopotamia as well.
7. For more on progressive Christian support for Wilsonian internationalism, see Richard Gamble, *The War for Righteousness* (Wilmington, Del.: ISI Books, 2003), pp. 149–232, and Andrew Preston, *Sword of the Spirit, Shield of Faith: Religion in American War and Diplomacy* (New York: Anchor Books, 2012), pp. 253–90.
8. As quoted in Gamble, p. 189.
9. Henry Churchill King, *For a New America in a New World* (Paris: Young Men's Christian Association, 1919), p. 16. This analysis owes much to an essay by historian Leonard V. Smith entitled 'Wilsonian Sovereignty in the Middle East: The King–Crane Commission Report of 1919' in *The State of Sovereignty: Territories, Laws, Populations*, ed. by Douglas Howland and Luis White (Bloomington: Indiana University Press, 2009), pp. 56–74.
10. MS King, Box 132, fol. 'Information about H.C. King by: D M Love, Ned King, other'. See also MS Lybyer, Box 16, fol. 'Doc. File #1 (1–61)', Doc. #33

'Who's Who', pp. 12a (1–2); and Donald M. Love, *Henry Churchill King of Oberlin* (New Haven: Yale University Press, 1956), pp. 211, 259–60.
11. MS King, King–Crane Commission Microfilm Reel Section A, 'Diary to Wife', 3 April 1919.
12. See Leo Bocage, 'The Public Career of Charles R. Crane' (unpublished doctoral dissertation, Fordham University, 1962), David Hapgood, *Charles R. Crane: The Man Who Bet on People* (Washington DC: The Institute of Current World Affairs, 2000). and Normal E. Saul, *The Life and Times of Charles R. Crane, 1858–1939: American Businessman, Philanthropist, and a Founder of Russian Studies in America* (Lanham, MA: Lexington Books, 2013).
13. MS Lybyer, Box 16, fol. 'Transcript of Diary: Mch 31–Sep. 15, 1919', 31 March 1919.
14. MS Lybyer, Box 8, fol. 'Misc. notes 1918–1919 (bundle)', likely 10 April 1919.
15. MS Lybyer, Box 16, fol. 'Doc. File #1 (1–61)', Doc. #33 'Who's Who', p. 12c. For a recent discussion of Lybyer's book, see Zachary Lockman, *Contending Visions of the Middle East: The History and Politics of Orientalism* (Cambridge: Cambridge University Press, 2004), pp. 103–4.
16. MS Lybyer, Box 16, fol. 'A.H.L. to C.A.L. March–May 1919', letter to Clara Lybyer, 1 April 1919.
17. MS Lybyer, Box 17, fol. 'Diary', 3 April 1919, and Box 16, fol. 'A.H.L. to C.A.L. March–May 1919', letter to Clara Lybyer, 6 April, 1919.
18. MS Lybyer, Box 17, fol. 'Diary', 1 April 1919.
19. Boston, Howard Gotlieb Archival Research Center, Boston University, MS William Yale Papers, Box 8, fol. 10 William Yale unpublished autobiography,, Chapter 11, pp. 1–2. Hereafter referred to as MS Yale-Boston.
20. MS Lybyer, Box 17, fol. 'Diary', 1 April 1919.
21. MS Lybyer, Box 16, fol. 'Doc. File #1 (1–61)', Doc. #33 'Who's Who', p. 12e.
22. MS Yale-Yale, Box 2, fol. 48 'Letter of Identification of William Yale', 13 July 1917, and MS Lybyer, Box 16, fol. 'Doc. File #1 (1–61)', Doc. #33 'Who's Who', p. 12f.
23. MS Westermann, 'Diary', 12 January 1919.
24. MS Yale-Boston, Box 8, fol. 10, Yale autobiography, Chapter 11, p. 19.
25. Information compiled from MS Lybyer, Box 16, fol. 'Doc. File #1 (1–61)', Doc. #33 'Who's Who' and various other sources.
26. 'Report of the American Section of the International Commission on Mandates', *FRUS PPC*, XII, pp. 751–2. Hereafter referred to as 'King–Crane Report'. The report oddly leaves out the names of Dorizas and Lambing, though these two did certainly start the journey with the commission. Little record exists of them during the journey.
27. MS Lansing, Reel 1, 'Peculiar Prejudices of the President', 20 March 1919.
28. MS King, King–Crane Commission Microfilm Reel Section A, 'Diary to Wife' 6 April, 23 April 1919.

29. Palo Alto, Hoover Institution, Stanford University, MS Donald Brodie Papers, Box 1, fol. 10 'Mr. Crane as Mandate commissioner', p. 1. Hereafter referred to as MS Brodie.
30. MS Lybyer, Box 16, fol. 'A.H.L. to C.A.L. March–May 1919', letter to Clara Lybyer, 6 April, 12 April, 22 April, and 15 May 1919.
31. Washington D.C., Library of Congress, MS Montgomery Family Papers, Box 6, fol. 'George R. Montgomery Family Correspondence 1919–1921', letter to Helen Montgomery, 27 April 1919. Hereafter known as MS Montgomery.
32. MS Yale-Boston, Box 8, fol. 10, Yale autobiography, Chapter 11, pp. 1–2.
33. MS King, King–Crane Commission Microfilm Reel Section A, 'Diary to Wife', 3 & 8 April 1919.
34. MS Westermann, 'Diary', 4 April 1919.
35. MS Lybyer, Box 17, fol. 'Diary', 12 April 1919.
36. MS Westermann, 'Diary', 4 and 12 April 1919.
37. Howard, *King–Crane*, pp. 43–5.
38. MS Westermann, 'Diary', 12 and 13 April 1919.
39. MS Yale-Yale, Box 6, fol. 20, 'Explanation of the American Division on Western Asia'.
40. MS Lybyer, Box 17, fol. 'Diary', 14 April 1919.
41. NA-ACNP, Reel 183, 'Committees and Commissions, Mandates in Turkey', Wilson to Grew, 15 April 1919.
42. MS Lybyer, Box 17, fol. 'Diary', 16 April 1919.
43. MS Lybyer, Box 16, fol. 'A.H.L. to C.A.L. March–May 1919', letter to Clara Lybyer, 15 April 1919. The letter is dated 15 April but was written over several days.
44. MS Lybyer, Box 17, fol. 'Diary', 16 April 1919.
45. MS King, King–Crane Commission Microfilm Reel Section A, 'Diary to Wife', 19 April 1919.
46. MS Lybyer, Box 16, fol. 'A.H.L. to C.A.L. March–May 1919', letter to Clara Lybyer, 15 & 18 April 1919.
47. MS Lybyer, Box 16, fol. 'A.H.L. to C.A.L. March–May 1919', letter to Clara Lybyer, 20 April 1919.
48. MS Lybyer, Box 17, fol. 'Diary', 19, 21, and 23 April 1919.
49. MS Lybyer, Box 16, fol. 'A.H.L. to C.A.L. March–May 1919', letter to Clara Lybyer, 20 April 1919, and Helmreich, p. 73.
50. MS King, King–Crane Commission Microfilm Reel Section A, 'Diary to Wife', 22 April 1919.
51. MS Lybyer, Box 16, fol. 'A.H.L. to C.A.L. March–May 1919', letter to Clara Lybyer, 20 April 1919.
52. NA-ACNP, Reel 183, 'Committees and Commissions, Mandates in Turkey', Lybyer to Grew, 23 April 1919.
53. Andrew and Kanya-Forstner, pp. 193–6, Helmreich, pp. 70–3, and Russell, pp. 34–8. Quotes from Andrew and Kanya-Forstner.

54. MS Lybyer, Box 16, fol. 'A.H.L. to C.A.L. March–May 1919', letter to Clara Lybyer, 28 April 1919.
55. MS King, King–Crane Commission Microfilm Reel Section A, 'Diary to Wife', 30 March and 3 April 1919.
56. MS Lybyer, Box 16, fol. 'A.H.L. to C.A.L. March-May 1919', letter to Clara Lybyer, 28 April 1919.
57. MS Montgomery, Box 6, fol. 'Family Correspondence 1919–1921', Montgomery to Helen Montgomery, 30 April and 4 May 1919.
58. MS Brodie, Box 1, fol. 10 'Mr. Crane as Mandate commissioner', p. 1, and MS Crane, Box 13, fol. 18, 'Charles R. Crane to Cornelia W. Smith Crane', 28 April 1919.
59. MS Lybyer, Box 16, fol. 'A.H.L. to C.A.L. March–May 1919', letter to Clara Lybyer, 23 April 1919.
60. MS Crane, Box 4, fol. 4, C. Snouck Hurgronje to Charles R. Crane, 8 May 1919.
61. MS Crane, Box 15, fol. 15, Woodrow Wilson to Charles R. Crane, 22 May 1919.
62. MS Lybyer, Box 16, fol. 'A.H.L. to C.A.L. March–May 1919', letter to Clara Lybyer, 9 May 1919.
63. King to Wilson, 6 May 1919, *PWW*, 58, p. 493.
64. 'Council of Four', 5 May 1919, *FRUS PPC*, V, pp. 466–8.
65. MS Lybyer, Box 16, fol. 'A.H.L. to C.A.L. March–May 1919', letter to Clara Lybyer, 11 May 1919.
66. MS Lybyer, Box 16, fol. 'Document File 2', Frankfurter to Wilson, 8 May; Wilson to Frankfurter, 13 May; Frankfurter to Wilson, 14 May; Wilson to Frankfurter, 16 May 1919.
67. MS Westermann, 'Diary', 4 April 1919.
68. 'Council of Four', 5 and 6 May 1919, *FRUS PPC*, V, pp. 465–9, 483–4.
69. Helmreich, pp. 94–101.
70. MS Lybyer, Box 16, fol. 'A.H.L. to C.A.L. March–May 1919', letter to Clara Lybyer, 27 May 1919.
71. Helmreich, pp. 94–8, and 'Council of Four', 19 May 1919, *FRUS PPC*, V, p. 718.
72. 'Council of Four', 13 May 1919, *FRUS PPC*, V, pp. 581–4.
73. 'Council of Four', 14 May 1919, *FRUS PPC*, V, p. 614.
74. 'Council of Four', 17 May 1919, *FRUS PPC*, V, pp. 690–701.
75. Westermann quoted in MS Lybyer, Box 16, fol. 'Diary', 23 May 1919.
76. 'Council of Four', 19 May 1919, *FRUS PPC*, V, pp. 708–11, 716–21.
77. MS Westermann, 'Diary', 16 May 1919.
78. MS Lybyer, Box 16, fol. 'A.H.L. to C.A.L. March-May 1919', letter to Clara Lybyer, 14 May 1919.
79. MS Lybyer, Box 17, fol. 'Diary', 17 May 1919.
80. MS King, King–Crane Commission Microfilm Reel Section A, 'Diary to Wife', 18 May 1919.

81. MS Montgomery, Box 6, fol. 'Family Correspondence 1919–1921', Montgomery to Helen Montgomery, 21 May 1919.
82. MS Lybyer, Box 16, fol. 'A.H.L. to C.A.L. March–May 1919', letter to Clara Lybyer, 11, 14, and 18 May 1919.
83. See MS Lybyer, Box 16, fol. 'Document File 1', document #26 entitled 'The Dangers to the Allies from a Selfish Exploitation of the Turkish Empire', May 1919. No date is given for the delivery of this document. Harry Howard has claimed 'May 1' but is likely mistaken because King stated that he was 'Working on reasons for proposal breaking up of the Turkish Empire' in mid-May. See MS King, King–Crane Commission Microfilm Reel Section A, 'Diary to Wife', 17 May 1919. The five main members of the commission had a meeting on 19 May in which they expressed agreement that the proposals for the split of the Ottoman lands that had appeared in the Parisian press would be disastrous, likely prompting the submission of this document. See MS Lybyer, Box 17, fol. 'Diary', 19 May 1919.
84. MS Lybyer, Box 17, fol. 'Diary', 20 May 1919, and MS King, King–Crane Commission Microfilm Reel Section B, King to W. F. Bohn, 23 May 1919.
85. MS Westermann, 'Diary', 19 May 1919.
86. MS Lybyer, Box 16, fol. 'A.H.L. to C.A.L. March–May 1919', letter to Clara Lybyer, 22 May 1919.
87. 'From the Diary of Colonel House', 20 May 1919, *PWW*, 59, p. 318.
88. MS Lybyer, Box 16, fol. 'A.H.L. to C.A.L. March–May 1919', letter to Clara Lybyer, 22 May 1919.
89. MS Lybyer, Box 16, fol. 'Document File #2', Hogarth to Lybyer, 21 and 22 May 1919. 22 May is undated but states 'Thursday 11pm', which is likely 22 May.
90. King to House, 21 May 1919, in *King–Crane Commission Digital Collection*, http://www.oberlin.edu/library/digital/king-crane/. accessed 20 December 2011. Hereafter know as *KC Digital Collection*.
91. King to House, 22 May 1919, *KC Digital Collection*, accessed 20 December 2011.
92. MS Lybyer, Box 17, fol. 'Diary', 20 and 21 May 1919.
93. 'Council of Four', 21 May 1919, *FRUS PPC*, V, pp. 756–68, 772–3.
94. 'Council of Four', 22 May 1919, *FRUS PPC*, V, pp. 807–12.
95. MS Lybyer, Box 17, fol. 'Diary', 22 May 1919.
96. MS King, King–Crane Commission Microfilm Reel Section B, document #102, entitled 'Memorandum of Points Desired to be taken up with the President'.
97. MS Westermann, 'Diary', 22 May 1919.
98. MS Frankfurter, Reel 15, Frankfurter to Brandeis, 25 May 1919.
99. MS Crane, Box 4, fol. 4, Felix Frankfurter to Charles R. Crane, 23 May 1919.
100. MS Frankfurter, Reel 15, Frankfurter to Brandeis, 25 May 1919.
101. NA-ACNP, Reel 544, 'Political Conditions Palestine', 'Hedjaz Delegation' to Wilson, 23 May 1919.

102. NA-ACNP, Reel 544, Faysal to the peace conference, received by the American delegation on 6 June 1919.
103. MS Montgomery, Box 6, fol. 'Family Correspondence 1919–1921', Montgomery to Helen Montgomery, 29 May 1919.
104. MS Lybyer, Box 16, fol. 'A.H.L. to C.A.L. March–May 1919', letter to Clara Lybyer, 29 May 1919.
105. MS Yale-Boston, Box 8, fol. 10, Yale autobiography, Chapter 11, p. 5, and NA-ACNP, Reel 183, 'Committees and Commissions, Mandates in Turkey', Westermann to Bowman, 29 April 1919.
106. NA-ACNP, Reel 183, 'Committees and Commissions, Mandates in Turkey', cable to American Legation in Bucharest, 26 May 1919.
107. MS Lybyer, Box 17, fol. 'Diary', 29 May 1919.
108. 'Council of Four', 31 May 1919, *FRUS PPC*, VI, pp. 132–3, 137.
109. MS King, King–Crane Commission Microfilm Reel Section B, King to W. F. Bohn, 26 May 1919.
110. MS Lybyer, Box 16, fol. 'A.H.L. to C.A.L. March–May 1919', letter to Clara Lybyer, 22 April 1919.
111. MS Westermann, 'Diary', 7 May 1919.
112. MS Lybyer, Box 16, fol. 'A.H.L. to C.A.L. March–May 1919', letter to Clara Lybyer, 25 May 1919.
113. Andrew and Kanya-Forstner, p. 197.
114. Cooper, *Woodrow Wilson*, p. 490.
115. 'Council of Four', 25 June 1919, *FRUS PPC*, VI, p. 675.

Chapter 5   Pre-Journey Opinions

1. MS Lybyer, Box 16, fol. 'A.H.L. to C.A.L. March–May 1919', letter to Clara Lybyer, 28 April 1919.
2. Frederic Lees in his introduction to P.J. Baldensperger, *The Immovable East: Studies of the People and Customs of Palestine* (London: Sir Isaac Pitman & Sons, 1913), p. xiii.
3. Donald Brodie, 'Notebook concerning the King–Crane Commission' in *KC Digital Collection*, accessed 20 December 2011.
4. MS Yale-Yale, Box 6, fol. 13, 'Notes on a conversation between William Yale and Emir Faisal, 1919 February 13'.
5. MS Lybyer, Box 15, fol. 'May 1919', Lybyer's notes, 5 May 1919.
6. 'The Plan of the "New Syria National League" for the Future Government of Syria', 15 March 1919 in *KC Digital Collection*, accessed 4 January 2012.
7. MS Lybyer, Box 16, fol. 'Folder Transcript of Diary: Mch 31–Sep. 15, 1919', 28 May 1919, and Box 15, fol. 'May 1919', Lybyer's notes, 28 May 1919.
8. MS Frankfurter, Reel 15, Frankfurter to Brandeis, 25 May 1919, and Ben Halpern, *A Clash of Heroes: Brandeis, Weizmann, and American Zionism* (Oxford: Oxford University Press, 1987), p. 194.

9. Kamal Madhar Ahmad, *Kurdistan during the First World War* trans. by Ali Maher Ibrahim (London: Saqi Books, 1994), pp. 196–8, Helmreich, pp. 203–5, and MacMillan, pp. 455–8.
10. MS Lybyer, Box 15, fol. 'May 1919', untitled notepad, and Donald Brodie, 'Notebook concerning the King–Crane Commission' in *KC Digital Collection*, accessed 20 December 2011. Quotes from Lybyer.
11. MS Lybyer, Box 15, fol. 'May 1919', untitled notepad, and Donald Brodie, 'Notebook concerning the King–Crane Commission' in *KC Digital Collection*, accessed 20 December 2011. Quotes from Lybyer.
12. MS Lybyer, Box 15, fol. 'May 1919', untitled notepad, and Donald Brodie, 'Notebook concerning the King–Crane Commission' in *KC Digital Collection*, accessed 20 December 2011. Quotes from Lybyer, except 'strong government …' from Brodie.
13. MS Lybyer, Box 15, fol. 'May 1919', untitled notepad, and Donald Brodie, 'Notebook concerning the King–Crane Commission', *KC Digital Collection*, accessed 20 December 2011. Quotes from Lybyer, except 'liberalism …' from Brodie.
14. MS Lybyer, Box 15, fol. 'May 1919', untitled notepad, and Donald Brodie, 'Notebook concerning the King–Crane Commission' in *KC Digital Collection*, accessed 20 December 2011. Quotes from Brodie.
15. MS Lybyer, Box 16, fol. 'Diary', 23 May 1919.
16. MS Lybyer, Box 16, fol. 'A.H.L. to C.A.L. March–May 1919', letter to Clara Lybyer, 25 May 1919.
17. MS Lybyer, Box 16, fol. 'Diary', 23 May 1919.
18. Albert Howe Lybyer, *The Government of the Ottoman Empire in the Time of Suleiman the Magnificent* (Cambridge: Harvard University Press, 1913), pp. 8–9.
19. Albert Lybyer, 'Turkey and the Great War', *City Club Bulletin* (Chicago), 19 February 1917, pp. 57–9, in MS Lybyer, Box 10, fol. 'Published Articles, 1910–1921, 1936, 1942 (manuscripts)'.
20. MS Yale-Yale, Box 2, fol. 4, 'Report #1' to Department of State entitled 'The Syrian Question', 29 October 1917.
21. MS Yale-Yale, Box 2, fol. 45, 'The Near East & The Western World', 16 December 1918; and Box 2, fol. 46, 'An Arab Empire', 18 December 1918.
22. MS Lybyer, Box 16, fol. 'Document File 1', document #26 'Dangers', May 1919.
23. On this point, see Smith, 'Wilsonian Sovereignty in the Middle East'.
24. Henry Churchill King, 'Grounds of Hope in the Present Crisis', in *President Wilson and the Moral Aims of the War* (New York: Fleming H. Revell Company, 1918), p. 79.
25. Hapgood, p. 51.
26. For the best summary of this, see Makdisi, *Faith Misplaced*, pp. 19–146.
27. MS Lybyer, Box 16, fol. 'Document File 1', document #26 'Dangers', May 1919.
28. MS Yale-Yale, Box 6, fol. 28, 'Report on Syria', p. 1.
29. See Manuel, pp. 238–50 (quote on p. 239) and Oren, pp. 386–90. Other such assessments include Brecher, *Reluctant Ally*, and Stuart E. Knee, 'The King–

Crane Commission of 1919: The Articulation of Political Anti-Zionism', American Jewish Archives, 29 (1977), pp. 22–53.
30. David Lloyd George, *The Truth about the Peace Treaties*, II (London: Victor Golliancz Ltd), pp. 1071–2.
31. A piece of evidence for this contention comes from the statement of an important 'interdenominational Missionary Conference' that took place in Souk El Gharb, Lebanon on 16–18 July 1919. At this conference, which was comprised of 'practically the entire Protestant missionary body in Syria' (both American and British), the missionaries produced a statement endorsed 'by a unanimous vote' which was sent to the King–Crane Commission. The plea of this body was simple: that no matter which country or countries served as a mandatory power in the region, missionaries should be granted 'absolute freedom so that Protestants may give the type of Education for which they stand', hence seemingly showing antipathy primarily to the perceived threat from a French (Catholic) mandate in the region. See MS Crane, Box 4, fol. 5 'Incoming Correspondence', 'Resolutions of Conference of British and American Missionary Societies', 21 July 1919.
32. 'King–Crane Report', *FRUS PPC*, XII, p. 792.
33. The spelling 'antisemitism' has been preferred to 'anti-Semitism' following the arguments of Mark Raider in *The Emergence of American Zionism* (New York: New York University Press, 1998), p. 12 and Ben Halpern in 'What Is Antisemitism?', *Modern Judaism*, 1, no. 3 (December, 1981), pp. 251–62.
34. Quoted in Brecher, *Reluctant Ally*, p. 19.
35. Ibid., pp. 49–52.
36. MS Crane, Box 8, fol. 8, Crane to Wilson, 24 March 1913, and Hapgood, pp. 44–5.
37. New York, Columbia University Rare Book and Manuscript Library, Bakhmeteff Archive, MS Charles Crane Papers, Box 1, Crane to Josephine Crane Bradley, 23 July 1916.
38. See Brecher, *Reluctant Ally*, p. 51.
39. The few scholars who have studied Crane in depth agree on this point. See Bocage, pp. 312–15 and Saul, pp. 269–70.
40. Stuart Knee, *Zionist Dissent*, pp. 16–20.
41. See Oren, pp. 276–80, 361; and Egal Feldman, *Dual Destinies: The Jewish Encounters with Protestant America* (Urbana: University of Illinois Press, 1990), pp. 162–74.
42. MS Yale-Yale, Box 2, fol. 27, 'Zionism and Palestine', 22 April 1918.
43. MS Yale-Yale, Box 7, fol. 6, 'Report upon Just and Practical Boundaries for Subdivisions of the Turkish Empire by W. L. Westermann and Others'.
44. At some point during the peace conference, Yale and Westermann critically annotated a draft proposal for a pro-Zionist Palestine mandate written by Felix Frankfurter, indicating that they were somewhat critical of his wording. They did not indicate disagreement with its overall content, however. See MS Yale-Yale, Box 3, fol. 3, 'Felix Frankfurter's Project of Mandate form for Palestine' with notes by Yale and Westermann.

45. MS Lybyer, Box 16, fol. 'Document File 1', document #26 'Dangers', May 1919.
46. MS Yale-Yale, Box 2, fol. 22, 'Notes prepared for H. Gary for a personal letter to Robert Lansing, Sec. of State', 18 March 1918.
47. MS Yale-Yale, Box 2, fol. 45, 'The Near East & The Western World', 16 December 1918.
48. MS Montgomery, Box 6, fol. 'Family Correspondence 1919–1921', letter to Helen Montgomery, 2 March 1919.
49. MS Lybyer, Box 16, fol. 'Document File 1', document #26 'Dangers', May 1919.
50. MS Yale-Yale, Box 2, fol. 45, Yale's report to the State Department entitled 'The Near East & the Western World', 16 December 1918.
51. MS Lybyer, Box 16, fol. 'Document File 2', document written by Lybyer entitled 'Suggestions in Regard to the Turkish Situation', 20 May 1919.
52. MS Crane, Box 8, fol. 12, Charles R. Crane to Mr. A.J. Gardiner, Editor of the *London Daily News*, 10 March 1919.
53. MS Lybyer, Box 16, fol. 'Document File 1', document #26 'Dangers', May 1919.
54. MS Yale-Yale, Box 2, fol. 2, report to the State Department entitled 'The Syria Question', p. 12.
55. MS Montgomery, Box 6, fol. 'Family Correspondence 1919–1921', letter to Helen Montgomery, 2 March 1919.
56. MS Lybyer, Box 16, fol. 'Document File 1', document #26 'Dangers', May 1919.

Chapter 6   Istanbul and Palestine

1. MS Lybyer, Box 16, fol. 'A.H.L. to C.A.L. March–May 1919', letter to Clara Lybyer, 8 June 1919, and MS Montgomery, Box 6, fol. 'Family Correspondence 1919–1921', letter to Helen Montgomery, 9 June 1919.
2. Keith David Watenpaugh, *Being Modern in the Middle East: Revolution, Nationalism, Colonialism, and the Arab Middle Class* (Princeton: Princeton University Press, 2006), p. 138.
3. James Gelvin, *Divided Loyalties: Nationalism and Mass Politics in Syria at the Close of Empire* (Berkeley: University of California Press, 1998), pp. 32–5.
4. MS Montgomery, Box 6, fol. 'Family Correspondence 1919–1921', Montgomery to Helen Montgomery, 1 June 1919.
5. MS Crane, Box 13, fol. 18, 'Charles R. Crane to Cornelia W. Smith Crane', 31 May 1919.
6. 'American commissioner in Constantinople (Heck) to American Ambassador in France (Sharp)', 4 January 1919, *FRUS PPC*, II, pp. 280–3.
7. Harry N. Howard, *Turkey, the Straits, and U.S. Policy* (Baltimore: The Johns Hopkins University Press, 1974), pp. 68–9.

8. College Park, Maryland, United States National Archives, Microfilm M-353 (US State Department, 1910–1929) Reel 7, Ravndal to the Secretary of State, 24 and 30 May 1919. Hereafter referred to as NA-Consular Records.
9. MS Lybyer, Box 16, fol. 'A.H.L. to C.A.L. March-May 1919', letter to Clara Lybyer, 8 June 1919.
10. MS Lybyer, Box 16, fol. 'Diary', 6–7 June 1919. Quote in MS Montgomery, Box 6, fol. 'Family Correspondence 1919–1921', Montgomery to Mary (sister), 9 June 1919.
11. MS Yale-Boston, Box 8, fol. 10, Yale autobiography, Chapter 11, pp. 7–9.
12. Mohammad Muslih, 'Arab Politics and the Rise of Palestinian Nationalism', *Journal of Palestine Studies*, 16, no. 4 (Summer, 1987), p. 82. See also Gelvin, *Divided*, p. 27 and Philip Khoury, *Urban Notables and Arab Nationalism: The Politics of Damascus 1860–1920* (Cambridge: Cambridge University Press, 1983), pp. 78–82.
13. Gelvin, *Divided*, pp. 61–3, and Khoury, pp. 78–86.
14. Ibid., pp. 144–53. Quotes on pp. 144 and 145.
15. Russell, pp. 42–66, 81–5.
16. For further explanation of these political currents, see Allawi, pp. 229–39.
17. NA-Consular Records, Aleppo (RG 84, UD 81, vol. 53), 'Political and Economical Conditions [in Aleppo]', 31 May 1919.
18. Abigail Jacobson, *From Empire to Empire: Jerusalem between Ottoman and British Rule* (Syracuse: Syracuse University Press, 2011), pp. 152–9, Ann Moseley Lesch, *Arab Politics in Palestine, 1917–1939: The Frustration of a National Movement* (Ithaca: Cornell University Press, 1979), pp. 83–4, Muhammad Muslih, *The Origins of Palestinian Nationalism* (New York: Columbia University Press, 1988), pp. 158–74, and Yehoshua Porath, *The Emergence of the Palestinian-Arab National Movement* (London: Frank Cass, 1974), pp. 89–92. Quote in Jacobson, p. 154.
19. MS Frankfurter, Reel 15, Frankfurter to Brandeis, 25 May 1919; and Jerusalem, Israel, Central Zionist Archives, L3/472, cable from Frankfurter to Harry Friedenwald (acting head of the Zionist commission in Jerusalem), 13 June 1919. Hereafter referred to as CZA.
20. The Zionist Commission was established in March 1918 in order to advise the British government on the implementation of the Balfour Declaration. It was already quite active in the region by 1919 and was the predecessor of the Jewish Agency for Israel. See Neil Caplan, *Futile Diplomacy: Vol. 1, Early Arab-Zionist Negotiation Attempts 1913–1931* (London: Frank Cass, 1983), p. 32.
21. CZA, L3/472, cable from Weizmann to Friedenwald, 21 June 1919.
22. 'Future Administration of Certain Portions of the Turkish Empire under the Mandatory System', *PWW*, 56, pp. 272–5.
23. 'King–Crane Report', *FRUS PPC*, XII, p. 752.
24. For a summary of this tradition, see Nora Lafi, 'Petitions and Accommodating Urban Change in the Ottoman Empire' in *Istanbul as seen from a distance. Centre and Province in the Ottoman Empire*, ed. by Elisabeth Özdalga et al. (Istanbul: Swedish Research Institute, 2011), pp. 73–82 and Yiğit Akın, 'Reconsidering

State, Party, and Society in Early Republican Turkey: Politics of Petitioning', *International Journal of Middle East Studies* 39 (2007), pp. 435–57. See also Watenpaugh, p. 103.
25. NA-ACNP, Reel 183, 'Committees and Commissions, Mandates in Turkey', King to Grew, 3 May 1919.
26. NA-Consular records, Aleppo (RG 84, UD 81, vol. 53), Polk to Jackson (Consul at Aleppo), 8 May 1919.
27. NA-Consular Records, Jerusalem (RG84, UD453, 'Correspondence, American Consulate Jerusalem 1919, part 3'), Glazebrook to State Department, 25 June 1919.
28. 'King–Crane Report', *FRUS PPC*, XII, p. 849.
29. MS King, Box 132, fol. '"War & Trip Abroad"—notes and the like', Notes entitled 'Outlines of address, etc.', p. 13.
30. 'King–Crane Report', *FRUS PPC*, XII, p. 751.
31. MS Lybyer, Box 16, fol. 'Diary', 26 June 1919.
32. 'King–Crane Report', *FRUS PPC,* XII, p. 771.
33. MS Lybyer, Box 16, fol. 'Diary', 16 June 1919.
34. MS Yale-Boston, Box 8, fol. 10, Yale autobiography, Chapter 11, p. 10.
35. MS Lybyer, Box 16, fol. 'Aug 1–7, 1919', document entitled 'List of Delegations received by the American commission in Syria'.
36. Watenpaugh, p. 152 n. 41.
37. MS Lybyer, Box 16, fol. 'Folder Transcript of Diary: Mch 31–Sep. 15, 1919', 9–12 June 1919.
38. MS Lybyer, Box 16, fol. 'Folder Transcript of Diary: Mch 31–Sep. 15, 1919', 9–12 June 1919.
39. MS King, Box 132, fol. '"War & Trip Abroad"—notes and the like', Notes entitled 'Outlines of address, etc.', p. 3,, and 'King–Crane Report', *FRUS PPC*, XII, p. 848–9.
40. MS Lybyer, Box 16, fol. 'Folder Transcript of Diary: Mch 31–Sep. 15, 1919', 10 June 1919, and Manuel, pp. 123–31.
41. CZA, L4/794, 'Statement by Mr. S. Hoofien to the American Member of the Inter-National commission on Mandates in Turkey', Jaffa, 11 June 1919.
42. CZA, L4/794, 'The Demands of the Moslems of Jaffa', 10 June 1919.
43. Russell, pp. 40, 61. This will be discussed further in Chapter 7.
44. MS King, Box 132, fol. '"War & Trip Abroad"—notes and the like', Notes entitled 'Outlines of address, etc.', p. 5.
45. CZA, L3/340, Harry Friedenwald to the 'Inneractions Committee' of the Zionist commission in Paris, 20 June 1919.
46. MS King, Box 132, fol. '"War & Trip Abroad"—notes and the like', Notes entitled 'Outlines of address, etc.', pp. 6–7.
47. 'Mr. C. R. Crane and Mr. H. C. King to the commission to Negotiate Peace', 20 June 1919, in 'King–Crane Report', *FRUS PPC,* XII, p. 748. This is dated 20 June *FRUS PPC* but, according to King's records, was 'sent June 12' (see a copy of this telegram in MS King, Box 128, fol. 3).

48. MS Lybyer, Box 16, fol. 'A.H.L. to C.A.L. March–May 1919', 'Tentative Conclusions after three days at Jaffa', 13 June 1919, likely sent with letter to Clara Lybyer, 9 July 1919.
49. CZA, L3/340, undated document titled 'An Account of the Visit of the Vaad Hazmani' [Jaffa, 11 June 1919], p. 5.
50. MS Lybyer, Box 16, fol. 'Diary', 13 June 1919.
51. MS Lybyer, Box 16, fol. 'June, 1919', document entitled 'Addresses Rishon', 13 June 1919.
52. MS Crane, Box 13, fol. 18, Crane to Cornelia W. Smith Crane, 15 June 1919; and MS Montgomery, Box 6, fol. 'Family Correspondence 1919–1921', Montgomery to Helen Montgomery, 16 June 1919.
53. MS Lybyer, Box 16, fol. 'Diary', 13 June 1919; and MS Lybyer, Box 16, fol. 'A.H.L. to C.A.L. March–May 1919', letter to Clara Lybyer, 16 June 1919.
54. CZA, L3/340, unsigned letter to the 'Inneractions Committee' of the Zionist commission in Paris, 20 June 1919, p. 4.
55. CZA, L4/794, undated document entitled 'Last informations [sic] concerning the arabic [sic] demands from the peace conference delegation'. The agent did not mention how he obtained this information.
56. MS Lybyer, Box 16, fol. 'Diary', 14 and 16 June 1919.
57. MS Lybyer, Box 16, fol. 'Document File 2', document entitled 'A statement presented to the representatives of the Allies at the Peace Confe-rence [sic] held in Paris, by the Christians and Mohammedan delegates of Southern Syria known as Palestine'.
58. CZA, L4/794, 'Reception of the Arabic Youth Association by the American Section of the Inter-Allied Delegation for Mandates in Turkey', 19 June 1919.
59. CZA, L4/794, 'Reception of the Moslem Delegation by the American Section of the Inter-Allied Delegation for Mandates in Turkey', 16 June 1919. Transcripts of testimony often alternate between French and English.
60. CZA, L4/794, 'Reception by the American Section of the Inerallied [sic] commission for the Mandates in Turkey of the Islamo Christian Association', 16 June 1919.
61. 'King–Crane Report', *FRUS PPC,* XII, p. 758.
62. CZA, L3/340, Harry Friedenwald to the 'Inneractions Committee' of the Zionist commission in Paris, 24 June 1919.
63. MS Lybyer, Box 16, fol. 'Document File 1', document entitled 'Statement to: The International commission on Mandates in Turkey American Section by Zionist commission to Palestine June 1919'.
64. CZA, L3/340, Harry Friedenwald to the 'Inneractions Committee' of the Zionist commission in Paris, 20 June 1919.
65. CZA, L4/794, 'A report by Rabbi Danon about his interview with the American commission', undated, likely 20 June 1919.
66. CZA, L3/340, Harry Friedenwald to the 'Inneractions Committee' of the Zionist commission in Paris, 24 June 1919.
67. MS Lybyer, Box 16, fol. 'Diary', 15 June 1919.

68. MS Lybyer, Box 16, fol. 'A.H.L. to C.A.L. March–May 1919', letter to Clara Lybyer (his wife), 16 June 1919.
69. MS Crane, Box 13, fol. 18, Crane to Cornelia W. Smith Crane, 15 June 1919.
70. MS Lybyer, Box 16, fol. 'A.H.L. to C.A.L. March–May 1919', letter to Clara Lybyer (his wife), 18 June 1919.
71. MS Montgomery, Box 6, fol. 'Family Correspondence 1919–1921', Montgomery to Helen Montgomery, 16 June 1919. For an overview of these views of Jerusalem, see Oren, pp. 159–62.
72. MS Lybyer, Box 16, fol. A.H.L. to C.A.L. May–Sept. 1919, letter to Clara Lybyer, 18 June 1919.
73. CZA, L4/794, 'Visit of the American commission to Hebron', 24 June 1919.
74. CZA, L4/794, Statement of 'The Jewish Community of Hebron', 17 June 1919.
75. MS Lybyer, Box 16, fol. A.H.L. to C.A.L. May–Sept. 1919, letter to Clara Lybyer, 18 June 1919.
76. CZA, L4/794, report on 'Tuesday 17 and Wednesday 18 June'.
77. MS Lybyer, Box 16, fol. 'Aug 1–7, 1919', document entitled 'List of Delegations received by the American commission in Syria', and MS Lybyer, Box 16, fol. 'Diary', 17 June 1919.
78. MS Lybyer, Box 16, fol. 'Diary', 21 June 1919.
79. CZA, L4/794, 'Questions of the Interallied commission and Replies of the representatives of the Jews of Acre', 24 June 1919.
80. CZA, L4/794, S. Nibashan to Zionist commission, Jerusalem, 23 June 1919.
81. CZA, L4/794, Mr. Montagu D. Eder to Friedenwald, 27 June 1919.
82. CZA, L3/426, Zionist intelligence summary entitled 'The American Section of the International commission and the Situation'.
83. CZA, L4/794, document entitled 'Report on the Fellahin question and the American Section of the International commission on Mandates in Turkey'.
84. CZA, L3/426, undated document entitled 'Report' and signed by 'a Reliable Informant'.
85. CZA, L3/340, Petition of the Moukhtar of Makd Mina, 29 June 1919.
86. CZA, L3/340, Petition from the Sheik of Katrah, 'June 1919'.
87. 'King–Crane Report', *FRUS PPC*, XII, p. 758.
88. See Jacobson, *From Empire to Empire*, pp. 159–67.
89. MS Montgomery, Box 6, fol. 'Family Correspondence 1919–1921', Montgomery to Roger Montgomery, 24 June 1919.
90. MS Lybyer, Box 16, fol. 'A.H.L. to C.A.L. March–May 1919', letter to Clara Lybyer, 26 June 1919.
91. MS Montgomery, Box 6, fol. 'Family Correspondence 1919–1921', Montgomery to Giles Montgomery, 24 June 1919.
92. MS Crane, Box 13, fol. 18, 'Charles R. Crane to Cornelia W. Smith Crane', 24 June 1919.
93. MS Lybyer, Box 16, fol. 'Diary', 17 June 1919, and MS Lybyer, Box 16, fol. 'July, 1919', document entitled 'Notes-Palestine'.

94. MS Crane, Box 13, fol. 18, 'Charles R. Crane to Cornelia W. Smith Crane', 19 June 1919.
95. 'King–Crane Report', *FRUS PPC*, XII, p. 850.
96. Gelvin, *Divided*, p. 82.
97. Eugene Rogan, *Frontiers of the State in the Late Ottoman Empire: Transjordan, 1850–1921* (Cambridge: University of Cambridge Press, 1999), pp. 242–3.
98. CZA, A153/44, 'Statement of the meeting of the Representatives of the Jewish Community of Jerusalem with the American Section of the Inter-Allied commission on Mandates in Turkey', 19 June 1919.
99. 'King–Crane Report', *FRUS PPC*, XII, p. 758.

Chapter 7   Syria and Lebanon

1. MS Crane, Box 13, fol. 18, 'Charles R. Crane to Cornelia W. Smith Crane', 24 June 1919.
2. MS Yale-Boston, Box 8, fol. 10, Yale autobiography, Chapter 11, pp. 15–17.
3. CZA, L4/794, document entitled 'I. Report on Journey through Syria', pp. 1 3.
4. This is based on a comparison of the Damascus newspaper transcripts provided by Elmaleh to the Zionist commission in CZA, L4/794, document entitled 'I. Report on Journey through Syria', pp. 5–6: 'Questions of the commission to the Christian Moslem Society of Jerusalem' from an unnamed newspaper in Damascus, with CZA, L4/794, 'Reception by the American Section of the Inerallied [sic] commission for the Mandates in Turkey of the Islamo Christian Association', 16 June 1919.
5. CZA, L4/794, document entitled 'I. Report on Journey through Syria', pp. 1–10.
6. CZA, L4/794, document entitled 'I. Report on Journey through Syria', pp. 1–3, 8–10.
7. MS Lybyer, Box 16, fol. A.H.L. to C.A.L. May–Sept. 1919, letter to Clara Lybyer, 26 June 1919.
8. MS Yale-Boston, Box 8, fol. 10, Yale autobiography, Chapter 11, p. 15.
9. MS Lybyer, Box 16, fol. 'Document File #1', document #51 entitled 'Distributed in the Bazaars of Damascus'.
10. MS Lybyer, Box 16, fol. A.H.L. to C.A.L. May–Sept. 1919, document entitled 'The Apparent Situation at Syria, July 1 1919'. See also Eliezer Tauber, *The Formation of Modern Syria and Iraq* (Newbury Park, England: Frank Cass, 1995), pp. 18–20.
11. MS Yale-Boston, Box 8, fol. 10, Yale autobiography, Chapter 11, p. 18.
12. MS Lybyer, Box 16, fol. A.H.L. to C.A.L. May–Sept. 1919, letter to Clara Lybyer, 26 June 1919.
13. MS Lybyer, Box 16, fol. A.H.L. to C.A.L. May–Sept. 1919, letter to Clara Lybyer, 26 June 1919, and MS Yale-Boston, Box 8, fol. 10, Yale autobiography, Chapter 11, p. 18.
14. MS Lybyer, Box 16, fol. 'Diary', 26 June 1919.

15. MS Lybyer, Box 16, fol. 'Document File #1', document #52 entitled 'Interview of commissioners, Advisers present, with the Kadi, Mufti, and six others of the Ulema of Damascus, at the Damascus Palace Hotel, at four o'clock p.m.', 26 June 1919.
16. MS Lybyer, Box 16, fol. 'Document File #2', document entitled 'Program at Damascus', and fol. 'Diary', 27 and 28 June 1919.
17. CZA, L4/794, document entitled 'I. Report on Journey through Syria', p. 12.
18. MS Lybyer, Box 16, fol. 'Diary', 25 June 1919.
19. MS Lybyer, Box 16, fol. 'Document File #2', document entitled 'Translation of Newspaper Article, June 27th, 1919, Damascus, Syria'; and MS Lybyer, Box 16, fol. 'Document File #1', document #52 entitled 'Interview of commissioners, Advisers present, with the Kadi, Mufti, and six others of the Ulema of Damascus, at the Damascus Palace Hotel, at four o'clock p.m.', 26 June 1919.
20. MS Lybyer, Box 16, fol. 'Doc. File #2', document entitled 'Notes on Interview of commissioners, Advisers present, with General Gabriel Haddad Pasha', 27 June 1919.
21. CZA, L4/794, document entitled 'I. Report on Journey through Syria', pp. 6–14.
22. MS Lybyer, Box 16, fol. A.H.L. to C.A.L. May–Sept. 1919, letter to Clara Lybyer, 29 June 1919.
23. MS Montgomery, Box 6, fol. 'Family Correspondence 1919–1921', Montgomery to Helen Montgomery, 3 July 1919.
24. MS Lybyer, Box 16, fol. A.H.L. to C.A.L. May–Sept. 1919, letter to Clara Lybyer, 29 June 1919, and MS Yale-Boston, Box 8, fol. 10, Yale autobiography, Chapter 11, pp. 19–20. James Gelvin discusses the invention of the 'May 6 martyr' tradition in *Divided Loyalties*, pp. 175–81.
25. MS Lybyer, Box 16, fol. 'Diary', 30 June 1919. On Allenby's position, see *FRUS PPC,* XII, p. 855.
26. Elizabeth Thompson, *Colonial Citizens: Republican Rights, Paternal Privilege, and Gender in French Syria and Lebanon* (New York: Columbia University Press, 2000), p. 128.
27. MS King, King–Crane Commission Microfilm Reel Section B, King to W. F. Bohn, 23 July 1919.
28. MS Montgomery, Box 6, fol. 'Family Correspondence 1919–1921', letter to Helen Montgomery, 3 July 1919.
29. MS Lybyer, Box 16, fol. 'Diary', 1 July 1919, and Box 16, fol. 'Petitions, Addresses to K-C Com. Arabs, Jews, Christians', petitions entitled 'Credentials of Christians from Kerak'.
30. See MS Brodie, Box 1, fol. 11, document entitled 'Ajarma tribe Amman'; MS King, Box 128, fol. 5, document entitled 'Nadi al-Arabi Aman'; MS Lybyer, Box 16, fol. 'Petitions, Addresses to K-C Comm.', document entitled 'Municipality of Amman'.
31. MS Lybyer, Box 16, fol. 'Diary', 1 July 1919.
32. MS Lybyer, Box 16, fol. 'Diary', 1 July 1919.
33. MS Yale-Boston, Box 8, fol. 10, Yale autobiography, Chapter 11, pp. 20–1.

34. MS Lybyer, Box 16, fol. A.H.L. to C.A.L. May–Sept. 1919, letter to Clara Lybyer, 9 July 1919.
35. Eliezer Tauber states that 69 actually attended, while Philip Khoury notes that 89 attended. See Tauber, pp. 16–20, and Khoury, pp. 86–8.
36. Allawi, pp. 239–42, Gelvin, *Divided*, pp. 166–8, and Russell, pp. 61–3. For the full text of the 'Program' see 'King–Crane Report', *FRUS PPC*, XII, pp. 779–81.
37. MS Lybyer, Box 16, fol. 'Doc. File #1 (1–61)', document entitled 'Emir Faisal to the American commission (Copied verbatim)'.
38. MS Lybyer, Box 16, fol. 'Diary', 3 July 1919.
39. MS Lybyer, Box 16, fol. 'Diary', 4 July 1919.
40. MS Yale-Boston, Box 8, fol. 10, Yale autobiography, Chapter 11, pp. 23–4.
41. MS Lybyer, Box 16, fol. A.H.L. to C.A.L. May–Sept. 1919, letter to Clara Lybyer, 9 July 1919.
42. MS King, King–Crane Commission Microfilm Reel Section A, King Diary, 6 July 1919.
43. MS Lybyer, Box 16, fol. 'A.H.L. to C.A.L. March–May 1919', letter to Clara Lybyer, 9 July 1919.
44. 'Mr. C. R. Crane and Mr. H. C. King to the commission to Negotiate Peace', 10 July 1919, in 'King–Crane Report', *FRUS PPC*, XII, pp. 749–50.
45. MS Yale-Boston, Box 8, fol. 10, Yale autobiography, Chapter 11, p. 25.
46. MS Yale-Yale, Box 1, fol. 6, Yale to William Westermann, 8 July 1919.
47. CZA, L4/794, document entitled 'I. Report on Journey through Syria', pp. 14–15.
48. MS Lybyer, Box 16, fol. 'A.H.L. to C.A.L. March–May 1919', letter to Clara Lybyer, 9 July 1919.
49. Zamir, *Lebanon*, pp. 64–70.
50. CZA, L4/794, document entitled 'I. Report on Journey through Syria', pp. 16–17.
51. CZA, L4/794, document entitled 'I. Report on Journey through Syria', pp. 18, 24.
52. 'King–Crane Report', *FRUS PPC*, XII, p. 760.
53. MS Yale-Boston, Box 8, fol. 10, Yale autobiography, Chapter 11, pp. 24–5.
54. MS Lybyer, Box 16, fol. 'Diary', 7 July 1919.
55. MS Lybyer, Box 16, fol. 'Doc. File #2', document entitled 'Program, Beirut 1919'.
56. CZA, L4/794, document entitled 'I. Report on Journey through Syria', pp. 19–20.
57. MS Lybyer, Box 16, fol. 'Diary', 7 and 9 July 1919.
58. CZA, L4/794, document entitled 'I. Report on Journey through Syria', pp. 23–4.
59. MS Lybyer, Box 16, fol. 'Doc. File #2', document entitled 'Program, Beirut 1919'.
60. MS Lybyer, Box 16, fol. 'Diary', 8 July 1919.
61. MS Lybyer, Box 16, fol. 'A.H.L. to C.A.L. March–May 1919', letter to Clara Lybyer, 9 July 1919.
62. MS Yale-Boston, Box 8, fol. 10, Yale autobiography, Chapter 11, pp. 25–6.
63. MS Montgomery, Box 6, fol. 'Family Correspondence 1919–1921', Montgomery to Helen Montgomery, undated letter from Beirut.

64. MS Lybyer, Box 16, fol. 'Diary', 2 July 1919.
65. MS Lybyer, Box 16, fol. 'A.H.L. to C.A.L. March–May 1919', letter to Clara Lybyer, 14 July 1919.
66. MS Lybyer, Box 16, fol. 'A.H.L. to C.A.L. March–May 1919', letter to Clara Lybyer, 9 July 1919.
67. MS Yale-Boston, Box 8, fol. 10, Yale autobiography, Chapter 11, p. 26.
68. MS Lybyer, Box 16, fol. 'Diary', 10 July 1919.
69. MS Lybyer, Box 16, fol. 'Diary', 11 July 1919.
70. MS Montgomery, Box 20, 'Subject File King–Crane Commission', third folder, documents entitled 'Zahleh July 11, 1919, and 'Moalaka July 11, 1919'.
71. MS Lybyer, Box 16, fol. 'Diary', 12 July 1919.
72. MS Lybyer, Box 16, fol. A.H.L. to C.A.L. May–Sept. 1919, letter to Clara Lybyer, 14 July 1919.
73. MS Lybyer, Box 16, fol. A.H.L. to C.A.L. May–Sept. 1919, letter to Clara Lybyer, 14 July 1919.
74. MS Lybyer, Box 16, fol. 'Diary', 13 July 1919.
75. MS Montgomery, Box 20, 'Subject File King–Crane Commission', third folder, document entitled 'Alexandretta July 13, 1919'.
76. MS Montgomery, Box 20, 'Subject File King–Crane Commission', third folder, documents entitled 'Les Turks d'Alexandrette & d'Antioche' and 'Alexandretta July 13, 1919'.
77. MS Lybyer, Box 16, fol. A.H.L. to C.A.L. May–Sept. 1919, letter to Clara Lybyer, 14 July 1919 and Box 16, fol. 'Diary', 14 July 1919. Few notes on the Latakia delegations remain.
78. MS Montgomery, Box 6, fol. 'Family Correspondence 1919–1921', Montgomery to Helen Montgomery, 15 July 1919.
79. MS Lybyer, Box 16, fol. 'Diary', 12 and 14 July 1919.
80. MS Yale-Boston, Box 8, fol. 10, Yale autobiography, Chapter 11, p. 26.
81. MS Lybyer, Box 16, fol. A.H.L. to C.A.L. May–Sept. 1919, letter to Clara Lybyer, 14 July 1919.
82. MS Lybyer, Box 16, fol. 'Diary', 13 July 1919.
83. MS Lybyer, Box 16, fol. 'Diary', 12 July 1919.
84. MS Lybyer, Box 16, fol. 'A.H.L. to C.A.L. March–May 1919', letter to Clara Lybyer, 17 July 1919.
85. MS Lybyer, Box 16, fol. 'Diary', 16 July 1919.
86. MS Lybyer, Box 16, fol. 'A.H.L. to C.A.L. March–May 1919', letter to Clara Lybyer, 17 July 1919.
87. MS Lybyer, Box 16, fol. 'Diary', 16 July 1919.
88. MS Lybyer, Box 16, fol. 'Diary', 16 and 17 July 1919.
89. NA-Consular Records, Aleppo (RG 84 UD 81), Jesse B. Jackson, report to State Department, 21 July 1919.
90. See Gelvin, *Divided*, p. 45.
91. CZA, L4/794, document entitled 'I. Report on Journey through Syria', pp. 25–6.

92. MS Lybyer, Box 16, fol. 'A.H.L. to C.A.L. March–May 1919', letter to Clara Lybyer, 17 July 1919.
93. MS Lybyer, Box 16, fol. 'Diary', 17 July 1919.
94. Watenpaugh, pp. 150–3.
95. MS Lybyer, Box 16, fol. 'Diary', 18 and 19 July 1919.
96. MS Lybyer, Box 16, fol. 'July, 1919', notes on 'Mesopotamians'.
97. CZA, L4/794, document entitled 'I. Report on Journey through Syria', p. 28.
98. NA-Consular Records, Aleppo (RG 84 UD 81), Jesse B. Jackson, report to State Department, 21 July 1919.
99. MS Montgomery, Box 20, 'Subject File King–Crane Commission', third folder, document entitled 'July 19, Aleppo to Adana 1919'.
100. MS Lybyer, Box 16, fol. 'Diary', 18 July 1919.
101. MS Lybyer, Box 16, fol. 'Diary', 20 and 21 July 1919.
102. MS Montgomery, Box 20, 'Subject File King–Crane Commission', third folder, document entitled 'Adana'.
103. MS Lybyer, Box 16, fol. 'Diary', 22 July 1919.
104. 'King–Crane Report', *FRUS PPC*, XII, pp. 763–4.
105. MS Crane, Box 8, fol. 14, Crane to Mildred N. Page, 29 July 1919.
106. 'King–Crane Report', *FRUS PPC*, XII, pp. 758–63.
107. Ibid., pp. 759–61.
108. Yuval Ben-Bassat and Fruma Zachs, 'From Şikayet to Political Discourse and 'Public Opinion': Petitioning Practices to the King–Crane Commission', *New Middle Eastern Studies*, 4 (2014), http://www.brismes.ac.uk/nmes/archives/1296, pp. 6, 16.
109. CZA, L4/794, document entitled 'I. Report on Journey through Syria', pp. 30–1.
110. 'King–Crane Report', *FRUS PPC*, XII, p. 760. Only 20.12 per cent of the petitions stated an opinion for or against Zionism.
111. CZA, L4/794, document entitled 'I. Report on Journey through Syria', p. 31.
112. MS Lybyer, Box 16, fol. 'A.H.L. to C.A.L. March–May 1919', letter to Clara Lybyer, 9 July 1919.

Chapter 8   Istanbul, Paris and the Recommendations

1. MS Lybyer, Box 16, fol. A.H.L. to C.A.L. May–Sept. 1919, letter to Clara Lybyer, 23 July 1919.
2. MS Yale-Boston, Box 8, fol. 10, Yale autobiography, Chapter 11, p. 28.
3. MS King, King–Crane Commission Microfilm Reel Section A, 'Diary to Wife', 23 July to 21 August 1919.
4. MS Lybyer, Box 16, fol. 'A.H.L. to C.A.L. March–May 1919', letter to Clara Lybyer, 10 and 14 August 1919. Historian Leonard Smith has also identified the writing style of the report as distinctly King's. See Smith, 'Wilsonian Sovereignty in the Middle East'.

5. MS Lybyer, Box 16, fol. 'Diary', 20 August 1919.
6. MS Lybyer, Box 16, fol. 'Diary', 1 August 1919, and MS King, King–Crane Commission Microfilm Reel Section A, King Diary, 26–30 July 1919.
7. MS Montgomery, Box 6, fol. 'Family Correspondence 1919–1921', letter to Helen Montgomery, 24 August 1919.
8. See MS Lybyer, Box 16, fol. 'Diary', 31 July to 1 August, 14 August 1919.
9. MS Lybyer, Box 16, fol. 'Diary', 6 August 1919.
10. NA-ACNP, Reel 183, 'Committees and Commissions, Mandates in Turkey', Memo to the American Commissioners entitled 'Return of the Mission on Mandates in Turkey', 5 August 1919, and 'Minutes of the Daily Meetings of the commissioners Plenipotentiary', 6 August 1919 in *FRUS-PPC*, XI, p. 358.
11. 'Minutes of the Daily Meetings of the commissioners Plenipotentiary', 2 August 1919 in *FRUS-PPC*, XI, p. 357.
12. NA-ACNP, Reel 183, 'Committees and Commissions, Mandates in Turkey', Polk to Ravndal, 15 August 1919.
13. See MS Lybyer, Box 17, fol. 'Aug. 1–7 1919' and fol. 'Aug. 8–31, 1919' for transcripts of the interviews with these groups.
14. MS Lybyer, Box 16, fol. 'Diary', 6 August 1919.
15. MS King, King–Crane Commission Microfilm Reel Section B, document (untitled) # 376, and MS Lybyer, Box 16, fol. 'Diary', 31 July 1919. For more on the effect of the Armenian Genocide on the United States, see Peter Balakian, *The Burning Tigris: The Armenian Genocide and America's Response* (New York: Harper Collins, 2003), pp. 277–96.
16. MS Lybyer, Box 16, fol. 'July, 1919', notepad labeled 'Notes at Consple', interview with Zeinel Abeddin Irfani Bey.
17. MS Lybyer, Box 16, fol. 'July, 1919', interview with Ali Kemal Bey.
18. MS Lybyer, Box 16, fol. 'Diary', 19 August 1919.
19. MS Lybyer, Box 16, fol. 'July, 1919', document entitled 'Interview with Essad Pasha' and others.
20. MS Montgomery, Box 20, King–Crane Commission, fol. 2, Petition from an unnamed Turkish group in French, 18 August 1919. Lybyer also noted the existence of this argument in his diary on 12 August. See MS Lybyer, Box 16, fol. 'Diary', 12 August 1919. This is also repeated on numerous other occasions, as recorded in MS Lybyer, Box 16, fol. 'July, 1919', notepad labeled 'Notes at Consple'.
21. MS Lybyer, Box 16, fol. 'July, 1919', document entitled 'Interview with Ahmed Riza Pasha', 31 July 1919.
22. MS Montgomery, Box 20, King–Crane Commission, fol. 2, untitled document stating what was likely the commission's statements to Turkish delegations they saw in Istanbul.
23. MS Montgomery, Box 20, fol. 2, letter from an Armenian delegate (name indecipherable) to Montgomery, 1 August 1919.
24. MS Lybyer, Box 16, fol. 'Aug 1–7, 1919', document entitled 'Interview with Armenian Huncakists', 1 August 1919.

25. MS Lybyer, Box 16, fol. 'Aug 1–7, 1919', document entitled 'Interview with Armenians represented by Gregorian Patriarch', 1 August 1919.
26. MS Lybyer, Box 16, fol. 'Aug 1–7, 1919', transcripts of various interviews with Armenians.
27. MS Lybyer, Box 17, fol. 'Aug 8–31, 1919', document entitled 'Interview with Sheikh Riza Effendi of Kirkup, and Baban Zadeh Hikimet of Suleimanieh', 12 August 1919.
28. MS Lybyer, Box 17, fol. 'Aug 8–31, 1919', document entitled 'Interview with Kurdish Democratic Party', 11 August 1919.
29. MS Lybyer, Box 17, fol. 'Aug 8–31, 1919', document entitled 'Interview with Greek Patriarch', 1 August 1919.
30. MS Lybyer, Box 17, fol. 'Aug 8–31, 1919', document entitled 'Interview with the Greek Smyrna Committee', 1 August 1919.
31. MS Lybyer, Box 17, fol. 'Aug 8–31, 1919', document entitled 'Interview with Mr. Bambahas, Greek lawyer', 12 August 1919.
32. MS Lybyer, Box 16, fol. 'Aug 1–7, 1919', document entitled 'Interview with Chaldean Clergyman' and Box 17, fol. 'Aug 8–31, 1919', document entitled 'Interview with Kurdish Democratic Party', 11 August 1919.
33. MS Lybyer, Box 16, fol. A.H.L. to C.A.L. May–Sept. 1919, letter to Clara Lybyer, 26 July 1919.
34. MS Lybyer, Box 16, fol. 'Diary', 7, 13, and 17 August 1919.
35. MS Crane, Box 4, fol. 1, 'Fourteen Reasons for an American Mandatory [sic] over Turkey', January 1919.
36. MS Lybyer, Box 16, fol. 'Aug 1–7, 1919', document entitled 'Interview with Miss Graffam', 6 August 1919.
37. George White to the International Commission on Mandates in Turkey, 16 August 1919, in *KC Digital Collection*, accessed 13 May 2012.
38. MS Lybyer, Box 17, fol. 'Aug 8–31, 1919', Pears to Montgomery, 21 August 1919.
39. MS Lybyer, Box 16, fol. 'Diary', 6 August 1919.
40. Ibid., 14 August 1919.
41. Ibid., 16 August 1919.
42. Ibid., 1 August 1919.
43. Ibid., 12 August 1919.
44. MS Crane, Box 8, fol. 14, Crane to Mildred N. Page, 5 September 1919.
45. MS Lybyer, Box 16, fol. 'Diary', 21–27 August 1919.
46. MS Crane, Box 8, fol. 12, Cable: Crane to Wilson, 31 August 1919.
47. NA-ACNP, Reel 183, 'Committees and Commissions, Mandates in Turkey', Grew to Secretary of State, 20 September 1919.
48. See Charles A. Selden, 'Our Cuban Record Appeals to Turks', *New York Times*, 31 August 1919, http://www.nytimes.com, accessed 8 July 2008.
49. 'Minutes of the Meeting of the commissioners and Technical Advisers of the American commission to Negotiate Peace', 24 September 1919, *FRUS PPC*, XI, pp. 432–3, and Charles A. Selden, 'French Offended by Emir's Arrest

Assert Crane was Duped', *New York Times*, 3 September 1919, http://www.nytimes.com, accessed 8 July 2008.
50. MS Crane, Box 8, fol. 14, Crane to Mildred N. Page, 5 September 1919.
51. See MS Lybyer, Box 16, fol. 'Diary', 29 August to 6 September 1919.
52. John Milton Cooper, *Breaking the Heart of the World: Woodrow Wilson and the Fight for the League of Nations* (Cambridge: Cambridge University Press, 2001), pp. 187–9, 198.
53. MS Yale-Yale, Box 6, fol. 28 'Report on Syria, Palestine, and Mount Lebanon for the American commissioners' and 'Conclusions'. Quotes on p. 18 and p. 1 respectively.
54. MS Montgomery, Box 20, King crane Commission, fol. 2, document entitled 'Report on Syria'. Quote on p. 8.
55. MS Montgomery, Box 20, fol. 2, 'Non-Arab Portions of the Ottoman Empire'.
56. 'King–Crane Report', *FRUS PPC*, XII, pp. 787–97.
57. Ibid., pp. 841–8.
58. Ibid., pp. 799–802.
59. Ibid., pp. 787–8.
60. Ibid., pp. 848–63.
61. See Gelvin, 'Ironic Legacy'.
62. Fromkin, pp. 435–40, Morris, pp. 92–111, and Zürcher, pp. 143–65.
63. See, for example, MS King, Correspondence Microfilm Reel 13, Crane to King, 11 May 1922. In this letter, Crane lamented the growing tensions in the region.
64. MS King, Correspondence Microfilm Reel 13, King to Crane, 18 November 1919, and MS Brodie, Box 1, fol. 7, King to Wilson, 10 September 1919.
65. Richard Gottheil, 'The Crane-King Report', *The New York Times*, 12 December 1919, http://www.nytimes.com accessed 7 June 2010.
66. MS King, Correspondence Microfilm Reel 8, Brodie to King, 5 November 1921.
67. 'Only America can save Armenia', *The New York Times*, 5 April 1920, http://www.nytimes.com, accessed 1 July 2008, and H. I. Katibah, 'The French in Syria', *The New York Times*, 1 August 1920, http://www.nytimes.com, accessed 1 July 2008.
68. Stephen Duggan, 'The Syria Question', *Journal of International Relations*, 11:4 (April, 1921), pp. 571–88, quote on pp. 583–4.
69. In 1934, Brodie (then secretary to Charles Crane) asked diplomat Stanley Hornbeck to see if the King–Crane Commission Report was in the State Department files. Hornbeck learned that a signed copy was in the files, though it bore 'no endorsements of any kind'. Palo Alto, Hoover Institution, Stanford University, MS Stanley Hornbeck Papers, Box 35, fol. 'Brodie, Donald M.', Hornbeck to Brodie, 15 December 1934, and internal 'Division of Near Eastern Affairs' memo, 14 December 1934.
70. MS King, Correspondence Microfilm Reel 8, Brodie to King correspondences between 15 June and 8 July 1922, and MS Crane, Box 4, fol. 18, Wilson to

Crane, 6 July 1922. It is difficult to tell what the President meant by 'timely' here, but he could have been referring to the debate in the US Congress over a resolution backing Zionism, the drafting of the terms for the Palestine Mandate by the League of Nations, or the continued unsettled nature of the Turkish situation.

71. 'First Publication of the King–Crane Report on the Near East', *Editor & Publisher*, 2 December 1919, and MS King, Correspondence Microfilm Reel 8, Fenton Dowling to Crane, 21 November 1922. See also MS Lybyer, Box 17, fol. 1923, 'Memorandum regarding publication of King–Crane Report' by Donald M. Brodie, undated.
72. William T. Ellis, 'Crane and King's Long-Hid Report on the Near East', *The New York Times*, 3 December 1922, http://www.nytimes.com, accessed 8 June 2008, and MS Brodie, Box 1, fol. 6, Brodie to James W. Brown, 29 November 1922, Brodie to William T. Ellis, 29 November 1922, and Brodie to Fenton Dowling, 14 December 1922.
73. 'The Crane-King Report', *The New York Times*, 20 August 1922, http://www.nytimes.com, accessed 8 June 2008.
74. MS Lybyer, Box 17, fol. '1922', transcriptions of 'Editorial, *New York Evening Post*, 31 August 1922, The Asia Minor Mandates' and Donald M. Brodie to the *New York Evening Post*, 1 September 1922. Yale was unaware of this controversy and later stated that he did not intend his memorandum to be a 'minority report'. See MS Lybyer, Box 3, fol. 'Howard, Harry N.', Howard to Lybyer, 24 July 1941.
75. MS Lybyer, Box 17, fol. '1923', Lybyer to William Westermann, 31 January 1923.
76. MS Lybyer, Box 16, fol. '1923', Westermann to Lybyer, 12 January 1923.
77. Samuel Untermyer, 'Zionism and the Crane Report' in *The Forum* 69, no. 1 (January 1923), pp. 1120–36.
78. MS Lybyer, Box 17, fol. '1923', Lybyer to William Westermann, 31 January 1923.

Chapter 9   Accounting for the Differences 1: The Ability to Become Modern

1. 'King–Crane Report', *FRUS PPC*, XII, p. 834.
2. Ibid., p. 841.
3. MS Brodie, Box 1, fol. 2, incomplete draft of King–Crane Commission history, undated, pp. 20, 23.
4. 'King–Crane Report', *FRUS PPC*, XII, p. 786.
5. Americans of African, Asian, or other origins did not figure significantly in this elite national image of the era. See Jackson Lears, *Rebirth of a Nation: The Making of Modern America, 1877–1920* (New York: Harper Perennial, 2009), pp. 93–132.

6. MS Yale-Yale, Box 1, fol. 6, Yale to Westermann, 8 July 1919.
7. Marshall Hodgson, 'Modernity and the Islamic Heritage' in *Rethinking World History: Essays on Europe, Islam, and World History* (Cambridge: Cambridge University Press, 1993), p. 234.
8. 'King–Crane Report', *FRUS PPC*, XII, p. 851.
9. MS Montgomery, Box 20, fol. 'King–Crane Commission' [second folder], 'Report on Syria', p. 3.
10. MS Montgomery, Box 20, fol. 'King–Crane Commission' [second folder], 'The Attitude toward Zionism', p. 3.
11. MS Crane, Box 8, fol. 14, Crane to Mildred N. Page, 1 June 1919.
12. MS Brodie, Box 1, fol. 2, incomplete draft of King–Crane Commission history, undated, p. 20.
13. MS Yale-Boston, Box 8, fol. 10, Yale autobiography, Chapter 11, p. 22.
14. MS Yale-Yale, Box 1, fol. 6, Yale to Westermann, 8 July 1919.
15. MS Yale-Boston, Box 8, fol. 10, Yale autobiography, Chapter 11, p. 12.
16. MS Crane, Box 8, fol. 14, Crane to Mildred N. Page, 9 July 1919.
17. MS Crane, Box 8, fol. 14, Crane to Mildred N. Page, 29 July 1919.
18. MS Crane, Box 13, fol. 18, Crane to Cornelia W. Smith Crane, 19 June 1919.
19. MS Crane, Box 13, fol. 18, Crane to Cornelia W. Smith Crane, 15 June 1919.
20. MS Lybyer, Box 16, fol. A.H.L. to C.A.L. May–Sept. 1919, letter to Clara Lybyer, 18 June 1919.
21. MS Lybyer, Box 16, fol. 'Folder Transcript of Diary: Mch 31–Sep. 15, 1919', 28 and 30 June 1919.
22. MS Brodie, Box 1, fol. 2, incomplete draft of King–Crane Commission history, undated, p. 20.
23. MS Crane, Box 13, fol. 18, Crane to Cornelia W. Smith Crane, 24 June 1919.
24. MS Crane, Box 20, fol. 15, Charles Crane's unpublished memoirs, p. 233.
25. MS Brodie, Box 1, fol. 2, incomplete draft of King–Crane Commission history, undated, p. 23.
26. MS Yale-Yale, Box 6, fol. 28, 'Report on Syria, Palestine and Mt. Lebanon for the American commissioners', p. 21.
27. MS Montgomery, Box 6, fol. 'Family Correspondence 1919–1921', Montgomery to Helen Montgomery, 24 June 1919.
28. 'King–Crane Report', *FRUS PPC*, XII, p. 839.
29. MS Lybyer, Box 16, fol. 'Folder Transcript of Diary: Mch 31–Sep. 15, 1919', 30 June 1919.
30. MS Brodie, Box 1, fol. 2, incomplete draft of King–Crane Commission history, undated, p. 3.
31. MS Crane, Box 8, fol. 14, Crane to Mildred N. Page, 29 July 1919. Crane's ellipsis.
32. 'Mr. C. R. Crane and Mr. H. C. King to the commission to Negotiate Peace', 10 July 1919, *FRUS PPC*, XII, p. 750.
33. MS Lybyer, Box 16, fol. 'Document File 1', document #54 entitled 'Speech of the Emir Faisal', 'about 1 July 1919' [actually 3 July].

34. CZA, L4/794, 'Reception by the American Section of the Inerallied [sic] commission for the Mandates in Turkey of the Islamo Christian Association', 16 June 1919.
35. CZA L4/794, letter from the Zionist Delegation of Jerusalem to the King–Crane Commission as an addendum to their testimony, 20 June 1919.
36. CZA L51/325, 'Statements by Mr. S. Hoofien to the American Members of the Inter-National commission on Mandates in Turkey', Jaffa, 11 June 1919.
37. CZA L4/794, letter from the Zionist Delegation of Jerusalem to the King–Crane Commission as an addendum to their testimony, 20 June 1919.
38. CZA A153/44, 'Statement of the meeting of the Representatives of the Jewish Community of Jerusalem with the American Section of the Inter-Allied commission on Mandates in Turkey, June 1919'.
39. CZA L3/340, 'An account of the visit of the Vaad Hazmani', undated, Jaffa [meeting occurred 11 June 1919].
40. CZA L4/794, letter from the Zionist Delegation of Jerusalem to the King–Crane Commission as an addendum to their testimony, 20 June 1919. For the report see, CZA L4/794, Dr Hillel Yofe, 'Report on Sanitary Condition of Palestine and the part played by the Jews', 23 June 1919.
41. MS Yale-Yale, Box 7, fol. 6, 'W.L. Westermann and Others, Report Upon Just and Practical Boundaries for Subdivisions of the Turkish Empire', pp. 1–3.
42. MS Yale-Yale, Box 6, fol. 28, 'Report on Syria', pp. 20–1.
43. 'King–Crane Report', FRUS PPC, XII, pp. 781–2, 836.
44. MS Yale-Yale, Box 6, fol. 28, 'Conclusions', p. 6.
45. 'King–Crane Report', FRUS PPC, XII, pp. 776, 790.
46. Ibid., p. 840.
47. MS Lybyer, Box 16, fol. 'Document File #1 (62–85)', document #72, telegram from Crane to Wilson, 29 July 1919. Drafts of this telegram in Lybyer's handwriting show that he and Crane wrote it together. See MS Lybyer, Box 16, fol. A.H.L. to C.A.L. May–Sept. 1919, document entitled 'Draft of additional paragraph suggested by Lybyer', 29 July 1919.
48. 'King–Crane Report', FRUS PPC, XII, p. 840.
49. Ibid., p. 814.
50. MS Brodie, Box 1, fol. 2, incomplete draft of King–Crane Commission history, undated, pp. 17–18.
51. MS Montgomery, Box 20, fol. 'King–Crane Commission' [second folder], 'The Non-Arab Portion of the Ottoman Empire', pp. 1–7.
52. MS Lybyer, Box 16, fol. A.H.L. to C.A.L. May–Sept. 1919, letter to Clara Lybyer, 17 July 1919.
53. MS Lybyer, Box 16, fol. 'Diary', 20 July 1919.
54. MS Brodie, Box 1, fol. 2, incomplete draft of King–Crane Commission history, undated, p. 17.
55. 'King–Crane Report', FRUS PPC, XII, p. 812.
56. MS Yale-Yale, Box 6, fol. 28, pp. 789–90.
57. MS Yale-Yale, Box 6, fol. 28, p. 814.

58. Ibid., pp. 836, 840.
59. MS Yale-Yale, Box 6, fol. 28, 'Conclusions', p. 6; Box 1, fol. 6, Yale to Westermann, 8 July 1919; and Box 6, fol. 28, 'Report on Syria', p. 2.
60. MS Montgomery, Box 20, fol. 'King–Crane Commission' [second folder], 'Report on Syria', pp. 1–7.
61. For more on this, see Justin McCarthy, *The Turk in America: The Creation of an Enduring Prejudice* (Salt Lake City: The University of Utah Press, 2010), pp. 105–64.
62. 'King–Crane Report', *FRUS PPC*, XII, p. 810.
63. MS Brodie, Box 1, fol. 2, incomplete draft of King–Crane Commission history, undated, pp. 12–13, 17–18.
64. 'King–Crane Report', *FRUS PPC*, XII, pp. 810–12, 818.
65. James Bryce and Arnold Toynbee, *Armenian Atrocities: The Murder of a Nation* (London: Hodder & Stoughton, 1916).
66. 'King–Crane Report', *FRUS PPC*, XII, pp. 812–16.
67. MS Montgomery, Box 20, fol. 'King–Crane Commission' [second folder], 'The Non-Arab Portion of the Ottoman Empire', p. 1.
68. MS Brodie, Box 1, fol. 2, incomplete draft of King–Crane Commission history, undated, p. 14.
69. 'King–Crane Report', *FRUS PPC*, XII, pp. 773, 787, 851.
70. Ibid., p. 817. Turkey here refers to the whole Ottoman Empire.
71. MS Brodie, Box 1, fol. 2, incomplete draft of King–Crane Commission history, undated, p. 27.
72. MS Crane, Box 8, fol. 12: 'CRC Letters 1919 January to December', Crane to Woodrow Wilson, 10 July 1919.
73. See E. Evans Pritchard, *The Sanusi of Cyrenaica* (London: Clarendon Press, 1954).
74. 'King–Crane Report', *FRUS PPC*, XII, p. 817.
75. Ibid., p. 796.
76. Ibid., p. 750.
77. Ibid., p. 844.
78. Ibid., p. 861.
79. Ibid., p. 791.
80. Maxime Rodinson, *Europe and the Mystique of Islam*, trans. by Roger Veinus (London: I.B. Taurus, 1988), pp. 60–67.
81. MS Montgomery, Box 20, fol. 'King–Crane Commission' [second folder], 'Report on Syria', pp. 1–4.
82. MS Yale-Yale, Box 6, fol. 28, 'Report on Syria', pp. 1, 18–19; and MS Yale-Yale, Box 1, fol. 6, Yale to Westermann, 8 July 1919.
83. MS Yale-Yale, Box 6, fol. 28, 'Report on Syria', p. 19.
84. MS Yale-Yale, Box 6, fol. 28, 'Report on Syria', p. 18.
85. MS Yale-Yale, Box 6, fol. 28, 'Conclusions', p. 5.
86. MS Yale-Yale, Box 6, fol. 28, 'Conclusions', pp. 5–6.

87. Rodinson, p. 63.
88. CZA, L3/340, unsigned letter to the 'Inneractions Committee' of the Zionist commission in Paris, 20 June 1919, pp. 2–3.
89. MS Crane, Box 13, fol. 18, Crane to Cornelia W. Smith Crane, 19 June 1919.
90. 'King–Crane Report', FRUS PPC, XII, pp. 792–5.
91. MS Lybyer, Box 16, fol. 'Folder Transcript of Diary: Mch 31–Sep. 15, 1919', 13 June 1919.
92. CZA, L3/340, undated document titled 'An Account of the Visit of the Vaad Hazmani' [Jaffa, 11 June 1919], pp. 3–4.
93. MS Lybyer, Box 16, fol. 'Doc. File #1 (1–61)', Doc. #52 'Interview of commissioners, Advisers present, with the Kadi, Mufti, and six others of the Ulema of Damascus, at the Damascus Palace Hotel, at four o'clock p.m. June 26 1919.'
94. 'King–Crane Report', FRUS PPC, XII, p. 794.
95. MS Lybyer, Box 16, fol. 'A.H.L. to C.A.L. March–May 1919', letter to Clara Lybyer, 16 June 1919.
96. MS Lybyer, Box 16, fol. 'Folder Transcript of Diary: Mch 31–Sep. 15, 1919', 12 June and 14 June 1919.
97. MS Montgomery, Box 20, fol. 'King–Crane Commission' [second folder], 'The Attitude toward Zionism', pp. 2–4; MS Montgomery, Box 20, fol. 'King–Crane Commission' [second folder], 'Report on Syria', pp. 3–4, 8; MS Lybyer, Box 16, fol. 'Document File 1' (1–61), Document 57 'Questions on Zionism', pp. 1–3.
98. MS Lybyer, Box 16, fol. 'Document File 1' (1–61), Document 57 'Questions on Zionism', pp. 1–3.
99. MS Yale-Yale, Box 6, fol. 28 'Report on Syria- Conclusions', pp. 1–3.
100. This analysis mirrors general observations about Western colonial administrators made by Partha Chatterjee in *The Nation and its Fragments: Colonial and Postcolonial Histories* (Princeton: Princeton University Press, 1993), pp. 17–18.
101. On this last point, see Ann Stoler's 'Racial Histories and Their Regimes of Truth'.

Chapter 10   Accounting for the Differences 2: The King–Crane Commission and Wilsonian Ideals

1. 'Secretary's Notes [...] Thursday, 6 February, 1919' FRUS PPC, III, p. 889.
2. As cited in the 'King–Crane Report', FRUS PPC, XII, p. 781.
3. MS House, Box 201, fol. 2/569, 'Wilsonian League' to Wilson, 5 December 1918.
4. MS Lybyer, Box 17, fol. 'Aug 8–31, 1919', document entitled 'Interview with Kurdish Democratic Party', 11 August 1919.
5. 'King–Crane Report', FRUS PPC, XII, pp. 787–8.

6. CZA, L4/794, 'Report on the reception of the Arab-Orthodox delegation by the American Section of the International commission for mandates in Turkey', Jerusalem, 16 June 1919.
7. MS Yale-Boston, Box 8, fol. 10 Yale autobiography, Chapter 11, pp. 12–13.
8. 'King–Crane Report', *FRUS PPC*, XII, pp. 752–64, 771. It should be noted that it is unclear what exactly the commission was counting when, for example, they claimed that they received 1863 petitions from 442 groups (see pp. 757 and 761 for these numbers). For this reason, this study does not base any of its claims specifically on the commission's statistics.
9. 'King–Crane Report', *FRUS PPC*, XII, pp. 789–96.
10. Ibid., pp. 820–1.
11. Ibid., pp. 834–6.
12. Ibid., p. 789.
13. Ibid., pp. 789–90, 833, 836–7, 840.
14. Ibid., pp. 789–93.
15. Ibid., pp. 806, 814, 820.
16. Ibid., pp. 820, 833, 836.
17. CZA A153/44, 'Statement of the meeting of the Representatives of the Jewish Community of Jerusalem with the American Section of the Inter-Allied commission on Mandates in Turkey, June 1919'.
18. MS Yale-Yale, Box 6, fol. 28, 'Conclusions', pp. 1–3.
19. MS Yale-Yale, Box 6, fol. 28, 'Conclusions', p. 6.
20. MS Yale-Yale, Box 6, fol. 28, 'Report on Syria', p. 12.
21. MS Yale-Yale, Box 6, fol. 28, 'Conclusions', p. 7.
22. MS Montgomery, Box 20, fol. 'King–Crane Commission' [second folder], 'Non-Arab Portions of the Ottoman Empire', pp. 1–6.
23. MS Montgomery, Box 20, 'The Attitude toward Zionism', p. 3.
24. MS Montgomery, Box 20, 'Report on Syria', p. 3.
25. MS Montgomery, Box 20, 'Report on Syria', p. 8.
26. See Chapter 6.
27. MS Montgomery, Box 20, fol. 'King–Crane Commission' [second folder], 'The Attitude toward Zionism', pp. 3–4.
28. See Frank Ninkovich, *The United States and Imperialism* (Malden, MA: Blackwell Publishers, 2001), pp. 214–20; Michael Hunt, *The American Ascendancy: How the United States Gained and Wielded Global Dominance* (Chapel Hill, N.C.: The University of North Carolina Press, 2007), pp. 57–62; Walworth, pp. 65–81; MacMillan, pp. 108–12; and Manela, pp. 28–43.
29. Among these were the Japanese quest for the German holdings in the Shandong Peninsula, the French desire for the previously German colony of Cameroon, numerous Italian claims to the Balkans and Anatolia, and Greek claims to Anatolia. See MacMillan, pp. 108–12, 288–314, 335–47, 357–76.
30. 'King–Crane Report', *FRUS PPC*, XII, pp. 807–10.
31. Ibid., pp. 807–10, 816–17.
32. Ibid., pp. 829–31.

33. MS Brodie, Box 1, fol. 2, incomplete draft of King–Crane Commission history, undated, pp. 14–15.
34. 'King–Crane Report', *FRUS PPC*, XII, pp. 785–6.
35. Ibid., p. 818.
36. Ibid., pp. 848–50.
37. MS Yale-Yale, Box 6, fol. 28, 'Report on Syria', pp. 14–15.
38. 'King–Crane Report', *FRUS PPC*, XII, p. 796.
39. MS Crane, Box 8, fol. 14, Crane to Mildred N. Page, 9 July 1919.
40. MS Brodie, Box 1, fol. 2, incomplete draft of King–Crane Commission history, undated, p. 28.
41. 'King–Crane Report', *FRUS PPC*, XII, pp. 796, 843–8, 855.
42. Ibid., pp. 844–6.
43. MS Crane, Box 8, fol. 12: 'CRC Letters 1919 January to December', Crane to Woodrow Wilson, 10 July 1919.
44. MS Yale-Yale, Box 1, fol. 6, Yale to Westermann, 8 July 1919.
45. MS Lybyer, Box 16, fol. 'Folder Transcript of Diary: Mch 31–Sep. 15, 1919', 25 July 1919.
46. MS Yale-Yale, Box 6, fol. 28, 'Conclusions', p. 4.
47. MS Montgomery, Box 20, fol. 'King–Crane Commission' [second folder], 'Report on Syria', pp. 7–8.
48. The terms ethnic and civic nationalism are employed here not as an endorsement of their existence but because they exemplify the commission members' thinking. A good summary of the problems with these terms can be found in Anthony D. Smith, *Nationalism*, 2nd edn (Cambridge: Polity Press, 2010), pp. 107–10.
49. MS Yale-Yale, Box 2, fol. 45, 'The Near East & The Western World', 16 December 1918; and Box 2, fol. 46, 'An Arab Empire', 18 December 1918.
50. MS Yale-Yale, Box 1, fol. 6, Yale to Westermann, 8 July 1919.
51. MS Yale-Yale, Box 6, fol. 28, 'Report on Syria', pp. 16–22.
52. MS Yale-Yale, Box 6, fol. 28, 'Report on Syria', pp. 16–18.
53. MS Montgomery, Box 20, fol. 'King–Crane Commission' [second folder], 'The Attitude toward Zionism', p. 3.
54. 'King–Crane Report', *FRUS PPC*, XII, pp. 786, 788.
55. Ibid., pp. 758, 791–2, 858–9.

Chapter 11 Conclusion

1. Perhaps the most emphatic voicing of this viewpoint is Kedourie, pp. 139–47.
2. This analysis echoes that of Russell, p. 89 and Gelvin, *Divided*, pp. 167–8.
3. For more on this, see Andrew Patrick, 'The Zionist Commission and the Jewish Communities of Greater Syria in 1919', *Jerusalem Quarterly*, 56 & 57 (2013), pp. 107–17.
4. Love, *Race over Empire*, p. 12.

SELECTED BIBLIOGRAPHY

Manuscripts

Albert H. Lybyer Papers, University of Illinois Archives, Urbana-Champaign, IL.
American University of Beirut Library Archives and Special Collections, Photos and Postcards, Beirut, Lebanon.
Charles Crane Papers, Bakhmeteff Archive, Columbia University Rare Book and Manuscript Library, New York.
Colonel E.M. House Papers, Sterling Memorial Library, Yale University, New Haven.
Crane Family Papers, Bakhmeteff Archive, Columbia University Rare Book and Manuscript Library, New York.
Donald M. Brodie Miscellaneous Papers, Hoover Institution Archives, Stanford University, Palo Alto, CA.
Felix Frankfurter Papers, Library of Congress (Madison Building), Washington D.C.
Henry Churchill King Papers, Oberlin College Archives, Oberlin, OH.
King–Crane Commission Digital Collection, Oberlin College Archives, Oberlin, OH, http://www.oberlin.edu/library/digital/king-crane/.
Michael 'Mike' Dorizas Papers, Historical Society of Pennsylvania, Philadelphia.
———, University Archives and Records Center, University of Pennsylvania, Philadelphia.
Montgomery Family Papers, Library of Congress (Madison Building), Washington D.C.
Robert Lansing Papers, Library of Congress (Madison Building), Washington D.C.
Stanley Hornbeck Papers, Hoover Institution Archives, Stanford University, Palo Alto, CA.
United States Department of State, Central Files, United States National Archives, College Park, MD.
———, Consular Records (Aleppo, Beirut, Constantinople, Damascus, Jerusalem), United States National Archives, College Park, MD.
———, General Records of the American Commission to Negotiate Peace, United States National Archives, College Park, MD.

William Linn Westermann Papers, Columbia University Rare Book and Manuscript Library, New York.
William Yale Papers, Howard Gotlieb Archival Research Center, Boston University, Boston.
———, Milne Special Collections and Archives, University of New Hampshire Library, Durham, NH.
———, Sterling Memorial Library, Yale University, New Haven.
Zionist Commission Papers, Central Zionist Archives, Jerusalem, Israel.

Printed Contemporary Sources

Bryce, James, and Arnold Toynbee, *Armenian Atrocities: The Murder of a Nation* (London: Hodder & Stoughton, 1916).
Edward M. House, *The Intimate Papers of Colonel House: Volume IV, The Ending of the War June 1918-November 1919*, ed. by Charles Seymour (London: Ernest Benn Limited, 1926).
King, Henry Churchill, 'Grounds of Hope in the Present Crisis', in *President Wilson and the Moral Aims of the War* (New York: Fleming H. Revell Company, 1918).
———, *For a New America in a New World* (Paris: Young Men's Christian Association, 1919).
Lloyd George, David, *The Truth about the Peace Treaties*, 2 vols (London: Victor Gollancz Ltd, 1938).
Paul Mantoux, *Paris Peace Conference 1919: Proceedings of the Council of Four (March 24-April 18)*, trans. by John Boardman Whitton (Geneva: Librairie Droz, 1964).
The New York Times, New York, USA.
Nicolson, Harold, *Peacemaking 1919* (London: Constable & Co., 1933).
Papers Relating to the Foreign Relations of the United States, The Paris Peace Conference, 1919, 13 vols (Washington: Government Printing Office, 1942).
Wilson, Woodrow, *Papers of Woodrow Wilson*, ed. by Arthur Link, 69 vols (Princeton: Princeton University Press, 1966–94).

Selected Secondary Sources

Ahmad, Kamal Madhar, *Kurdistan during the First World War*, trans. by Ali Maher Ibrahim (London: Saqi Books, 1994).
Akın, Yiğit, 'Reconsidering State, Party, and Society in Early Republican Turkey: Politics of Petitioning', *International Journal of Middle East Studies* 39 (2007), 435–57.
Aksakal, Mustafa, *The Ottoman Road to War in 1914* (Cambridge: Cambridge University Press, 2008).
Allawi, Ali A. *Faisal I of Iraq* (New Haven: Yale University Press, 2014).
Ambrosius, Lloyd, 'Wilsonian Diplomacy and Armenia' in *America and the Armenian Genocide of 1915*, ed. by Jay Winter (Cambridge: Cambridge University Press, 2003), 113–45.
Anderson, Benedict, *Imagined Communities: Reflections on the Origin and Spread of Nationalism* (London: Verso, 2006).
Andrew, Christopher M., and Alexander Sydney Kanya-Forstner, *France Overseas: The Great War and the Climax of French Imperial Expansion* (London: Thames and Hudson, 1981).

Antonius, George, *The Arab Awakening: The Story of the Arab National Movement* (Beirut: Librairie du Liban, 1969).
Balakian, Peter, *The Burning Tigris: The Armenian Genocide and America's Response* (New York: Harper Collins, 2003).
Ben-Bassat, Yuval and Fruma Zachs, 'From Şikayet to Political Discourse and "Public Opinion": Petitioning Practices to the King–Crane Commission', *New Middle Eastern Studies*, 4 (2014), http://www.brismes.ac.uk/nmes/archives/1296.
Bocage, Leo, 'The Public Career of Charles R. Crane' (unpublished doctoral dissertation, Fordham University, 1962).
Brecher, Frank W., 'Revisiting Ambassador Morgenthau's Turkish Peace Mission of 1917', *Middle Eastern Studies*, 24, no. 3 (July, 1988), 357–63.
———— *Reluctant Ally: United States Foreign Policy Toward the Jews from Wilson to Roosevelt* (New York: Greenwood Press, 1991).
Burgoyne, Elizabeth, *Gertrude Bell: From her Personal Papers*, 2 vols (London: Ernest Benn, 1961).
Cabrera, Miguel A., *Postsocial History: An Introduction* (Lanham, Maryland: Lexington Books, 2005)
Campos, Michelle, *Ottoman Brothers: Muslims, Christians, and Jews in Early Twentieth-Century Palestine* (Palo Alto: Stanford University Press, 2011).
Caplan, Neil, *Futile Diplomacy: Vol. 1, Early Arab-Zionist Negotiation Attempts 1913-1931* (London: Frank Cass, 1983).
Chatterjee, Partha, *The Nation and Its Fragments: Colonial and Postcolonial Histories*, 4th edn (Princeton: Princeton University Press, 1993).
Christison, Kathleen, *Perceptions of Palestine: Their Influence on U.S. Middle East Policy*, (Berkeley: University of California Press, 2001).
Cohen, Naomi, *The Americanization of Zionism, 1897–1948* (Hanover and London: Brandeis University Press, 2003).
Cooper, John Milton, *Breaking the Heart of the World: Woodrow Wilson and the Fight for the League of Nations* (Cambridge: Cambridge University Press, 2001).
———— 'A Friend in Power? Woodrow Wilson and Armenia' in *America and the Armenian Genocide of 1915*, ed. by Jay Winter (Cambridge: Cambridge University Press, 2003), 103–12.
———— *Woodrow Wilson: A Biography* (New York: Vintage Books, 2009).
Darwin, John, *Britain, Egypt and the Middle East: Imperial Policy in the Aftermath of War 1918–1922* (New York: St Martin's Press, 1981).
Degler, Carl N., *In Search of Human Nature: Decline and Revival of Darwinism in American Social Thought* (Oxford: Oxford University Press, 1991).
DeNovo, John A., *American Interests and Policies in the Middle East, 1900–1939* (Minneapolis: University of Minnesota Press, 1963).
Deringil, Selim, *The Well-Protected Domains: Ideology and the Legitimation of Power in the Ottoman Empire 1876–1909* (London: I.B.Tauris, 1999).
Dirlik, Arif, Vinay Bahl, and Peter Gran, eds., 'Is there history after Eurocentrism? Globalism, postcolonialism, and the disavowal of history', in *History After the Three Worlds: Post-Eurocentric Historiographies*, 2nd edn (London: Rowman & Littlefield, 2000), 25–47.
Dodge, Toby, *Inventing Iraq: The Failure of Nation Building and a History Denied* (New York: Columbia University Press, 2003).
Duggan, Stephen, 'The Syria Question', *Journal of International Relations*, 11:4 (April, 1921), 571–88.

Dyer, Gwynne, 'The Turkish Armistice of 1918: 1: The Turkish Decision for a Separate Peace, Autumn 1918', *Middle Eastern Studies*, 8 (1972), 143–78.

—— 'The Turkish Armistice of 1918: 2: A Lost Opportunity: The Armistice Negotiations of Moudros', *Middle Eastern Studies*, 8 (1972), 313–48.

Evans, Laurence, *United States Policy and the Partition of Turkey 1914–1924* (Baltimore: The Johns Hopkins Press, 1965).

Evans-Pritchard, Edward E., *The Sanusi of Cyrenaica* (London: Clarendon Press, 1954).

Fairclough, Norman, *Discourse and Social Change* (Cambridge: Polity Press, 1993).

Feldman, Egal, *Dual Destinies: The Jewish Encounter with Protestant America* (Urbana: University of Illinois Press, 1990).

Foucault, Michel, *The Archaeology of Knowledge* (London: Tavistock Publications, 1972).

Fromkin, David, *A Peace to End All Peace: The Fall of the Ottoman Empire and the Creation of the Modern Middle East* (New York: Holt Paperbacks, 2001).

Gamble, Richard, *The War for Righteousness* (Wilmington, Del.: ISI Books, 2003).

Gelfand, Lawrence E, *The Inquiry; American Preparations for Peace, 1917–1919* (New Haven: Yale University Press, 1963).

Gelvin, James L., 'The Ironic Legacy of the King–Crane Commission', in *The United States in the Middle East: A Historical Reassessment*, ed. by David Lesch (Boulder, Colorado: Westview Press, 1995), 13–29.

—— *Divided Loyalties: Nationalism and Mass Politics in Syria at the Close of Empire* (Berkeley: University of California Press, 1999).

Giddens, Anthony, *The Consequences of Modernity* (Cambridge: Polity Press, 1991).

Gong, Gerrit W., *The Standard of 'Civilization' in International Society* (Oxford: Clarendon Press, 1984).

Grabill, Joseph L., *Protestant Diplomacy and the Near East: Missionary Influence on American Policy, 1810–1927*, Minnesota Archive Editions (Minneapolis: University of Minnesota Press, 1971).

Grose, Peter, *Israel in the Mind of America* (New York: Alfred A. Knopf, 1984).

Haddad, Farid S., *A First Class Man in Every Particular: Dr. Sami I Haddad* (Paradise Valley, Arizona: Sami I. Haddad Memorial Library, Shad Board, 2001).

Halpern, Ben, 'What Is Antisemitism?', *Modern Judaism*, 1, no. 3 (Dec., 1981), 251–62.

—— *A Clash of Heroes: Brandeis, Weizmann, and American Zionism* (Oxford: Oxford University Press, 1987).

Hapgood, David, *Charles R. Crane* (Washington D.C.: Institute of Current World Affairs, 2000).

Helmreich, Paul, *From Paris to Sevres: The Partition of the Ottoman Empire at the peace conference of 1919-1920* (Columbus: Ohio State University Press, 1974).

Hixson, Walter L., *The Myth of American Diplomacy: National Identity and U.S. Foreign Policy* (New Haven: Yale University Press, 2009).

Hobsbawm, Eric, *The Age of Empire: 1875–1914* (New York: Vintage, 1989).

Hodgson, Marshall G.S., *Rethinking World History: Essays on Europe, Islam and World History* (Cambridge: Cambridge University Press, 1993).

Horsman, Reginald, *Race and Manifest Destiny: Origins of American Racial Anglo-Saxonism* (Cambridge: Harvard University Press, 1981).

Howard, Harry N., 'An American Experiment in Peacemaking: the King–Crane Commission', *Muslim World*, 32 (1942), 122–46.

────── *The King–Crane Commission: An American Inquiry in the Middle East* (Beirut: Khayats, 1963).
────── *Turkey, the Straits and U.S. Policy* (Baltimore: Johns Hopkins University Press, 1974).
Howarth, David, *Discourse* (Buckingham: Open University Press, 2000).
────── 'Applying Discourse Theory: the Method of Articulation', in *Discourse Theory in European Politics: Identity, Policy, and Governance*, ed. by David Howarth and Jacob Torfing (New York: Palgrave MacMillan, 2005), 316–49.
Howe, Frederic C., *The Confessions of a Reformer* (New York: Charles Scribner's Sons, 1925).
Hunt, Michael H., *Ideology and U.S. Foreign Policy* (New Haven: Yale University Press, 1987).
────── *The American Ascendancy: How the United States Gained and Wielded Global Dominance* (Chapel Hill: The University of North Carolina Press, 2007).
Jacobs, Matthew, *Imagining the Middle East: The Building of an American Foreign Policy, 1918–1967* (Chapel Hill: University of North Carolina Press, 2011).
Jacobson, Abigail, *From Empire to Empire: Jerusalem between Ottoman and British Rule* (Syracuse: Syracuse University Press, 2011).
Jacobson, Matthew Frye, *Whiteness of a Different Color: European Immigrants and the Alchemy of Race*, New edition (Cambridge: Harvard University Press, 1998).
────── *Barbarian Virtues: The United States Encounters Foreign Peoples at Home and Abroad, 1876–1917* (New York: Hill and Wang, 2001).
John, Robert and Sami Hadawi, *The Palestine Diary 1914–1945: Britain's Involvement* (Beirut: The Palestine Research Center, 1968).
Kaiwar, Vasant, and Sucheta Mazumdar, 'Race, Orient, Nation in the Time-Space of Modernity', in *Antinomies of Modernity: Essays on Race, Orient, Nation*, ed. by Vasant Kaiwar et al. (Durham: Duke University Press, 2003), 261–98.
Kaplan, Robert D., *The Arabists: The Romance of an American Elite* (New York: The Free Press, 1993).
Kark, Ruth, *American Consuls in the Holy Land 1832-1914* (Jerusalem: The Magnes Press, 1994).
Kassir, Samir, *Beirut* (Berkeley: University of California Press, 2010).
Kayali, Hasan, *Arabs and Young Turks: Ottomanism, Arabism, and Islamism in the Ottoman Empire, 1908–18* (Berkeley: University of California Press, 1997).
Kedourie, Elie, *England and the Middle East: The Destruction of the Ottoman Empire, 1914–1921* (London: Bowes & Bowes, 1956).
Khalidi, Rashid, *Palestinian Identity: The Construction of Modern National Consciousness* (New York: Columbia University Press, 1997).
────── *Resurrecting Empire: Western Footprints and America's Perilous Path in the Middle East* (London: I.B.Tauris, 2004).
Khoury, Philip, *Urban Notables and Arab Nationalism: The Politics of Damascus 1860–1920* (Cambridge: Cambridge University Press, 1983).
────── *Syria and the French Mandate: The Politics of Arab Nationalism 1920–1945* (Princeton University Press, 1987).
Knee, Stuart, 'The King–Crane Commission of 1919: The Articulation of Political Anti-Zionism', *American Jewish Archives*, 29 (1977), 22–53.
────── *The Concept of Zionist Dissent in the American Mind 1917–1941* (New York: Robert Speller & Sons, 1979).

SELECTED BIBLIOGRAPHY

Knock, Thomas J., *To End All Wars: Woodrow Wilson and the Quest for a New World Order* (Princeton: Princeton University Press, 1995).

Laclau, Ernesto, and Chantal Mouffe, *Hegemony and Socialist Strategy: Towards a Radical Democratic Politics*, 2nd edn (London: Verso, 2001).

LaFeber, Walter, *The Cambridge History of American Foreign Relations: The American Search for Opportunity, 1865–1913*, vol. 2 (Cambridge: Cambridge University Press, 1995).

Lafi, Nora, 'Petitions and Accommodating Urban Change in the Ottoman Empire' in *Istanbul as seen from a distance. Centre and Province in the Ottoman Empire*, ed. by Elisabeth Özdalga et al. (Istanbul: Swedish Research Institute, 2011), 73–82.

Lears, Jackson, *Rebirth of a Nation: The Making of Modern America, 1877–1920* (New York: Harper Perennial, 2009).

Leftwich, Adrian, *States of Development: On the Primacy of Politics in Development* (London: Polity Press, 2001).

Lesch, Ann Moseley, *Arab Politics in Palestine, 1917–1939: The Frustration of a National Movement* (Ithaca: Cornell University Press, 1979).

Little, Douglas, *American Orientalism: The United States and the Middle East since 1945*, 3rd edn (Chapel Hill: University of North Carolina Press, 2008).

Lockman, Zachary, *Contending Visions of the Middle East: The History and Politics of Orientalism* (Cambridge: Cambridge University Press, 2004).

Longrigg, Stephen Hemsley, *Syria and Lebanon Under French Mandate* (London: Oxford University Press, 1958).

Love, Donald M., *Henry Churchill King, of Oberlin* (New Haven: Yale University Press, 1956).

Love, Eric T.L., *Race over Empire: Racism and U.S. Imperialism, 1865–1900* (Chapel Hill: The University of North Carolina Press, 2004).

Lybyer, Albert Howe, *The Government of the Ottoman Empire in the Time of Suleiman the Magnificent* (Cambridge: Harvard University Press, 1913).

MacMillan, Margaret, *Peacemakers: Six Months That Changed the World: The Paris Peace Conference of 1919 and Its Attempt to End War* (London: John Murray Publishers Ltd, 2003).

Makdisi, Ussama, *The Culture of Sectarianism: Community, History, and Violence in Nineteenth-Century Ottoman Lebanon* (Berkeley: University of California Press, 2000).

—— *Artillery of Heaven: American Missionaries and the Failed Conversion of the Middle East* (Ithaca, NY: Cornell University Press, 2008)

—— *Faith Misplaced: The Broken Promise of U.S.–Arab Relations: 1820–2001* (New York: Public Affairs, 2010).

Mandel, Neville, *The Arabs and Zionism before World War I* (Berkeley: University of California Press, 1976).

Manela, Erez, *The Wilsonian Moment: Self-Determination and the International Origins of Anticolonial Nationalism* (Oxford: Oxford University Press, 2007).

Manuel, Frank E., *Realities of American-Palestine Relations* (New York: Public Affairs Press, 1949).

Mazower, Mark, *No Enchanted Palace: The End of Empire and the Ideological Origins of the United Nations* (Princeton: Princeton University Press, 2009).

McCarthy, Justin, *Muslims and Minorities: The Population of Ottoman Anatolia and the End of the Empire* (New York: New York University Press, 1983).

―――― *The Turk in America: The Creation of an Enduring Prejudice* (Salt Lake City: The University of Utah Press, 2010).

Mitchell, Timothy, *Colonising Egypt* (London: University of California Press, 1991).

―――― 'The Stage of Modernity', in *Questions of Modernity*, ed. by Timothy Mitchell (Minneapolis: University of Minnesota Press, 2000), 1–34.

Monroe, Elizabeth, *Britain's Moment in the Middle East 1914-1956* (London: Chato and Windus, 1963).

Morris, Benny, *Righteous Victims: A History of the Zionist-Arab Conflict, 1881–2001* (New York: Vintage, 2001).

Mosse, George L., *Toward the Final Solution: A History of European Racism* (Madison: University of Wisconsin Press, 1985).

Muslih, Muhammad, 'Arab Politics and the Rise of Palestinian Nationalism', *Journal of Palestine Studies*, 16 (1987), 77–94.

―――― *The Origins of Palestinian Nationalism* (New York: Columbia University Press, 1988).

Nevakivi, Jukka, *Britain, France and the Arab Middle East 1914–1920* (London: The Athlone Press, 1969).

Ninkovich, Frank, *The United States and Imperialism* (Malden: Blackwell Publishers, 2001).

Omi, Michael, and Howard Winant, *Racial Formation in the United States: From the 1960s to the 1990s*, 2nd edn (New York: Routledge, 1994).

Oren, Michael B., *Power, Faith, and Fantasy: America in the Middle East: 1776 to the Present* (New York: W.W. Norton & Company, 2007).

Patrick, Andrew J., 'The Zionist Commission and the Jewish Communities of Greater Syria in 1919', *Jerusalem Quarterly*, 56 & 57 (2013), 107–17.

―――― '"These people know about us": A Reconsideration of Attitudes towards the United States in World War I-Era Greater Syria', *Middle Eastern Studies*, 50, No. 3 (2014), 397–411.

Porath, Yehoshua, *The Emergence of the Palestinian National Movement 1918–1929* (London: Frank Cass, 1974).

Preston, Andrew, *Sword of the Spirit, Shield of Faith: Religion in American War and Diplomacy* (New York: Anchor Books, 2012).

Quataert, Donald, *The Ottoman Empire 1700–1922*, 2nd edn (Cambridge: Cambridge University Press, 2005).

Raider, Mark, *The Emergence of American Zionism* (New York: New York University Press, 1998).

Reimer, Michael, 'The King–Crane Commission at the Juncture of Politics and Historiography', *Critique: Critical Middle Eastern Studies*, 15 (2006), 129–50.

Reinharz, Jehuda, *Chaim Weizmann: The Making of a Statesman* (Oxford: Oxford University Press, 1993).

Renton, James, *The Zionist Masquerade: The Birth of the Anglo-Zionist Alliance 1914–1918* (London: Palgrave Macmillan, 2007).

Rodinson, Maxime, *Europe and the Mystique of Islam*, trans. by Roger Veinus (London: I.B.Tauris, 1988).

Roediger, David R., *Working Toward Whiteness: How America's Immigrants Became White: The Strange Journey from Ellis Island to the Suburbs* (New York: Basic Books, 2005).

Rogan, Eugene L., *Frontiers of the State in the Late Ottoman Empire: Transjordan, 1850–1921* (Cambridge: Cambridge University Press, 1999).

────── *The Arabs: A History* (New York: Basic Books, 2009).
Rosenberg, Emily, *Spreading the American Dream: American Economic & Cultural Expansion 1890–1945* (New York: Hill and Wang, 1982).
Russell, Malcolm B., *First Modern Arab State: Syria and Faysal, 1918–1920* (Minneapolis: Bibliotheca Islamica, 1985).
Sachar, Howard M., *The Emergence of the Modern Middle East: 1914–1924* (London: Penguin Press, 1969).
────── *A History of the Jews in America* (New York: Vintage Books, 1993).
Salibi, Kamal, *The History of Modern Jordan* (London: I.B.Tauris, 1998).
Saul, Normal E., *The Life and Times of Charles R. Crane, 1858–1939: American Businessman, Philanthropist, and a Founder of Russian Studies in America* (Lanham, MA: Lexington Books, 2013).
Schlicher, Linda Schatkowski, 'The Famine of 1915–1918 in Greater Syria', in *Problems of the Modern Middle East in Historical Perspective: Essays in Honour of Albert Hourani*, ed. by John Spagnolo (Reading: Ithaca Press, 1992), 229–58.
Shafir, Gershon, *Land, Labor and the Origins of the Israeli–Palestinian Conflict, 1882–1914* (Berkeley: University of California Press, 1996).
Shapiro, Michael, *Reading the Postmodern Polity: Political Theory as Textual Practice* (Minneapolis: University of Minnesota Press, 1991).
Shorrock, William I., *French Imperialism in the Middle East: The Failure of Policy in Syria and Lebanon, 1900–1914* (Madison: University of Wisconsin Press, 1976).
Smith, Anthony D., *Nationalism*, 2nd edn (Cambridge: Polity Press, 2010).
Smith, Leonard V., 'Wilsonian Sovereignty in the Middle East: The King–Crane Commission Report of 1919' in *The State of Sovereignty: Territories, Laws, Populations*, ed. by Douglas Howland and Luis White (Bloomington: Indiana University Press, 2009), 56–74.
Smith, Michael Llewellyn, *Ionian Vision: Greece in Asia Minor 1919-1922* (New York: St Martin's Press, 1973).
Steed, Henry Wickham, *Through Thirty Years 1892–1922: A Personal Narrative*, 2 vols (London: William Heinemann, 1924).
Stoler, Ann, 'Racial Histories and Their Regimes of Truth', *Political Power and Social Theory*, 11 (1997), 183–206.
Suny, Ronald Grigor, Fatma Muge Gocek, and Norman M. Naimark (eds), *A Question of Genocide: Armenians and Turks at the End of the Ottoman Empire* (Oxford: Oxford University Press, 2011).
Tamari, Salim, *Year of the Locust: A Soldier's Diary and the Erasure of Palestine's Ottoman Past* (Berkeley: University of California Press, 2011).
Tauber, Eliezer, *The Arab Movements in World War I* (London: Frank Cass, 1993).
────── *The Formation of Modern Syria and Iraq* (Newbury Park, England: Frank Cass, 1995).
Taylor, Charles, *Modern Social Imaginaries* (Durham: Duke University Press, 2004).
Thompson, Elizabeth, *Colonial Citizens: Republican Rights, Paternal Privilege, and Gender in French Syria and Lebanon* (New York: Columbia University Press, 2000).
Thronveit, Trygve, 'The Fable of the Fourteen Points: Woodrow Wilson and National Self-Determination', *Diplomatic History*, 35, no. 3 (June, 2011).
Tibawi, A.L., *American Interests in Syria 1800–1901* (Oxford: Clarendon Press, 1966).
────── *Anglo-Arab Relations and the Question of Palestine 1914–1921* (London: Luzac & Company, 1978).

Traboulsi, Fawwaz, *A History of Modern Lebanon* (New York: Pluto Press, 2007).

Turki, Benyan Saud, *The King–Crane Commission* (Kuwait: Kuwait University, Authorship, Translation and Publication Committee, 1999).

Untermyer, Samuel, 'Zionism and the Crane Report' in *The Forum*, 69, no. 1 (January 1923), 1120–36.

Urofsky, Melvin, *American Zionism: From Herzl to the Holocaust* (Lincoln: University of Nebraska Press, 1975).

Wallerstein, Immanuel, *The Modern World-System II: Mercantilism and the Consolidation of the European World-Economy, 1600–1750* (New York: Academic Press, 1980).

—— *The Modern World-System III: The Second Era of Great Expansion of the Capitalist World-Economy, 1730s–1840s, With a New Prologue* (San Diego: University of California Press, 2011).

Walworth, Arthur, *Wilson and His Peacemakers: American Diplomacy at the Paris Peace Conference, 1919* (New York: W.W. Norton & Company, 1986).

Watenpaugh, Keith David, *Being Modern in the Middle East: Revolution, Nationalism, Colonialism, and the Arab Middle Class* (Princeton: Princeton University Press, 2006).

Westrate, Bruce, *The Arab Bureau: British Policy in the Middle East 1916–1920* (University Park, Pennsylvania: Pennsylvania State University Press, 1992).

Williams, Raymond, *Keywords: A Vocabulary of Culture and Society*, Rev Sub (London: Flamingo, 1983).

Winant, Howard, *Racial Conditions: Theory, Politics, Comparisons* (Minneapolis: University of Minnesota Press, 1994).

—— 'Racial Formation and Hegemony: Global and Local Developments' in *Racism, Modernity and Identity on the Western Front*, ed. by Ali Rattansi and Sallie Westwood (Cambridge, MA: Polity Press, 1994).

Yale, William, 'Henry Morgenthau's Special Mission of 1917', *World Politics*, 1, no. 3 (April, 1949), 308–20.

Yapp, M.E., *The Making of the Modern Near East 1792–1923* (London: Longman, 1987).

Zamir, Meir, *The Formation of Modern Lebanon* (Ithaca: Cornell University Press, 1985).

—— 'Faisal and the Lebanese Question, 1918–1920', *Middle Eastern Studies*, 27, No. 3 (July, 1991), 404–26.

Zeine, Zeine N., *The Struggle for Arab Independence: Western Diplomacy and the Rise and Fall of Faisal's Kingdom in Syria* (Beirut: Khayats, 1960).

Zürcher, Erik J., *Turkey: A Modern History*, Revised Edition (London: I.B.Tauris, 2004).

INDEX

Abbasids, 250
Acre, 116, 123, 124, 126
Adana, 159, 160, 197, 238
Africa, 83, 173, 206, 241
Ainab, 151
Aintab (Antep, Gaziantep), 105
Albania, 17, 95
Aleppo, 103, 105, 153, 155–59
Alexandretta, 152–54, 197
Algeria, 17, 197
Allenby, General Edmund, 19, 20, 29, 44, 45, 63, 74, 75, 98, 123, 139, 152, 154
American Colony, Jerusalem, 121
American Committee for Armenian and Syrian Relief (ACASR), 19, 22, 40, 157
American Red Cross, The, 116
American West, 11, 245
American University of Beirut, *see* Syrian Protestant College
Amman, 139, 140
Anatolia, 2, 18–22, 30, 35, 36, 41, 46, 67, 68, 71, 73, 79, 83, 85, 87, 96, 98, 101, 165–67, 169–172, 176–78, 184, 198, 206, 228, 229, 232, 245–47
Anatolia College (Marsovan), 172
Anderson, Sarah, 100

Anglo-French Declaration (1918), 21, 38, 46,
Anglo-Palestine Company, 194
Anglo-Saxons, 13, 56, 86, 183
'Aniza Tribes, 158
Antioch, 153
antisemitism, 91, 260
Antonius, George, 3
Arab Awakening, The, 3
Arab Club, The, 102, 103, 132, 134
Arab Empire, 209, 210, 249, 250
Arab uprising (2011–present), 6
Arabs, 3, 5, 25, 34, 36–38, 48, 56, 69, 84, 85, 88, 89, 93, 105, 111, 112, 118, 124, 128, 129, 131–33, 140, 144, 153, 156, 158, 162, 175, 177, 178, 194–97, 199, 202, 205–11, 214, 215, 218–20, 230, 237, 248–54, 257, 258, 260–62
Armenians and Armenia, 2, 19, 25, 28, 30, 31, 39, 41–43, 45, 46, 50, 59, 65, 67, 71, 79, 80, 81, 83, 85–87, 89–90, 98, 101, 105, 156, 157, 159, 167–72, 176, 177, 179, 196–201, 203, 204, 226, 227, 229, 230, 232, 233, 235, 237, 240, 245–47, 254, 260

Armenian massacres, 31, 41, 42, 90, 101, 156, 168, 169, 171, 172, 200, 204, 226, 232
Armenian Orthodox Church, see Gregorian Church
Armenian refugees, 157, 159, 200
Article 22 (of the League of Nations Covenant), 106, 133, 142, 225
Asia Minor, see Anatolia
Assyrians, 83, 84, 171
Austria-Hungary, 9, 15, 18, 26, 32, 238

Baabda, 151
Baalbek, 143
Baghdad, 177
Baker, Ray Stannard, 52, 53, 63, 179, 180
Baldensperger, P.J., 79
Balfour, Arthur, 47, 50
Balfour Declaration, 21, 26, 66, 114, 231, 236
Balkans, 16–18, 54, 95
Balkan Wars, (1912–13) 17
Barton, James, 35, 40
Basra, 18, 177
Bedouins, 19, 140
Beersheba, 123, 188, 249
Beirut, 20, 22, 38, 101, 105, 108, 136, 143–151, 154, 156, 157, 177, 230
Bell, Gertrude, 48–50
Beqa'a Valley, 143, 151
Bible, The, 53, 79, 80, 187
Bitlis, 170
Black Sea, 18, 41, 74, 81, 87, 176, 177, 200, 229, 230, 235
Bliss, Daniel, 38
Bliss, F. J., 80
Bliss, Howard, 28, 29, 38, 39, 41, 42, 45, 58, 90
Bliss, General Tasker H., 29, 35, 38
Boas, Franz, 14
Bolsheviks, 15, 21
Bosphorus, 18, 168, 231, 241

Bowman, Isaiah, 30
Brandeis, Louis, 25, 48, 73, 74, 91, 92, 99
Brenier, Henri, 49, 61
Brindisi, 40
Bristol, Admiral Mark, 100, 171
Britain and the British, 1, 15–23, 26–30, 32, 36, 38–40, 42–59, 56, 61–65, 70–73, 75–76, 79, 81, 83, 85–89, 93–97, 101, 102, 106, 108, 109, 111, 113–117, 119, 122, 123, 125, 127–129, 131–133, 135, 138–42, 144, 145, 149, 151, 153, 157, 158, 161, 163, 171, 174–178, 180, 193, 209, 210, 215, 220, 223, 234, 238, 239, 242–48, 251, 254, 262
Brodie, Donald, 58, 65, 123, 146, 150, 154, 165, 166, 174, 179, 180, 182, 185, 187, 189, 190, 192, 200, 203–6, 241, 244
Brown, James W., 179
Bryce, James, 204
Bulgaria, 17–19, 99
Bullitt Mission (1919), 32
Buxton, Harold, 79
Buxton, Noel, 79

de Caix, Robert, 49, 60, 61, 70
Caliphate, 65, 67, 68, 89
Caucasus, 18, 65, 176
Central Powers, 18,
Chaldeans, 171, 201
Chaplin, Charlie, 63
Chicago, 54, 88, 190
Childs, W.J., 79
China, 54
Chirol, Sir Valentine, 49
Christians and Christianity, 13, 14, 16, 23, 26, 53, 60, 80, 84, 85, 87–90, 92, 103, 105, 107, 113, 114, 116–19, 121, 123–25, 127, 130, 132, 133, 135, 140, 145, 148,

151, 152, 163, 172, 183, 185, 187, 192, 193, 195–202, 204–12, 214, 216, 218, 220, 230, 234, 235, 240, 243, 250, 251, 260
Church of the Holy Sepulchre, 121
Cilicia, 20, 41, 46, 197
Circassians, 154, 197
Clemenceau, Georges, 21, 22, 38, 40, 42, 43, 45, 47, 48, 50, 52, 60, 61, 63, 67, 68, 70–72, 75, 76, 239
Colorado, 174
Committee of Union and Progress (CUP), 16–18
Constantinople College, 54, 63, 99–101, 165, 172, 173
Constantinople, *see* Istanbul
Constantinopolan State, 2, 87, 176, 241
Constanza, 74, 99
constitutional monarchy, 177, 207
Constitutional Revolution (1908), 16
Cornwallis, Colonel Kinahan, 141
Council of Four, 30 (n.4)
Council of Ten, 30 (n.4)
Crane, Charles R., 3, 7, 51, 54, 55, 57–60, 62, 63, 65, 70, 72–75, 77, 78, 89, 91, 95, 99, 101, 105, 107, 108, 113, 115, 117, 121, 123, 127, 129, 130, 131, 133, 138, 139, 141, 144–46, 150, 153, 154, 159, 160, 165–67, 172–76, 178–180, 182, 187–90, 192, 197, 199, 202–207, 210–15, 220, 225–33, 237, 239–42, 244–48, 252–55, 259–61, 263
Crane, Richard, 174
Cuba, 244, 245, 247
Czechoslovakia, 174

al-Dajani, Arif Pasha, 117, 118
Damascus, 38, 81, 105, 108, 113, 116, 119, 123, 124, 126, 128, 130–43, 145–48, 150, 151, 154, 156, 157, 178, 189, 191, 192, 197, 214, 249, 252

Damascus Conference, *see* Syrian Congress
Damascus Program, 142, 143, 146, 148, 151, 152, 154, 157, 158, 162, 201, 210, 223, 257
Dana, Selim, 146, 147
'The Dangers to the Allies from a Selfish Exploitation of the Turkish Empire', 69, 79, 86, 89, 93, 94, 96, 97, 239
Danon, Haham Bashi Nissim, 120
Dardanelles, 18, 19, 24, 35, 168, 231, 241
Darwin, Charles, 12
'Daughters of the Martyrs', 137, 138
Dead Sea, 126
democracy, 32, 66, 91, 108, 161, 170, 176, 177, 184, 185, 193, 206, 207, 224, 230, 238, 244, 245, 253
Denikin, General Anton, 173, 174
Dera'a, 139, 140
discourse, 5 (n. 10)
Diyarbekir, 170
Dodge, Cleveland, 23
Dome of the Rock, 121
Dominian Commission, 35, 41, 52
Dominian, Leon, 30, 32, 35
Dorizas, Michael, 57, 58
Druze, 105, 134, 149, 189, 251
Duggan, Stephen, 179

Eastern Question, The, 9, 240, 241
Editor and Publisher, 179, 180
education (as a feature of modernity), 25, 120, 135, 184–86, 192, 194, 199, 209, 224, 230, 245, 249, 252
Egypt, 17, 19, 30, 49, 53, 61, 62, 94, 135, 173, 206, 209, 247
Ellis, William T., 180
Elmaleh, Abraham, 131–33, 136, 145–47, 149, 151, 153, 156–58, 162
Enver Pasha, 18
Erzerum, 170
d'Espeyran, Sabatier, 49

Factory Commission (1911), 32
al-Fatat, 102, 118
Faysal, Amir, 19, 20, 22, 28, 32–38, 45, 47–49, 61, 63, 64, 69, 74, 76, 81, 82, 89, 101–3, 112–16, 118, 119, 125, 127, 128, 131–34, 136, 139, 141–44, 161, 163, 175, 177, 178, 185, 192, 193, 207, 210, 223, 243, 248–53, 257
Farhi, Joseph, 146, 147
Fellahin, 125, 187, 189, 216
Ferid Pasha, Damad, 101
feudalism, 190
Four Point Address, 34, 35
Fourteen Points, 23, 47, 50, 67, 241
Forum, The, 180
France and the French, 1, 2, 16–22, 27–9, 32–34, 36, 38–40, 42–49, 52, 53, 60–65, 67, 68, 70–73, 75, 76, 81–83, 85–88, 93–97, 101, 106, 108, 109, 113, 114, 124, 125, 130, 132–34, 138–55, 157–59, 161–63, 174–80, 189, 193, 209, 210, 220, 223, 235, 238, 239, 242–45, 247, 248, 254, 262
Frankfurter, Felix, 48, 49, 66, 73, 74, 82, 103
French mandate, 48, 85, 125, 144, 146, 147, 152, 157, 161, 175, 177, 242, 243
Friedenwald, Dr. Harry, 119, 120
Future of Constantinople, The, (by Leonard Woolf) 241

Gates, Caleb, 66, 81, 85, 90
Gauvain, Auguste, 49
Gaza, 123
Gaziantep, *see* Aintab
Gelvin, James, 3 (n. 8), 102, 128, 178
Georges-Picot, Francois, 33, 61, 64, 123, 147, 148
Georgia and Georgians, 167, 171

Germany and Germans, 9, 15, 16, 18, 26, 30, 32, 33, 52, 56, 91, 94, 159, 184, 238
Glazebrook, Otis, 105, 109, 116
Gottheil, Richard, 91, 179
Goût, Jean, 33, 61
Government of the Ottoman Empire in the Time of Suleiman the Magnificent, The, (by Albert Lybyer), 55, 87, 88
Graffam, Mary, 172
Great Britain, *see* Britain and the British
Greece and the Greeks, 16, 17, 21, 22, 30, 32, 35, 36, 57, 67, 83, 86, 87, 90, 95, 100, 101, 114, 167, 171–73, 177, 178, 198, 199, 201, 204, 223, 230, 240, 241
Greek Catholics, 107, 113, 123, 134, 149
Greek Orthodox, 107, 113, 134, 149, 152, 153, 155
Gregorian Church, 170, 197
Gregorian Patriarch of Istanbul, 170
Grew, Joseph, 41, 55, 62, 174

Haddad Pasha, Gabriel, 135, 136
Haddad, Sami, 7, 58, 108, 123, 146, 152, 165, 166, 225
Hama, 154
Harvard University, 53, 55
Hashemites, 32, 252
Haydar, Rustem, 34, 69
Hebron, 121–23, 187, 188, 191, 225
Heck, Louis, 83, 84
Hejaz, 19, 28, 37, 74, 81, 86, 119, 149, 197, 253
Hodgson, Marshall, 186
Hogarth, David, 62, 64, 70
Homs, 154, 156
Hoofien, Sigfried, 109–112, 119, 194
Hôtel de Crillon, 47, 63
House, 'Colonel' Edward, 23, 29, 34, 35, 43, 47, 49, 52, 54, 62, 69, 70, 73, 215
Howard, Harry N., 2
Howe, Frederic C., 35, 40

INDEX

Hunchak Party (Armenian), 170
Hurgronje, C. Snouck, 65, 80
al-Husayni, Kamil, 116
al-Husayni, Musa, 119
Hussein-McMahon Correspondence, 21
Hussein, Sharif, 21, 33, 34, 44, 89, 177, 210, 250

Illinois, University of, 55, 59
imperialism, 3, 9, 12, 13, 17, 24, 48, 76, 82, 83, 86, 88, 91, 93–95, 97, 184, 199, 209, 210, 220, 221, 223, 238–48, 253, 254, 261
India and Indians, 17, 49, 53, 67, 68, 73
Indian Muslim Delegation (at the Paris Peace Conference), 67, 68, 73
Inquiry, The, 29, 30, 32, 39, 41, 55, 68, 75, 84, 196
Iran, *see* Persia
Iraq, *see* Mesopotamia
Islam and Muslims, 14, 17, 67, 73, 80, 84, 85, 87–90, 99, 102, 103, 112, 113, 116–19, 123, 125, 127, 130, 132, 134, 135, 139, 145, 148, 149, 158, 175, 183, 187, 191–93, 195, 197–212, 214, 218–20, 235, 240, 243, 246–254, 259–63
Israel, 2, 16, 111, 131, 160, 162, 256, 262
Istanbul, 2, 18, 20, 23, 40, 43, 54–57, 63, 67, 73, 75, 81, 85, 98–101, 109, 114, 159, 164–73, 176, 240–42, 246, 260
Italy and Italians, 1, 17, 18, 20–22, 27, 32, 35, 36, 45, 52, 53, 56, 65–68, 70, 71, 73, 75, 83, 86, 94, 95, 97, 223
Izmir, *see* Smyrna

Jackson, J.B., 103, 155, 156
Jacobson, Matthew Frye, 14
Jaffa, 101, 104, 107–15, 117, 118, 121, 125, 194, 213, 215
Jamal Pasha, 18, 19, 33, 137

Jenin, 123
Jerusalem, 7, 18, 56, 99, 105, 108, 115–125, 128, 131, 132, 137, 188, 193, 194, 215, 233
Jews, *see* Judaism
Jordan, 2, 16, 20, 21, 128, 160, 161
Jordan River, 126
Journal of International Relations, 179
Judaism and Jews, 1, 3, 6, 14, 21, 25, 26, 30, 43, 47–49, 66, 91–93, 99, 103–5, 109–29, 131–34, 136, 146, 147, 149, 151, 153, 156–58, 162, 175, 185, 189, 193–95, 197, 198, 201, 209, 211–220, 226, 231, 233–37, 246, 251, 257, 258, 260–62

Kalvarisky, Chaim, 125
Katibah, H.I., 179
Kattah, 126
Kedourie, Elie, 3 (n. 8), 257 (n. 1)
Kemal, Mustafa, 172
Kerak, 139, 189
Kharput, 170
King, Henry Churchill, 52–55, 57–60, 62–65, 68–73, 77–80, 82, 89, 92, 101, 105–8, 113–15, 117, 123, 126, 128, 129, 139, 141, 144–46, 150, 151, 153, 165–69, 171, 173–76, 178–80, 182, 184–86, 190, 197, 199, 201–8, 210, 211, 213–15, 220, 226–33, 237, 239–42, 244–48, 252–55, 259–61, 263
King–Crane Commission Report, 1–4, 6, 79, 91, 128, 142, 144, 160, 164–67, 171, 173, 174, 176–82, 184–6, 190, 199–208, 211–15, 224, 227–33, 237, 240–42, 244–46, 252, 253, 259–61
Kirkuk, 170
Kurdistan and Kurds, 28, 83, 84, 167, 167, 170, 171, 201, 224, 231, 233, 247
Kut, 19

Lambing, Ross, 58, 108
Lansing, Robert, 26, 29, 33, 35, 38, 40–43, 58, 59
Latakia, 152–55
Lausanne, The Treaty of, 178
Lawrence, Captain T.E., 19, 33, 34, 38, 37, 47–49, 56, 63
League of Nations, The, 29–31, 37, 46, 74, 78, 106, 116, 133, 142, 157, 174–77, 216, 224, 225, 228, 230, 235, 241, 251, 254
League of Nations Covenant, The, 37, 78, 106, 116, 133, 142, 225
Lebanon, 2, 3, 16, 20, 21, 37–40, 61, 86, 105, 130, 135, 143–55, 160–63, 175–77, 197–99, 201, 209, 210, 230, 234, 243, 254, 257
Libya, 16, 17, 173, 206
Lloyd George, David, 15, 21, 22, 37, 38, 43–47, 49, 50, 52, 63, 64, 65, 67, 68, 70–72, 75, 76, 239
London, 57, 189, 190
Ludd, 107, 113
Lutfallah, Michel, 141
Lybyer, Albert, 55–70, 74–79, 81, 87, 88, 95, 100, 108, 109, 114, 115, 117, 121, 123, 127, 129, 133–41, 143–46, 149–55, 157, 159, 163, 166–69, 171, 173–76, 180–82, 188, 191, 192, 197, 199, 200, 202–07, 210, 211, 213–15, 220, 226–33, 237, 239–242, 244–48, 252–55, 259–261, 263

Magdala, 126
Magie, David, 30, 73, 84
Makdisi, Ussama, 3, 14
mandates, 2, 30, 31, 37, 39, 43–49, 65–67, 70–73, 81–87, 93, 96–98, 101, 102, 104, 106, 109, 111, 113, 114, 116, 119, 125, 128, 130, 134–136, 139, 142, 144, 146–49, 151, 152, 154, 157–59, 161, 169–72, 175–78, 184, 185, 190, 193, 195, 202, 207, 210, 217, 218, 223–25, 228, 229, 232, 234, 235, 237, 238, 241–48, 250–52, 254
Manuel, Frank, 3, 90
Maronites, 113, 114, 123, 152
Marsovan, 172
Mary Magdalene, 126
Masaryk, Thomas, 174
McMahon, Sir Henry, 62, 64
Mecca, 21, 33, 34, 89, 192, 252
Mediterranean Sea, 41, 67, 81, 87, 176, 200, 229, 235
Mersin, 159
Mesopotamia, 2, 16, 17, 19–21, 30, 31, 37, 39, 44–46, 48, 50, 61, 71, 83, 83, 85, 86, 94, 98, 158, 165–67, 172, 176, 177
Mezes, Sidney, 68
Millet, Phillippe, 49
missionaries, 3, 11, 21, 22, 23, 30, 35, 53, 56, 65, 79, 80, 85, 90, 92, 159, 172, 185, 203, 260, 261
Mitchell, Timothy, 5
modernity and modernising, 5, 9–11, 13, 14, 16–18, 25, 28, 36, 41, 42, 85, 87–90, 93, 97, 99, 110, 112, 120, 122, 135, 162, 175, 182–222, 234, 237, 244–46, 248, 249, 252, 259–63
Montgomery, George R., 8, 56–59, 65, 68, 74, 75, 77, 78, 81, 89, 93, 94, 96, 99, 100, 108, 115, 117, 121, 123, 126, 129, 137, 139, 141, 144–46, 148, 149, 151, 153, 155, 157, 159, 165–67, 174–76, 180, 182, 186, 188, 190, 196, 200–2, 204, 205, 208, 209, 211, 212, 215–18, 220, 226, 233, 235–37, 239, 243, 246–48, 251–55, 261–63
Moore, Laurence, 57, 58, 100, 139, 146, 155, 165, 172, 173, 188
Morgenthau, Henry, 23, 85, 86

Mosul, 22, 170, 177
Mu'allaqa, 151
Muslim-Christian Association, 103, 117, 119, 132, 193
Muslims, *see* Islam and Muslims

Nablus, 116, 123
Nassif, Suleiman Bey, 116
nationalism, 15, 25, 32, 85, 89, 92, 95, 102, 108, 115, 116, 122, 124, 128, 132, 136, 137, 139, 141, 142, 144, 146–48, 157, 162, 163, 171, 175, 177, 178, 192, 201, 216, 221, 223, 234, 244, 248–253, 257
Native Americans, 12
Nazareth, 123, 124
Near East Relief, *see* American Committee for Armenian and Syrian Relief
Nestorian Christians, 201
Netherlands, The, 109
'The New Syria National League', 82
New York Evening Post, 180
New York Times, The, 174, 179, 180
Nicholas II, Tsar, 54
'Night of Power', 130
Ninkovich, Frank, 10, 238

Oberlin College, 53, 55, 58, 59
Occupied Enemy Territory East (OETA East), 20, 161
Occupied Enemy Territory South (OETA South), 20, 161
Occupied Enemy Territory West (OETA West), 20, 161
oil, 22, 23, 56, 83, 173
Arabian Nights, 79
Oren, Michael, 3, 90
Orlando, Vittorio, 52, 75
Ottoman Empire, 1, 2, 4–7, 9, 10, 15–26, 28–52, 55, 56, 58, 61, 64–98, 101–3, 105, 108, 109, 113, 119, 135, 136, 141, 153, 159, 162, 164–72, 176–78, 182–85, 187, 190, 191, 193, 195, 196, 198, 200, 201, 203–5, 209, 211, 215, 216, 219, 222–26, 229, 231–34, 238–41, 242–48, 253, 254, 256, 257, 259, 261, 263

Palestine, 1–3, 16, 17, 20–22, 26, 30, 31, 37, 39, 43, 45, 46, 47, 49, 50, 56, 66, 80, 82, 86, 92, 93, 101, 103–5, 108–136, 144, 147, 156, 157, 160, 161, 163, 172, 175, 176, 178, 187, 189, 193, 194, 197, 211–18, 220, 227, 228, 230, 231, 233–37, 242, 243, 246, 249–52, 254, 257, 261, 262
Pan-Arabism, 249
Pan-Islamism, 89, 249, 250
Paris Peace Conference, 1, 7, 22, 26, 28–78, 80–85, 91, 93, 95, 100, 101, 118, 119, 148, 167, 173, 174, 179, 215, 223–25, 238, 249
Patrick, Mary Mills, 172, 173
Pears, Sir Edwin, 100, 101, 172
Persia, 17, 61, 197
petroleum, *see* oil
Philippines, 11, 13, 32, 244, 245–47
Philippines Commission (1899), 32
Pichon, Stéphen, 39, 42–44
plebiscites, 31, 32, 34–108
pogroms, 233
Poland, 133, 148, 233, 235
Princeton Theological Seminary, 55
Princeton University, 30
Protestants (from Greater Syria), 107, 123, 149, 151, 158, 197

race, 5, 12–16, 36, 41, 88, 110, 118, 157, 172, 183–85, 193, 195–222, 259, 261
Ramadan, 99, 130, 133, 136
Ramallah, 123, 125
Ramleh, 105, 107, 113
Ramsay, William, 79
Ravndal, Gabriel Bie 32, 100

Religion and religious groups, 5, 12–17, 26, 39, 41, 60, 66, 79, 84, 87–90, 92, 93, 102, 105, 108, 118, 119, 123, 141, 149, 167, 175, 183–85, 190, 193, 195–222, 224, 226, 227, 231, 238, 245, 249, 252, 259, 261
Rihbany, Abraham Mitrie, 82
Rishon LeZion, 115
Riza Pasha, Ahmet, 169
Robert College, 54, 55, 57, 63, 66
Rodinson, Maxime, 208, 211
Rogan, Eugene, 128
Roman Catholics, 111, 149
Romania, 99
Rome, 35, 40
Rome, Ancient, 30, 143
Rosenberg, Emily, 11
Russia, 16–18, 20, 21, 32, 44, 54, 83, 91, 101, 133, 170, 173, 189, 197, 235

Saudi Arabia, 16
self-determination ('desires' or 'wishes of the people', 'consent of the governed'), 3, 5, 14–16, 31, 34, 35, 37, 39, 44, 47, 50, 61, 63, 74, 76, 80, 87, 95, 96, 98, 102–4, 106, 108, 111, 114, 117, 118, 133, 164, 211, 213, 215, 217, 221–238, 254, 255, 257, 260, 261, 262
Senussis, 173, 206, 207
Sevres, The Treaty of, 178
Schiff, Jacob, 91
Scotland, 84
Scutari College, 100
Shahbandar, Dr. Abd al Rahman, 141
Shapiro, Michael, 5
Shiite Islam, 151, 197, 235
Sivas, 172
Smith, G.A., 79
Smyrna, 21, 35, 67, 87, 100, 101, 114, 171, 177, 199, 230, 240

social imaginary, 5, 9, 10, 16, 90, 183, 184, 187, 212, 218–20, 258, 259, 261
Spaffords, 121
Standard Oil Company of New York, 22, 56, 173
Steed, Henry Wickham, 49
Straights, The, 18, 19, 24, 35, 168, 231, 241
Suez Canal, 17–19
Sulaymaniyah, 170
Supreme Council (of the Paris Peace Conference), 30, 32, 35–37, 39–47, 49–50, 52, 65, 67, 68, 71, 72, 75, 81, 223
Sykes, Sir Mark, 33
Sykes-Picot Agreement, 21, 22, 33, 43, 44, 60, 61, 72
Syria and Greater Syria, 2, 3, 5–7, 16–22, 28, 30, 31, 33, 34, 37–39, 42, 44–49, 52, 56, 58–62, 64–66, 68, 69, 71, 72, 74–76, 81–85, 87–89, 93, 94, 98, 101–105, 107–67, 172–80, 185, 188, 190, 192, 193, 196–201, 204, 206–13, 215, 217, 219, 223, 225, 227–231, 234, 235, 237, 239, 241–53, 256–58, 260–62
Syrian Catholics, 149
Syrian Congress, 112, 113, 116, 118, 124, 126, 128, 130, 141, 142, 144, 146, 156, 223, 257
Syrian Protestant College, 28, 38, 58, 85, 96, 135
Szold, Robert, 119

Tagi, Soliman, 105, 107
Taylor, Charles, 5
Tel Aviv, 115
Thrace, 16
Tolstoy, Leo, 54
Toren, Paul, 58, 166
Toynbee, Arnold, 62, 63
Transjordan, *see* Jordan

INDEX

Triple Entente, 18, 41, 72
Tripoli, 135, 152–54
Tunisia, 17
Turkey and Turks, *see* Ottoman Empire
Twain, Mark, 13

Ummayad Mosque, 133
United Kingdom, *see* Britain and the British
United States of America and Americans, 1–3, 5–7, 9–16, 18, 19, 22–27, 29, 30, 32–38, 40–44, 48, 51–58, 61–76, 78, 80–87, 89–92, 94–97, 100–3, 105, 106, 108, 109, 111, 114, 116, 117, 119, 121, 124, 131–36, 139, 140, 142, 144, 147–49, 151, 156, 157, 159, 161, 166–74, 176–80, 183–87, 189, 192, 193, 195, 196, 200–3, 206–8, 210–12, 215, 217, 218, 220, 223, 224, 228, 229, 238, 242–48, 254, 256, 259, 260, 262, 263
Untermeyer, Samuel, 180
USS *Dupont*, 173
USS *Hazelwood*, 159
Utilitarianism, 117, 215, 236

Vaad Ha'ir (Beirut), 146, 147
Venizelos, Eleutherios, 35, 36

Watenpaugh, Keith, 98, 108
Weizmann, Chaim, 73, 103
Westermann, William, 30, 33, 34, 36, 39–41, 47, 48, 50, 52, 55, 56, 58–61, 63, 67–69, 72–76, 81, 83, 84, 93, 115, 129, 145, 180, 196, 197, 246, 249
White, George, 172
White, Henry, 29, 35, 40, 42
Wilsonian League (Turkey), 223
Wilson, Woodrow and Wilsonian ideals, 1, 3, 4, 6, 14–16, 23–76, 86, 89, 93, 95, 96, 106, 109, 114, 142, 144, 145, 151, 169, 173, 174, 178–80, 183, 192, 199, 206, 215, 222–46, 253–55, 261–63
Wise, Rabbi Stephen, 26
women (delegations of), 107, 139, 149, 158
Woolf, Leonard, 241
World War I, 1, 6, 7, 9, 10, 14–16, 18–29, 31, 32, 35, 37, 41, 43, 51, 53–57, 62, 67, 76, 78, 83, 88–92, 94–98, 102, 109, 135, 140, 145, 149, 157, 168, 172, 175, 185, 201, 203, 207, 210, 222, 224, 226, 233, 238, 240, 243–45, 253, 263

Yale, William, 7, 56–59, 75, 77, 78, 81, 83–85, 88–90, 92–96, 101, 104, 108, 116, 120, 123, 124, 129, 131, 133, 134, 136, 138–41, 143–46, 148–52, 154, 155, 159, 165, 166, 173–75, 180, 182, 185–87, 190, 196–98, 201, 202, 204, 208–12, 217, 218, 220, 225, 226, 233–35, 237, 239, 242, 243, 246–55, 261–63
Yemen, 16, 17
'Young Arabs', 131, 175, 210, 211, 250, 251
Young Men's Christian Association (YMCA), 52
Young Turks, 16, 66, 169, 210, 249

Zahleh, 151
Zionism, 1–3, 5, 6, 21, 23, 25, 26, 28, 29, 43, 47–49, 61, 66, 73, 74, 82, 90–93, 99, 103, 105, 107, 109–129, 131–34, 136, 137, 142, 144–47, 149, 156–58, 161, 162, 176–80, 186, 192–95, 205, 209, 211–20, 229, 231, 233–37, 248, 250, 251, 257, 258, 260–62
Zionist Commission, 104, 107, 113, 115, 118–21, 125, 162, 257
Zionist Organisation 43, 119
Zwemer, Samuel 80

www.ingramcontent.com/pod-product-compliance
Lightning Source LLC
Chambersburg PA
CBHW070014010526
44117CB00011B/1568